Race, Rights, and Rifles

CHICAGO STUDIES IN AMERICAN POLITICS

A series edited by Susan Herbst, Lawrence R. Jacobs, Adam J. Berinsky,
and Frances Lee; Benjamin I. Page, editor emeritus

∴

Race, Rights, and Rifles

∵

THE ORIGINS OF THE NRA AND
CONTEMPORARY GUN CULTURE

Alexandra Filindra

THE UNIVERSITY OF CHICAGO PRESS

CHICAGO AND LONDON

The University of Chicago Press, Chicago 60637
The University of Chicago Press, Ltd., London
© 2023 by The University of Chicago
Published 2023
Printed in the United States of America

32 31 30 29 28 27 26 25 24 23   1 2 3 4 5

ISBN-13: 978-0-226-82874-9 (cloth)
ISBN-13: 978-0-226-82876-3 (paper)
ISBN-13: 978-0-226-82875-6 (e-book)
DOI: https://doi.org/10.7208/chicago/9780226828756.001.0001

Library of Congress Cataloging-in-Publication Data

Names: Filindra, Alexandra, author.
Title: Race, rights, and rifles : the origins of the NRA and contemporary
    gun culture / Alexandra Filindra.
Other titles: Chicago studies in American politics.
Description: Chicago : The University of Chicago Press, 2023.
    | Series: Chicago studies in American politics | Includes
    bibliographical references and index.
Identifiers: LCCN 2023001533 | ISBN 9780226828749 (cloth) |
    ISBN 9780226828763 (paperback) | ISBN 9780226828756 (ebook)
Subjects: LCSH: National Rifle Association of America. | Firearms
    ownership—United States—Philosophy. | Citizenship—United
    States. | Racism—United States.
Classification: LCC HV7436 .F457 2023 | DDC 363.330973—dc23/
    eng/20230307
LC record available at https://lccn.loc.gov/2023001533

♾ This paper meets the requirements of ANSI/NISO Z39.48-1992
(Permanence of Paper).

To Xanthi, who raised me to be curious and care.
To Alexandros and Melina. May they be virtuous citizens.

The soldier is, at the same time, a citizen. He thinks of his country and of his party; he talks politics; he reads almost every day the gazettes brought to the camps by intrepid little carriers; he often sends a correspondence to the journals; he communicates military impressions to the Senators and his plans of campaign to chiefs the most elevated in grade.

LT. COL. FERDINAND LECOMTE, Report on the US Civil War, 1862

Negro manhood says, "I am an American citizen." Modern Democracy says, "You are not." Negro manhood says, "I demand all my rights, civil and political." Modern Democracy says: "You have no rights except what I choose to give you. . . ." Negro manhood says, "I will exercise the rights vouchsafed." Modern Democracy says, "If you do, I will mob and murder you."

BENJAMIN TANNER, *Christian Advocate* Editor, 1868[1]

We cannot outnumber the negroes. And so, we must either outcheat, outcount, or outshoot them!

CLAUDE KITCHIN, Democratic Party Executive Committeeman,
Laurinburg, NC, Political Rally, 1898[2]

Proud Boys, stand back and stand by.

PRESIDENT DONALD J. TRUMP, presidential debate, September 29, 2020

Contents

Abbreviations

AMR	Ascriptive Martial Republicanism
AR	Ascriptive Republicanism
BAFTE	Bureau of Alcohol Firearms Tobacco and Explosives
BLM	Black Lives Matter
BPP	Black Panther Party
CMP	Civilian Marksmanship Program
CRT	Critical Race Theory
CSA	Confederate States of America
DAR	Daughters of the American Revolution
DCM	Directorate of Civilian Marksmanship
FBI	Federal Bureau of Investigation
FFA	Federal Firearms Act (1938)
GAO	Government Accounting Office
GCA	Gun Control Act (1968)
ICR	Inclusive Civic Republicanism
IRS	Internal Revenue Service
NAACP	National Association for the Advancement of Colored People
NBPRP	National Board for the Promotion of Rifle Practice
NGA	National Guard Association
NFA	National Firearms Act (1934)
NRA	National Rifle Association
SCLC	Southern Christian Leadership Conference
SCV	Sons of Confederate Veterans
SNCC	Student Nonviolent Coordinating Committee
UDC	United Daughters of the Confederacy
UFA	Uniform Firearms Act (1926)
UMA	Uniform Militia Act (1792)
USCT	United States Colored Troops
WAC	Women's Army Corps

Introduction

In May 2000, at the National Rifle Association's (NRA) National Convention in Charlotte, North Carolina, the organization's president, Charlton Heston, concluded his speech by clutching a handcrafted flintlock rifle and bellowing defiantly: "from my cold, dead hands!" The image has become iconic—a symbol of Americanism and patriotism to some and militarism to others. That night, like so many more that followed over the next several years, Heston would channel the ancient heroes that made him famous. Once again he was a Roman legionnaire, raising his sword and fighting to the death for freedom and the Republic. Much as the infamous Emperors of yore did in ancient Rome, corrupt elites in Washington, DC and Hollywood were plotting to subvert treasured American institutions, and the aging Cincinnatus had once again put down his plow. He had "enlisted as sentinel" to guard the gates of the Republic.[1] He was warning its people of the mortal danger that lay within.[2] Each time Heston raised his shaking arm, fist tight around the elegantly carved body of the rifle, the crowd ate it up, enthusiastically applauding in delight.

Humans are not "a perfect species, capable of coexisting . . . under everlasting peace," the NRA elder proclaimed. Humans are "egotistical, corruptible, vengeful, sometimes, even a bit power-mad."[3] Given the frailty of human nature and the temptation of vice, concentrating power in the hands of the few was dangerous for institutions. A nation where "police, military, and government agents are allowed the force of arms and individual citizens are not" is vulnerable to corruption. A political class that controls lethal force is empowered to dominate the people rather than represent their interests. It becomes "big brother knows best," its authority enforced with "powder and ball." [4]

Since humans are not always virtuous, preserving democratic freedom requires active and conscious effort. "It takes courage," Heston told his rapt audience. It takes constant alertness to politics; "[the] red, white, and blue stand for valor, purity, and vigilance." It is the courage displayed by "soldiers in distant trenches."[5] For the aging warrior of the NRA, an armed citizenry embodied manly courage and honor. "Muskets in the hands of farmers, not trained soldiers or police" is what enabled those who assembled at Concord Bridge to "[stand] their ground, as if to say 'don't tread on me.'"[6] This virtue and political responsibility, Heston tells us, develops when "young men [look] upon the ownership of tools ranging from a rifle to a spear to a bow and arrows as a rite of passage into manhood and the adult world." Through training with arms, "a boy make[s] a transition to responsible manhood."[7]

For Heston, and the NRA, the right to bear arms, codified in the US Constitution's Second Amendment, is the country's "first freedom"—an absolute right. "The right to keep and bear arms is the only right that allows 'rights' to exist at all. It is the right that . . . creates the absolute capacity to live without fear." The right to bear arms "makes us equal when divisions of power are assessed. To those who desire a cultural hierarchy with an elite in power, a gun is a threatening symbol of *equality* of power" (emphasis in the original). If citizens are barred from owning firearms, all other freedoms—including the rights to vote, worship, and speak freely—become vulnerable to elite repression.[8]

What makes Americans virtuous, according to Heston, is their commitment to a shared set of values and a common identity—a shared understanding of peoplehood. These values are encoded in the country's founding documents. They were developed by "a bunch of wise, old, dead, white guys"—people who shared Heston's and the model NRA member's beliefs and physical features, even their age.[9] These values are not negotiable or subject to interpretation. Much like the Ten Commandments, they are written in stone—and it is "absurd" to even try to analyze them.[10] This expression of peoplehood inheres in the America that "[Americans] built." It is the America "where you could pray without feeling naive, love without being kinky, sing without profanity, be white without feeling guilty, own a gun without shame, and raise your hand to say so without apology."[11] This masculine, Christian, and proudly, unapologetically White America, Heston believed, is what guns in civilian hands and the courage to use them are meant to protect.

Heston warns that cosmopolitan and multicultural political elites introduce corruption into the soul of the Republic. By attacking traditional notions of what it means to be an American, these forces are not truly striving for political equality but branding many Americans as "lesser citizens," degrading their status and contributions to the polity. "We are in danger of becoming numbed by the barrage of cultural messages being hurled at us by the elitists—messages that make the majority feel like they're the minority," he warned. These forces assault American political virtue and "rob" citizens "of the courage of their convictions. Our pride in who we are and what we believe has been ridiculed, ransacked, and plundered." The consequences of this assault on tradition are dire for the Republic. Citizens have become willing "to tolerate the erosion of our freedom. . . . Heaven help the God-fearing, law-abiding, Caucasian, middle class, Protestant (or even worse evangelical) Christian, the Midwestern or southern (or even worse rural) hunter, apparently straight or admitted heterosexual gun-owning (or even worse NRA-card-carrying) average working stiff, or even worse still male working stiff, because not only do you not count, you're a downright obstacle to social progress."[12]

Heston's ideology that combines faith in the ability of gun owners to discern what is good for America with a deep suspicion of the national government and its motivations is antithetical to modern notions of state organization.[13] However, this ideology is popular with his NRA audience, whose members jumped to their feet and applauded Heston at every event he headlined. This ideology has also been popular with militia groups, from the 1990s extremists in Michigan and the West to modern-day Proud Boys and Oath Keepers.[14] Elements of this culture are reflected in modern White Christian nationalism.[15]

These groups are not alone in embracing these ideas. In May and June 2021, I fielded a nationally representative survey and found that almost four in ten contemporary White Americans share this worldview—especially (but not exclusively) Republicans. They believe that being a "true American citizen" combines patriarchal authority, Christianity, Whiteness, and militarized political engagement, especially owning firearms. Almost two-thirds (60 percent) of White people who embrace this ideology prioritize the right to bear arms over other rights, much as Heston did. To them, it is "the first freedom." Also, like Heston, more than half (54 percent) of White people who embrace this worldview believe that the government is so powerful that people need guns to protect themselves from it.

At the same time, supporters of this ideology endorse draconian policies that empower citizens to act as political vigilantes: 71 percent believe that there should be "laws that protect citizens who shoot at protesters whom they think are violent and threatening private property"—practically endorsing immunity for vigilantism. Similarly, 43 percent are so concerned with protecting their White heritage that they support "laws that classify as terrorism any activity that promotes beliefs and ideologies that criticize America's White and European heritage." More ominously, 46 percent of White people who share Heston's view of politics believe that the QAnon conspiracy whose adherents attacked the US Capitol on January 6, 2021, is "a group of patriots dedicated to exposing the corruption of the deep state." The vast majority (78 percent) judge twice-impeached Donald Trump among the country's best presidents.

The historical record suggests that militarized conceptions of political membership like those documented in the survey can influence citizens' political behavior in ways detrimental to democracy. More than once, groups of Americans have taken up arms against their political institutions. The most devastating such event was the Civil War, but it is far from the only one. American history is marked by vigilante violence targeting people of color, armed labor strife, citizen rebellions, political assassinations, and at least one successful armed overthrow of an elected government.[16] The January 6 attack on the US Capitol may have been shocking to many and a terrible omen for the future of American politics, but it is not unique in character or intent.

But where does this ideology that links suspicion of government authority, human fallibility, martial virtue, and Eurocentric values come from? And why has it captivated so many people—even motivating an attack on the US Capitol?

IDEOLOGICAL TRADITIONS IN AMERICAN POLITICS

Many contemporary observers—including scholars, ordinary people, and many members of the NRA itself—believe that American gun culture is closely tied to American traditions of individualism and libertarianism. Such accounts of gun culture emphasize the role of beliefs grounded in self-sufficiency, hard work, and moral independence as the foundation of people's commitment to gun rights.[17] Other observers suggest it is a gun-centric ideology that the NRA created.[18] Yet, recent US Supreme Court decisions notwithstanding, historians and political theorists agree that little connects liberal individualism to America's gun culture.[19]

I argue that this gun-centric ideology rests on a very old, but different foundation. In this book, I will show that the NRA's worldview is the modern expression of an ideological system that fused the classical republican citizen-soldier ideal—the foundation of democracy—with American White male supremacy. I call this mixed ideology *ascriptive martial republicanism* (ascriptive republicanism, for short) because it weights martial expressions of citizenship proportionately more than civic participation and recognizes as "true citizens" only those who fulfill specific identity-based criteria—key among them, being male and White.

By "worldview" or "ideology," I mean a set of ideas that have some internal coherence and seek to describe and explain the nature of the social world. Alternately called "causal stories," "political narratives," "legitimizing myths," "stories of peoplehood," "constitutive norms," or "political languages," these moral constructs help us determine what behavior should be punished or rewarded, who deserves access to collectively held resources, and who should be offered full social, economic, and political rights (and why). They answer questions about what is just, fair, and legitimate. Ideologies tend to undergird institutions and laws that enable societies to incentivize and reward conformity and punish deviance. In short, these ideas justify a polity's structural organization and social hierarchy. [20]

Ideologies consist of repertoires involving symbols, myths, and narratives that produce and reproduce how members of a culture define social and moral worth. This language gives meaning to social action and creates a sense of common cause and community among participants. This political vernacular is not random; it is deeply embedded in the broader culture that gives rise to social movements. Intimate knowledge of the culture is required to understand the relative significance of the political meanings encoded in these stories and to be mobilized by them. Historians have observed that political narratives often create "usable" history or a "usable past": they selectively emphasize, embellish, or silence the historical record in ways that allow groups to create positive, diachronic links between a heroic past and today's political actors. This continuity through time allows groups to make claims to moral authority for their actions and political goals today, based on their claims to be the "true" heirs or "true" representatives of a political community.[21]

As human beings, we have an innate disposition to understand the world in normative terms and, often, to rely on affect and emotion rather than reason in our social judgments. As a result, expressing interests and justifying social and political privileges in the language of morality and values has many benefits. Translating interests into the language of values can help increase issue salience. The point of contention is no longer material; rather, it is the defense of closely held moral standards. Transforming a political argument into a moral one also forecloses many response options, allowing the state a lot less latitude in dealing with moralized issues. At the same time, this process can transform petty grievances into grand causes. If moral intuition is innate, moral arguments are more accessible than interest-based arguments to broad audiences. People are more likely to have strong negative emotional responses to perceived violations of society's moral code, and these emotions can help sustain mobilization. This "translation" process is not necessarily strategic, although political elites can and do behave instrumentally. [22]

Classical liberalism understands political membership based on in-dependence, political equality, and "negative liberty," or the absence of government involvement in citizens' daily lives. The institutions that Americans built are supposed to reflect this ideal: they are described as egalitarian, voluntary, and requiring minimal government involvement. Public authority is responsible for keeping the community safe from inter-nal and external foes and protecting people's rights to property. In a liberal polity, citizens do not have duties to the community; their primary respon-sibility is to pursue their self-interest.[23]

Although classical liberalism assigns a minimal role to state authority, little in this theory suggests that as citizens, individuals are duty-bound to bear arms and be vigilant against political corruption, or that they have any civic duties at all. In fact, the classical liberal state's primary responsibility is to provide security of life and property through professionalized institu-tions such as courts, police, and the military so that citizens can remain free to pursue their economic self-interest.[24] Classical liberalism views citizens as individuals who pursue personal economic gain, rather than splitting their time and attention between private and public functions.

Liberals—or what today we call libertarians—are not likely to associate good citizenship with gun ownership and using arms to stand up to govern-ment corruption. "Civic duty" and "collective responsibility" are not terms commonly associated with liberal thought. Liberals do not generally think of themselves as "sentries" who "stand guard" at the gates of the Republic—like NRA leaders Charlton Heston and Wayne LaPierre have done for de-cades.[25] But this language of duty and civic obligation is everywhere you look in the gun world. The gun rights discourse emphasizes a right to pro-tect against government tyranny and a civic responsibility to do so using both the ballot and the bullet. The NRA's flagship publication, *The Ameri-can Rifleman*, is brimming with exhortations to civic duty and the necessity for military preparedness among civilian men. The "most sacred" duty of the citizen, declared the magazine, was the protection of the "freeman's ballot" against "internal and external enemies." In this view, "no moral law or common law" can "entirely delegate this right and duty to mercenaries" and professional soldiers.[26]

The emphasis on manhood and honor pervasive in the gun culture is another clue of an inconsistency between the egalitarianism inherent in liberal theory and contemporary gun narratives. Mostly, gun myths and narratives associate citizenship with men, not women.[27] Even when gun narratives mention women, it is not as citizens with duties and obligations or as soldiers. Instead, women are mentioned as either the objects of men's sexual fantasies or victims of violence.[28] NRA narratives also imply a racialized view of citizenship, focusing not just on men but on White men.[29] As I will examine later in this book, pictures of non-White people in NRA magazines are conspicuous in their absence. People of color are rarely (if ever) discussed in the context of political membership—as soldiers or citizens or even voters. Where NRA narratives do imply race, it is usually in stories of how "law-abiding citizens" deter attacks by racialized others: thugs, criminals, felons, terrorists, or rioters. Native Americans are the perennial enemy whose destruction is a source of the armed White man's honor.

In this book, I will show how the militarized understandings of political membership prominent in NRA narratives and embraced by many White Americans fit within a broader ideology—one that I call *ascriptive martial republicanism*—that has its roots in the American Revolution. This ideology represents the syncretic combination of two worldviews that were influential at the time (and remain so today): martial republicanism and White male supremacy.

Martial republicanism is a system of thought associated with Aristotle, Cicero, and Machiavelli. It is an ideology that predates liberalism—a product of the Enlightenment—and the establishment of the modern nation-state. Martial republicanism emerged long before the Industrial Revolution and modern forms of warfare. In short, it is a very old idea. Unlike liberalism, which emphasized negative liberty, republicanism understood citizens as bearers of rights and *duties*. The duties of citizenship included political participation and military service. A good citizen would train at arms in times of peace to be ready to distinguish himself as a hero in war. Much like Heston, republican theorists believe that practicing with arms, or military preparedness, endowed male citizens with political virtue or "honor," making them enlightened stewards of the public good in politics.[30]

Unlike liberalism, which emphasizes individual interests, republicanism has a robust understanding of the public good and differentiates it from private interests. Liberalism views the pursuit of self-interest as a positive for society; for republicans, though, pursuing personal gain is evidence of moral corruption and is therefore a threat to the Republic. Virtuous citizens can differentiate between personal gain and the public good and subordinate their interests to the collective. "Our country includes family, friends, and property, and should be preferred to them all," is how republicans envisioned the relationship between the individual and the state.[31] It was a man's willingness to embrace the public good and sacrifice his life for the nation that made him a virtuous decision-maker at the ballot box. A nation's independence and liberty thus depended on cultivating virtue in its citizens. Dependent citizens were destined for moral and physical slavery.[32]

The tracts of the founding era are replete with republican arguments and narratives. The country's intellectual and political founders were very concerned about political virtue and how to inculcate and protect it. Benjamin Rush hoped that men would train to be "republican machines"—selfless, rational, and unemotional protectors of the Republic. These themes were so central to the rhetoric of the early Republic that foreign observers of early American politics picked up on the importance of republicanism. Alexis de Tocqueville, a great admirer of the American democratic experiment, discussed American republicanism at length, extolling Americans' civic involvement and commitment to military preparedness. He dedicated entire chapters to the American military tradition of the citizen-soldier and the country's refusal to establish a large professional army, which republicans viewed as a source of corruption.[33]

Political, non-militarized republican ideals—civic education, civic engagement, voluntarism—are central to several twentieth-century explanations of American democracy. For example, in *The Civic Culture*, a book that has influenced generations of social scientists, Gabriel Almond and Sidney Verba argued that American political culture is characterized by a strong sense of patriotism, social and political duty, and corresponding high levels of political and social participation. They viewed this civic culture as the apex of democracy. In this culture, citizens do not merely obey the law or focus exclusively on their interests; they view the law as central to preserving their social and individual commitments and actively shaping the polity. These ideals and relationships allow political members to sustain trust in each other and safeguard civil authority.[34] Ideals focused on nonviolent political engagement, inclusivity, and respect for cultural others are also central to the discourse of the civil rights movement and the feminist movements of the mid-twentieth century.[35]

Republican ideology is thus the foundation of modern participatory democracy. As such, it carries the promise of inclusivity and can be enticing to majority groups and minorities alike. Its most inclusive forms suggest that any member of society who fulfills their obligations to the polity can be called a citizen and make claims against the state. Any human being, regardless of race, gender, class, sexual orientation, or religion, is entitled to full membership in the American polity if they hold up their end of the bargain: if they work hard, are independent, care about fellow citizens, contribute to society, pay their taxes, and vote. Indeed, this promise of inclusivity animated African American men and White women to use republicanism as a vehicle to achieve political rights—a topic the book touches on but does not delve into very deeply.[36] But inclusivity is possible yet not *necessary* for republican systems—and broad inclusivity was not a constitutive part of the early American polity.

Unlike the liberal myth, which focuses on individuals and their relationship to the state, the republican myth requires a moral theory of the people who deserve citizenship: a peoplehood. Who constitutes the civitas, the body politic? What kinds of people could develop the political virtue required for republican governance? White Americans of the revolutionary generation, most of them men, provided the dominant answer to this question and the one that shaped the country's institutions. They stressed that only people with a specific combination of beliefs, aspirations, and character traits could be transformed into "republican machines." But who were these people?

In addition to republicanism, American political culture was founded on hierarchical beliefs about race and gender (and Christian religion—often a stand-in for Whiteness[37]) that situated White men at the top of the social pyramid, vesting them with citizenship rights. This ideology is called "ascriptive" because it places moral value on traits that people are born with—characteristics that are "ascribed" to them at birth. These are traits difficult, if not impossible, to change, such as race, gender, religion, or ethnicity. Ascriptive ideologies use these characteristics to determine who is a good citizen and who is not, who deserves membership in the polity, and who is destined to moral, if not physical, slavery. Therefore, ascriptive ideologies explain and justify systems of social stratification that are based not on merit but on social identities.[38]

In the United States, a "creative synthesis" brought together two popular ideological streams at the time of the Revolution, and the combined ideology became the foundation for the country's citizenship institutions.[39] Republican ideology created the scaffolding and ascriptive ideas filled in the gaps and defined American peoplehood—the meaning of who is a "true" American. Americans found their "republican machines" in a mix of religious, gendered, and racial ideas that elevated White Anglo-Saxon Protestant males as the prototypical republican citizens. In this ascriptive republican ideological system, White men were the citizen-soldiers: the virtuous bearers of rights and duties to the Republic, including the right to bear arms.

These ideas about honor, arms, and status are foreign to a liberal ideology that celebrates the equality of all individuals under the law and has no place for manly armed virtue. Today, we think democratic rights and racial/masculinist thinking are opposites. The ideas of rights and freedom associated with democracy carry a positive valence, while ideologies that valorize race and gender are proscribed. Yet, ascriptive ideologies emerged at a time when both ideological streams were positively viewed. In fact, ascriptive republicanism rests on the belief that rights, race, and honor are positive values that are inseparable at their core. As a result, ascriptive republicanism operated both as a principle to organize resistance against oppression and as a system of racialized and gendered injustice. What Edmund Morgan identified as the key paradox of American politics—the co-existence of freedom and slavery—is thus the logical structure that undergirds ascriptive republicanism: freedom requires slavery.[40]

Some authors claim that American ideas of martial honor, manhood, and virtue were exclusively rural and Southern.[41] In fact, honor and political virtue were traits cherished across the nation by rich and poor alike. It was far from unusual for members of the country's political elite to use violence to restore their honor.[42] The West Indies–born New Yorker Alexander Hamilton died in a duel. Even Abraham Lincoln was challenged to a duel. If the honor culture was exclusive in any way, it was that it applied exclusively to White men—it was a vital component of the system of White supremacy. Honor, chivalry, or manly "integrity" was the basis for social equality among White men across social ranks. As a result, White men of all classes—from farmers to preachers to future presidents—took slights to their honor seriously, much as they sought to extinguish any traces of honor from the lived experience of the enslaved.[43]

Given the centrality of honor in American social and political life, it was not White men alone who sought to prove their honor and manliness for political aims. Many Black men aspired to honor and manliness. For example, Frederick Douglass believed that armed service was the primary vehicle through which Black men could prove their political worth. But neither society nor the law allowed for that option. In a White polity, violence by a Black man could never be righteous—something Douglass knew all too well.[44] White people thought Black folks had tolerated and even *chosen* the dependency and purported protection of chattel slavery over the hard work and self-sufficiency of republican freedom. As a result, arms in the hands of Black people could never be in the service of liberty.[45] This is the irony to which this book returns time and again: White resistance to the idea that Black people could behave virtuously explains why even though Black people of both sexes served in almost all American wars, their service received minimal recognition in the official records.[46]

Unlike African Americans who were excluded from political virtue, White women did have a role in the Republic, albeit a subordinate one, as "republican mothers" and wives who instilled republican spirit and honor in their sons through modesty and chastity. They could use firearms in social life—for sport or protection—but not "bear" arms in defense of the nation.[47] The American rules of conduct in war reflected this view of women as "noncombatants" in need of protection even as women were unofficially used in military roles from nurse to soldier to spy.[48] It took more than a century for women to be officially included in the US military forces in 1948; they were only allowed to join combat units in 2015.[49]

THE INSTITUTIONALIZATION OF ASCRIPTIVE REPUBLICANISM

In this book, I will pay particular attention to how ascriptive republicanism became embedded in institutions, including the NRA, and how institutions have preserved and transmitted this ideology. Ascriptive republicanism did not structure only social relationships. Rather, it was etched in America's laws, military institutions, and martial traditions, which further linked the idea of political freedom to White male supremacy. The Founders knew that a professional standing army offered superior performance—but often in service to tyrants. Consequently, guided by republican ideals, they preserved the conscript citizen militia system and linked military service to political rights. Federal and state laws and constitutions established Whiteness and maleness as preconditions for both dimensions of republican citizenship. States required White males to enroll in the militia if they were to have a right to vote. In turn, White men of lower socioeconomic classes used their military service in the Revolution to advocate for their full political inclusion.[50]

Gun rights mythology has turned the "minuteman"—the (White) revolutionary citizen-soldier—into the freedom-loving, liberal-individualist gun owner archetype. According to this mythology, the minutemen were expert shooters, having learned to use the rifle in the private domain, relying on guns for protection and food. The responsibility of providing for a family and the discipline developed in learning to shoot for survival endowed these men with the "common sense" required to recognize the corruption of King George III and the bravery to fight against government abuse.[51] The rifle is "an emblem" of independence, responsibility, and democratic equality in this story.[52] Yet, the revolutionary militiamen were state-trained conscript soldiers mostly from urban settlements, not rugged woodsmen who learned the art of the rifle in the wild.[53]

Furthermore, contrary to NRA mythology, the state militias had limited military use. They were underfunded, underregulated, and undertrained. Conscripted soldiers were expected to purchase service weapons, which many couldn't afford. Refusal to serve was a long-standing problem that states addressed with fines and penalties or substitution rules—but generally with little success. As voting citizens, White men resisted the obligations imposed on them by their governments.[54] Despite its military limitations, though, the militia was of great *political* significance. First, the militias operated as recruitment pools for future political leaders and functioned as military enforcers for political parties and police auxiliaries for local communities. Second, they were a corporeal representation of the republican citizenship ideal: a symbol of the political power of White men and a focus on the aspirations of those excluded from citizenship. Their elaborate uniforms and weapons highlighted the social distance between the "true" American citizens—White men—and others in society. The militias learned, reproduced, and reinforced racial, gender, and class hierarchies through parades, musters, election-day service, and other performative acts.[55]

A critical irony that the book highlights but does not analyze in detail is that from early on, African Americans—and even White women—embraced martial republican ideals as a means toward political incorporation and equality. Republican ideology and the public symbolism of the militia appealed to all excluded groups because they seemed to offer the promise of inclusion to those who embraced the ideals of commitment to liberty and sacrifice for the common good. This is the deceptive promise of this ideological system because it obscured the interconnection between freedom and White male supremacy. Republicanism offered the promise that women and people of color could control their destinies; yet, in its ascriptive form, the ideology reserved freedom from domination by others for White men alone.[56] Marginalized groups hoped to achieve political inclusion by making claims of worthiness based on military service. However, ascriptive republicanism is a perilous worldview because it includes and excludes people from political membership based on more than one identity dimension. Political scientists would call it an "intersectional" ideology because it operates simultaneously along two (or more) axes of exclusion/inclusion.

In this worldview, race and gender operate together, not individually. Some people may meet the inclusion criteria along one dimension but fail on another. The result is an ideology that can appear egalitarian and appealing to many women and people of color. From Black abolitionists to Black Power proponents to Supreme Court Justice Clarence Thomas, many African Americans have been drawn to the patriarchal authority and honor symbolized by the virtuous armed man.[57] Yet ascriptive martial republicanism legitimizes social inequalities and valorizes White male supremacy.

Ascriptive republicanism offered marginalized groups the illusion of inclusion but never true equality. Even as it held the promise of ascribing *some* value under limited circumstances to some of the disadvantaged, ascriptive republicanism continued to justify and institutionally reinforce their marginalization and political exclusion. As a result, struggles by marginalized groups to be included in political membership on the grounds of their demonstrated commitment to martial republican values ironically bolstered the dominance of White men. It was not until the 1960s and 1970s, when the civil rights and women's rights movements of that era advanced a comprehensive new vision of citizenship based on nonviolence, anti-militarism, multiculturalism, and acceptance of cultural, gender, and racial differences, that ascriptive republicanism met with powerful opposition in American culture.[58]

One of the most poignant examples of how ascriptive republicanism operated in service to racial *inequality* by opening small political spaces for non-White people is the case of the Buffalo Soldiers and their state-level "brothers"—the Black state volunteer or "National Guard" groups. The Buffalo Soldiers were African American US Army regiments created after the Civil War. During the same period, African Americans organized volunteer militia groups at the state level. In both cases, these units represented the institutionalization of African American martial citizenship even as Black people continued to lack political rights. For those who participated in these military units and for many in the Black community who financed and supported these groups out of their meager resources, armed service to the nation was proof that African American *men* deserved political membership. Many in the African American community believed that military service would bring racial equality, and many in the White community resisted it for the same reason.[59] But Black military service was also service to White supremacy. Ironically, these African American volunteers participated in the slaughter of Native Americans in the West and America's quest for empire in Cuba and the Philippines, a war which some White supporters described as "conquest, extension, appropriation, annihilation, and even the extermination of inferior races."[60] White state authorities also used Black militia units to suppress labor activism among Black workers.[61]

How can an ideology that emerged in the eighteenth century continue to influence politics in the twenty-first? The preservation and continued dominance of ideologies that justify an existing social order depend on formal and informal social learning processes. In short, they are taught in families, churches, schools, national celebrations and monuments, and political campaigns.[62] The ascriptive republican model was preserved and disseminated into the twentieth century by the US military establishment, the educational system, and popular culture.[63] Many a schoolbook extolled the rugged, self-sufficient White woodsmen who fought the Revolution and settled the "Wild" West. According to twentieth-century schoolbook accounts, these rugged woodsmen, armed only with their civilian-life weapons, "ax and rifle (in the use of which weapons they have never been equaled)," and "unorganized and uncaptained"—that is, without any institutional support—"subdue[d] a continent" and spread democracy, capitalism, and independence across the land.[64] Never mind that the Americans would have lost the Revolution if not for French support. And never mind that the federal government planned and organized many aspects of Western expansion.[65] This ideal of (White) honor and manhood is evident even in contemporary gun ads targeting "a man's man," urging him to buy the "BRO-Tyrant" assault rifle.[66] It is also evident in political ads using military imagery and implied armed violence to address political disagreements and conflict.[67]

In this book, I will show that a key agent of transmission of ascriptive republican ideology has been the National Rifle Association. The NRA was a quasi-military, federally subsidized organization born out of the militia system of the late nineteenth century. The organization's mission was to preserve the republican citizen-soldier system by encouraging White male citizens to develop shooting skills. Long after the military and the education system abandoned ascriptive republican ideology—at least overtly[68]—under pressure from the progressive movements of the 1960s and 1970s, the NRA remained a key vector for the preservation and dissemination of these ideas to the broader public. Since the 1980s, NRA ideology that links firearm ownership to responsible citizenship has found its way into the Republican Party platforms, messaging, and policy proposals.[69] More recently, with the NRA weakened and distracted due to infighting and lawsuits, the Republican Party has taken the lead on reinforcing the absolutist messaging.[70]

The NRA's vision of citizenship reflects the American ascriptive republican tradition. For more than a hundred years, the organization believed that political virtue was developed by taking up shooting sports and hunting to prepare men for military service. The exemplar of the virtuous citizen was "the rifleman," the disciplined, rational, expert marksman. In this view, firearms were *instrumental* to political virtue, as shooting contributed to moral development, making men virtuous republican citizens. Thus, legislation that put roadblocks on White men's access to firearms and discouraged them from taking up shooting was detrimental to the Republic and put the country on a path to political corruption and tyranny.

The contemporary NRA narrative, which developed in the 1990s and is also reflected in Republican Party ads and communications, hasn't changed much from the earlier version, but it is different in one important way. This new ascriptive republican narrative presents firearms as *intrinsic* rather than instrumental to liberty. Gone are the days when the "riflemen" were expected to spend their weekends hunting or at the range. The modern virtuous citizen need not participate in military preparedness or even shooting sports. Gun ownership in itself is sufficient to make a person into a virtuous citizen. The consumer choice of *purchasing* a firearm is all it takes to qualify a citizen as politically virtuous. These contemporary virtuous citizens are not morally (and sometimes not even legally) required to know how to use, store, and maintain their firearms. In fact, the NRA has vigorously fought against legislation that imposes such requirements on gun owners, and Republican-controlled legislatures have followed suit. This, even while industry surveys suggest that fewer than half of gun owners are knowledgeable about firearms.[71]

Even though it no longer emphasizes military preparedness, the NRA narrative has preserved many ascriptive republican elements. It emphasizes gun owners' duty to the public good and their responsibility to use arms and the ballot box to protect the polity from political corruption. It is also a narrative that implicitly (if not explicitly) legitimizes a social hierarchy presided over by White men. Starting with the magazine's title, "The American Rifleman," the organization has envisaged the citizen-soldier as male—a *White* man. For the most part, women have no political role in the NRA's vision of the Republic. As citizens, women are suspect because their emotionalism and lack of "common sense" turn them into "naïve do-gooders," vulnerable to corruption. They are therefore relegated to the private domain as putative victims of crime or objects of men's illicit sexual desire. Only through firearms ownership can they achieve a sense of social "equality," as guns are thought to erase the physical power differentials between the sexes.

If women are marginalized in the world of the NRA, people of color are practically nonexistent. Going back to the early twentieth century, mentions of non-White people are exceedingly rare. Yet, the absence of mentions and pictures of African Americans and other racial minorities in *The American Rifleman* does not mean that gun rights narratives are race neutral. NRA narratives are implicitly racialized. First, volunteering for armed service was insufficient to make a man politically virtuous; he also had to be a "rifleman"—a shooting expert. In the early twentieth century, African Americans sought to join the ranks but were relegated to labor duty. At the same time, NRA narratives limited the scope of political virtue only to those privileged (White) men in the services who received expert training in shooting.

THE STRUCTURE OF THIS BOOK

The book consists of three key sections. The first section draws on primary and secondary historical sources to describe ascriptive republican ideology, explain its origins, situate it in American institutional development, and account for its persistence today. The second section uses primary sources, including NRA reports and publications, to tell the association's history and provide an in-depth analysis of its ascriptive republican narratives. The third section focuses on public opinion. Using an original national survey of White Americans, I demonstrate the prevalence of ascriptive republican ideology in the White public and its relationship to gun-related beliefs, policy preferences, and attitudes about democratic norms and political violence.

Chapter 1 defines and outlines the premise of martial republican ideology, emphasizing four concepts central to this worldview: the dyads of virtue/corruption and freedom/slavery. I argue that early republican theory associated political virtue with readiness to sacrifice for the Republic and political corruption as selfishness and prioritizing personal gain over the public good. Independence—not relying on others for material security—and preparedness defined the virtuous republican citizen. By contrast, dependence led to corruption and slavery. The emphasis on republicanism was instrumental in expanding democracy, sustaining the politics of social deference, and fueling the American quest for empire.[72]

Chapter 2 discusses how the ideas of virtue/corruption and freedom/slavery became intertwined with race and gender hierarchies—the ascriptive dimension of American martial republicanism. Specifically, the chapter focuses on how Whiteness and virtue were juxtaposed to Blackness and slavery. Perversely, slavery was portrayed as the result of choice, and Black resistance to slavery was misconstrued while Black military service in American wars was erased. This chapter draws on analysis of historic texts that are undoubtedly painful to read; however, an analysis of the ideology and assumptions that underwrite these texts helps us to evaluate how claims are marshaled today and how sanitized stories have inflamed White political grievances.[73]

Chapter 3 traces how ascriptive republicanism became embedded and reproduced in the country's military institutions, specifically the state militia. The early Republic hosted a multitude of military organizations; some were conscripted (the "enrolled militia") and others were self-organized and loosely regulated volunteers (the "volunteers" or "National Guards"). The enrolled and volunteer militia throughout the nineteenth century were inefficient and ineffective military institutions. The reliable backbone of the American forces in the Revolution was not the militia but the professional soldiers, men whom revolutionary pamphleteers described as people who "dislike labor," were "the dregs of the people," and just like slaves, "have relinquished voluntarily the blessings of freedom."[74] Ironically, the nineteenth-century militia was undertrained, underfunded, and underregulated by cash-strapped and administratively weak states. Their perseverance resulted from their political utility as symbols of White male martial citizenship and authority. Militia units taught, reproduced, and reinforced American social hierarchies. In the words of Edmund Morgan, they were "school[s] of subordination" and a "prop for deferential politics."[75]

Although the military was a key institution for reproducing ascriptive republicanism, it was not the only one. Chapter 4 discusses the role of historical analysis, school textbooks, novels, films, and public memory in teaching, reproducing, reinforcing, and disseminating ascriptive republican ideology well into the modern era. School textbooks, especially those promoted by Southern women's organizations keen on creating and maintaining a positive, democratic, and romanticized view of the Confederacy (known as "the Lost Cause"), taught young pupils myths about White valor at arms in the Revolution, the Civil War, and Reconstruction well into the twentieth century.[76] Monuments to Confederate heroes and loyal slaves also helped preserve ascriptive republican ideology.[77] So did Civil War reenactments and other commemorations popular to this day, especially among participants in the NRA gun culture. Books and movies, such as Dixon's *The Clansman* and Mitchell's *Gone with the Wind*, reinforced these ideas at the broader public level.[78]

Chapter 5 discusses the ascriptive republican origins of the NRA, from its emergence as a "quasi-governmental" organization to its modern-day political outsider pretense. The NRA was founded in 1871 by National Guardsmen whose vision was to create virtuous citizen-soldiers by incentivizing the country's adolescent and adult (White) men to take up the sport of rifle shooting. The National Guard—the country's most powerful lobbying group through the mid-twentieth century[79]—became the backbone of the NRA's membership and influence. Their combined lobbying—a privilege that Progressive reforms denied the US Army—led to a federally granted monopoly over the sale of Army surplus weapons and ammunition to civilian shooters. This program helped the group build its civilian membership and political base—creating the conditions to make the NRA the political powerhouse it is today.

Chapter 6 discusses the evolution of the NRA's membership. Founded as a military organization, the NRA had little room for women or African Americans as members and competitors, even though the bylaws did not explicitly exclude these groups. The NRA did not need to formally exclude them because, through the 1940s, the Army did so (from combat infantry units), and participation in many NRA-sponsored events was meant for active-duty soldiers and those who could be drafted as riflemen—White men. Even after the desegregation of the military and the recruitment of more women, the NRA remained an organization focused on White men. My analysis of the visual content of *The American Rifleman* and *America's 1st Freedom* documents how rare pictures of women and people of color, both relative to White men and in absolute terms, are on the cover and the pages of the magazines.

Chapters 7 and 8 provide a detailed analysis of the NRA's ascriptive republican narratives. The chapters focus on the main elements of ascriptive republicanism, explaining how the organization conceptualized political virtue and corruption. I pinpoint the similarities and differences between the republican ideology of the early Republic and the NRA's ascriptive republicanism. Specifically, chapter 7 shows the remarkable consistency with which the NRA has conceptualized the political world for over 150 years. One key difference is that the early NRA story locates the source of political virtue not in compulsory military service—as was the case in the Revolutionary era—but in marksmanship skills developed in the private domain. The *choice* to learn how to shoot and to be prepared for war is the foundation of political virtue. In the contemporary narrative, the organization has decoupled virtue and military service by associating virtue with the consumer act of purchasing a firearm. Neither marksmanship nor even training is necessary for gun ownership and the acquisition of political virtue. Yet, the message remains the same: a man learns to decipher and defend democratic institutions through engagement with arms.

Chapter 8 analyzes the NRA's understanding of political corruption, focusing on the groups that the association understands as vectors of venality: criminals, do-gooders, fanatics, and extremists. Do-gooders—whom the NRA imagines to be women more than men—are not necessarily corrupt, but because they lack cold reason, they are easily influenced by the Republic's enemies. Fanatics are committed to gun control, but because of either naïveté or intention they do not understand the importance of civilian gun ownership for the health of the Republic. Extremists—a heavily racialized group—support gun control for political reasons: their goal is to subvert American democratic institutions. Criminals, another racialized category,[80] are presented as the beneficiaries of gun control laws and the government's excuse for disarming law-abiding citizens.

Chapter 9 delves deeper into the NRA's theory of democracy. According to the association, citizens have a right to armed insurrection when their institutions no longer represent their interests. The group defines political freedom as private gun ownership and insists on a bidirectional, causal relationship between the two: private gun ownership fosters democratic freedom, and democracy necessitates universal citizen access to firearms.

However, by decoupling gun ownership from military service, the NRA has created a series of gendered and racialized moral traps that the chapter identifies and analyzes. Ultimately, the NRA's insurrectionist narrative has no answer for two key questions: why were American White women excluded from the vote until 1920 and from full military membership until 1948 (and combat until 2015), when they could and did own firearms in the private domain? And why didn't White gun owners—the law-abiding, virtuous citizens—come to the aid of their Black brethren during slavery and Jim Crow? These issues highlight the ascriptive assumptions hidden in the NRA's republican stories. They also showcase the political dangers inherent in simplistic narratives that attribute chattel slavery and the Holocaust to the lack of guns among the affected populations instead of the ideological and institutional systems that justified and fostered these practices.[81]

Chapter 10 moves the analysis from the NRA narratives to contemporary White public opinion and asks whether ascriptive republicanism is a measurable ideology that can be identified through survey analysis. Building on extant work on American ideologies,[82] I use factor analytic techniques to show that beliefs associated with ascriptive republicanism are part of a coherent set of ideas in the public mind. Specifically, White Americans who believe gun ownership is "important" for making someone a "true American" also think that nativity, European ancestry, Christianity, and traditional gender roles are equally important. Ascriptive republicanism, as I define and measure it, is more prevalent among conservatives, Republicans, White people who live in rural America, and those who express an attachment to White identity or negative attitudes toward Black people. Ascriptive republicanism correlates positively with gun ownership, prioritizing gun rights over other rights, and viewing the NRA as a virtuous defender of the public good. Using experiments, I show that White Americans are more likely to perceive White gun owners as virtuous citizens ("good guys with guns") but Black gun owners as criminals, consistent with ascriptive republicanism. Furthermore, this is especially prevalent among those who embrace this worldview.

Chapter 11 focuses on the more profound and pernicious influences of the NRA's ascriptive republican ideology, which calls for a right to insurrection, on White Americans' support for political violence and antidemocratic policies, norms, and practices. The data show that White people who embrace ascriptive republicanism are more likely to support militarized policy ideas, such as "stand your ground" laws and even "extended stand your ground" proposals that immunize those who shoot and kill protesters. Furthermore, people who endorse ascriptive republicanism are more likely to believe that guns should be allowed in political spaces such as protests. My data also show that a small but not trivial percentage of White Americans are open to political violence and feel that it is a justified response under some circumstances. Openness to violent radicalization is stronger among White people who embrace ascriptive republicanism. Also, this same group is more likely to view the January 6, 2021, US Capitol events as "a rally by patriots" instead of a riot. The effect exists for Democrats as well as Republicans. As others have noted, there is a big gap between being open to political violence in a survey and threatening or harming others for political ends.[83] Nevertheless, these findings move beyond accounts focused on partisan social identity to underscore the danger to democratic institutions inherent in ideologies that associate private gun ownership with political virtue and claim that democracy affords people a right to use arms for political ends.

The good news in the data is that White Americans also embrace a second, competing form of republicanism—an ideology that I call inclusive civic republicanism (ICR). This ideology, shared by 79 percent of White Americans, fuses a commitment to peaceful political engagement, civic forms of voluntarism and participation, and strong beliefs in multiculturalism. ICR is negatively correlated with ascriptive martial republicanism, and the data show that it often counters or mitigates the latter's effect. It is through the rejection of ascriptive republicanism and the conscious embrace of this inclusive republican ideology that America may have a way out of the current crisis of democratic politics.

∴

Part One

HISTORICAL FOUNDATIONS

∵

CHAPTER 1

Republican Ideology in Early America

White Americans' obsession with firearms is often expressed not in the laissez-faire language of economic liberalism but in terms of duty, obligation, and patriotism. Gun rights principals describe the world as freedom-loving "good guys with guns" pitted against corrupt "anti-gunners," political elites and their sinister or naïve supporters. They say that these corrupt national and international elites, which the Republicans have branded "the swamp," want to impose political tyranny through gun control. In this dark and dangerous world where elected representatives cannot be trusted to act for the public good, "good guys with guns" must be vigilant. They should be ready for an armed revolution, if that is what it takes to restore democracy.

The anti-lockdown armed protests of 2020 and the attack on the US Capitol in 2021 used this language of revolution against tyranny. They carried signs saying, "We the People," "Tyrants Get the Rope," and "My Constitutional Rights Are Essential." Elsewhere in the country, at other state houses, the signs read "A Man Chooses, A Slave Obeys," or "What's the Fix? 1776."[1] They claimed to be responding to violations of democracy and to be "tak[ing] our country back" from corrupt politicians. "Hang Mike Pence," they chanted.[2]

And it is not only NRA leaders and followers who express a worldview linking gun ownership to a citizen's right to overthrow a "tyrant" and even to political violence more explicitly. Prominent members of the Republican Party, especially the Trump-aligned faction, express similar beliefs. In campaign ads and speeches, they characterize the Democratic Party and the federal government apparatus as "corrupt" or "tyrannical" and offer citizens' Second Amendment rights as a "remedy." For example, Rep. Lauren Boebert suggested that "the second amendment isn't about hunting, except hunting tyrants, maybe."[3] The pattern continued and intensified in the 2022 election cycle: Senate candidate Eric Greitens (R-MO) issued a video ad of himself, armed with a shotgun, and a group of men dressed in soldiers' gear breaking into a suburban house to "hunt for RINOs" (Republicans in name only).[4] Trump suggested that "second amendment people" should go after Hillary Clinton during the 2016 presidential campaign.[5] Senator Josh Hawley (R-MO), who pumped his fist in approval in the direction of the Capitol rioters, wants to restore American Christian manhood. Guns will transform American men into the masculine, self-sufficient, independent Roman plebeians whose discipline and willingness to sacrifice for the common good make them worthy participants in self-government.[6] Even the Supreme Court's *District of Columbia v. Heller* decision has endorsed civilian gun carry as a right to revolution, imagining that the virtuous "able-bodied men of the nation" will train and organize to prevent tyranny.[7]

I argue that the ideology that undergirds this regressive, gun-centered vision of the political world, where citizens have absolute and unquestionable "second amendment remedies" and are entitled to act as a check on government abuse through threats of physical violence, has no relationship to Lockean liberalism, which inspired the "American Creed" conception of American political culture.[8] Instead, this book demonstrates that American gun culture is steeped in a different and much older theory of politics: martial republicanism. Martial republicanism emphasizes the importance of a citizen's political virtue, a capacity developed through armed preparedness, in preserving democracy. However, republican ideology does not come with a pre-defined understanding of "the people" or peoplehood; it does not tell us who gets to be a citizen and who can become virtuous. In the United States, Americans of the Revolutionary era filled this "gap" by defining the virtuous citizen in ascriptive terms, and specifically, criteria based on race, gender, and (to a degree) religion. This chapter explains the fundamental tenets of republican ideology and situates this worldview in the American context.

MARTIAL REPUBLICANISM

Understanding ascriptive republican ideology requires explaining martial republicanism. Republicanism is the theory that undergirds democratic practice. For that reason, explaining how Americans—especially the White men who constituted the dominant group in society—understood democracy and its relationship to arms is the first step to understanding the contemporary White American obsession with firearms.

Today, we think of republicanism primarily as a commitment to civic engagement. It is keeping abreast of political developments and participation in the political life of the polity that defines the modern-day good American citizen. Going back to the 1960s, scholars have identified American democracy with the prevalence of this participatory "civic culture."[9] Republican theorists worry that democratic decline, division, and polarization, the ills of modern democracy, are related to the decline of people coming together in communities and interacting meaningfully as social and political members.[10]

However, early republican theories placed significant weight not only on political participation but also on service at arms—military service. Republicans were deeply concerned about preserving individual autonomy and liberty and consensual governance. Participatory forms of government, where the people collectively make decisions about their future, were desirable above all others. However, according to republicans, the problem with such regimes was their lack of longevity. Ancient and medieval republics promised individual liberty and self-governance, but soon gave way to absolutism.[11] Republican theorists thus sought to explain what caused republics to fail and what polities could do to preserve participatory, egalitarian institutions that represented the commonweal. Their story of politics incorporated historical time and rested on the idea that when people form social bonds of reciprocity and trust in each other as a community, they create their own morality—what we would call a "peoplehood."[12]

But what caused republics to fail? This premodern worldview, which emerged long before nation-states and industrial capitalist economies, not to mention assault rifles and nuclear weapons, explained the collapse of democratic institutions in citizens' nature, character, and behavior. Republicanism is an inherently pessimistic ideology: it views venality and corruption as constitutive parts of human nature. For republicans, political virtue—prioritizing the public good over self-interest—is not innate; it is cultivated. Much like Charlton Heston and the NRA, republican theorists believe that people become corrupt because they focus exclusively on self-interest at the expense of the public good. Elected leaders are entrusted with pursuing public welfare as defined by citizens engaged in political deliberation. However, these leaders and their followers could be tempted by narrow self-interest to pursue goals that subvert rather than promote the public good. The temptation of power and money ("luxury" in the era's language) is too great for most people to overcome. The "depravity of mankind," said Samuel Adams, lay in that people placed "ambition and lust for power above the law," thus endangering liberty.[13] Heston would agree.

VIRTUE AND CORRUPTION

Life in the Republic was characterized by an almost Manichean fight between virtue and corruption, good and evil. The temptation to succumb to vice and personal gain was high, so republicans placed great emphasis on virtue and its cultivation. The liberal theorist Locke defined virtue as opposition to social hierarchies based on heredity and social privilege. Religious faith and rationality enabled people to identify and promote the public good.[14] Other liberal theorists, such as Adam Smith, understood the public good to be the aggregation of individual personal interests.[15] In the republican view, by contrast, the public good was distinct from private interests. Furthermore, neither reason nor religion was strong enough to constrain the human desire for power, so neither could alleviate the danger to democratic institutions. For republicans, virtue derived from self-reliance and independence. In turn, independence was understood as autonomy or not being beholden to others for survival and prosperity. In the original stipulation, virtue was thus inherently aristocratic and exclusive, the purview of the propertied classes.[16]

Such elitist notions differentiated the gentlemen from the plebeians, attributing to the former a degree of moral superiority outside the commoner's reach. The republican model implied that only men of "property" and not wage-earners could be sufficiently independent and thus virtuous.[17] A wage-earner was beholden to employers; therefore, he could not be trusted to put the public interest ahead of his employer's. The poor and idle depended on the community or illicit activity and did not have the autonomy required to exercise the responsibilities of citizenship. Thus, the working classes and the poor could not be entrusted with the public good and governance. Modern-day political suspicion of those who depend on government beneficence and those with a criminal record is rooted partly in republican ideals. From this perspective, contemporary beliefs that Black people "choose" laziness and state dependence or that women seek too much power and "special treatment" resonate with republican beliefs about political virtue and corruption.[18] As we shall see, these beliefs have deep roots in the American experience.

Republican independence also required wisdom and courage in thought and opinion, and that the citizen remain disinterested, dispassionate, and enlightened. Independence ensured that citizens would make political decisions based on the public good rather than on narrow self-interest.[19] In one sense, contemporary calls for "civility" in political discourse have their roots in this worldview and its emphasis on enlightened, dispassionate citizens coming together to define and defend the public good. As we will see, the NRA's calls to listen to the "common sense" of the people "whose roots lay in the soil" over that of people living in the urban centers whom the group often deemed irrational or excessively self-interested or dependent on the state are modern versions of republican narratives.[20]

Armed preparedness was a second key source of moral strength and virtue. The training and discipline of armed service prepared citizens to defend the Republic. At the same time, one's readiness to make the ultimate sacrifice for the polity built the kind of public-spiritedness and enlightenment necessary for the virtuous pursuit of the public good.[21] Republicanism has its roots in ancient times when people could hardly imagine modern weapons and warfare. Theirs was the world of cannons, swords, and daggers—or, at best, early-technology pistols and rifles. Wars in the eighteenth and nineteenth centuries relied on large numbers of soldiers trained to march in formation and shoot in groups. Technological advances that transformed twentieth-century wars, such as rockets, airplanes, and cyberwarfare, were unknown to revolutionary pamphleteers in 1776. The soldier and his rifle were central to how people thought about war. This approach is also evident in the ideology of the NRA. During the first hundred years of the organization's history, armed preparedness in the form of rifle practice was a crucial feature of the NRA narrative, central to its conception of political virtue and enlightened citizenship. The idea that the man with the gun defends democracy is key in the contemporary NRA narrative as well, even though the group has replaced military preparedness with the consumer act of gun ownership and readiness to defend gun rights through political activism as the hallmarks of political virtue.

In republican ideology, the opposite of virtue is corruption. Republics are viewed as institutions that are vulnerable to internal and external threats. These threats arise from "corruption": groups and leaders—domestic and foreign—who are unenlightened and guided by emotion rather than reason, or those with ill intent who seek to replace republican freedom with "tyranny." In turn, republicans define "tyranny" as a government that does not represent the will of the body politic, and instead seeks to lavish its supporters (what today we may call "special interests," or "the swamp") with material benefits in exchange for power. These "others" are willing to betray republican freedom and to accept nondemocratic governance in exchange for personal benefit. Corruption emerges when citizens pursue private gain or "luxury" through the public sphere or when they are too weak in body and spirit to resist the power of others. As more citizens lose the vigilance and virtue associated with armed preparedness, the danger increases of losing political autonomy to a tyrant.[22] As the NRA warns, without an armed citizenry, democracy is in peril.[23]

Thus, money and power were thought to be key sources of corruption. The English republican tradition, which in many ways shaped the narratives of the American Revolution, was suspicious of centralized administration on the one hand and moneyed elites and commercialism on the other.

Aristocratic in character and rooted in defense of private property, republicanism resisted the taxes and public debt that the English government
expected for sustaining a professional army.[24] From a republican perspective, these policies drained the material and moral resources of the most
virtuous and independent class, the yeomanry or freeholders, while at the
same time centralizing power in the hands of a few government officials,
inviting corruption.[25]

Moreover, republican ideology held that a professional or "standing"
army—which at the time typically meant an army made up of mercenaries,
often recruited from outside the realm—bestowed excessive power upon
the few who controlled it, creating a power imbalance between the citizens
and their leaders.[26] A professional army consisted of men who viewed the
military as a job for pay, not as a duty, and who would work for the highest
bidder. Despots and demagogues could take control of the army and use it
to enslave the citizens and destroy the institutions of the Republic. Worse,
the existence of a professional army reduced the incentives for citizens to
train in arms and be ready to protect their polity. The result was a net loss
of public virtue, followed by civic and political apathy, and the Republic's
eventual collapse and replacement by tyranny. Military preparedness and
active engagement in political life were the twin rights and obligations of
republican citizenship, without which the Republic could not survive.[27]
In the same vein, the NRA today warns of the danger of a "police state"
with authority to confiscate citizens' arms. Mirroring republican themes,
the association warns that gun control makes citizens weak and apathetic,
more susceptible to tyranny, while an armed citizenry is a "great equalizer,"
counteracting the power of political elites.[28]

English republicanism, the source of many American republican ideas,
emerged out of the English Civil War and the clashes between Catholics
and Protestants that followed Elizabeth I's reign. During this time, English
defensive forces were organized as county militia led by the local gentry,
which led to regional power centers being represented in Parliament. In
1688, the Catholic King James II attempted to disarm the Protestant gentry
and consolidate power in the hands of the Catholic Royal Court, alarming
Parliament. Protestants sought external help in removing the King. After
James II abdicated, Parliament offered the throne to the Protestant Prince
William of Holland on the condition that he accept a declaration of rights.
The declaration said to contain all "traditional English rights" included a
guarantee that Protestants would be permitted to bear arms for their de-
fense "suitable to their condition and as allowed by law."[29]

In the middle and late seventeenth century, settlers brought with them
to America the lessons of the English Civil War.[30] These ideas acquired

added resonance in the context of the American Revolution when a standing army of Redcoats controlled by the King sought to impose royal tax policy by force.[31] The dispute started as a result of Britain's expectation that the colonists shoulder some of the cost of the Seven Years' War and other expeditions meant to protect the colonies from the Spanish, the French, and the Native Americans, but it escalated into a civil war that led to the establishment of an independent republic.[32]

The ardently republican founders and their heirs told the story of the American Revolution as a tale of political virtue winning over corruption. In revolutionary tracts and pamphlets, the British government, especially the Parliament, was portrayed as a corrupt and venal elite intent on destroying the colonies' autonomy and self-governance. In one sense, that narrative was not very different from contemporary stories about the corrupt "deep state," or the Washington "swamp." The colonists understood British efforts to quell the riots that erupted in Boston in the aftermath of the Tea Act of 1773 as an attempt to use a "standing army"—that is, the British Regulars—to take over colonial governance, dissolve elected assemblies, and confiscate private property directly and through arbitrary taxation. In their view, the corrupt English Parliament and Court had run out of opportunities to grant patronage and offices in England proper and thus needed to extract more resources from the American colonies.[33]

The American republican ideal defined and emphasized the moral distance between the virtuous (White) American Patriots and the venal British authorities. At a time of great uncertainty, the image of the armed citizenry, the citizen-soldiers, played an essential role in mobilizing colonists to join the Revolution rather than remain loyal to the Crown. It also offered reassurance of a future characterized by republican independence and liberty. Revolutionary narratives portrayed the militiamen as virtuous heroes—the heirs of Cincinnatus. These martial republican ideals became embedded in schoolbooks, novels, public monuments, and later, films. Charlton Heston's movies reflect this belief system; so do his ideas. It is the ideal of the independent (White) American yeomen who relied on their strengths and abilities—their mastery of the rifle, in the NRA's version of the myth—to conquer the land, protect their institutions, and defeat Britain. Economic and political independence allowed the colonists to develop dispassionate reason and use it to engage in martial preparedness and politics. In turn, the technical and moral skills associated with armed service made (White) American men worthy guardians of the public good, able to recognize corruption and rise against it.[34]

These beliefs were central in how the Patriots roused the colonists against Britain. American propagandists such as Josiah Quincy, John Hancock, and John Adams created a stark dichotomy between life in freedom as a citizen-soldier who defends civil liberties and slavery under a King and his standing army. These revolutionaries insisted that political freedom in America could only persist if the new state cultivated virtuous citizens. Only these honorable and martially trained republican men could recognize the dangers of political corruption and be ready to fight it politically and militarily.[35]

FREEDOM AND SLAVERY

In addition to virtue and corruption, American republican ideology engaged two other important political concepts: freedom and slavery. Freedom and slavery as political concepts are not dependent on race. Ideals of republican freedom date back to ancient Greece, long before the concept of race was developed as a political category. The institution of slavery predates the American experience and can be found in all regions of the world. However, American ascriptive republicanism strengthened the relationship between Blackness and slavery, and conversely, between freedom and Whiteness. In effect, White Americans developed an intersectional racialized and gendered theory of the Republic, which elevated White men alone as virtuous citizens.[36]

Freedom and slavery have had different meanings across time and space. Ancient Greek accounts defined freedom in the context of "unimpeded motion," the lack of obstacles to action. Slavery, by contrast, was defined in terms of externally imposed limitations on human action. Across many Western cultures, freedom and slavery have been posited as antonyms; in Greek and Latin, the word denoting freedom meant "not enslaved." Liberal thought defined freedom in negative terms. Rights, or the guaranteed absence of interference by civil authority, protected individual freedom. State limitations on human action—especially state interference with property ownership—led to slavery.[37]

The republican narratives of the Revolution recast the meaning of freedom as human capacity for independent action—that is, human agency. Unlike the liberal tradition, which viewed freedom and slavery as two contrasting outcomes resulting from actions of civil authority, American ascriptive republicanism placed freedom and slavery as the two ends of a continuum. The amount of freedom that an individual or a community enjoyed did not depend on external factors. Instead, it was endogenous to the people's character and their willingness to resist corruption. Tyrannical government, and thus slavery, always lurked in the Republic. Each citizen, and the citizenry as a body, resisted slavery by cultivating political and martial virtue. Individuals who did not take the appropriate steps to prevent corruption by cultivating virtue *chose* to be enslaved. Thus their enslavement was legitimate, because they consented to it through their behavior. In the words of Samuel Adams, "nations were as free as they deserved to be." Josiah Quincy held the same sentiment: "if the people of the Commonwealth of Massachusetts shall ever become slaves, it will be from choice and not from nature, it will be, not because they have not the power to maintain their freedom, but because they are unworthy of it."[38] These narratives emphasized that freedom was *not* a right of people as humans, but something learned or acquired through sacrifice and resistance. It was earned, not given.

Liberal thought understood freedom as a natural right inherent in humanity. Slavery resulted from civil authorities denying individuals their natural or "God-given" rights. However, the American republican tradition turned the relationship between freedom and slavery on its head, creating what Edmund Morgan has labeled "the American Paradox." American republicans did not recognize liberty as a God-endowed property of all human beings. Nor did they attribute slavery to choices by civil authority and institutions to which people did not consent. Instead, they attributed slavery to people's choices as individuals and as a body politic. It was their *choice not* to pursue political virtue that led to individuals' enslavement.[39]

In this sense, citizenship was not a status conferred by civil authorities but a perpetual practice, a performance that necessitated constant reinforcement. Veering away from practicing citizenship could lead to slavery, and the citizen would be complicit in this change of political status.[40] Today this comes through in the NRA's (and the Republican Party's) warnings that citizens must practice constant vigilance to avoid the "slippery slope" of gun control, confiscation, and tyranny. If contemporary gun owners are slacking in fulfilling their duties as citizens—if they don't vote, and don't contact their political leaders on behalf of gun rights—they may lose their freedom, and they will have only themselves to blame. Gun control, some Republicans warn, will make the citizenry "weak" and "vulnerable" to invasion.[41] Other Republicans have argued that the Second Amendment is "not subject to debate," it is an "absolute" right that "shall not be infringed," and that anyone who says otherwise is "a tyrant" seeking to take away people's liberty.[42]

In eighteenth-century American political discourse, the concept of slavery appears in almost every pamphlet and oration discussing citizenship, political rights, and constitutional principle. Economic dependency on faraway British creditors and increased transfers of property—and thus power—from the colonists to the Crown did not just threaten affluent colonists' quality of life. Economic dependency weakened human agency and made the colonists "tame and abject as the blacks we rule over."[43] Republican citizenship maximized the social and political distance between the deserving and the undeserving. In the international context, this meant the colonists on the one hand and the British sovereign on the other. In the domestic sphere, as chapter 2 explores in detail, it translated to White men on the one hand and women and African Americans (enslaved and free) on the other. In this sense, the coexistence of White freedom and Black slavery in the American context was not contradictory or paradoxical, as Morgan claimed, but rather mutually constitutive and reinforcing. It was a feature, not a bug.

In fact, these ideals were central to American Revolutionaries' thinking in 1776 and highly influential in how they sought to organize their society: how they explained the relative positions of White men, women, and African Americans in the social order. As I discuss in chapter 3, this ascriptive republican worldview also shaped the relationship between the body politic and the military forces, and between citizens and those who did not enjoy political membership.[44] The institutional embodiment of ascriptive republican ideology was the citizen-soldier—the militiaman or "minuteman" of Bunker Hill. The conscript militia of the early Republic, and the volunteer National Guards of the nineteenth century, the citizen-soldiers, represent the institutionalized form of this worldview. The NRA, a military "patriotic" organization, emerged out of the National Guards in the late nineteenth century with the goal of reforming the country's citizen soldiery and enhancing their shooting skills and political virtue. The group and, more recently, its Republican supporters have continued to this day to propagate this ideology linking arms and White manhood.

CHAPTER 2

An Exclusive Vision
of Virtue and Citizenship

As I discussed in the previous chapter, Revolutionary-era republican ideology rested on two sets of contrasting ideas: virtue/corruption and freedom/slavery. (White) Americans defined themselves and their adversaries—the British Crown and Parliament—in these terms. They developed a narrative explaining that the source and persistence of their political virtue were found in the citizen-soldiers' preparedness to defend the public good in politics and on the battlefield. It was (White) American men's commitment to political virtue that would ensure their republican freedom in the future. America's European antagonists relied on standing armies— "species of animals, wholly at the disposal of government"[1]—and therefore their people were neither virtuous nor free.

Republican ideals are not necessarily ascriptive, nor do they apply only to a group of people who share a gender, race, religion, or language. The draw of republicanism and what makes it the engine of democracy is that—in its most universal articulations—it confers membership on any person who behaves consistently with republican ideals. This inclusive vision of the "American Creed" suggests that anyone who fulfills their duties to the polity, regardless of their biological characteristics and social origins, deserves the title of citizen.[2] This ideal is central to *The Civic Culture*—America's civic nationalism—that mid-twentieth-century political scientists extolled as a model for the world.[3] It is also central to the reimagined understanding of membership that emerged with the civil rights and women's rights movements of the 1960s and 1970s. This new republicanism embraced civil participation, nonviolence, and multiculturalism and rejected racism, patriarchy, militarism, and armed violence. As we will see in chapter 10, this inclusive civic republicanism is alive and vital in White American public opinion and offers a solid counter to ascriptive republican ideology. But that is not the republicanism that the founding generation built.

Instead, White Americans of the Revolutionary era developed an ascriptive narrative that justified the elevation of White men alone to political citizenship and excluded African Americans and women. American ascriptive ideology described White men as freedom fighters who proved their deservingness for political membership on the battlefields of the Revolution. However, ascriptive republicanism portrayed African Americans as slaves by *choice*, who eschewed the risk and hardship of freedom and material and moral independence for the protection and dependence of slavery. The success of the narrative rested on denying and making invisible both the cruelty of slavery and the military service of Black men who have participated in every American war. This chapter thus exposes the dark underbelly of the American experience. As such, it is painful to read. However, this story is theoretically relevant and politically important for contemporary debates. Exposing the evil character of chattel slavery is important for dispelling contemporary myths promoted by the gun rights movement. As we will see, these myths deny the systemic nature of slavery, implying that it was a relationship between and among individuals—enslaved and slavemasters. As a result, they conclude that "if only" African Americans had firearms, they would not have been enslaved. This line of thinking comes dangerously close to blaming the enslaved for their predicament, rather than the White political system that enslaved them.

WHITE VIRTUE, WHITE FREEDOM

Republican notions of political equality have deep roots in America. Colonists from the British Isles did not understand themselves as citizens in the way the term came to be understood in the American Revolution. However, as Crown subjects, they knew themselves to have rights and obligations to the polity. By the seventeenth century, the terms "subject" and "citizen" were used interchangeably. Since the English Civil War, the idea of citizenship had been linked to republican equality—political members viewed each other as equals even if they viewed the Crown as a sovereign.[4]

Although the colonies reserved political participation for only a subset of White men, British law recognized indentured servants as freeborn English people and thus subjects. Half to two-thirds of Europeans who immigrated to the colonies before the American Revolution arrived on indenture contracts—not enslaved, but not free. In America, indentured servants were called "Redemptioneers" or "free-willers" to differentiate them from enslaved Black people. This status afforded them legal rights, including access to the courts, that were not available to slaves.[5]

Furthermore, the exigencies of colonial life meant that all White men, even indentured servants, could exercise the martial dimension of political membership. Rich White men sent their indentured servants to take their place in the militia, and in many places White indentures were expected to be familiar with the arms of war. Some colonial and early state laws allowed indentures to serve in the militia with written permission from their masters. When indentures gained freedom because of military service, masters received compensation.[6] In Virginia, the law required masters to pay "freedom dues" to every White male indentured servant who completed his contract and became free. These dues included a working musket. This requirement likely symbolized the former servant's admission into citizenship.[7]

After the Revolution, republicanism became the moral force behind the enfranchisement of all White males and the first wave of political and cultural democratization of American politics for those at the intersection of manhood and Whiteness. White men who did not own real property, including indentured servants, already understood themselves as citizens. Their service in the Revolution grounded these men's claims to republican virtuous citizenship. Institutional design reflected these bottom-up pressures from White men who fought at arms but whom colonial laws excluded from the franchise. Even before delegates arrived in Philadelphia for the Constitutional Convention, state constitutional conventions had begun debating the franchise's reach and whether those compelled to serve at arms should be enabled to have a say in politics. In Pennsylvania, militiamen's associations representing native-born White men and German immigrants petitioned the state assembly to ensure that "brave and spirited" men were enfranchised. Backed by Benjamin Franklin and Thomas Paine, militiamen argued for and eventually won state constitutions that extended political rights to most White men. In Maryland, militiamen marched to the polls, demanding the right to vote and threatening to lay down their arms if those rights were not granted. These militant displays influenced the delegates to the state constitutional convention, who consequently agreed to more inclusive citizenship rights that more closely reflected the republican ideal of the citizen-soldier.[8]

By the early decades of the nineteenth century, most White men had achieved access to both dimensions of republican citizenship: the bullet and the ballot. Native-born White men and European immigrants volunteered for federal service and organized volunteer militia companies to demonstrate their martial republican ethos. Militia service was significant for White immigrants who needed to prove their Whiteness and thus deservingness for political equality relative to Protestant Anglo-Saxons.[9] In part, volunteer militia service was popular because it reinforced White men's claims of political equality anchored in honor and virtue. Through militia service, men from various social backgrounds interacted as citizen-soldiers—that is, as political equals. These White men could be the NRA's "good guy with a gun." The proliferation of military titles, especially in the South, also helped shrink the social distance between White men, reinforcing bonds of White equality.[10]

In modern-day gun parlance, the right and duty to own and bear arms to defend the nation became a "great equalizer" among White men. Social class differences remained important, and social standing continued to matter within White male society regardless of how political membership was determined. However, expanding the circle of virtue to include almost all White men, poor and rich, immigrant and native-born, and to extend to them the opportunity to perform the rituals of republican membership on equal terms, created a *perception* of political equality within Whiteness. Perceived in-group equality also fostered greater in-group solidarity, which is visible even in modern politics.[11]

Political equality among White men strengthened the intersectional character of ascriptive republicanism. Ascriptive republican ideology uses more than one dimension to include and exclude categories of people from political membership. In political science, this makes it an ideology that exploits the meeting of two categories in distinguishing the "deserving" from the "undeserving." Status equality among White men strengthened the emotional bonds within this group. It also reinforced their attachment to the social stratification system, creating strong incentives for White men to view the political status quo as "natural" and legitimate.[12] Such attachments made cross-category alliances (between men and women, or White people and African Americans) far more challenging to develop. This pattern continues to be the case today.[13] Historically, the experience of Bacon's Rebellion that united White indentured servants and enslaved Black people in common cause became much more difficult, if not impossible, to repeat.[14] The democratization of White maleness maximized the social and psychological distance between White men and all women along the gender dimension and White men and Black men along the race dimension. On ascriptive republican terms, neither of these groups ("unenlightened and weak" women and "debased and violent" slaves) was morally equivalent to White men, nor could they ever develop the requisite political virtue for membership in the White male republic.

DEFINING WHITENESS AS PERFORMING MARTIAL CITIZENSHIP

Among men, Whiteness was not merely a precondition for possessing political virtue and being legally eligible for voting and military service (the responsibilities of republican citizenship). Instead, the performance of civic and military acts *defined* Whiteness for men, further strengthening the association between White men and political membership. Skin color was not always enough to make a social or legal determination of a person's race, which had implications for the individual's legal status in the polity. This problem arose because of individuals who were of mixed-race heritage, either Black and White parentage or even Black and Native American ancestry. Given the rampant sexual violence against enslaved women by White masters and overseers, it was not uncommon for children produced from such unions to have very light skin and Caucasian facial traits. In the absence of official state records (not to mention DNA tests), courts and observers relied on social behaviors and characteristics to determine the race of those not easily classified visually. Courts used witnesses' testimony on the petitioner's civility, cleanliness, and engagement with White people as an equal, among other traits, to determine the proper racial classification of individuals who could not be readily defined as either Black or White by their skin color alone.[15] Much as is the case today, violence and aggression were associated with Blackness and gentility and politeness with Whiteness.[16]

According to the legal historian Ariella Gross, "racial identity was neither a scientific fact nor a mere matter of documentation but rather a socially and legally defined status." Thus, racial identity and the way society classified members "rested on a deeper ideological commitment to race in which White equaled free (civic, responsible, manly) and black equaled slave (degraded, irresponsible, unfit for manly duties)." Furthermore, Whiteness had a prescriptive quality: people could lay possessive claims to Whiteness by "owning" it or by performing it through fulfillment of the obligations of republican citizenship.[17] Therefore, men who for various reasons did not fit the "White" category but were "other-White" or "off White"—like many White European ethnics and mixed-race people—could lay claim to Whiteness by performing it with arms in musters and holiday celebrations, or with a ballot at the voting booth. In modern gun culture terms, the "good guy with the gun" had to be a White man.

This bidirectional relationship between Whiteness and republican citizenship is evident in court cases where enslaved men sued to gain their freedom claiming they were White and thus wrongly enslaved. As proof of their Whiteness, men presented evidence of having performed citizenship, such as voting in elections or mustering with the militia. Regardless of their phenotype or social standing, proof that these individuals had exercised citizenship rights could only mean one thing: they had to be White. South Carolina did not even define one's status as "negro" through ancestry; instead, the state relied exclusively on behavior, reputation, and social standing. Court decisions freeing men from bondage would argue that "although of a dark complexion, [he] has been recognized as a White man, received into society, *and exercised political privileges as such.*"[18] Such determinations were based on the ascriptive republican assumptions that Black men were incapable of civic acts.

In contrast, honorable White men could not be prevented from performing the duties of citizenship without due process of law. Errors in either direction were not culturally permissible because they threatened the viability of the White Republic. If Black men could "pass" for White and the system could not weed them out from citizenship roles, the political virtue of the populace was under threat. Conversely, if White men who legitimately deserved citizenship were excluded because they were mistaken for Black men, this put the White man at threat of exclusion.

BLACK CHOICE, BLACK SLAVERY

Debates in politics and courts strengthened the link between White men and republican citizenship. Understanding how republican ideology was filtered through the ascriptive lens of White male supremacy requires a discussion of how this syncretic ideology explained the central concepts of republicanism discussed in the previous chapter: virtue and corruption, freedom and slavery. As I noted in chapter 1, martial republican narratives at the time of the American Revolution understood slavery—and thus freedom—not as the result of external coercion but rather as a *choice* by individuals and nations. A man remained free because he trained in arms and developed the political virtue required to fight for his freedom. Conversely, a man did not become enslaved because a more powerful entity enslaved him—he became a slave because he did not maintain vigilance, was lured by luxury and dependency, and allowed himself to be enslaved. The American ascriptive republican myth combined the idea of political freedom as a *choice* with the notion that the system of chattel slavery was benevolent and caring to reconcile contradictory beliefs about Black and White men.[19]

Ascriptive republicanism presupposed that White men's social and political dominance resulted from cultivating traits conducive to political virtue. White men were expected (and even required) to train at arms and through martial preparedness to preserve their commitment to the public good and democratic institutions. This willingness to die for the nation—an individual and collective choice—turned them into virtuous citizen-soldiers. By contrast, political freedom and republican institutions were "not only unsuited to the Negro but . . . poisonous to his happiness."[20] Furthermore, Black men were corrupt and undeserving of citizenship because they "chose" the dependence and safety provided by slavery. "Willing" submission to slavery meant Black men lacked moral fortitude, civic virtue, and manliness. In other words, they did not have the will and capacity to fight for their freedom.[21]

As the ascriptive myth told the story, the idleness and dependency of slave life were not conducive to the development of martial virtue, and thus Black men had opted out of the body politic. In this ideological context, African Americans' degenerated moral status and incapacity for virtue meant they deserved their position as slaves because they had brought it on themselves. Given these life choices, the inclusion of African Americans in political membership and armed service would be detrimental to the Republic.[22] In this view, three million White people achieved independence from the British, evidence that virtuous men could become free, but four million enslaved people had been incapable of securing their freedom—evidence of their dependency and acceptance of their status.[23]

Stereotypes of African Americans as too violent and too meek—a contradiction of little importance to ascriptive republican ideology—were deployed to justify Black dependency and exclusion from citizenship during slavery and the Jim Crow era. In one example of the dependent and weak narrative, New York Judge Edward Edmonds argued that "the Southern negroes are by nature gentle and kind. They are fond of children, of music, and of flowers. They are ever governed more by sentiment than by reason, more the creatures of emotions than judgment."[24] Fifty years later, Howard W. Odum, a noted progressive sociologist, leveraged the criminality stereotype to assert that "he [the Black man] has little conception of the meaning of virtue, truth, honor, manhood. He is shiftless, untidy, and indolent."[25] Even modern-day debates over the practice of kneeling to the national anthem—as many Black and some White athletes have done to protest police violence and racial inequality—evoke early American understandings of freedom and slavery. After all, as countless monuments tell us, soldiers—honorable men—salute the flag while standing; kneeling in front of authority is an attribute of subordination.

Perhaps because of their limited experience with enslaved people, Northerners generally thought of enslaved Black people as violent. Southerners, however, vacillated between the dangerous criminal, the cunning lazy hand, and the faithful slave who prioritized his owner's family over his own. There is little evidence that White Southerners existed in a persistent state of terror. Despite, or perhaps *because* of the pervasive surveillance to which they subjected their slaves, Southern plantation owners and their families famously kept their homes and bedrooms unlocked. This always surprised Northern visitors, who expected enslavers to be fearful of enslaved people with access to kitchen knives. Slave codes also changed in severity when slave revolts took place.[26]

Ironically, one of the many deep contradictions of ascriptive republican ideology is that it exalted White male idleness as the facilitator of civic virtue, while Black idleness was evidence of servility. Slavery made commitments to martial virtue possible for Southern men by freeing them up from the time demands of making a living. It afforded Southern White men "idle independence." The Southerner "delights in violent bodily exertion. . . . He is familiar with the use of arms, and as a child, he learned to risk his life in single combat," noted Alexis de Tocqueville.[27] Therefore not only did slavery afford White men the time and opportunity to engage in martial arts; this intense cultivation of martial virtue, so central to the republican spirit, made them averse to personal profit, venality, and political corruption. It was slavery—the domination of an entire race—that allowed White men to become virtuous republican citizens.[28]

Ascriptive republican ideology was founded on negating several historical realities written off or minimized in the historical record and public discourse. These include 1) the inhumanity and cruelty of slavery; 2) the history of African slave resistance to capture and enslavement; 3) the history of African American armed service; and 4) White people's betrayal of republican ideals evidenced in slavery and the politically motivated violence to which African Americans were subjected during the Jim Crow era. Most of these practices have stayed with us to the modern era. The resurfacing of ascriptive republicanism in the alt-right and politically motivated violence and vigilantism targeting primarily minorities are central to Trump- and post-Trump–era politics.[29]

Due to the anodyne way in which the institution of slavery and its consequences continue to be taught in American schools and the myth of the faithful, unresisting slave which persists to this day through popular culture and even beloved products such as "Aunt Jemima" pancakes and syrup, most Americans have only a vague idea of the true history of the Black experience in the country. The 2021 YouGov survey shows that almost one-fifth of White Americans (18 percent) have internalized the myth of the "loyal slave" and believe it to be "very or somewhat" true that "Black slaves enjoyed the protection of slave-masters who provided food and shelter in exchange for loyal service." Another 20 percent deemed this very pernicious story "somewhat false." I discuss the transmission and perseverance of these myths in chapter 4. For now, it suffices to say that the following sections are hard to read and may give rise to strong feelings. However, this information is not presented gratuitously; the history of chattel slavery along with the history of Black resistance and African American military service are key elements of the refutation of modern myths prevalent in the gun culture. More broadly, it works to refute the myth that gun ownership would have enabled the enslaved to take their proper place in American democracy.[30] This section argues that it is the other way around.

THE CRUELTY OF SLAVERY

Historians have shown that slavery induced conformity and discipline through social and ideological means. Pervasive physical violence (mostly short of death, as enslaved people were valuable property) was one tool slaveholders used to ensure compliance. But psychological violence in the form of extensive surveillance, depersonalization, dehumanization, and threats to the only meaningful social support system available to enslaved people—the family—were equally if not more important tools for obtaining their submission. Additionally, geography, isolation, exclusion from education, and the unavailability of committed White allies until the Civil War also hampered armed resistance by enslaved people.

Slaveholders' authority over the family unit was a critical means of slave control. The American Revolution increased political and economic equality among White men by doing away with the institutions of entail and primogeniture, which limited aristocratic families' control over slaveholding estates. These reforms democratized property ownership and decentralized political power by promoting the development of a White middle class—but they were devastating for enslaved Blacks and their families.[31] The elimination of primogeniture and entail created many more slaveowners, thus increasing White people's dependence on and support for the "peculiar" institution. Left with smaller estates and fewer restrictions, heirs required more work hours from slaves; as a result, they increased productivity through torture or rented underutilized slaves to other farmers. Owners also sold "unproductive" or resisting slaves to new, faraway markets. The result was that slave families were always in danger of being split up, which increased their vulnerability to the vicissitudes of enslavers' fortunes and the market.[32] In retaliation for a slave's escape or his participation in revolt, masters could not only punish him with beatings, mutilation, or death; they could also punish his parents, wife, and children with beatings or sale to a distant owner. Attachment to family explains why it was primarily young, single men who sought to escape or were active in rebellions.[33]

In addition to punishing family members, newly imported enslaved people from various parts of Africa were often quartered together. These people came from different, sometimes warring tribes who spoke different languages and had distinct customs. Such social differences made it

very difficult to build solidarity and cooperation among the first generation of enslaved people. Masters often forced slaves to beat underperform-
ing workers and runaways or "insolent" slaves in order to break bonds of
solidarity among them. Slaves were also forced to tell on others and even
chase after runaways, further undermining social trust—with long-lasting
consequences for the African American community. Furthermore, masters
depersonalized and dehumanized enslaved people, preventing them from
using their given names or calling them all the same nickname or same di-
minutive (e.g., "boy").[34]

Moreover, slaveholders often prohibited the education of enslaved
people, fearing that knowledge of sensitive information about the plantation, the colony, and its affairs could empower slaves. Education could also
improve communication and contact with abolitionist ideas and organizations, increasing the probability of revolts. Religious service attendance
was discouraged unless sermons were delivered by a White pro-slavery
preacher who taught slaves to expect deliverance in the next life through
submission to the master, not relief of suffering in the current one.[35]
Through such practices, slaveholders sought to inculcate among slaves the
belief that their status was just, natural, and deserved.[36]

Planters discouraged stable family units among enslaved people and
interfered with procreation. Slaves were not allowed to get formally mar-
ried because marriage was a right associated with citizenship and personhood, and recognition of slave marriages could threaten the chattel status
of slaves. Frederick Douglass and other former slaves have claimed that
planters "bred" enslaved women to sell their children, especially boys, for
profit. Such claims were probably part of abolitionist propaganda, a sen-
sationalization of slavery to elicit a sympathetic response from Northern
White audiences.[37] Yet there is extensive evidence that Black women, especially mixed-race women with fairer skin, were sold into sexual slavery.[38]
The extensive nonconsensual relationships between White slave-owners
and overseers with women slaves are not in dispute. The children of such
unions inherited their mother's slave status.

Slave colonies and states developed an extensive surveillance system
that engaged the entire White population and even enslaved people themselves. Not only did communities have regular slave patrols with extraordinary authority to punish without due process; White people were attentive
to slave movements, moods, and behaviors. Suspicions or rumors related
to insurrection were reported to authorities. Patrollers had broad authority
to enter private residences without a warrant and arrest and punish slaves
on a whim. Given the deep-seated fears of rebellion among White people,
it took no more than perceived "rudeness" or "insolence" by a slave to

imagine that an insurrection was in the making. This complex set of formal and informal institutions made it all but impossible for enslaved people to initiate a successful revolt.[39]

Slave-masters also used enslaved people against each other, fracturing bonds of trust and solidarity within the community.[40] Given the tight-knit and untrusting nature of slave communities, White people needed insider information to counter slave plans to revolt or harm masters and their families. Information from loyal slaves could help masters guard against harm. Slave codes created a system of incentives for loyal slaves who betrayed plots to authorities. White citizens frequently petitioned legislatures to emancipate loyal slaves who exposed conspiracies.[41] Slave cooperation with the slavery regime is understandable, given enslaved people's circumstances. But such behavior undoubtedly helped validate the ascriptive republican contention that faithful slaves chose slavery over freedom and could not be depended upon to act as independent citizens in a republic.

Contemporary psychological studies investigating the effects of state surveillance on minority populations help us understand how the social control of slavery impacted the beliefs, attitudes, and behaviors of enslaved people. Studies suggest that individuals subjected to constant surveillance suffer from extreme stress, which has significant adverse psychological and physical consequences impacting family and social relationships, job performance, aggression, and alcohol and drug use. As was the case among slaves, suicide is not infrequent among surveilled populations and victims of state violence. Coupled with people's tendency to rationalize and find justice in circumstances they perceive as unchangeable, the system of slavery created powerful institutional and ideological mechanisms of control that few could overcome.[42]

This historical account of slavery is not theoretically essential simply because it complicates and contradicts ascriptive republican narratives. It is important because slavery and Jim Crow are central in modern-day NRA and other elite narratives. Contemporary accounts among gun rights supporters, including NRA-affiliated legal scholars and principals, have focused on gun access as key to explaining the emergence and perseverance of Black slavery in America. From this perspective, the inaccessibility of firearms was a *primary cause* of Black disempowerment, political exclusion, and enslavement. Focused primarily on a White audience, proponents of this myth argue that a tyrannical yet impersonal state—not the democratically elected instrument of White society—had prevented a political minority from owning guns, and then took away all their political rights and enslaved them. Conversely, it was individual bad seeds— plantation owners, and later the Klan—who created this predicament for

Black folks. Black people could not defend themselves against the tyrant and the individual abuser because they had no firearms. Had Black people had access to firearms, they could have gained political equality at the point of a gun, the story goes.[43]

This narrative is false and pernicious because it willfully misrepresents the direction of political causation. White Americans developed an entire system of violent surveillance and control to *ensure* the subordination of Black people. A state that builds its social architecture on ascriptive republicanism cannot honor the demands for political membership—including service at arms—of those it believes to be morally and socially inferior. In short, it was not lack of access to firearms that kept enslaved people from securing their freedom—it was the system of slavery in which most if not all Southern Whites were socially and politically complicit. The American South may have had elections and certain other elements of democracy, but it was not a democratic polity until the latter third of the twentieth century.[44] Even after emancipation, White Southern society and its political representatives fought to maintain an exclusive, White republic. Armed Black men, the Black soldiers who fought in all American wars, the Buffalo Soldiers, and the Black militia, which emerged in the Civil War and remained active until 1904, could not overcome institutionalized White supremacy rule. Instead, they came to serve its interests in building the empire.

However, this simplistic narrative fulfills two important functions. First, it provides an allegory to fuel and sustain White grievances. White gun owners—like the slaves—are a political minority in danger of losing their status by submitting to a government that wishes to marginalize and exclude them from the body politic. However, unlike Black slaves, modern-day (White) gun owners will not succumb to political corruption and dependency; instead, they will fight for "freedom." Second, the story is likely quite effective in reinforcing the belief among many White gun rights activists and those who endorse ascriptive republicanism that their support for gun rights is prima facie evidence that they are not racists while their progressive opponents are biased not only against guns but also against minorities.[45] Such constructions can further deepen the gulf between the two camps as, in addition to other strong claims, they provide White gun rights supporters grounds to believe that they are on the right side of the race issue.

BLACK RESISTANCE TO SLAVERY

Black resistance to capture and slavery was persistent and endemic—contrary to ascriptive republican narratives. It started in Africa, where cap-

tured people fought their kidnappers, often to death. During "transporta-
tion," the era's term for the slave trade, Black resistance on the high seas
was so frequent that slave traders had to take out special insurance to cover
the cost of ships lost to slave uprisings. Slave resistance continued on plantations in the form of rebellions and escapes. In the smaller islands of the
West Indies, such as Barbados, armed resistance by slaves was so frequent
and bloody that many slaveholders took the opportunity to invest in the
newly opened lands of the Carolinas, where they hoped the terrain would
offer greater security against insurrections.[46]

Most often, Black resistance took the form of smaller acts of interference with the operation of slavery, such as strikes, theft, skirting work,
feigning illness, lying, arson, and other "weapons of the weak." These acts
had both material and psychological implications. First, they enabled enslaved people to survive using stolen food and stolen time to hunt, fish,
or do tasks for pay to supplement their personal and familial needs. Second, they signaled slaves' refusal to submit fully to the system of slavery.
Through small acts of resistance, slaves asserted their political personhood
and their "manhood" in the context of a system that required their complete subordination.[47]

According to the historian Terri Snyder, a key argument among proponents of slavery in the antebellum era was that if slavery were so degrading
and unbearable and Black men were manly and honorable, they would opt
for death by suicide. However, slaves were so cowardly that they elected
slave life. This argument goes against the reality of many Black suicides
documented by White people throughout the history of slavery in the
United States. For sure, slave suicides were not always political acts of resistance. Various triggers led people to commit suicide; however, the refusal
to admit that slaves *ever* committed suicide was a White political choice,
a way to buttress the ascriptive republican argument about the nature of
Black slaves.[48]

After the Revolution, Northern African Americans sought to undermine slavery and assert their political presence by assisting fugitive slaves.
Northern Black communities organized "safe harbor," material help, armed
defense, and legal support against claims based on the federal fugitive slave
acts. Assisting fugitive slaves and their families could put Northern African Americans in jeopardy, as a confrontation with law enforcement and
slave-catchers could lead to jail sentences or even death. Northern African
Americans also resisted slavery in the South and their second-class status
in the North through political means, demonstrating their aptitude with
the political participation dimension of republican citizenship. During the
antebellum era, African Americans organized countless petitions, letter-

writing campaigns, and protests exercising the prerogatives of citizenship that White society had not extended to them, insisting on their worthiness for republican membership.[49]

White people supported the ascriptive republican myth by presenting Black men as dependent, misrepresenting their commitment to freedom. In the ascriptive republican telling Black armed resistance did not exist,[50] or it was no evidence of a people fighting for freedom—rather a sign that weak and dependent people were manipulated into agitation. Black revolt had nothing to do with manliness, martial virtue, independent agency, or the desire for political freedom, the hallmarks of republican citizenship. Black violence was not to be interpreted in the context of the *political*, only in the context of the *social*. In that sense, it was evidence of Black manipulability, criminality, depravity, monstrosity, and lack of a moral compass.[51] Conversely, when Black violence was recognized as political, it was committed in service not of democratic ideals of equality and inclusion but of ideologies hostile to democracy. "We regard our negroes as JACOBINS," declared one Southern leader in 1822. "They are ANARCHISTS and the DOMESTIC ENEMY."[52]

A dramatic example of the profound contradiction in how White people sought to explain Black resistance was evident in the White elites' response to the Haitian Revolution (1790). Black slaves successfully thwarted French rule in a decade-long insurrection, and Haiti became the first Black-ruled independent state. White Americans stubbornly refused to accept that Blacks could possess political agency and the ability to be virtuous. White elites denied that enslaved people had organized the revolt, refusing to believe that Blacks had the autonomy and the moral capacity to resist their condition. In Thomas Jefferson's famous utterance, they also labeled the revolting slaves "cannibals" and characterized them as intent on "plunder, carnage, and conflagration." These labels are in stark contrast to the titles White elites reserved for themselves: "patriots" and "freedom-fighters."[53]

The live capture of revolting slaves was also interpreted through a social rather than a political lens: capture turned Black insurrectionists not into political prisoners but into docile cowards who feared death more than they desired freedom. If they did not attempt to escape their captors or commit suicide, this was seen as another signal that Blacks did not possess manliness and virtue. For example, Nat Turner was not man enough to resist to the death. His capture was perceived as evidence that he lacked virtue and thus deserved his slave status. These stories showed that race was built on a foundation of ascriptive republican ideology to deny Black slaves' humanity, virtue, manhood, and freedom.[54]

Not surprisingly, resistance to chattel slavery through escape was viewed as evidence of moral cowardice, if not a mental defect: according to the Southern physician Samuel A. Cartwright, given the benevolent nature of slavery, it was the disease of "*drapetomania*" that caused slaves to run away from their masters. The White consensus was that, given their effeminate nature and moral weakness, enslaved people did not run away of their own volition. They were most likely kidnapped or lured away by evildoers: the French or abolitionists.[55]

Defenders of violent repression promoted the same themes after the Civil War. Supporters of White supremacy suggested that slavery was *necessary* for White republican freedom. In this view, Haiti's history taught the likely future of the South after emancipation. The South should expect "dreadful deeds of riot, rape, robbery, incendiarism, and bloodshed" once "the civilizing and humanizing influences of the institution of Negro slavery" were interrupted. It was slavery that ensured "the absence of the quality of savage ferocity in the negro race in the South." The basis for "the kindness and loyalty felt and manifested by the former slave to his White friends in the South" was due "mainly to the courage and endurance of Southern White women and the manliness and patience of Southern White men."[56]

White Americans perceived lesser forms of resistance, the "weapons of the weak," through a similar lens. American ascriptive republican ideology allowed White people to dismiss such forms of resistance as biological and moral flaws, further reinforcing the belief that Black people did not possess virtue and were incapable of freedom, and that if freed, they would be a danger to the Republic itself. Cartwright had an explanation for slaves' resistance to forced work, too. They suffered from "dysaesthesia Aethiopis," which translates to Black (Ethiopian) abnormal sensation or insensitivity to work. Only under the firm control of the White man could Black slaves work effectively and efficiently. Thus passive forms of resistance reaffirmed ascriptive republican ideology, preserving the social and moral distance between Black and White.[57]

THE BLACK TRADITION IN ARMS

Since the colonial era, African Americans have enlisted and fought in all American wars. This history has been obscured and devalued by official records and ascriptive republican historians. Fighting on the American side could come with promises of freedom, so enslaved people took that path when available, and many fought with distinction. Although they were sometimes impressed, many more *chose* to enlist because the reward for service was freedom from slavery, even though such promises did not generally include acceptance into political membership. Northern and Southern colonies enlisted free and enslaved Black men in the Seven Years' War (1756–1763), which preceded the American Revolution. African Americans served in twenty-five different militia companies in New York and Connecticut. In Massachusetts, so many Black men gained freedom through service that Black enlistments contributed to a notable decline in the number of slaves in the colony.[58]

About 5,000 Black men served during the Revolution, representing various Northern state militias. Northern states contributed several integrated units, some of which served in battle, like the 1st Rhode Island Regiment. Many slaves and free Black men served in fully integrated state militia units. The northern colonial militia was integrated before the Revolution, and continued to be so during the war. Militia rosters listed a modest number of free African Americans and mixed-race ("mulatto") men. Yet, in a practice that persisted well into the twentieth century, Black volunteers were assigned primarily as infantry orderlies and body servants. African Americans served in support roles as wagon drivers, cooks, waiters, or foragers. The Continental Army rolls did not identify them by name: they just listed "A negro man." And although some Black men served in combat units, most Black soldiers until World War II were delegated to support positions that did not require arms or martial skills.[59] Black soldiers were "no more than equipment in the eyes of Whites."[60]

The recruitment of enslaved and free Black men to serve in the Revolution was a highly contested issue that threatened North-South relations and, by extension, the success of the Revolution. Although initially the Continental Army encouraged the recruitment of enslaved and free Black men, southern colonies resisted the practice, which they viewed as undermining their institutions. Southern threats forced the Continental Army to halt such recruitments. For the southern colonies, slavery was more important than freedom. General Washington was amenable only to an exception for Black men already in the ranks. "Whether it will be advisable to enlist any negroes in the new army? Or whether there be a distinction between such as are slaves and those who are free? Agreed unanimously, to reject all slaves, and, by a great majority, to reject negroes altogether," state the notes from the Continental Army internal discussions.[61]

Since most African Americans were enslaved, Army leaders believed that enlisting Black men could violate the property rights of southern slaveholders and lead to accusations that the federal army was a sanctuary for runaway slaves. This could keep the southern colonies out of the Revolution and possibly threaten the Patriots' chances. Ironically, southern freedom fighters were prepared to yield to a tyrannical King if it meant they would keep their human chattel. As a result, after independence was declared all states followed the federal rules and excluded Black men from the ranks for any subsequent recruitments. Some Southern states resisted enlisting not only slaves but also free Blacks, because that too contradicted ascriptive republican ideology. When some slaves tried to participate in military drills, they were punished severely, some even being put to death.[62]

Only the pressing need for soldiers in the face of early defeat in 1777–1778, coupled with the immense difficulty of attracting White volunteers, forced the Army to rescind its exclusionary policy on Black recruitment. With news of the British occupation of Savannah in December 1778, Congress and Washington's second-in-command, Alexander Hamilton, sought to convince Georgia and the Carolinas to accept the recruitment of enslaved men. Slave-owners would be compensated up to $1,000 for each able-bodied slave—an astronomical amount—and the army would liberate slave recruits at the end of the conflict. But this was not enough. Despite the existential danger to their sovereignty, Southerners refused slave recruitment. Southern White Americans were more concerned with the example and precedent set by freeing enlisted slaves. Adhering to their ethos of ascriptive republicanism, Southern White citizens insisted that since slaves were not citizens, their obligation to the master superseded any obligation to the community. But even in the North, the political significance of military service ensured substantial political resistance to Black recruitment. As a result, as the front moved to the South, even Massachusetts barred African Americans from the militia.[63]

In late 1777, the army reversed its policy to benefit White slave-owners and wealthy yeomen. The new policy enabled White men to avoid military service by sending Black slaves as substitutes or paying free Black men to replace them. An African American substitute was easier and cheaper to secure. Black men seeking freedom through martial valor fought to enlist, petitioning the Army and Congress to accept their service. Meanwhile, many White men stayed home, ignoring the lofty ideals that motivated their rebellion.[64]

The ironies do not end there. Raising White militia units had become so challenging that Virginia even contemplated offering enslaved people as bounty to White farmers in exchange for enlisting in the militia and fighting in the Revolution. These proposals suggest that Southern elites believed that the increase in social and material status accompanying slave-ownership would entice White men to accept the responsibilities that republican citizenship placed on them—not for glory but for social and economic prestige. White men required material and social rewards to perform the duties of freedom, while Black men sought to use sacrifice to prove they deserved freedom. The contradiction did not escape James

Madison. In response to the Virginia law, Madison asked, "would it not be as well to liberate and make soldiers at once of the blacks themselves as to make them instruments for enlisted White soldiers?"[65]

African Americans' service notwithstanding, ascriptive republicanism took legal form in the Uniform Militia Act of 1792 (UMA), which sought to enforce the Second Amendment to the US Constitution. As I will discuss in chapter 3, the UMA explicitly defined White men's duty to perform military service. State constitutions and laws mirrored the Act's racial requirements, resulting in the formal exclusion of Black men, enslaved or free, from military service. But official debarment did not mean that African Americans fought in no other American wars.

In the disastrous War of 1812, which culminated with the burning of Washington by the British, General Andrew Jackson sidestepped political objections and officially enlisted the support of free Black militia in the Battle of New Orleans. Louisiana, a former Spanish colony, maintained three militia companies composed of free Black men. Under Spanish authority, Black units served in a military capacity and as slave-catchers—one of the many ironies and complexities of racial history in the Americas.[66] The state dismantled these units in 1804 because of their incompatibility with ascriptive republican ideology. However, Louisiana sought to reinstate the Black militia on two occasions: first when a slave rebellion threatened the state in 1811, and second in the War of 1812. In September 1814, General Jackson formally asked for the Black militias' participation in the war effort. In a "Proclamation to the Free Colored Inhabitants of Louisiana," Jackson came close to recognizing Black rights to national citizenship and republican duties to bear arms. He addressed free Black men as Americans and "sons of freedom" who enjoy rights. Jackson characterized the UMA "a mistaken policy" that deprived free Blacks "of participation in the glorious struggle for national rights." Black men, the general declared, had an obligation "as a faithful return for the advantages enjoyed under [America's] mild and equitable government" to provide "valorous support" and help "defend our most inestimable blessing."[67]

Despite Black service in the War of 1812, and earlier in the Revolution, Black people's hopes of citizenship rights through military service were for naught. Ascriptive republican ideology remained dominant. The War Department issued regulations in 1820-1821 excluding African Americans from federal military service, and state militias followed suit. Only the US Navy allowed free Black men to join, in numbers equal to 5 percent of White enlistees. Therefore, fewer Black men served in the Mexican War. Despite the prohibition, free and enslaved African Americans attempted to cross the color line through unsanctioned enlistment. Even when Black men were not allowed to enlist, they were not absent from the war front. Instead, many Black men and several Black women participated in the Mexican War as slaves and servants, facing many of the same dangers and performing tasks necessary for the function of the army, but often without pay or recognition.[68]

The UMA's racial requirements were contested in the Civil War as the demand for soldiers to serve in the Union Army escalated. For quite distinct reasons, White people and African Americans in the North argued that Black military service was practicable and desirable, especially in this conflict over slavery. Early in the Civil War, President Lincoln and his cabinet were wary about enlisting Black troops, fearful that it could prompt border slave states still faithful to the Union to secede. Military leaders faithful to ascriptive republican ideology were ambivalent about the operational value of Black soldiers. They thought that neither free African Americans nor former slaves had the courage, discipline, and skills required of a professional soldier. As was the case in earlier conflicts, Black men were thought too unruly and too servile, simultaneously too strong and too weak. The prevailing belief was that they would be a hindrance rather than an asset to the armed forces. But in May 1863, five months after the Emancipation Proclamation went into force, the practical demands of the war overran ideological objections.[69]

THE IRONY OF ALLIANCES

Violence, dependency, and idleness were not the only attributes ascriptive republican myths used to explain and justify Black subordination and exclusion from political membership. These narratives also used the need of African Americans to develop alliances with White people such as the British, Native Americans, the abolitionists, or the USSR as evidence of venality, weakness, and dependency—further reasons to deny them political membership in the Republic.

Foreign allies were vital to the Revolution's success and the new nation's survival. Territory controlled by three powerful empires surrounded the United States. The British, French, and Spanish competed for power and territory, each with designs on the New World. In this context, the success of the American experiment depended on financial and political support from European allies. France, which competed with the British, secretly aided the Continental Army with supplies and materiel as early as 1776. By 1778, the French and the Americans had signed a treaty of alliance. Soon after, Spain and the Netherlands, engaged along with France in a global war against Britain, sent support to the fledgling nation.

In the context of ascriptive republican ideology, the need for such alliances was something of an embarrassment. It suggested that the Patriots did not have sufficient capacity to win their independence alone, and that they were forced into alliances with Catholic kingdoms. In many respects, Catholicism, with its dogma that the Pope is God's representative on Earth, represented the antithesis of White Protestant republican ideals. Yet, so dependent was the United States on its French allies that for a short time in 1781 it relinquished control of the peace negotiations to the French authorities.[70] This dependence on alliances is not discussed in ascriptive republican narratives insisting that the Patriots won the Revolution because of their political virtue and superior command of weaponry. Yet that is not how the African American experience is presented in such narratives.

As African Americans realized, and as the Civil War and the later civil rights movement (and even the twenty-first-century Black Lives Matter movement) showed, effective political mobilization required strong alliances with White people sympathetic to the cause of racial equality.[71] Both on the islands and on the mainland, the best chance at freedom came from alliances with European powers hostile to British and, later, American interests. On the continent, alliances with Native American tribes seeking to prevent further White incursion into tribal lands offered a path to freedom. Fighting on the side of European powers was especially attractive to enslaved men because it came with promises of freedom and shelter for Black soldiers and their families. Free and enslaved African Americans collaborated with the Spanish during the Seven Years' War in exchange for safe haven and freedom in Spanish-held Florida. When the British offered Virginia Tidewater–area slaves refuge and freedom in exchange for fighting against the Americans in the Revolution and the War of 1812, numerous slaves accepted the offer. During the Revolution, upward of 20,000 Black men served under the Crown.[72] During the antebellum era, African Americans worked closely with White abolitionists, and in the twentieth and twenty-first centuries with White supporters of racial equality and international movements for self-determination, to advance their claims to freedom and equal political membership.[73]

However, proponents of ascriptive republican narratives saw in these alliances confirmation of Black moral weakness and lack of political virtue. Slave rebellions and soldiering for the enemy were not evidence of moral independence and virtue; instead, they showed a people whom America's enemies could manipulate. Therefore, armed resistance to slavery only proved African Americans' moral weakness and unsuitability as political equals in the Republic.[74]

These narratives persisted even after the Civil War. In the waning days of

Reconstruction, a new political crisis overtook America. Industrialization had brought workers to Northern factories with a promise of stable wages and prosperity, but the reality was very different. Fueled by new ideas from European immigrants, American workers organized a powerful labor movement. The relationship between White laborites and Black workers was complex: in some places Blacks were accepted into unions, but in most they were not.[75] However, with the rise of new ideologies such as socialism and anarchism within the labor movement and society more broadly, White citizens adjusted the ascriptive republican narrative to meet the new environment. The enemy within was now the proponents of these new ideologies that were critical of American capitalism. According to this new version of the myth, the fledgling African American movement for political equality was not an authentic development. Instead, much as they had in the Revolution been manipulated by the British to attack the Patriots, now, goaded by laborite and socialist White agitators, Blacks planned armed insurrection to overthrow White supremacy and capitalism. This myth allowed White political elites to continue to blame African Americans for White-instigated riots.[76]

Even as commissions reported that White mobs were to blame for the violence, ascriptive republican themes predominated in Washington. In the 1920s and 1930s, some Southern Blacks did find in Communism the promise of social equality. Unlike the accommodationist vision, which required submission to Jim Crow, early Communism offered a worldview based on absolute race and class equality.[77] This is not how White authorities viewed it. Federal law enforcement believed that "red," socialist, and anarchist agitators organized and manipulated docile Black workers into violent anti-White action. Through the trope of Black violence, these agencies linked Communism and Black civil rights in an attempt to discredit both. In an extensive report to Congress on the violence of 1919, Attorney General A. Mitchell Palmer and the FBI's J. Edgar Hoover presented the race riots as the result of anti-American activism by Blacks goaded by White agitators bent on overthrowing the government.[78]

African Americans' efforts to build alliances with forces sympathetic to their cause of racial and political equality continued to be perceived as sedition by many White elites throughout the twentieth century. Through the 1960s, federal intelligence agencies sought to "prove" to the American public that Black movements for political equality and self-determination were little more than the result of foreign agitation and propaganda. The FBI tried hard to link Black leaders and movements to foreign interference in the American political process. Martin Luther King Jr. was supposed to be beholden to Russia and other foreign enemies;[79] Malcolm X was said to be a puppet of Middle Eastern and other Muslim countries intent on harming the United States by instigating Black supremacy.[80] The Chinese and the Russians supposedly manipulated and goaded the Black Panthers, who were nothing more than a criminal gang.[81] Castro must have been behind the Black Power demonstrations at the United Nations building.[82] For many White Americans, such groups were not motivated by sincere beliefs in anti-imperialism, anti-colonialism, racial equality, and liberation of subordinated groups. They were simply the puppets of America's foreign enemies, intent on destabilizing domestic politics. Even today, conservatives and the alt-right call BLM both socialists seeking to upend American democracy and an "extortionist ring" that "shak[es] down corporations and buy[s] themselves mansions."[83] Efforts to require that the history of slavery and Jim Crow be taught in schools are labeled "divisive" and un-American.[84] Such narratives underscore the belief that un-American forces influence African Americans' political behavior and that their demands are illegitimate and politically suspect, that they are undemocratic agitators serving the interests of some obscure political elite and expecting special treatment. They are not seen as democratic citizens petitioning their government for justice and equality.

WHITE POLITICAL VIOLENCE

Ascriptive republicanism emphasizes the "subversive" nature of Black violence and completely obscures the political nature of White violence. After the Civil War, White political violence emerged in response to emancipation and the presence of Black men in arms. In the name of democracy, honor, and valor, White men intimidated and often killed African Americans and their White Republican Party supporters. Whites branded such violence "a counterrevolution" and "a legitimate resistance to tyranny."[85] Politically motivated violence against Black men persisted through the Jim Crow era. Only in 2022 did Congress pass anti-lynching legislation that African Americans had advocated for since 1918.

During Reconstruction, Radical Republican governments in the South organized Black militia to protect Republican officials and voters—Black and White alike. During Reconstruction, the Union Army disbanded the Confederate forces and discharged White state militiamen. However, because of the perceived protection afforded to militias by the Second Amendment, the Republicans did not eliminate state companies; instead, they replaced the members lost with Black men and Union loyalists.[86]

White Southerners affiliated with the Democratic Party viewed Black militia not as representatives of political authority but as gangs of criminals intent on raping White women and killing White men. The brutality that occurred during Reconstruction was primarily White political violence; there is little evidence of Black militias abusing their authority and committing violent crimes. Murder and violence were rare, but were magnified by the hostile White Democratic press. The Black militia often used nonviolent means to signal their presence and newfound authority. For example, returning from musters in the evenings, they would make a ruckus by scraping bayonets against picket fences and beating the drum or having an entire band play as they marched. These petty displays of power caused immense consternation and resentment among White people, who understood them as a reminder of an unwelcome change in the social order. Most White citizens perceived the existence of Black men bearing arms in this era in the South as a moral and political threat, a devaluation of their cherished understanding of martial citizenship.[87]

In response, White Democrats organized paramilitary groups to defend White male supremacy. The Ku Klux Klan, along with the White Leagues and the Red Shirts, were White paramilitary organizations determined to avenge White manly honor and protect Southern political institutions from what they perceived as the corruption of a racially and politically integrated polity.[88] Some of these groups called themselves "the Minutemen" to reinforce their republican bona fides and their ties to the American Revolution.[89]

Klan supporters used the trope that Black people had no independent agency because of their choice of slavery over freedom to accuse Republicans of taking advantage of gullible and disloyal freedmen to establish one-party control—tyranny—in the South. In this view, Black suffrage "would ensure their [i.e., the Republicans'] so-called benefactors, absolute control . . . and that thus a Northern sectional party would govern the White people of the South absolutely and forever."[90] These groups and their White political allies portrayed the Black militias as a "standing army of negro soldiers"—the ultimate betrayal of republican ideals.[91] For White Democrats in the South, cooperation with federal authorities and the enfranchisement and arming of Black men constituted the highest form of political corruption.[92] White elites and the public believed that Republican leaders established Black militias to incite a race war. Such beliefs became integral to the "Lost Cause" myth of a virtuous and democratic South and persisted into the twentieth century.[93]

Because Republican authorities had banned White volunteer militias, paramilitary groups were organized as "rifle clubs"—civilian sports clubs not regulated by military laws. Local White "rifle clubs" maintained the pretext that they were civic clubs, not volunteer military organizations. For a paramilitary organization during this period, organizing itself as a "rifle club" was very advantageous because it evaded Union Army surveillance, and, as a "civic club," it was not tied to a specific ward or territorial unit.[94] These rifle clubs became the organizational basis for the Klan and other similar organizations—"the citizen-soldier at his most vicious."[95] The military nature of these social clubs was no secret: the records of the clubs explicitly outlined their purpose and goals.[96] Also, the conservative historian William Dunning, who chronicled the Reconstruction era using a "Lost Cause" lens, used the terms "rifle clubs," "White clubs," and Ku Klux Klan interchangeably.[97]

Across the South, armed White reactionaries patrolled neighborhoods and intimidated political gatherings of Republicans, Black and White alike. In South Carolina, more than 30,000 men were thought to be members of "rifle clubs" that claimed to be peacekeeping units and neighborhood protection groups, but were in many cases "night riders."[98] Historical records show that Southern Democratic politicians helped organize and arm such "rifle clubs" among native and immigrant White ethnics, to be used as an intimidation force during the 1876 election.[99]

Echoing ascriptive republican ideology, revisionist late-nineteenth-century commentators described these rifle clubs as "a band of comrades . . . actuated by a common spirit . . . and united in the determination to stand by each other . . . with arms in their hands, to protect their homes and families against aggression from negroes." It was "the magnificent manhood" of rifle club members—their republican virtue—that prevented local officials and even President Grant from forcing these groups into obedience. If the clubs were virtuous, Reconstruction was abusive, corrupt, and tyrannical: "the excesses of misgovernment, fraud, and corruption had grown so great, and the abuse of civilization had become so notorious as to revolt public sentiment."[100]

Some historians suggest that the individual rights narrative of the Second Amendment developed to justify the use of arms by paramilitary organizations antagonistic to Reconstruction governments and increase the appearance of legitimacy of such rifle clubs.[101] As the rifle club records suggest, White paramilitaries of the era appeared to interpret the Second Amendment in such a manner. Specifically, the clubs had embraced "the great American principle that the citizen has an inalienable right to *publicly* bear arms." Although the clubs alluded to an individual right to bear arms, the context for doing so was military, not civilian. "The Carolina Rifle Club had the honor of being the first military body of White men which paraded the streets of the city or the State, bearing arms and the first to march under the Confederate Banner."[102] As we will see, similar interpretations can be found in *Arms and the Man*, the NRA's first magazine.

White political violence against African Americans continued for almost a century after Reconstruction. Historians have documented hundreds of cases of race riots between the 1880s and the 1950s, instigated by rumors of impending Black "insurrection"—plans to attack the republican polity and impose tyranny. White racists instigated most race riots before the late 1960s, and most victims were Black people. In farming towns in the South, Black sharecroppers' and farmers' efforts to ensure better working conditions and higher prices for their products were perceived by White citizens as insolence and insurrection, provoking mob violence in Black neighborhoods. In cities, various interpersonal provocations, many imagined or rumored, led to tales of Black political conspiracies that mobilized White mobs.[103] Black soldiers wearing their United States military uniforms in public spaces was a trigger sufficient to spark a White riot—as was the case for many of the mob violence incidents that occurred in the "Red Summer" of 1919.[104] As the Chicago Commission on Race Relations Report bluntly stated in 1922, "many White Americans, while technically recognizing negroes as citizens, cannot bring themselves to feel that they should participate in government as freely as other citizens." This included not only political agency but also martial virtue: Blacks in arms were politically dangerous.[105]

Local police, political authorities, and White militia brought in to control the violence tolerated White riots. Local and national White authorities and the media presented these mob attacks as Black-initiated and -orchestrated. On several occasions, White police and militiamen joined in the attacks against Blacks, a fact reported in the Black press and in reports produced by investigative commissions charged with assessing the causes of the riots. In at least one case, the East St. Louis riots of 1917, White militiamen allowed White mobs to disarm them and these mobs used the militiamen's military weapons against Blacks. In another infamous case, the Wilmington, North Carolina riots of 1898, White people planned the violent overthrow of Black and White Republican elected officials. The coup organizers had purchased a Gatling gun (the era's rapid-fire military machine gun) and more than 2,000 Winchester rifles for the occasion.[106] As Thurgood Marshall noted in an article about the 1943 riots for the NAACP's *The Crisis*, police treated "all Negroes as looters" and White people as innocent bystanders who, even when intercepted at the scene of a riot, were often allowed to keep their firearms to defend themselves.[107] Marshall's criticism rings true eight decades later. In August 2020 the police in Kenosha, Wisconsin welcomed White militias as auxiliaries to help them guard against a multiracial group of BLM protesters whom they expected to turn violent. When an armed Kyle Rittenhouse approached police officers ready to turn in his military-style weapon and surrender after killing two men and wounding a third, they did not recognize him as the shooter and told him to move away from the scene.[108]

Calls for African Americans to get armed for self- and community protection were not viewed kindly by state and national authorities—Black gun carry was evidence not of political virtue but of mischief. Palmer and Hoover saw Black men's need for armed self-defense as evidence of "inflammatory sentiment" and "open defiance and a counsel of retaliation." Local authorities arrested Black leaders who urged armed self-defense on charges of sedition and inciting violence—an ironic parallel to the incidents of January 6, 2021, as brought to light in congressional investigations. Unlike armed White people, who were assumed to be defending themselves and their communities (or in the recent context of January 6 were called "peaceful tourists"), armed Blacks were at best divided into two groups: "the mob elements" who were "armed for war," and "the better elements" who were "armed in obedience to the first law of nature."[109]

Although these narratives are inherently and deeply contradictory, they created an insurmountable double bind for African Americans that persists today. Ascriptive republican narratives were inscribed in federal and state laws that governed military organization until the integration of the armed forces in 1948. Their echo exists in criminal law and police training and procedure. These narratives were passed down across generations of White Americans through military culture, gun culture, and institutions. As chapter 4 discusses, they survived into the late twentieth century in schoolbooks and educational curricula, public memory, and culture. The NRA played a pivotal role in disseminating these narratives as well. These ideals helped sustain the perception that the NRA's "good guy with a gun" was White and that a Black man could only be "a bad guy with a gun."

CHAPTER 3

Militias and the Institutionalization
of Ascriptive Republicanism

American ascriptive republican ideology appropriated the constitutive ideas of classical republicanism—virtue/corruption, freedom/slavery—and vested them with a worldview that understood human beings not as equals, but as organized in a hierarchy based primarily on race and gender. As I argued in chapter 2, republican ideology requires a "peoplehood": a definition of who the members of the democratic community can be and what sets them apart from outsiders. In the modern version of this republican narrative evidenced in *The Civic Culture*, America accepts as a citizen any person who demonstrates a commitment to its political ideals of inclusivity, equality, social and political participation, and positive patriotism. That is not the peoplehood that emerged out of the American Revolution, nor was it the peoplehood that Americans wrote into their institutions.

The people who constituted the American nation and had both the rights and obligations of political membership were White men. Early laws and constitutions linked the bearing of arms—mandatory military service—with the right to vote and limited both rights to White men. In turn, many White men of social rank took advantage of the provisions of an 1803 federal law to establish self-organized and self-funded volunteer militia groups that over time supplanted the "enrolled" or conscript militia.[1]

Ascriptive republican ideals were so deeply held in the United States that the institution of conscription remained on the books until 1903, long after state-enrolled militias had been informally abandoned in favor of volunteer units. Revolutionary-era Americans insisted that the enrolled militia were the bulwark of the country's defense against internal and external foes, when in reality they were ineffective, undertrained, badly armed, and underfunded. Military leaders from George Washington and Alexander Hamilton to foreign observers in the Civil War and late-nineteenth-century social critics complained that the militia was "tin soldiers": drunk, unruly, unreliable, and relatively useless.[2] But, as this chapter discusses, the militias were politically useful as the embodiment of America's ascriptive

republican ideology, representing, replicating, and enforcing social hierarchies. For that reason, despite frequent calls for their reform, they remained essentially the same for more than a century.

THE ENROLLED MILITIA

Among the many key questions that the Constitutional Convention was
called on to answer was the organization of the new nation's defensive
forces. The American colonists had developed a hodgepodge of institutions
to address internal and external dangers—from riots and slave rebellions to
Native American attacks and wars with European adversaries. The experience of the Seven Years' War had convinced the colonists of the benefits of
a professional army, a belief reinforced by the abysmal performance of the
militia in the Revolution. Ever the pragmatist, James Madison had no interest in entrusting the stability of the Republic to the virtue of its citizens.
Institutional brakes to power were much preferable to utopian attempts
to cultivate political virtue.[3] However, the martial republican fervor that
flooded the colonies in the wake of the Revolution propelled many to imagine a nation of virtuous citizen-soldiers whose training at arms would serve
as a bulwark against corruption in politics and war.[4]

In addition to the question of political virtue and corruption inherent
in armed men, the debates over the character of American military institutions were intertwined with debates over federalism and voting rights. A
single federal army could be militarily efficient and effective, but a "standing" army threatened the sovereignty of individual states. The colonies
that had just ousted the British monarchy were in no mood to entrust
the new nation's defense to a centralized institution accountable only to
the national government. One of the many compromises orchestrated in
Philadelphia was to establish two levels of defensive forces: a small federal
standing army and a much larger conscript state militia.

Conscription came with its own political issues: would men agree to
serve in the militia if the new Republic did not grant them full citizenship
rights? In the colonies, even though all White men thought of themselves
as "citizens," they did not all have political rights. Colonial laws had placed
a property restriction on the right to vote and imposed militia obligations
only on men of property. In early republican ideology, the citizen, the soldier, and the freeholder (the propertied man) were three sides of the same
entity. Property and self-interest through property were the foundation of
the citizen-soldier model. Tending to property and soldiering were integral
parts of citizenship.[5] However, the military mobilization required to fight
the Revolution empowered working-class White men to demand political

rights based on their military service.[6] The implications of unpropertied soldiers' claims to political membership were not universally welcomed. At the Constitutional Convention, conservatives like Madison feared popular democracy and argued for constitutional provisions that limited the franchise to property-holding White people. However, delegates from frontier areas pushed for practicality and principle. They argued that it would be impossible to sustain a conscript militia force with universal requirements—as prescribed by republican ideology—if these soldiers had no political rights.[7]

Conservatives lost that battle. The federal Uniform Militia Act (UMA) of 1792 required all free, able-bodied, White males ages 18–45 to be part of the enrolled militia and to supply their own weapons and ammunition. Some states extended the obligation to White male indentured servants.[8] The Act's ascriptive republican provisions were reflected in state laws and constitutions. Northern and Southern state constitutions granted the citizen-soldier "the right to bear arms in defence [*sic*] of himself and the state" and specified criteria for voting that included militia service. Such provisions linked the dual duties of republican citizenship to male Whiteness. For example, Mississippi's Constitution of 1817 specified that the right to the franchise belongs to "every free White male person" provided that these men "shall be enrolled in the [state] militia."[9] Similarly, the Connecticut Constitution of 1818 stipulated that the franchise belonged to "every White male citizen of the United States, who shall have gained a settlement in this State," and "having been enrolled in the militia, shall have performed military duty therein for the term of one year."[10] The Florida Constitution of 1839 is very similar: Article 6, Section 1 stipulates that "every free White male person . . . who shall be enrolled in the militia thereof shall be deemed a qualified elector."[11] Elsewhere, as in New York or Massachusetts, White men had to choose between militia service and a tax.

The conscript militia was not a new institution to the United States; what changed after the Revolution was that it became far more democratic. The "enrolled" militia had been the colonies' principal defensive and policing force. Before the American Revolution, English settlements in North America received the protection of the professional British Army, but this was mainly in the context of major wars with other European powers. The British Regulars were under the command of the King. They served the interests of the empire, not those of each colony—and the colonists knew it. Starting in the 1750s, they demanded control over the Regulars.[12] Although the colonists recognized the benefits of a professional military force, raising a "standing" army was financially prohibitive. Instead, they established conscript militia forces to defend urban settlements against slaves, Native

Americans, or other foes. In times of peace, the militia operated as police auxiliaries, especially in cases of emergency or civil disorder. The militia was responsible for slave patrols in the South, including monthly inspections of slave quarters for weapons and ammunition. The colonies also organized expeditionary militia forces to push westward, and these forces provided the basis for the organization of White civil authority in the new territories.[13]

Initially, much as was the case in England, it was propertied men who owed military service and had political rights; but over time, necessity required that White men of other classes—including indentured servants, in some cases—serve as well. The colonies' defensive needs and the colonists' expansionist aspirations made it necessary that most White men be conscripted.

Yet, lacking a sufficient tax base, colonies privatized the responsibility for weapons procurement—a practice enshrined in the new nation's UMA. Militia members were required to furnish their own military weapons and keep them in good working order, while the colonial (and later the state) authorities provided armories and some ammunition. Militias were also expected to organize regular drill exercises for each company and to participate in frequent "musters," or training and inspection exercises, for the whole body of the militia.[14] Militia service was part of the White man's civic duty.

THE MILITARY FAILURE OF THE ENROLLED MILITIA

From early on, the performance of enrolled militia in war, especially compared to the Regulars, was abysmal, exposing recruitment, training, and equipment problems. The ascriptive republican ideal that all White male citizens had an obligation to serve and, through service, to develop republican virtue proved problematic when put to the test. White Americans may have aspired to republican citizenship, but they behaved much more like liberal individualists. Collective action problems abounded. The gentry, who was supposed to make up the core of the enrolled militia, resisted leaving their farms and families behind and suffering the economic consequences of soldiering. Fines were not enforced frequently enough to make the yeomen change their minds, or even worse, they were enforced selectively only against less prominent men, thus fueling resentment.[15] This underscores the racial irony embedded in the history of American democratic politics: African American men demanded to be allowed to serve to prove their republican virtue, while many White men did everything possible to evade their obligations to the Republic.

Buying and maintaining military weapons was costly and further suppressed enthusiasm for service. Although a fair proportion of White American men owned firearms suited for private life, these were not typically usable in war, and their owners did not necessarily have the skills and training required to use military weapons.[16] Those who did not own firearms were forced to drill with brooms or corn stalks, which was embarrassing and was therefore another major disincentive. In times of prolonged peace, militiamen often sold their weapons or allowed them to rust—in contravention to federal and state laws—because they could not afford the maintenance and repairs.

Ironically, one of the very first laws that Congress enacted mandated a civilian gun registry—which is anathema to the modern-day gun rights movement and is seen as a sign of un-American and undemocratic intent. The UMA required militiamen to provide and maintain their service weapons; initially it included fines and penalties for men who did not adhere to these requirements and sold their firearms, but this latter provision was subsequently dropped. The lack of enforcement mechanisms—omitted over the objections of President Washington and other military leaders—was a key reason for the failure of the enrolled militia. However, to keep track, the annual military census mandated by Congress recorded both the number of militiamen in each state and the type, number, and quality of their equipment.[17]

Since these citizen-soldiers tended to be more engaged with their political rights than with their soldiery duties, they put pressure on elected officials for relief. Over time, citizens gained increased access to deferments, exemptions, and opportunities to avoid enrolled military obligations at the cost of a fine or fee. Members of the social elite took full advantage of these exemptions and sought to pay fines instead of serving, or they sent their indentured servants as replacements. Men from lower socioeconomic classes did not have the same opportunities. Increasingly, enrolled militia forces consisted of poor and disenfranchised White men who could not pay their way out of service.[18]

The neglect of the militia did not originate on the citizens' part alone. During the colonial era, theft and neglect of military equipment due to insufficient inventory control practices and shoddy accounting was so prevalent that Britain refused to send munitions, believing that the colonists would waste them. After the Revolution, states did not enforce the requirements of the UMA, nor did they institute penalties for those who did not own military equipment, fearing the wrath of voters faced with mounting financial obligations. In times of prolonged peace, governments cut budgets for armaments and limited their procurement and maintenance. Some

Figure 3.1 Satirical drawing from 1862 depicting what the
militia looked like in the 1830s, Library of Congress.

towns came to organize musters only once a year, which was insufficient
to train an effective defensive force. Federal records from the first half of
the nineteenth century show that Indiana did not have a single muster in
twelve years, while Connecticut recorded an annual turnover of 25 percent
of its militia officers.[19]

The enrolled militia was the subject of frequent ridicule (fig. 3.1). The
nineteenth-century press labeled the militia "rabble" or "scarecrow militia," "ragtail and bobtail assemblages armed with broomsticks and cornstalks and umbrellas."[20] In his humorous recollections of the militia of his
youth, Abraham Lincoln underscored how neglected and derided militia
were at the frontier. He talked about military parades where "the rules and
regulations [specified that], no man is to wear more than five pounds of
cod-fish for epaulets, or more than thirty yards of bologna sausage for a
sash."[21]

Even with deferments, incentives, and penalties, desertion was rampant. Citizen-soldiers did not want to commit long periods to military
activities, and initial enthusiasm for war waned once people experienced
the hardships of the battlefield. Militia companies refused to fight outside
the boundaries of their own colony, and ideals that tied the citizen-soldier
to his political community enabled them to do so. By the early eighteenth
century, the conscription system for raising a defensive army had all but

collapsed, as it was inadequate to sustain the demands of major wars. By the time of the French and Indian Wars, there was a growing consensus in the colonies that compulsory service was unenforceable and an inefficient means to secure the defense of the land.[22] With the possible exception of Southern slave patrols, enrolled citizen militia had atrophied for decades before the Revolution, replaced by volunteer companies. In the South, there was a perennial fear that without a large and constant patrol presence, slave rebellion was imminent—but even there the level of surveillance declined significantly in periods of domestic tranquility.[23]

The lack of commitment and training did not escape army officers, who viewed professionals as more effective and dependable soldiers in battle than the militia. On the eve of the Revolution, colonial military leaders were in full agreement that disciplined and trained professional soldiers were far more effective and reliable than the enrolled militia. The professionals understood how to operate under a central command structure. They were well-acquainted with weapons of war and their use. They were disciplined and experienced. In the summer of 1776, General George Washington expressed his full contempt for the militia. He told the Continental Congress that, in his experience, the militia were "hurtful upon the whole" and "no militia will ever acquire the habits necessary to resist a regular force." For Washington, the militia "will never answer your expectations, no dependence is to be placed upon them; they are obstinate and perverse."[24] He was not wrong: at Bunker Hill, even though the colonists inflicted heavy casualties on the British, the Americans were forced to retreat because of desertions in the ranks and a refusal of nearby militia companies to come in aid of the combatants.[25] Washington went so far as to reject an offer by the ladies of Philadelphia to provide the militiamen with a cash allowance based on funds that the women had raised. Fearing that the men would use the money for liquor, he told the women to provide articles of clothing instead.[26] The criticism from another experienced military commander, Alexander Hamilton, was equally biting. "I expect we shall be told that the militia of the country is the natural bulwark and would be at all times equal to the national defence [sic]. This doctrine, in substance, had like to have lost us our independence," he proclaimed.[27] Both leaders persistently asked for a "select militia," the eighteenth-century term for a trained, disciplined reserve force. The clearest evidence of the militia's failure came in the War of 1812. After a strong performance in New Orleans, they were defeated by the British in numerous subsequent battles, enabling the enemy to march to Washington and burn down the capital. At that point, it became clear to federal officials that militia were inadequate for the defense of the country.[28]

The consensus among military leaders before, during, and long after the Revolution was that the enrolled militia was a failed military institution that needed to be replaced by a professional army.[29] However, political ideology proved stickier than military experience. The martial republican fervor that accompanied the Revolution made such proposals nonstarters. Revolutionary tracts ignored the role of foreign money and the alliance with France or the professionally trained Continentals, promoting instead the myth that it was the republican political virtue inherent in colonial institutions such as the militia that won Americans' independence. In the new federal structure, a standing army would only mean replacing one tyrant (the King) with another (the federal government) while political virtue weakened. Reality notwithstanding, republican ideology held that the political security of the Republic required the citizen-soldier. Despite elite and popular criticism, the UMA remained on the books until 1903. Its requirement that citizens must own and maintain their military weapons—a requirement made partially obsolete by federal funding of the militia in 1808—endured as a symbol of republican civic responsibility.[30]

VOLUNTEER MILITIA

An 1803 federal law enabled states to accept volunteer companies as part of the militia. As a result of this new law, volunteer companies, which had developed initially in New England and operated in parallel with the enrolled militia, mushroomed across the country. As the American military slowly professionalized in fits and spurts following the Civil War, the country experienced a parallel growth in militia companies, which did not subside until the 1903 Dick Act—the law that reorganized and federalized the militia. Thus, for about a century the United States had several types of military organizations, operating under different command structures and playing various domestic roles. The federal armed forces consisted of professional soldiers who engaged primarily in defensive and offensive wars as the country pursued territorial expansion in the West and imperial designs elsewhere.[31] The state militia forces were the remnants of the old colonial system of the enrolled militia, constitutionally mandated but disorganized, underfunded, and ineffective. And the volunteers were self-organized groups that showed great variability in skills and performance, but were overall not very effective either.

Volunteer companies were especially popular in cities and larger towns because they allowed men of means to fulfill their military obligations on their own terms, dodging the stricter requirement imposed by military efficiency and uniformity. Far from being the NRA's ruggedly individualistic woodsmen, the "Minutemen" and other volunteer companies of that nature were deeply embedded in urban communities and meant to provide public safety and local defense along with socialization and networking opportunities.[32]

Friends and neighbors banded together to have fun doing martial activities that they enjoyed, rather than to undertake the disciplined and regimented training required by the army. All it took to form a volunteer company was an ambitious and enterprising man who would recruit members and act as "captain," and a little political sway. The men decided what kind of military unit they wanted to be (e.g., artillery, cavalry, or infantry) without concern for actual state needs. Once formed, a company had to petition the state assembly for authorization to be part of the state militia. Legislatures faced with electoral pressures and meager finances typically granted the permits to White men. Not unlike contemporary militias, nineteenth-century groups determined the nature and extent of their activities, as well as the arms they were willing to purchase. Some groups were wealthy enough to buy heavy artillery and cannons; others paraded with brooms. In addition to the mandated annual musters, volunteer companies undertook other activities, such as rifle practice and parade drilling.[33] Loose regulation notwithstanding, these units were military companies subject to military oversight, and they were counted on to support the state's defensive needs. That is not the status of contemporary militia groups such as the Proud Boys and the Oath Keepers.

But rich or poor, the groups' greatest delight was in designing their uniforms—colorful outfits, with gold and lace trim and feathered hats. Gilbert and Sullivan's Major-General Stanley in *The Pirates of Penzance* is a close approximation to the typical nineteenth-century volunteer officer's get-up. As a result, if the UMA had created as many armies as states, the 1803 law enabled the creation of as many armies as local communities. Some described militia parades as displaying all the colors of the rainbow.[34]

During the Jacksonian era, bowing to pressure from voters-soldiers, states started to replace the enrolled militia with volunteers, implicitly recognizing that the conscripted militia model had failed. Volunteer companies adopted the name "the National Guards" to differentiate themselves from the disparaged enrolled militia.[35] As we shall see in chapter 5, the NRA emerged out of the National Guard system as an organization focused on improving military education and soldier discipline and ethos—the same problems that Washington and Hamilton had identified as endemic a century earlier.

Volunteer militia companies were state-subsidized private policing forces and armed preparedness units. Since these were voluntary, not state-mandated institutions, the internal composition of the units was determined by the members alone. In the context of White supremacy and nativism, volunteer militia units formed along ethnic lines, as White ethnics who were not welcomed in Anglo units opted to form their own organizations. As soon as one ethnic group organized a company, there was pressure for others to follow. Through volunteer militia service, new immigrants assimilated into American political culture and showed their political legitimacy and deservingness for republican American citizenship. At the same time, militia units offered a safe space for co-ethnics to socialize far from the hostility of the native population and the pressures for immediate assimilation.[36]

With industrialization, units formed along class-based ideological lines as well. Labor activists organized their own militia groups to project and amplify the power of workers relative to industry and the state. Participants in these militia organizations often came from within White immigrant communities, but what bonded members together was laborism, not ethnicity. At the same time, growing fears of riots by "anarchists, internationalists, and nihilists" led businesses in Northern cities to organize their own militias to fight the labor movement, often with active support from states.[37]

Volunteer militia companies were embedded in and reflected the social hierarchies of their communities. Volunteer companies operated much like private fraternal martial clubs, similar to other fraternal organizations and burial societies. Such groups developed their own constitutions and rules, and until the late nineteenth century they were subject to minimal state or federal regulation. Companies had strict recruitment criteria based on social standing and reputation. Their leaders tended to be planters, lawyers, doctors, and other respected citizens—the urban elite. They adopted distinctive uniforms, unique vocabularies, and a set of club-specific traditions. The uniforms, titles, and insignia denoted social status, not military rank or merit. These groups were hierarchical and exclusive externally, but participatory and relatively democratic internally—in some ways, mirroring American society. By liberally assigning titles, they offered White men a sense of belonging to a group of equals and the means to enhance their social status relative to society at large and to develop a business and social network useful to their professional careers.[38]

Social differences between volunteer companies were accentuated by differences in resources, which affected groups' preparedness and appearance. Many did receive weapons and ammunition from government authorities, but never very much and often on an unequal basis. For the most part, companies relied on community fundraising events to finance their activities. Drilling competitions that involved cash prizes were also a big draw, as companies stood to make significant sums. As a result, militias were more frequently found at picnics, lecture series, balls, cotillions, and banquets, and performed at parades, on national holidays, at various local commemorations, and in competitions, rather than in active duty or military training.[39]

NRA ascriptive republican mythology asserts that weapons were important to the "minuteman" because they enabled him to provide food and security for his family, and through these responsibilities to develop political virtue.[40] The historical reality is quite different. Then as now, training and dexterity in firearms was not a top priority for most people—contemporary surveys suggest that less than half of gun owners believe themselves to be knowledgeable about arms.[41] Military weapons, along with uniforms, were essential to these militia companies because they augmented the pageantry involved in musters and militia celebrations, thus increasing the social status of the group. The historian Harry Laver offers an example that suggests that the primary motivations for the establishment of militia groups were social and political, not military. Specifically, one company leader professed that in his company "[we are not] military men, nor [do we] know what are the requirements of the law in relation to the public arms . . . [but we] would be gratified in obtaining [guns] at as early a period as practicable."[42] Similarly, John Hope Franklin explains how elaborate militia costumes could be: "He wore white pants, white vest, blue cloth coat trimmed in red and brass buttons. His hat was crescent shape with a cockade, with a silver eagle on one side and a large white feather tipped with red. He wore a sword and belt and a ruffled shirt and high boots."[43]

Despite their popularity and the relatively more generous financial support they received (primarily thanks to private donations) compared to the enrolled militia, volunteer companies were only somewhat more effective as military units than the conscripts. Participation in volunteer companies was often spurred by motivations other than a desire to be a soldier. Some men joined for social reasons, to showcase their social status or develop a social network. Others enjoyed the camaraderie and the esprit de corps, as well as the formal trappings of the uniform. As a result, participation was inconsistent, driven by the demands of private life and the strength of one's social ambitions.

Given the lofty republican rhetoric with which the militias have been shrouded, especially in recent years, it is ironic that many White men became citizen-soldiers to avoid a different duty of citizenship: serving on a jury. For de Tocqueville, jury duty was where men learned "not to shirk responsibility." Such practices sustained "a virile disposition without which political virtue does not exist."[44] But for late-nineteenth-century White men it was just an annoying obligation. As an inducement to military service, states offered volunteers exemptions from jury service and substantial property tax discounts. These incentives were pushed heavily by military reformers concerned about the deterioration of the volunteer militias.[45]

Consistent with republican ideology, volunteer (and conscript) companies' primary obligation was to their city or town; therefore they could refuse to serve in emergencies outside the local community, and many of them did so. State legislatures wary about the effect at the ballot booth of changing such provisions of the militia laws refrained from any reforms. Not surprisingly, foreign observers noted that militia members who fought in the Civil War lacked solidarity with other companies, which led to brawls. Echoing George Washington's complaints about the Revolution-era militia, observers mentioned that militiamen were frequently and excessively drunk "to the extent of falling on the spot by the side of their guns."[46]

By the time the militia were federalized and officially named "the National Guard" by the Dick Act in 1903, there was a strong public and elite consensus that they were inept, violent, and partisan—characteristics incompatible with an effective military force, let alone with lofty republican ideals. According to the historian Jerry Cooper, militia responses to public order emergencies lacked "mobilization plans, centralized command and control, logistical support, tactical training, and discipline."[47] It is not surprising, then, that the public called them "tin soldiers" and thought of their members as "fanatics who were mentally unbalanced."[48] These characterizations are far closer to modern-day perceptions of the citizen militia groups in the West and upper Midwest, or the Oath Keepers and Proud Boys more recently, than the cherished legend of the republican citizen-soldier of revolutionary tracts and storybook accounts.[49]

Militia reform was finally passed in 1903 after the monumentally chaotic mobilization in the Spanish-American War and the war in the Philippines—wars meant to demonstrate (White) American manliness and preserve it for generations to come.[50] As the US was preparing to land in Cuba, volunteer companies showed up with unserviceable, out-of-date equipment and heavy wool uniforms completely unsuitable for the tropics; many were also lacking crucial inoculations. Reports showed that many militiamen failed physical fitness tests, and as many as 40 percent of the volunteers had never drilled or fired a gun.[51]

The Dick Act of 1903 officially created and consolidated the "National Guard" and eventually subsumed volunteer militia organizations under a national military system, setting federal standards for training and organization and providing federal funds for recruits' salaries and equipment, and for armory construction. The law divided the militia into the organized militia (the National Guard) and the unorganized militia (draft-age males). This latter group became the key target market for a fledgling quasi-governmental organization born out of the National Guard: the NRA.

The federal government standardized and supervised the equipment and training of all reserve units and required that states provide equal support to all units that remained after the reorganization. The National Defense Act of 1916, which was enacted on the eve of World War I, nationalized the state militia units and waived the territorial service limitations that had plagued every administration since the late eighteenth century. It also integrated them into the national defense command structure of the War Department and the Army. State legislatures' acceptance of federal funds and supervision was a tacit acknowledgment of the militia's nationalization.[52] As we will see in chapter 5, both laws were in good part the result of intensive lobbying by two interrelated organizations: the National Guard Association (NGA) and the NRA. Both saw great direct material benefits from this military reorganization.

Figure 3.2 shows schematically the evolution of the state militia, both the enrolled and the volunteer corps. The enrolled militia declined steadily through the early national era. As of the early nineteenth century the number of volunteer groups increased steadily, and their presence spiked markedly during the Civil War. In 1903, the volunteer National Guards were federalized under the US Army and became the Army reserve corps, but retained the National Guard name. Thereafter, the size of the National Guard was determined centrally based on the War Department's needs and

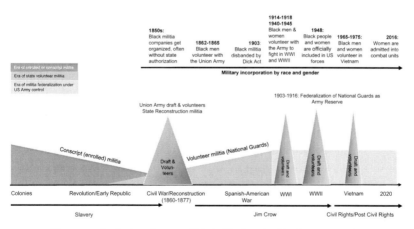

Figure 3.2 Evolution of state militia in black and white (1770s–2020).

expectations. Numbers surged during the two world wars and Vietnam, but after the conclusion of each war, the National Guard size shrank to peacetime numbers.

This timeline reflects primarily the experience of White militia forces. As I will discuss in the next section, Black militia companies formed in the late antebellum era in anticipation of the Civil War. Most Black companies did not receive state authorization but persisted nonetheless—evidence of the value Black communities placed on martial citizenship, but also a testament to the loose regulatory enforcement by states. The number of Black volunteers skyrocketed during the Civil War, but only a few companies remained active in the North and the South after Reconstruction, primarily due to state neglect and Black communities' financial weakness. The reorganization of the National Guards in 1903 did away with most Black militia companies. Black men and some (mostly White) women served in World War I and World War II, but mostly in noncombat roles. Both groups were officially incorporated into the US military in 1948; however, women had to wait until 2016 to be allowed into combat units and become full citizen-soldiers analogous to the NRA's "riflemen."

AFRICAN AMERICANS' ENROLLED AND VOLUNTEER MILITIA SERVICE

Even though they had served in every American war, African American men officially gained the right to serve at arms only in the middle of the Civil War, and only in noncombat roles. For them, military service and political rights remained decoupled until the 1960s. During the colonial era, free Blacks served in integrated enrolled militia units in the North. In the South, only Spanish-controlled New Orleans maintained a free Black regiment along with Black slave-catching units—a testament to the complex reality of race in early nineteenth-century America. This Black militia was disbanded following the Louisiana Purchase, but it was recalled to active duty twice: once in 1811 to help put down a slave rebellion, and again in 1812 to help Andrew Jackson fight the British in the Battle of New Orleans.[53]

During the antebellum era, free Black volunteer militia companies developed in the Northeast. In defiance of the racial limitations of the UMA and related state statutes, African Americans in the North organized "vigilance committees" and militia units as early as the 1830s. These units assisted in protecting and transporting fugitive slaves as well as deterring and intercepting slave-catchers. By engaging in the rituals of martial citizenship, they also promoted martial republican ideals and showcased African Americans' deservingness for political membership. Vigilance committees proclaimed that their mission was to protect the "rights and safety of blacks." Especially in the 1850s, conflicts erupted between federal agents, slave-catchers, and armed Black mobs determined to protect and rescue fugitive slaves. W. E. B. DuBois and the historian Herbert Aptheker have credited these battles over fugitive slaves with creating solidarity and a shared racial consciousness among African Americans.[54]

As early as 1853, African Americans in Ohio and Massachusetts unsuccessfully sought to change the law so that free Blacks could bear arms and form volunteer militia companies. When permission was not forthcoming, Black men formed their militia units anyway. Advocating for the tenets of inclusive republicanism, African Americans in the North who viewed military service as a visible and public display of citizenship strenuously objected to their exclusion from service. According to the former slave and Black abolitionist William J. Watkins, they wanted Whites to "regard us as . . . men who knowing our rights, dare, all hazards, to maintain them. We are entitled to ALL the rights and immunities of CITIZENS OF MASSACHUSETTS [as] law-abiding, tax-paying, liberty-loving, NATIVE-BORN, AMERICAN CITIZENS."[55]

Abolitionists in Massachusetts even sought state approval to form a Black militia company; in 1855, when that permission was not forthcoming, they formed the Massasoit Guard anyway. The Black historian William Cooper Nell documented several Black militia units present in New York, such as the Attucks Guards, the Hannibal Guards, and the Free-Soil Guards. Scholars have also identified Black militia units, some state-approved and others unsanctioned, in Cleveland and Cincinnati, Ohio; in Providence, Rhode Island; in New Bedford, Massachusetts; in Albany, New York; in Reading and Harrisburg, Pennsylvania; in Patterson, New Jersey; and in Detroit, Michigan.[56]

Anticipating the advent of the Civil War, these groups formed to help Black men learn the art of bearing arms. The units were community-funded and -supported and played a significant political role as symbols of martial citizenship. Despite the poverty of the Black community, militiamen donned the kind of elaborate uniforms that were typical of militias in that era. Although many drilled with broomsticks and cornstalks, others managed to procure weapons—some had axes, but others had muskets. Much like White nineteenth-century militia companies, Black groups sought to project and perform respectability, solidarity, and martial citizenship to signal their deservingness for equal political membership.[57]

The Congressional Reconstruction era was the only time in American history when African American rather than White military forces represented the primary, official embodiment of state-sanctioned violence in an entire section of the country. The participation of White militia in the Civil War on the side of the Confederacy left Radical Reconstruction authorities with a dilemma. In the post-conflict context, enforcement of Reconstruction laws and political authority required establishing an effective force that would counter the White paramilitary organizations that had sprouted across the South. White Southerners viewed Radical Republican governors as usurpers of power, sidelining democratic institutions and forcefully imposing the will of a hated minority on the majority. Thomas A. Hendricks of Indiana captured this view when he accused his colleagues in Congress of "[having] attempted to reverse the American doctrine and to declare that by force the power of the states shall be placed in the hands of the minority, stripping classes of the right to participation in the government, and then by force governing them." A force that consisted of Northern "carpetbaggers," Southern Republican sympathizers or "scalawags," and newly freed Black men would face determined resistance and terrorism from White people committed to racial supremacy.[58]

The historian Otis Singletary has documented the history of the Black militia during Reconstruction, highlighting how these groups were perceived differently by various White political actors. For Radical Republicans, the Black militia was not only a means of imposing social order and combating growing White political violence, especially the emergent Ku Klux Klan, but also a tool for developing a key constituency within a hostile political terrain. In essence, the Republican Southern strategy of the era consisted of inculcating martial citizenship among Black men, ensuring their political membership, and providing a degree of social welfare support to the freed people, who had a position akin to refugees. The Republicans used the militia, the Freedmen's Bureau, and the Union Leagues to advance their political agenda. It is important to note that unlike prewar militia, Reconstruction forces were modeled after the US Army and were expected to abide by the rules of war as set out in the "Lieber Code."[59] Thus, their role was not merely to maintain domestic order and act as police. The Reconstruction militia provided Black men with invaluable experience in political organizing and leadership and taught them the importance of martial citizenship.[60]

In some states, Black militia were organized as official state forces. In others, such as in Alabama, they were volunteer troops not officially sanctioned by the state. In some states, like Tennessee, Black militia had a primarily political function—monitoring elections and bringing Republican constituents safely to the polls. In North Carolina, they also staged local operations against the Klan, which lasted for several years until President Grant put entire counties under martial law and sent in federal forces. In

Texas, Black militia became the enforcers of martial law, which had been declared by Republican Governor Edmund J. Davis in an attempt to protect the political rights of African Americans against White armed violence. When Davis lost the gubernatorial election, Black troops were used in a battle against White Democrats over the statehouse. In Louisiana, where Republicans were divided between radicals and moderates, when the two factions fought against each other Black militia participated in street battles in support of both camps.[61]

Before the Jim Crow system hardened, from 1877 through the early years of the twentieth century, African Americans organized and maintained volunteer militia companies in nine of the eleven states of the former Confederacy. Black militia companies were also common in Northern states where Black communities were sufficiently large to absorb the costs. Many more requested permission to form militias, but state authorities turned them down, citing lack of arms availability. The historian Bruce Glasrud has labeled these groups "the Brothers of the Buffalo Soldiers." Ironically, Black militia companies served in the Spanish-American War because some Southern states could not find enough White recruits; White men, secure in their political status, did not volunteer in sufficient numbers.[62]

In the North and the South, the Black militia companies that formed by the end of Reconstruction fulfilled mostly ceremonial functions: they participated in parades, commemorations, national holidays, and other community events. Their principal purpose was to enable Black men to perform martial citizenship in the same way that White men had done for centuries. In many communities, especially in the South, Black men were barred from the franchise, but militia service opened another road to claiming honor, virtue, and republican citizenship.[63]

Even their ceremonial participation was almost always segregated. Black militias marched and paraded in Black public spaces and competed in "sham battles" and shooting competitions against other Black companies. In the rare cases when Black and White militias participated in the same event, the Black militia had to follow the White companies, and White militiamen often refused to salute their Black counterparts.[64]

The costs of setting up and maintaining a militia organization in the nineteenth century were substantial for any community. In theory, the state budget absorbed the cost of leasing an armory and procuring weapons and ammunition. However, state appropriations were never sufficient in practice, and companies had to pay for weapons, weapon repairs, uniforms, and other incidental costs. Participation was also time-consuming, especially for a community made up of working-class people who labored long hours. Militia participation required weekly drills, summer training, and many social and fundraising events. These costs were a challenge for any White company; for Black companies, they represented significant impediments simply because the size of the middle class was so small. The fact that Black communities across the country chose to underwrite this type of civic involvement, despite their limitations and the indignities faced by Black militiamen, attests to the social and political importance of the institution.[65]

Figure 3.3 is a drawing from 1876, now housed at the Library of Congress, that depicts a scene after a Black militia drill in Philadelphia during the Centennial celebrations. In contrast to the militia of the 1830s, here militia men wear formal uniforms that recall those of the Union Army. The African Americans in the drawing display all the trappings of Victorian-era respectability: the women are dressed in fancy, high-quality dresses, and the men wear well-maintained uniforms. Even the children are well-dressed and well-behaved, all contrary to the stereotypical portrayals of African Americans of the era. In reality, Black militia had been prevented from drilling on Independence Day in Philadelphia for most of the nineteenth century. Their presence in the Centennial festivities was an anomaly. Contemporaneous sources also noted that African Americans celebrated the day in segregation.[66]

Black companies persisted because of the potent political symbolism

Figure 3.3 The American Centennial Festival Exhibition: Scene in Fairmount Park, Philadelphia—Negro militia after drill. From *The Illustrated London News*, May 13, 1876, 465. Library of Congress.

associated with military service and the opportunity these organizations provided for socializing, exercising social leadership, and advancing economically and socially through networking. The Black community recognized militia participation as part of an effort to gain the respect and acceptance of the White community and the political establishment. Attesting to the political importance of military service, lithographs of Black militia units adorned most African American homes of this era. Consistent with republican ideology, militia service was evidence that Black men chose independence and patriotism, which made them deserve citizenship rights. According to the historian Eleanor Hannah, Black communities had "faith in the ability of military service to confirm and preserve their claims to equality, citizenship, and manhood. . . . African Americans struggled on because a militia company was a tangible demonstration of their independence . . . they believed that the role of the citizen-soldier in civic pageantry, especially parades, and the responsibilities of the citizen-soldier for national defense placed the militia squarely in the midst of the general debates about who was a citizen, what was responsible citizenship, and how a citizen might be made." In insisting on the same public expressions of citizenship as White men, Black men expressed their deep-seated belief that by acting out "responsible citizenship and disciplined manhood" in the public theater, they defended their political rights as citizens.[67]

THE POLITICAL SUCCESS OF THE MILITIA

If the militia were so inept on the battlefield, why did states support the institution for so long? Why didn't they enact laws to centralize and professionalize the militia, force them to adopt uniform dress and armament, turn them into a standing army? The answer lies in the institution's political role. Today, we are accustomed to thinking that the US has always had a complete separation between the military and politics. The federal military command's subordination to the president signifies this separation. But that is not the full story. In fact, a very different picture emerges when we consider the role that state-sanctioned armed bands of men played in nineteenth-century political life.

First, the militia had an important political function as police auxiliaries helping to suppress politically motivated violence such as political protests, insurrections, and race riots. Second, the militia acted as the armed units of political parties, intimidating opponents and rallying supporters to the polls. Third, parties recruited candidates among militia officers. Fourth, militia drills and parades were important social events that brought out the entire community. Political candidates used such events to generate support for their party. These events also served to reinforce ascriptive republican ideals as armed White men were the focus, and women and Black folks sat on the sidelines. Finally, as White ethnics organized their own units, participation in the militia became an important vehicle for the political and social incorporation of immigrants and their induction into the system of ascriptive republicanism.

The political centrality of the militia is the reason volunteer groups were obsessed with social appearances. Drilling with brooms and cornstalks was humiliating, while drilling with muskets projected power and authority. These weapons acted as symbols of the citizen-soldiers' status as responsible and patriotic members of society—as good citizens. Uniforms and weapons emphasized the social distance between White men and others and underscored distinctions in class and rank *between* White men. In the process, these occasions reinforced and ritualized the relationship between guns, race, and manhood.[68]

The first duty of the militia was to suppress political violence. Most famously, both in the colonial era and after the Revolution, militia forces suppressed rebellions organized by disadvantaged White citizens. The deployment of the militia enabled established authorities to marginalize yeomen and working-class White people and to ignore the grievances that had moved them to take up arms. Militia forces suppressed Bacon's Rebellion (1676), the Regulators (1771), Shays' Rebellion (1787), and the Whiskey Rebellion (1794). In the late nineteenth century, the militia suppressed labor strikes and intervened in a variety of other episodes of unrest, including race riots. The militia were also employed to respond to prison riots, bank robberies, civil rights protests, and a variety of other social disturbances.[69] In the twenty-first century, the National Guard has also been deployed on the Southern border to prevent undocumented migration from Mexico and Central America. Most recently, the Washington, DC, National Guard was called in to protect the US Capitol and other government buildings in the aftermath of the January 6, 2021, insurrectionary attack by supporters of former president Donald Trump.

In the nineteenth century, it was political violence in the form of ethnic/race riots and labor strikes that often required militia involvement. Abolitionism and emancipation on the one hand, and industrialization and the labor movement on the other, deepened social cleavages in American politics and gave rise to many more incidents of social violence. Before the Civil War, ethnic riots involved White groups, and race riots targeted abolitionists. After the Civil War and Reconstruction, as the Jim Crow regime hardened, racial violence took the form of lynchings and race riots targeting African Americans.[70]

By the 1860s, only a handful of major cities had professional police forces and armed constabularies, and those were very expensive to maintain. Police departments, much like fire departments, were centers of political patronage and were heavily involved with urban machine politics. As a result, police could not always be trusted to handle major urban disturbances. Since in many cases racial and labor strife also implicated partisan leanings, elected officials often expected that the police would take sides. In many such cases, the state militia was called in to assist. But militia participation in race riots was selective: when the fighting was between Blacks and Native Americans, as it often was before the 1830s, or when it involved attacks against abolitionists, the militia was rarely called in; however, when riots involved Blacks and the Irish, towns often sent in units (fig. 3.4).[71]

The historian Jerry Cooper identified 411 cases of civil disorder between 1868 and 1899 in which the militias were called in to assist. Of those, 218 corresponded to race-related mass violence, 118 related to labor unrest, 15 were identified as "handling Indian difficulties," and 20 were considered election-related violence, which also could have had racial or ethnic components.[72] Militia training manuals of the era emphasized the units' role in riot control and quashing of street brawls. In the 1870s, cities also called in regular Army units to assist with labor strikes. Contemporary comparisons between Army and militia responses to railroad unrest showed that the Army could control riots using much less violence and causing no deaths, while the militia shot hundreds of people. This led to proposals to expand

Figure 3.4 Riot in Philadelphia, June [i.e., July] 7, 1844
/ H. Bucholzer. Library of Congress.

the Army and to use it for domestic social control, but this was a no-go for Southern congressmen still reeling from Reconstruction.[73]

When political parties developed after the Revolution, militias became central to the political process. Militia clubs were a launching pad for ambitious local politicians, a ready-made electoral political base, and a means to distribute political patronage. Militia musters, parades, and social events were political spectacles that political parties could not afford to lose. Such occasions attracted large crowds, who enjoyed the military parade with all its pomp and circumstance and listened to political speeches. On election day, militia officers marched their companies and other voters to the polls, and captains worked with local party bosses to deliver votes. Militias were also used to intimidate the opposition and keep them from voting. They were an incredibly effective means of political organizing—so much so that for over one hundred years, state legislatures and Congress resisted efforts to fold them into the professional army and turn them into effective military units.[74]

During Reconstruction and the latter part of the nineteenth century, the use of the militias for partisan violence came into sharp focus. Republican governors in Southern states organized Black militia forces to supplement the Union Army in enforcing Black political rights and protecting the Republican Party's supporters. In some states, the militia operated as a governor's army to prevent Democratic paramilitary mobilization and to intimidate Republican opponents in intra-party conflicts. In some border states—such as Kentucky, which remained loyal to the Union and thus avoided the Reconstruction process—state-approved militia companies became the military arm of local Democratic Party leaders. These militia groups worked in concert with paramilitary White supremacist groups in suppressing the African American and White Republican vote. Peaceful political parades and demonstrations meant to create enthusiasm among Black voters before the election were met with extreme violence.[75]

The militia and militia events were sites of political socialization for White men. These institutions were steeped in ascriptive republican ideology and recreated and reinforced existing social hierarchies. Men from similar economic and demographic backgrounds came together to socialize but also to practice an ascriptive republican form of citizenship. Volunteer militia companies functioned as centers for instruction about and ritualized performance of gendered and racialized American martial ideologies. Participation in militia companies taught political subjects their proper role in the community and conditioned them to admire and support social superiors and resent and shun social inferiors. As the historian Carole Emberton argues, especially in the South the militia and the slave patrol were vital sources of political socialization, as they "brought White men together under a common purpose and taught them the fundamental lessons of discipline and hierarchy. Although the citizen-soldier ideal embodied in militia duty claimed to equalize men of all ranks in the performance of their republican duty, it remained an institution deeply involved in the replication of social and political status."[76]

Other experts have reached similar conclusions. The historian John Hope Franklin argued that the militia had a social and political function more than a military role: they acted to reinforce social hierarchies and promote exclusionary notions of patriotism and community. These clubs taught participants how to behave as was expected of White men and how to interact appropriately with others in the community.[77] Edmund Morgan reminds us that militia musters were "schools of subordination," occasions that visibly reaffirmed social hierarchies. According to Morgan, the most valuable service rendered by the militia was "reconciling the incongruity of popular sovereignty with a hierarchical society."[78]

In many towns, the volunteer militia became an essential mechanism for newly arrived European immigrant men's social and political incorporation in two ways. First, White ethnics set up their own volunteer militia companies according to the model provided by Anglo companies. Through these organizations, White ethnic men learned to perform martial Whiteness. These militia groups also became politically connected to urban machines such as New York's Tammany Hall, introducing White ethnics to partisan politics. Second, in the latter part of the nineteenth century, many White ethnics joined the labor movement. Because labor strikes often drew in the state militia and industry-organized militia groups, laborites organized their own volunteer militia forces. In fact, the development of the labor movement accounts for part of the increase in the popularity of militarism in the late nineteenth century. The need to suppress and resist racial and labor strife created incentives for citizens to establish new volunteer militia companies.[79]

Ironically, the popularity of the militia among newly arrived European immigrants as a means of political incorporation and empowerment became central to the first attempt by states to assert better control over the volunteers. Especially after the Civil War, the proliferation of White ethnic militias and their involvement in race and labor strife became alarming to elected officials. State authorities became concerned that they were losing control over the volunteers, since some organized for the explicit purpose of countering the authority of industry and its political supporters. The volunteer militia system was incentivizing the development of armed groups that did not necessarily share the dominant political ideology. These groups sought to operate as rival sites of power and to use their access to weapons to produce greater social and economic equality and inclusion. These developments provided the impetus for states to rein in the militia and impose greater regulation and control. States sought to do away with practices that allowed citizens to organize militia groups without the express consent of the state. In *Presser v. Illinois* (1886), the US Supreme Court upheld an Illinois statute that prohibited men from forming private military companies without state approval. Presser led an armed parade of the socialist German workers' organization *Lehr und Wehr Verein* (Education and Defense Society) in Chicago without permission. The Court's decision affirmed that private militia could not operate without state approval. It also suggested that the state could delegate authority to use violence based on its own ideological, partisan, and social criteria. The *Presser* decision led all fifty states to enact bans on unauthorized private militias, effectively disbanding labor-supported companies.[80]

This was the institutional, political, and ideological context that gave rise to the National Rifle Association. The terrible performance of many volunteer companies in the Civil War prompted a group of National Guard officers to propose their own solution to the perennial problems of the militia. The association was founded as a "patriotic," quasi-governmental organization dedicated to teaching shooting skills and developing political virtue among the volunteers and the military-age civilian men eligible for a war draft. As we will see in chapter 5, the NRA was a product of the American military establishment, and it is the US military's ascriptive republican worldview that it carried forward from the nineteenth to the twenty-first century.

The NRA has been one key vector for the preservation and transmission of ascriptive republican ideology. As I discuss in chapter 4, in addition to the military itself, other key conduits of this worldview were the public education system, which after the Civil War yielded to the influence of organizations dedicated to the myth of the "Lost Cause" (the idea that the Confederacy fought for the protection of local democracy, not slavery) and the preservation of the Southern memory. In addition to working through school boards to adopt schoolbooks friendly to their interpretation of the Civil War and race relations, organizations such as the United Daughters of the Confederacy (UDC) built monuments to Confederate soldiers and loyal slaves across the South. The myths of the Old South were also preserved in popular culture—from movies to novels read by several generations of Americans.

CHAPTER 4

Cultural Transmission

So far, we have seen that a new ideological system emerged at the time of the American Revolution that combined elements of martial republicanism (a worldview that understood citizenship in terms of one's responsibility to armed readiness) and White male supremacy (a worldview arguing that only White men could develop the political virtue necessary for armed service and democratic politics). African Americans had chosen the "protection" and "dependence" of chattel slavery over the hardship of freedom and independence. White men who used armed violence were understood as seeking political liberty. Despite a long history of resistance to slavery and valorous military service to the colonies and the United States, Black men who engaged in armed violence were viewed as criminals or "cannibals," in Jefferson's words. Yet, how could these ideas that originated so long ago still be influential today? How can a significant minority among the White public today embrace ascriptive republicanism? After all, slavery ended in 1863, and the Jim Crow era concluded in 1954. Women gained the right to vote in 1920—more than a century ago. African Americans and women today serve in the military as equals; they vote, run for office, and have the same political rights as White men. White Americans have also accepted that African Americans are not biologically inferior and should have equal political rights and be treated equally by the government.[1] The world has changed a great deal since the late eighteenth century.

Ideologies of inequality are not easy to dismantle. Scholars argue that institutionalized systems of inequality are maintained because there are persuasive ideologies that rationalize inequities as natural or deserved. These "legitimizing myths" serve to preserve rather than challenge social hierarchies. Thus, ideologies define which traits, behaviors, and actions are appropriate and legitimate social and political expressions, and which are not, thus undergirding systems of social control. In this context, group-based stereotypes—as "good guys" and "virtuous," or as "corrupt," "lazy," and "criminals"—are used to justify and legitimize group differences in treatment and outcomes.[2] People from both advantaged and disadvantaged groups come to accept and internalize inequality as normal, legitimate, and just. In fact, studies show that marginalized groups are *more* likely to endorse ideologies that justify inequities than are members of advantaged groups.[3]

Ascriptive republicanism has been one such legitimizing ideology preserved and transmitted through institutional and social processes. The American military, especially the militia system, served as a critical mechanism for preserving and transmitting ascriptive republican ideology. Through volunteer militia service, White American men reinforced their dominant social and political position relative to women and minority groups and taught the rules of White male supremacy to White male ethnics. Important as it was, the military was only one mechanism through which ascriptive republican ideology was preserved and transmitted both intergenerationally and—equally important—to subordinated groups.

Such beliefs are transmitted and reinforced by social learning processes, such as popular culture and the teaching of history and civics in the classroom. Movies, newspapers, magazines, and popular fiction, along with state-sanctioned educational materials, teach Americans from a very young age about the structure of the social system and provide ideological justifications for it. Public memory preserved in monuments, museums, parades, and other public events also serves as a powerful system of ideological transmission across time and space. After all, the reader should recall that Confederate monuments continue to litter the American landscape even after recent efforts to dismantle many of them. As I discuss in later chapters, the NRA has also served as a mechanism for transmitting ascriptive republican ideology. Most importantly, even after other transmission mechanisms became sites of ideological contestation and were forced to accommodate and transmit viewpoints that challenged ascriptive republican ideology, the gun culture and the NRA remained largely insular and unaffected by such challenges.

SCHOOL BOOKS AND EDUCATIONAL CURRICULA

School curricula and readings targeted at children are key vectors of political socialization for young people. History and civics books, along with children's fiction, are prescriptive—they teach young minds "how things are done" and how people are expected to behave. These materials operate in the context of a legitimizing ideology: they explain and promote society's values. According to the sociologist Gordon Kelly, within children's fiction, authors "may also renew their own commitment to certain principles of social order—for example, shaping their fictional response, in part, to meet threats posed by alternative belief systems."[4] Parental choices regarding how to address issues of race relations and American racial history are also consequential. Recent research conducted in the wake of the Black Lives Matter movement documents the ambivalence and difficulty many White parents have in explaining this political context to their children.[5]

Unlike European countries, the United States does not have a national school curriculum in history and the social sciences. Except for the early twentieth century, when the federal government produced textbooks meant to promote the "Americanization" of immigrants, there have not been federal standards for curriculum. American federalism ensures that decisions about schoolbooks' content are made at the state and local levels. The decentralization of educational curricula has made it difficult to create uniform standards for the interpretation of American history. The country has not coalesced around a single "truth." People disagree about what it means to be an American and what elements of the past are essential for students to know. From patriotic societies to the Chamber of Commerce to immigrant, feminist, and minority rights organizations, a variety of groups have sought to challenge the historical orthodoxy presented in schoolbooks, with varying degrees of success.[6] Most recently, we have witnessed this division over the "truth" of American history and what our children should be exposed to in schools, in the controversies over the *New York Times*'s "1619 Project" and fabricated concerns that Critical Race Theory (CRT), a form of analysis used by legal scholars, has permeated the public school curriculum.[7]

Drawing on contemporary historiography and social science research, the "1619 Project" focused on the centrality of race and slavery in the history of American economic and political development, emphasizing the structural nature of racism in American society. For its proponents, the project was an effort to introduce anti-racism principles into the public discourse.[8] In other words, the project sought to refute ascriptive republican ideology. However, this is not what conservatives saw. White conservatives criticized the project as "racist" and "divisive," and questioned the social and political effects of introducing such a perspective to schoolchildren.[9] In the year following its inception, right-wing activists sought to trace the intellectual origins of the "1619 Project" and the anti-racism movement more broadly to an academic theory, extensively used in legal scholarship since the 1990s, known as CRT.[10] According to the Project's and CRT's detractors, such ideas are promoted by an elite "seeking to reengineer the foundation of human psychology and social institutions through the new politics of race." In this view, this type of analysis of America's racial history is "poisonous" and "an existential threat" to the country because it teaches hate and inequality.[11] This desire to hold the line against fragmentation by privileging the ascriptive republican truth of the country's founding was evident in laws banning the teaching of "critical race theory" and, in some states, removing a variety of lessons related to the women's rights and civil rights struggles.[12] The laws limit how teachers discuss ideas such as racial privilege, explicit or implicit bias, discrimination, and oppression. Some laws impose financial penalties on schools that do not comply. This same desire for uniformity and protection of a sacred White European past is evident in a substantial portion of the White public. A recent national survey shows that 30 percent of White Americans believe that issues of racial inequality should never be taught in schools. Another 15 percent concede that such issues should be taught, but only "a little."[13] In my 2021 national survey, 26 percent of all White Americans, and 43 percent of those who embrace ascriptive republican ideology, support "laws that classify as terrorism any activity that promotes beliefs and ideologies that criticize America's White and European heritage."

The CRT controversy is neither the first nor the last one to erupt over education policy and the content of schoolbooks. Concerns about how American history was taught in schools emerged early on in US history. A republican society was obligated to create republican citizens—evervigilant (White) men, ready to protect political virtue. The Founders may have been critical of each other in real life—Benjamin Rush was not a fan of George Washington's war strategy—but they agreed that the security of the republic depended on all republican citizens learning to cherish the same political principles—the same version of "the truth." The past was treated as a usable form of the present from which we can extract elements to weave an "eternal truth."[14] Each generation added some elements to these fundamental historical "truths," the interpretations of the past that political actors of the present believed were best suited to unify a racially and socially diverse society even as the winds of social change continued to blow. State laws and constitutions thus banned perspectives—sectarian, partisan, or political—that contradicted this orthodoxy.[15]

States and local communities have understood well that through the teaching of history, people create political subjects and preserve or change social structures. As a result, local and state leaders selected authors and books that represented their views of the past—a process that continues to this day.[16] These texts promoted a simplistic, heroic narrative of the American Revolution as a "White, [male], Anglo-Saxon, Protestant pageant" that celebrated the virtuous White and male citizen-soldier. They described the War of Independence as a crusade waged by virtuous White men against tyranny, a fight against "the badge of slavery" or the yoke forced on the colonists by Parliament. These men were portrayed as "uncaptained" rugged individualists—that is, independent people not coerced or helped by state authority—who developed political virtue by mastering the use of the rifle in private life.[17] These narratives almost completely excised African Americans from the heroic American narrative and relegated women to roles as wives and mothers of famous White men.[18]

From children's books to NRA accounts, authors often adopted a universalistic language to explain the Revolution—the Patriots were "fighting for rights . . . for men and women and children all over the world," one 1943 book stated. No longer could "a handful of men" have "power over thousands," the text taught, ignoring the reality of Jim Crow.[19] This type of storytelling concealed the ascriptive nature of American republicanism and allowed authors to obviate what Edmund Morgan has called "the American paradox"—the realization that in America, White freedom rested on Black unfreedom.[20] Well into the 1950s, these officially sanctioned accounts presented slaveholders as virtuous champions of freedom, never grappling with the contradiction between the rhetoric and the Founders' behavior. Others simply do not include African Americans in the narrative, rendering them invisible and therefore morally unproblematic.

Equally insidious was the "Lost Cause" narrative that dominated the portrayal of slavery, the Civil War, Reconstruction, and the Jim Crow era in historiography and textbooks alike. The "Lost Cause" is a revisionist, ascriptive republican narrative that Southern White people developed in the latter part of the nineteenth century to justify the moral legitimacy of racial segregation and Black political repression. The "Lost Cause" myth held that noble Southern men fought the Civil War not to protect slavery, but rather to defend local self-determination and democracy from federal encroachment—what they called "states' rights." The Southern plantation system was portrayed as a gentle and cultivated society of fair dames and brave, freedom-loving cavaliers surrounded by loyal and kindly slaves. Southern men were virtuous because they trained in the art of war; this allowed them to be enlightened political stewards. Slavery was presented as a protective and enlightening institution: masters cared for their slaves in the same way they cared for children. They provided shelter and food along with guidance to help slaves transition from savagery to civilization.[21] In exchange, slaves willingly submitted to their condition and loved and supported their masters. Since Black slaves chose slavery and dependence, they could not be trusted with the obligations of political freedom—the ballot and the bullet.

Before the war started, Confederate leaders such as Jefferson Davis and

Alexander Stephens were clear that slavery was the reason for the South to rise against the Union. In his "Cornerstone" speech, delivered in Savannah, Georgia, on March 21, 1861, Stephens rejected the egalitarian principles of the "old confederation," the United States. The Confederacy, he asserted, "is founded upon exactly the opposite idea; its foundations are laid, its cornerstone rests, upon the great truth that the negro is not equal to the White man; that slavery . . . is his neutral and normal condition."[22] By the end of the war, both Confederate leaders had changed their minds. With slavery gone, social norms changed in the country, and conceding that a war that killed 620,000 people was fought over slavery conferred no honor on the cause. The new narrative insisted that the war was fought over democracy: the rights of the people to make sovereign decisions about the form of their government—states' rights.[23]

The Progressive school of historiography, which dominated academia in the early part of the twentieth century, allowed the "Lost Cause" myth to persist. For the Progressives, the war resulted from a clash between economic forces. Plantation agriculture and industrial capitalism—two distinct and competing ways of organizing economic life—fought for political dominance, and Northern industrialism won. From this vantage point, slavery was not central to the war. It only represented the labor system of the plantation economy, not so different from the "wage slavery" of the factory floor.[24]

Influential Southern historians embraced and propagated the economic explanation. For them, the Confederacy fought for the constitutional principle of democratic self-governance and "the preservation of a stable, pastoral, agrarian civilization" against "the overbearing, acquisitive, aggressive ambitions of an urban-industrial Leviathan."[25] Among revisionists, chattel slavery was seen as a minor contributor to Southern life and the causes of the war. Its role was only in exciting extremists on both sides. If anything, it was abolitionists and fire-eaters (ardent supporters of slavery) who polarized the sections, forcing the South into a corner, which led to the conflict. From this perspective, the South fell victim to self-righteous Northern attacks in a "war of Northern aggression."[26]

And it was not only the causes of the conflict that came under the revisionist analysis that was reflected in school textbooks. In a parallel development, the Dunning school of historiography gave academic credence to the myth that Black political leadership in the South during Reconstruction represented the hallmark of corruption and mismanagement, which justified Black political exclusion and repression.[27] In the Dunning school's telling, the South honorably accepted its defeat and agreed to do right by the freedmen to ensure sectional reconciliation and restore the

Union. However, Radical Republicans in Congress dismantled Southern governments and forced Black political rights through illegitimate means. Tyrannical radical governments consisting of corrupt Northern "carpet-baggers," Southern White "scalawags," and illiterate and politically inept Black people compromised Southern freedom and virtuous republican governance. Historians placed undue emphasis on rapes of White women by Black men, thus offering justification for lynchings and White political violence. In this view, racial equality and democracy threatened the purity of the White race, and consequently the stability of American civilization.[28] "Liberty without anarchy," or "ordered liberty," required rigid racial stratification with Whites at the helm—a point made over and over in the late nineteenth and early twentieth centuries in the justifications of the "White Man's Burden" for empire.[29]

Following earlier ascriptive republican narratives, Dunning school historians argued that the freedmen were incapable of self-government, freedom, and political membership. Blacks did not have the education, refinement, or intellectual capacity to exercise the political rights Northerners had bestowed on them. At best, Black men were the victims of Radical Republican manipulation and corruption—a narrative that persists into modern times. In response to this degradation of their republican institutions, honorable White Southern men came together to defend "home rule" and their states' rights—euphemisms for White supremacy. Progressive-era historians told a similar story about Reconstruction, except that the driver behind Northern Radical Republican machinations was not Black equality but the imposition of Northern-style capitalism on the South.[30]

According to the historian Eric Foner, the Dunning school of Reconstruction history "was not just an interpretation of history. It was part of the edifice of the Jim Crow System which followed Reconstruction." The Dunning school sought to validate Southern political suppression of African Americans, arguing that because Black people supported illegitimate "carpetbagger rule," they abused their voting privileges. Dunning school history offered "a justification for the White South resisting outside efforts in changing race relations because of the worry of having another Reconstruction." Dunning school myths were taken as axiomatic, unquestioned in Supreme Court cases that decided on the scope and meaning of the Reconstruction Amendments, which were meant to safeguard Black Americans' republican citizenship. These decisions had enormous implications for the political rights of African Americans.[31]

A lone critical voice presenting Reconstruction as an idealistic project to establish a more democratic society was the Black activist and sociologist W. E. B. DuBois, who called out the field as incapable of "conceiv[ing]

Negroes as men." A new narrative on Reconstruction that dismissed the premise of Southern republican honor had to wait until the civil rights movement.[32] Yet, even after the civil rights era, versions of the "Lost Cause" myth persisted among some academics.[33]

Dunning school historians, as well as activists who dabbled in local history, were drafted to write many of the history and civics books used in American classrooms for much of the twentieth century. The Southern Historical Society was dedicated to the reinterpretation of both the Civil War and sectional reconciliation from a "Lost Cause" perspective.[34] Conservative White organizations such as the Sons of Confederate Veterans (SCV), the United Daughters of the Confederacy (UDC), and the Daughters of the American Revolution (DAR), dedicated to the preservation of Southern historical memory and ascriptive republicanism, worked through local school boards to revise curricula in ways that glorified the Confederacy. UDC activists used their influence over the Southern school market to pressure Northern publishers to revise their narration of the Civil War to present the South as an honorable region fighting for civil liberties rather than defending slavery.[35] One such text, *Cavalier Commonwealth: History and Government in Virginia*, published in 1957 and used for almost two decades, signaled its ideology in the title. According to the text, slaves "did not work so hard" because they needed not "worry about losing [their] jobs." According to the book, "the slave enjoyed what we might call comprehensive social security," which included "plentiful food," "adequate clothing," a "warm cabin," health protections, and "carefree leisure."[36]

Ascriptive republican myths, including the "Lost Cause," were also preserved and reproduced through various educational institutions tied to the military. First, these myths were incorporated into military education. Southern students and Army officers dominated military academies and training programs. They brought their culture of honor, chivalry, valor, and veneration of the Confederacy to these institutions, and these traditions persist in many schools today.[37]

Even contemporary history books do not adequately explain the country's racial history. A review of history books conducted by the Southern Poverty Law Center (SPLC) shows that most school textbooks today fail to explain how the ideology of White male supremacy was used to justify slavery. The emphasis is more on abolitionism than on the structure and effects of the peculiar institution. The report also suggests that the country's later racial history, from Reconstruction to the civil rights movement, is taught without a deeper context. The "Lost Cause" is deeply entrenched in how students are taught American history. The result is that very few students (8 percent) recognize slavery as the principal cause of the Civil

War, and equally few understand that a constitutional amendment was required for its eventual abolition.[38] Some widely used contemporary history
books describe enslaved Africans as "immigrants" and suggest that Southern White people resisted Reconstruction because it was costly and could
require higher taxes.[39]

Public opinion data show that a significant minority of White Americans do not recognize historical myths as such. My 2021 survey shows that
24 percent of White Americans and 37 percent of those who embrace ascriptive republicanism believe that "Black slaves enjoyed the protection of
slave-masters who provided food and shelter in exchange for loyal service."
Similarly, 36 percent of all White people and 51 percent of those who score
high on ascriptive republican beliefs think that "the Civil War was fought to
preserve the democratic rights of Southern states, not because of slavery."
Finally, 22 percent of all White people and 34 percent of those who embrace ascriptive republicanism believe that "when the Pioneers settled the
West, these lands did not belong to anyone"—a myth central to the NRA's
narrative.

PUBLIC MEMORY

The preservation and social transmission of ascriptive republican myths
was accomplished not just by education, but by public memory. By "public memory" historians mean how social groups and communities tell the
story of their past and how they recall their ancestors' lived experiences.
Communities often institutionalize this public memory in celebrations, rituals, monuments, and even advertising that continue to frame the past in
ways consistent with the community's ideology. Therefore, public memory
is neither scientific nor neutral: it is an attempt to use the past to justify and
legitimize (or disrupt and change) the present social organization. According to the historian John Bodnar, public memory is the product of "a political discussion" focused on society's "organization, [the] structure of power,
and the very meaning of the past and present," and its function is "to me-
diate the competing restatements of reality these antinomies express." In
this sense, public memory is "an ideological system with special language,
beliefs, symbols, and stories" that people use to select among competing
interpretations of the past and present.[40] In this case, public memory reflected the ideology of ascriptive republicanism.

The Union may have won the war, yet postwar politics wasn't built on
the repudiation of the South and its institutions. Sectional reconciliation,
a key objective of Northern and Southern White people, was built on extolling the soldier's honor, regardless of what side he fought on. Military

virtue provided an ostensibly nonpolitical moral high ground on which to build reunion. Military leaders on both sides embraced the decontextualized honorable soldier narrative as a vehicle for sectional integration and the preservation of White supremacy. Starting in the 1870s, Memorial Day commemorations in the South and North honored the virtuous fallen citizen-soldier regardless of what political cause he fought for. The cult of fallen virtuous soldiers included annual veterans' celebrations where old soldiers recounted their war experiences, memorials to fallen heroes, and countless opportunities for Southerners to shape a narrative around virtuous soldiers whose righteous cause was defeated by a tyrannical industrialized military machine. The rebel soldiers were "heroic victims of colossal Yankee machines and venal Republican tyranny." This veneration of soldiering devoid of politics enabled the normalization of the Lost Cause.[41]

Adherents of the "Lost Cause" myth did much of the cultural work that shaped public memory about the system of slavery, the origins of the Civil War, and the failure of Reconstruction. Tourist guides of the Old South; museums, statues, and memorials dedicated to the Confederacy; and Civil War reenactments reinforced ascriptive republican myths of Southern honor and armed virtue, the loyal slave, and Black people's moral failings.[42]

These expressions of public memory did not stop after Civil War soldiers and their descendants passed on. Most Southern states memorialized the Confederacy in memorials and official state holidays.[43] As recently as 2001, a Florida courthouse installed a mural that included depictions of Klansmen. The guidebook for the painting explained in typical ascriptive republican terms that during Reconstruction, "lawlessness among ex-slaves and troublesome White people was the rule of the day." The White Southerners were the victims, as "no relief was given by the carpetbag and scalawag government or by the Union troops." White people formed "secret societies claiming to bring law and order to the county. One of these groups was the Ku Klux Klan." The guidebook admits that the Klan "sometimes took vigilante justice to extremes," but justified White violence by falsely claiming that this "was sometimes the only control the county knew over those outside the law." The book goes on to further excuse and exalt the Klan: "since then, it has become the subject of legend rather than a cause of fear."[44] A penumbra of this mythology is evident even in twenty-first-century Supreme Court cases. For example, in *Virginia v. Black*, 538 U.S. 343 (2003), a 6-3 majority determined that cross burnings, even those by the Klan, are not necessarily meant to intimidate but can be cultural or ideological expressions of "group solidarity."

Civil War reenactments also sought to preserve the memory of the "noble past," the Confederacy, and the Old South.[45] Such rituals started even before the Civil War concluded. These events have allowed thousands of civilians to participate in and relive a sanitized, memorialized experience of Civil War battles.[46] Reenactments continue to be popular. In addition to annual reenactments of battles of military significance, Confederate re-enactors replay minor battles in which the Confederacy won as a way to express their nostalgia and pride in their Confederate heritage.[47] These re-enactments focus on accurately replicating the material conditions under which the battles took place: the firearms, uniforms, unit organization, and strategy are central concerns. But the deliberate eschewing of politics does not mean that politics is absent from these performances. The "authentic-ity" pursued by participants often reflects their political views about the conflict.[48] Civil War reenactments reproduce the Confederacy materially and psychologically, reinforcing ascriptive republican beliefs about the "Lost Cause."[49]

In addition to reenactments, the North-South Skirmish Association (N-SSA), founded in 1950, organizes annual skirmishes, events meant to encourage people to learn how to use historical weapons. The N-SSA is focused primarily on the accurate use of Civil War–era weapons and sec-ondarily on the accurate representation of uniforms and equipment. These events attract not only Civil War devotees but members of gun clubs, since the skirmishes include shooting competitions. In fact, the N-SSA has been an NRA member and exhibitor at the association's annual convention. Ar-ticles on Civil War skirmish events have been featured in *The American Rifleman*.[50] Such events exist at the intersection of gun culture and the cel-ebration of Southern manly honor and pride.

The "Lost Cause" myth, and the image of the noble, patriotic cavalier, continue to be influential within the gun culture. As a product of the post–Civil War era military establishment, the NRA embraced and reproduced ascriptive republican narratives, including the "Lost Cause." As early as 1917, it described the Civil War as "the war between the states," a nod to post-Reconstruction reconciliationist narratives.[51] Stories suggested that the Civil War was meant not to end slavery but "to test a great principle of government," that is, Southern states' right to home rule.[52] C. B. Lister, the magazine's chief editor in the 1930s and 1940s, ranked Robert E. Lee among the country's venerated heroes along with Lincoln, Washington, and Ham-ilton, praising his "respectability, courage, and unselfish patriotism."[53] In recent years, as part of the celebration of 150 years since the Civil War, NRA magazines have advertised a variety of Confederate memorabilia, a testa-ment to the continued popularity of the ascriptive republican myth of the "Lost Cause" among its readers. Advertisements sell the "official" Stone-wall Jackson and Robert E. Lee bronze tributes, the Robert E. Lee collector knife, official ring, official watch, and official canteen.[54] The NRA does not endorse these products. However, at a minimum, advertisers believe that NRA members are a receptive audience for their Confederate memorabilia. In a modern twist to ascriptive republicanism, gun ads urged consumers to buy a specific assault rifle brand and "be a man among men." Others stated, "consider your man card re-issued" upon purchase of a given brand.[55]

THE MYTH OF THE BLACK CONFEDERATE

Ascriptive republicanism did not guide only the portrayal of the White South—the noble, virtuous freedom fighters. Depictions of African Americans as brave soldiers were integral to the "Lost Cause" myth—anchoring Southern republicanism. Of course, adherents to the cult of the Confederacy did not celebrate the valor of Black Union soldiers—more than 200,000 of whom fought in the war. Instead, the myth celebrates Black men who fought on the side of the Confederacy.

The myth of the Black Confederate soldier is no more than that: a myth. Some slaves did indeed join their masters in camp during the Civil War. However, these slaves were not there voluntarily, nor did they perform a soldier's duties. This does not mean that their service was not valuable; quite the opposite is true. However, these men were impressed into service and were not performing the duties of republican citizenship. Near the end of the war, recognizing that defeat was likely, Confederate military leaders proposed the arming and conscription of enslaved men. However, Confederate political authorities rejected the plan precisely because it conflicted with the ascriptive republican ideology on which the polity was founded. Arming slaves and accepting that they could be virtuous soldiers contradicted the myth that Black people chose slavery and were incapable of martial virtue. So central was this ideology to the Confederate project that Confederate political leaders chose defeat over giving republican citizenship—and the right to bear arms—to enslaved Blacks.[56]

After Reconstruction, as Southerners reshaped the memory of the Civil War and refashioned it into a war for "states' rights" and local democracy, the presence of Black slaves in Confederate military camps took on new meaning—as a moral justification of slavery. The "Lost Cause" posited that the Old South was a kind and gentle society where White people cared deeply for the well-being of their Black slaves, and the enslaved responded to White people's protection and support with loyalty. The Southern way of life, slavery included, was an ideal democratic system that protected even those at the very bottom of the social pyramid. According to this myth, slaves benefited from the system of chattel slavery and were as committed to its preservation as White people were. The "Black Confederate" became an important symbol for legitimizing slavery and the Confederacy. If Black slaves were so committed to the institutions of the Old South as to have fought on the side of the Confederacy, then the real motives of the North in engaging in the Civil War could not have been expanding freedom and democracy. Instead, the story went, the North sought to impose its version of tyranny on Southern society.

Thus, the Black Confederate took his place as an important and venerated figure in the Civil War pantheon and became a tool for system justification. Local and national monuments to Confederate "heroes" included loyal slaves. In 1914, the UDC memorialized the loyal slave in a monument in Arlington National Cemetery dedicated to the "Lost Cause." Today, pictures of this monument, along with other artifacts purporting to show Black Confederate soldiers and stories of various former slaves said to be the life stories of Black Confederates, fill the internet. Websites and publications at the intersection of gun politics and the Civil War are particularly intent on promoting this myth.[57] Even more perversely, supporters of the Black Confederate myth praise the Confederacy for supposedly having integrated military units, while Black men served in segregated units in the Union Army.[58] This allows modern-day supporters of the "Lost Cause" to justify their admiration for the Confederacy and to explicitly or implicitly accept the validity of Black exclusion from republican citizenship.

Here it is important to note that during Reconstruction, a small number of African Americans supported the Democratic Party despite its White supremacist ideology. Some even donned red shirts, the emblem of violent White supremacist suppression in the region, supporting Wade Hampton's Redemptioneers in South Carolina.[59] Grasping these men's motivations is crucial and constitutes a fascinating complexity of the story of ascriptive republican politics and the ideology's function as system justification. Understanding these African Americans can also help shed light on Black conservatives today. Historians suggest that a combination of resentment of Republican abandonment, desire for status, patronage, and coercion may have motivated African American men to support the Democratic Party in this period. Many Black Democrats of this era belonged to the Black elite: they were freeborn, had economic standing, and sought to protect their financial well-being at all costs. Some blamed the Republicans for fostering racial divisions rather than promoting economic well-being. In fact, Hampton used former slaves' disillusionment with the Republicans as a recruitment tactic, stressing peace and a common identity as Southerners. These cases highlight the multiple forms that political agency can take, as both resistance and compliance.[60] However, the fact that a small number of African Americans sided with the Democrats during Reconstruction and even into the Jim Crow era does not validate the ascriptive republican narratives of the Lost Cause myth. More than anything, it reinforces the common perception among African Americans that peace and prosperity could only arise if they submitted to White rule.[61]

POPULAR CULTURE

"There was a land of Cavaliers and Cotton Fields called the Old South. Here in this pretty world, Gallantry took its last bow. Here was the last ever to be seen of Knights and their Ladies Fair, of Master and Slave. Look for it only in books, for it is no more than a dream remembered. A Civilization gone with the wind" read the opening credits of the popular and (at the time) critically acclaimed 1939 film *Gone with the Wind*. The movie sold more than 25 million tickets in the first year of its release. In the past eighty years, more than 200 million people have seen the film. Along with D. W. Griffith's 1915 *Birth of a Nation*, the story of Rhett Butler and Scarlett O'Hara represents classic portrayals of the "Lost Cause" narrative in film. In these films, one finds noble White Confederate soldiers fighting for the preservation of an idyllic way of life, faithful slaves who defend their masters, vicious and corrupt Union soldiers intent on raping Southern women and Southern lands, and virtuous Klansmen protecting White women from the rapacity of freed slaves.

These two films may be the most popular articulations of the "Lost Cause" and the ascriptive republican myth, but they are not alone. According to the historian Glenda Elizabeth Gilmore, Southern "Lost Cause" culture migrated north along with Southern White intellectuals and artists in award-winning plays such as *Porgy* (later adapted by George Gershwin as *Porgy and Bess*) and *Green Pastures*. The themes found a home in the writings of Northern artists such as Eugene O'Neill.[62] Books and movies such as Thomas Dixon's *The Clansman, An Historical Romance about the Ku Klux Klan*, Disney's *Song of the South* (1946), and *Gods and Generals* (2003) have reproduced the ascriptive republican mythology of the Old South.[63] In such stories, Confederate soldiers have been transformed into popular heroes—"good guys with guns." Such is the case of the Confederate guerilla leader Jesse James, son of a prominent slaveholding family in Missouri, who committed several atrocities against civilians and Union soldiers during the Civil War. Yet popular culture has turned James into a nineteenth-century Robin Hood who robbed trains to take from rich bankers and robber barons and give to the poor.[64]

And it was not only stories written for adults that glorified the Old South. Children's fiction—a key vector of political socialization for young people—contained similar portrayals. "Blackface" and stereotypical Black clowns were ever-present in adult and children's fiction. Other Black characters included menial workers, agricultural laborers, or criminals. According to the education sociologist Donnarae MacCann, out of 137 children's books targeting White boys (Black children were an infinitesimal proportion of the readership in the late nineteenth and early twentieth centuries), 92 percent included Black characters. These characters were there not to teach tolerance and inclusivity but to reinforce ascriptive republican ideals. Mark Twain's classic, *Huckleberry Finn*, read by generations of American children, employs many of the same minstrel-type portrayals of Black folks.[65]

Throughout the twentieth century, America kept changing. A new inclusive narrative of democratic membership developed in the trenches and foxholes of World War I and World War II, where Black soldiers fought shoulder to shoulder with White men to preserve the democratic ideal. This narrative was etched in the suffragettes' white dresses and the uniforms of General Pershing's "Hello Girls."[66] America's new story of political membership—a story of pluralism and inclusion—was institutionalized first in the integration of the Armed Forces, soon after in the Supreme Court's rejection of segregation, and then in the Civil and Voting Rights Acts of the 1960s. As this new ideology fought for dominance, African Americans, women, immigrants, and other groups whose voices and stories had been excluded from official histories fought hard for new interpretations and new "truths." As a result of these struggles, state institutions such as the military and the public education system began to reflect less the ascriptive republican narrative and to allow space for new voices and participants. To be sure, neither institution faithfully reflects America's complex social tableau. School textbooks, in particular, seem just to overlay a patina of pluralism and inclusion over the core ascriptive republican narrative.[67] In the military, the ranks look more like American society than the leadership, but even that varies by branch of the service.

One institution has remained faithful to ascriptive republican ideology from the nineteenth to the twenty-first century: the NRA. A patriotic organization with military roots and an ambition to teach patriotism and the art of rifle shooting to draft-age men, the NRA was a key vector for transmitting ascriptive republican ideology. As I discuss in chapter 5, the organization used its ties to the military and political establishment to develop the civilian market. Through the 1960s, the NRA remained a recipient of exclusive subsidies and a loyal citizen-soldier to the federal government. But as the ideology of the federal government and the military changed in response to social and technological change, the NRA turned its sights on the government, becoming a critical voice in opposition.

∴

Part Two

THE ORIGINS AND
WORLDVIEW OF THE NRA

∵

CHAPTER 5

The Emergence of the NRA

As I have noted, republican ideology is grounded in two sets of opposi-
tional concepts: virtue/corruption and freedom/slavery. First, it emphasizes that the Republic's moral and physical security depends on its citizens' political virtue. The possession of political virtue enables citizens to
recognize and combat corruption—the foe of republican politics. Citizens
are virtuous when they choose to fight at arms for freedom and independence. The virtuous citizen is engaged and vigilant. He knows that corruption always lurks in a republic; thus, the virtuous citizen actively protects
the public good with the ballot and the bullet. Republicans understand
human nature as weak and easily influenced by the promise of personal
gain. A pivotal threat to republican freedom is dependency or slavery. It
comes from people who put their narrow self-interest ahead of the polity
and choose to depend on others for their livelihood, well-being, and safety.
Such people are always motivated to pursue riches or "luxury" at the expense of the public good.

American Revolutionary narratives melded republican ideology with
White male supremacy. The result was a republican ideology that attributed political virtue to White men, recognizing only this group as capable
of developing it. In this worldview, not only did White men have the physical strength required to train at arms and become effective soldiers, but
they alone had the moral capacity to recognize the importance of republican freedom and defend it even at the expense of personal gain. White
men maintained their virtue and commitment to the public good through
political engagement and military preparedness. Women lacked the physical strength to train in arms and the moral capacity for unemotional reason or "common sense." These traits made women naturally dependent on
their fathers and husbands, and thus unsuitable for political life. African
American men may have had the physical strength to bear arms, but they
had chosen slavery and dependence.

At the time of the American Revolution, adherents of ascriptive republicanism believed that conscription was necessary to maintain the public virtue of citizens. Unless the country's White men were required to develop martial skills and prepare for war in times of peace, their political virtue would wane. Without enrolled militiamen, the country would have to entrust its military security to a professional or "standing" army. A professional soldier—a volunteer—was a vector of political corruption because, for him, soldiery was a job, not a civic obligation. Professional soldiers depended on the government for their pay, which made them dependent on ambitious, self-interested elected officials. Thus, a professional army had no incentive to protect the public good and uphold the rule of law.

Americans designed their military institutions based on their ascriptive republican ideals. However, their experience with the conscript state militia forced them to adjust their institutions and ideology. As we saw in chapter 3, the enrolled militia proved militarily inept, as conscripts lacked interest, incentives, and equipment. Much like today, ideology is insufficient to get people who own guns to train in their use. A recent survey sponsored by the gun industry showed that less than half of gun owners are knowledgeable about firearms.[1] Since those liable for service also had a right to vote, states had little incentive to impose severe penalties for noncompliance. By the Civil War, the enrolled militia had been supplanted by self-organized and self-sustained volunteer companies, which came to be known as the National Guards. With the growth of voluntarism, ascriptive republican ideology adapted to the changing landscape. Choice rather than obligation came to be viewed as the source of political virtue. This is the social and political context that gave rise to the NRA.

AN ASSOCIATION IN THE SERVICE OF GOVERNMENT

The NRA—"a patriotic association," as its early annual reports state—was founded in New York in 1871, while Radical Reconstruction sought to transform the South. In many respects, the association was a product of the American Civil War and the era's ascriptive republican ethos. Its founders, two militia officers, General George Wingate and Col. William C. Church, who was also a correspondent for New York papers, experienced firsthand the dearth of marksmanship skills among the Union Army's volunteer militiamen. The Confederate Army prided itself on its officers' marksmanship skills. According to the "Lost Cause" myth, the Confederacy lost the war only because the Union Army had greater numbers and technology.[2] For Church and Wingate, the lack of similar skills among Union soldiers had brought the Union perilously close to defeat. Freedom could have submitted to slavery because Union citizen-soldiers were insufficiently trained, disciplined, and virtuous.[3]

For most of the nineteenth century, the country's defensive forces consisted of a small professional army, enrolled militia, and local volunteers. Militias were not adequately trained or armed by the states to fulfill the needs of a war-bound army, and their decentralized, republican structure was not suited to the organization of an efficient nineteenth-century military. The military strategy of the eighteenth and early nineteenth centuries required that infantrymen advance in line or column formation and fire their weapons in volleys in the enemy's direction ("firepower" or "mass fire"). According to the military theory of the era, what won battles was not marksmanship; training in collective formation skills was believed to be far more critical than sharpshooting.[4]

Despite their limited military utility and state and federal neglect, state militias persisted because of their political and social usefulness. As discussed earlier, militia often operated as police and fire department auxiliaries. They helped quash labor strife and race riots.[5] Militia companies served as hubs for political organizing and cultivated candidates for office. As a result, the militia functioned like social and political clubs for White men. Given the political importance of the militia, state officials resisted calls to address the issue of militiamen's operational deficiencies. This resistance was attributed to the cost of creating effective military units and the fear of a backlash from citizen-soldiers, many of whom saw themselves more as citizens with some law enforcement responsibilities that added excitement to their lives than as actual soldiers.[6]

Given that states generally lacked coordinated training for militia units and sufficient appropriations for defense, Church and Wingate envisioned a public-private partnership: the NRA would overlay its programs and services onto the existing institutional structure. The association would train National Guardsmen and draft-age men in "the most important part of the drill of a soldier: marksmanship on a scientific basis." As the NRA bylaws specified, training would take place with military rifles and pistols. Every year, National Guardsmen, US Army riflemen, and civilians of military age would gather for a national competition and training event. Participants would receive instruction, practice their skills, compete for individual and team trophies and prizes, have fun, and network. Such events would merge sport and play with military and citizenship education. For Church and Wingate, marksmanship contributed to creating good soldiers and developing good republican citizens with the independence, discipline, and virtue required for a well-functioning republic.[7]

The NRA's original vision was to create an organization to serve the needs of the military and the National Guard. Church and Wingate thought that cash-strapped state authorities would outsource the task of marksmanship training to a private nonprofit. The NRA would fund its operations through a mix of state and federal subsidies and membership and participation fees. National Guard members would be offered discounted membership and admissions fees and would be encouraged to join the association as units. Their civilian target audience was not the general public. The civilians the NRA had in mind were not working-class; instead, they were middle- and upper-middle-class men who had leisure time and could afford to partake in an expensive form of recreation, and who might be interested in forming a National Guard company.

Church and Wingate pursued state- and federal-level relationships in developing the NRA. Both were well-connected New Yorkers, so their first step was to lobby the state of New York for financial support to establish a shooting range suitable for championships. The range would feature established teams, and would enable militiamen and civilians to train in rifle practice. In response to their lobbying, the state of New York appropriated $25,000 (equivalent to $500,000 today) to establish the NRA's shooting range in 1872.

The newly founded association sought to ensure its success by closely tying itself to the military establishment. In claiming the moniker of a "patriotic association" and even fashioning military-style uniforms for its civilian members, the NRA branded itself as a military organization, a promoter to the nation of ascriptive republican citizenship in the form of rifle practice. It courted top military officers for leadership positions to sustain this image and to increase the group's prestige and influence. Former general and president Ulysses Grant, General Ambrose Burnside, and General Philip Sheridan, among many others, served as NRA presidents. State Adjutant Generals, the chief administrative officers of each state's National Guard, were invited to be ex officio NRA Board members.

The association's future came under serious threat in the 1890s because of internal and external developments, revealing the inherent vulnerability of the state-based, militarized patriotism the NRA espoused. The national military establishment became divided over the NRA on philosophical and political grounds. Some among the US Army top brass were not convinced that infantrymen needed to be trained in rifle usage, especially not by a private contractor. Many Army leaders believed that soldiers needed collective skills for massed fire, not aimed fire. Militia officers and some recruits came from middle- and upper-middle-class backgrounds, but the Army drew enlistments from the lower socioeconomic strata. Many top officers doubted that any training would be sufficient to make marksmen of poor and working-class infantry volunteers, even with more accurate weapons. The Army's refusal to recognize the NRA as a military organization added to the association's travails.[8]

Additionally, the NRA experienced internal disagreements about the overrepresentation of New Yorkers in the membership. In the late nineteenth century, many rival organizations had sprung up in various states. At a time when sectional attachment was important, the overrepresentation of New Yorkers in the organization's leadership prompted resistance. Teams from other states resented the prominence and dominance of the New York National Guard at the NRA range, and their participation became less enthusiastic over time. In addition, philosophical disagreements over emphasizing military exercise and thus tying the group very closely to the military or sports-style long-range shooting, which would attract civilians, brought the organization close to bankruptcy.

However, the most severe blow to the NRA's ambitious plans to become the de facto marksmanship trainer for the National Guard came with Alonzo Cornell's election as governor of New York. A fiscally conservative Republican who slashed state budgets beyond anything that the state had seen, Cornell saw no use for militia training. In his view, the National Guard's purpose was symbolic, "to show itself in parades and ceremonies . . . their only function will be to march a little through the streets." The state cut its appropriations for NRA matches and introduced requirements that soldiers' participation would also involve drilling and marching—critical components of nineteenth-century militia training. Essentially, New York State sought to turn NRA matches into the Guard's annual training camp, which had implications for the ability of civilians to participate. The exclusion of civilians from NRA events threatened to cut off a key market. By 1892, the NRA had suspended its operations in New York and moved its matches to New Jersey under the auspices of that state's Rifle Association.[9]

Once the strategy of tying its fate to New York had failed, the organization set its sights on Washington, DC as a source of money, stability, and legitimacy. At this time, the federal government did not have the financial power it would gain with the income tax amendment, nor did it have today's regulatory reach. However, Congress played the principal role in designing national defense policy. During this period of American expansionism and imperial ambitions, with ongoing Indian wars in the West and military adventures in Cuba and the Philippines, there was significant pressure to reform, expand, and enhance the nation's professional and citizen soldiery.

The early cold reception from the US Army notwithstanding, the NRA reorganized itself in 1900, further developing its ties to the national military establishment. The secretary of war and all general officers of the US Army and West Point were ex officio Board members, giving them a consultative role and a stake in the organization's operation. Furthermore, the secretary of war was given authority to select members of the Board of Trustees, strengthening the ties between the national defense agencies and the NRA. The organization also cultivated relationships with Congress, prominent lawyers, judges, and other members of the capital elite.[10]

The NRA's capacity to tie itself to the federal military establishment was facilitated by the lack of partisan polarization on issues relevant to the association's agenda. First, gun control policy was not on the horizon yet as a national political concern. The NRA's key focus was defense policy, specifically the training protocols for the National Guard and draft-age civilians—not regulating the civilian use of firearms. Second, the Republican Party dominated presidential politics between 1860 and 1932; only two Democrats won the presidency during this entire period. Although the Democratic Party of the early twentieth century was anti-militaristic (meaning hostile to a large professional army) and anti-imperialist, it was not hostile to the National Guard, which it viewed as the bedrock of America's defense system. By the time of the Wilson administration, the Army's embarrassing campaign in Mexico to capture Pancho Villa and, more importantly, the advent of World War I had paved the way for stronger support for militarism and recognition that military preparedness was vital for the United States to win the war.[11]

DRAWING ON THE POLITICAL POWER OF THE MILITIA

The group's close relationship with the National Guard Association (NGA) was crucial for the NRA's future economic viability and transformation into a mass membership organization. General Wingate promoted the establishment of the NGA at the same time that he and Church were founding the NRA. The goal of the NGA was to organize the guardsmen politically and use them as a base to advocate in Congress and state assemblies for the interests of the National Guard. In time, the NGA became one of the most successful mass membership–based interest groups in American politics. As noted in chapter 3, states and the federal government had neglected the volunteer state militia, which was undertrained, underfunded, and ridiculed. Federal appropriations had been set at $200,000 in 1808 and had not been increased in seventy years. Wingate and his counterparts in other state Guards envisioned the 115,000-strong militia as the country's reserve force of citizen-soldiers, fully trained in marksmanship and able to hold their own in battle.[12]

The NRA and the NGA, and the NGA's successor organizations, shared ideology, leadership, membership, and goals. This amplified the NRA's access and influence in Washington, DC, and enhanced the rifle group's legitimacy. Also, local National Guard companies across the country re-named themselves National Guard Rifle Associations, adding to the NRA's name recognition and popularity. These groups' accomplishments in local matches and other engagements reflected positively on the NRA through their shared name. In this way, the NRA label became synonymous with marksmanship and patriotic duty—a schoolhouse reinforcing the legiti-macy of existing social hierarchies.[13]

The post–Civil War era reinvigorated interest in the volunteer militia. As discussed in earlier chapters, White men (including many immigrant groups) and some African Americans organized volunteer militia compa-nies to project manhood, respectability, and republican virtue. The militia's training emphasized drilling and marching, not shooting rifles, which the NRA and the NGA considered a significant obstacle to the Guards' profes-sionalization. For both organizations, marksmanship was a skill crucial for the battlefield and moral education, which men needed in order to develop patriotism and be good citizens.

The National Guard viewed itself as the epitome of republican citizen-ship. The militias' core values were physical fitness, discipline, individual self-reliance, and manly virtue. Humorous pamphlets of the era under-scored the ascriptive republican narrative. They portrayed (White) recruits as lazy and effeminate men who joined the Guard to avoid the responsi-bilities of citizenship, especially jury duty, but emerged from the training muscular, manly, war-ready, and attractive to women.[14] These portrayals are not very different from contemporary gun ads. In ascriptive republican terms, the Guard understood its role as instilling a set of moral values, or political virtue, in citizen-soldiers. Through militia service, men developed a common understanding of the public good and the means to achieve it. An article outlining the moral tenets of the organization proclaimed that "WE BELIEVE IN THE MORAL INFLUENCE FOR GOOD of the citizen soldiery—that the armory and the parade ground, so far from constituting places of contamination, comprehend schools wherein the members of the National Guard may learn their duty to God and man."[15] Rifle practice was central to the National Guard's vision of instilling republican virtue into the country's young men. According to the same article, "WE BELIEVE IN RIFLE PRACTICE as an important element of National Guard education—

its benefits in promoting manliness, healthfulness, self-reliance, coolness, nerve, and skill."[16]

Reforming the Guards became increasingly salient in the late nineteenth century, as racial and labor strife came to demand the involvement of military forces. The political scientist William Riker directly attributed the National Guard's elevation on the state and national political agenda to the industrial violence of the 1870s and 1880s. The Posse Comitatus Act of 1878, part of the political compromise that ended Reconstruction in the South, practically prohibited the engagement of federal forces in domestic disturbances. Southern Democrats keen on preventing the federal government from using the US Army to enforce the Reconstruction Amendments supported the Act. So did some Northerners concerned about using federal troops to quash labor unrest in 1877. Restrictions on the use of federal troops in domestic conflicts meant that the militia became the primary responders in such crises, which seemed to be occurring more frequently.[17]

A second factor hobbled the US Army's political clout: the army could not lobby Congress directly. In 1873, the secretary of war issued orders prohibiting officers and enlistees from contacting Congress on military issues without permission from army leadership. However, since the National Guard as a state institution was not part of the federal armed forces, such prohibitions did not apply. Even after its reorganization and integration into the federal structure, the Guard remained a state institution not subject to political engagement prohibitions except when the president called it to active duty. The National Guard's institutional position (guaranteed in the Constitution), its clout as a component of the national defense, its exemption from lobbying restrictions or even to the requirement of registering as a lobby, and its large membership of officers and soldiers, many with social and political connections, combined to make it one of the most successful lobbying forces in the United States.[18]

These changes in the political environment provided an opportunity for the National Guard to pressure Congress and state governments for more resources and a thorough modernization without giving up the institution's republican roots. The Guards sought to walk a fine line between federalization, professionalization, and maintaining the militia's citizen-soldier character. Federalization meant resources and better weapons and training, which the Guards wanted. But the federal government imposed federal rules on the selection of officers (rather than election by company members) and a commitment to participating in military campaigns outside the Guards' home state, which many Guards resented.

Soon after its establishment, the NGA began to lobby Congress, seeking recognition for the Guards as the only state militia—which would be a de facto elimination of the conscript system mandated by the UMA. This demand was both symbolic and substantive. Technically, the provisions of the US Constitution, as implemented in the UMA, required that *all* White males serve in the militia. The Militia Act of 1862 extended the obligation to Black men. Over time, the conscription system was largely abandoned, but this was not reflected in law. Thus, the NGA sought official recognition of volunteers as the country's citizen-soldiers. This official act would ensure that all state defense resources would be channeled to volunteer companies. At the same time, this demand was significant because it suggested the ideological shift that had taken place over the preceding century.

Deviating from the revolutionary generation's republicanism, which viewed military service as an obligation of citizenship, but consistent with the attitudes of the late nineteenth century, the NGA and the NRA linked virtue *with choice*. They argued that conscription was impossible in the United States because of citizen resistance. Americans did not want to be forced into service; they wanted to have the freedom to choose soldiery. In this revisionist ascriptive republican view of the late nineteenth century, not all American men had the innate character and virtue required for military service. Thus, conscription could weaken rather than strengthen American defense by enlisting morally weak men. Americans of the late eighteenth century expected that all White male citizens would accept the duty of soldiering. African Americans and women were excluded from citizenship, and therefore conscription did not apply to them. In the late nineteenth century, however, to the well-known practical problems with conscription—free-riding, underfunding, and under-training—came to be added that African Americans might well have to be included in a conscript army, and thus afforded claims to full political membership. Choice and voluntarism provided a new way for ascriptive republicanism to justify the exclusion and subordination of Black men from a critical dimension of republican citizenship—at least discursively, if not historically.[19]

The need to rely on volunteers introduced two interrelated challenges: recruitment into the National Guard and training of the volunteer militias. For the NGA and the NRA, marksmanship programs addressed both goals, as rifle competitions could be "an inducement" to recruit a "better class of men" to the Guards and improve citizen-soldiers' military education, enhancing their utility in war. Since requiring "military education" and service was not realistic or desirable, the American government could instead encourage its male citizens to train at arms by turning rifle shooting into a sport. Proponents of marksmanship training offered that given the impossibility of conscription, "the encouragement of rifle firing as a military sport affords the government of a free country the opportunity to give the male citizen fit for military service at least part of the training which is necessary in war."[20]

The ascendancy of Theodore Roosevelt to the presidency after McKinley's assassination was a boon for both the NRA and the NGA. An avid shooter, a supporter of rifle matches, and a firm believer in the ascriptive republican tradition, Roosevelt was impressed with the skills exhibited by the teams that trained and participated in NRA-sponsored events. A former New York State National Guardsman himself, Roosevelt had experienced the disastrous mobilization of the volunteer militia in the Spanish-American War both as assistant secretary of war and as commanding officer of the "Rough Riders." As a result, Roosevelt favored federalization and professionalization of the Guards, including rifle practice. Another significant ally was Representative Charles Dick (R-OH), the chairman of the House Committee on the Militia. Dick was also a former National Guardsman, a veteran of the Spanish-American War, adjutant general of the Ohio National Guard, and, for several years, president of the NGA. Between Dick and Roosevelt, the political circumstances were ideal for the NRA and the NGA to influence Congress.[21]

INSIDER POLITICS

Today, the NRA presents itself as an "outsider" critic of the Washington establishment, an independent actor that perceives the government as corrupt, overbearing, and a threat to citizens' republican virtue. In 1902, the NRA was a supplicant seeking recognition, greater integration with the military, and direct and indirect financial assistance from the federal government. During this period, the NRA's goal was to persuade the federal government to foster "the enlargement and scope of the National Rifle Association and its influence upon rifle practice." The group hoped to secure "the support of the United States government." According to the NRA, by "stamp[ing] the proposal plan with the approval of the President and Secretary of War," it would increase its prominence "before the country."[22]

A 1904 article in the *Washington Tribune* exemplifies the enthusiastic support the NRA's ideas were met with in the political world and the defense establishment's seemingly high hopes for a civilian marksmanship program.

> The War Department has taken a very important step forward in the direction of educating American youth in rifle shooting by the approval of a system for a "National Marksman's Reserve." The object of this is the encouragement of the science of marksmanship, and if the plans result as

anticipated, it will in a few years produce in the United States 1,000,000 men who will have for practical purposes on the battlefield nearly all the requirements for the most efficient soldiers in the world.[23]

This story suggests that the War Department had accepted the idea of a public/private partnership and had come to view the NRA as a private contractor to whom the training of the nation's reserve military would be outsourced. No evidence substantiates the provenance of the figure of one million citizen-soldiers emerging from such a program. At best, it reflects the enthusiasm for rifle practice among President Theodore Roosevelt's political advisers and the NRA more than any realistic estimate of such a program's effectiveness.

The NRA's influence in subsequent policy formation is evident when we compare the group's direct advocacy, the NGA's proposals, and the ideas emanating from the War Department. This is not to say that the NRA convinced the War Department of the soundness of rifle practice as a solution to the problems with the National Guard and military preparedness more broadly. Instead, all three shared the same ascriptive republican worldview: they believed that republican virtue requires martial preparedness, and the state should encourage its (White) male citizens to engage in rifle practice for this purpose. This ideological congruence led to fewer resistance points to the idea of a private organization acting as the exclusive firearms trainer of the citizen-soldiers.

Today, the NRA operates in a contested ideological environment where its worldview is not the dominant paradigm. Alternative ideological systems provide powerful policy prescriptions for the problems the organization has identified as central, such as crime and political corruption. In today's climate, the NRA needs to leverage its membership and donations to candidates to prevent policy changes antithetical to its agenda and to push for proposals consistent with its views. But in 1902, the organization operated in an environment (the defense establishment) dominated by one set of ideas: ascriptive republicanism. Since the NRA mainly consisted of military officers, it had insider access to power. This shared worldview and ease of access made it much easier for the organization to achieve its goals quickly.

The NRA's civilian marksmanship plans were echoed in proposals by the NGA and an independent report commissioned by the War Department. This congruence further illustrates the similarity in ideology and goals across the three institutions. There is little chance that these proposals were created independently. Much as the NRA suggested, the proposals focused on the UK and Switzerland as likely models for emulation. Ideologically neutral actors would have engaged in a broader comparative review meant to establish what military model best served the goal of effectiveness given rapidly changing military technology. However, such an inquiry would have necessitated questioning the martial republican commitments that all three institutions—and much of the broader American society—shared. Specifically, the proposals would have had to question whether a large standing army might be preferable to a decentralized system of volunteer militias. But this would be anathema to a republican nation. Instead, the NGA and the War Department focused on countries that relied on citizens rather than professional soldiers. Then, they identified models that they found desirable because the models were consistent with their republican ideological commitments, not because of their performance.

In addition to a civilian marksmanship program, the NRA proposed establishing a federal committee within the Department of War responsible for promoting rifle practice. This recommendation, too, found its way into the other organizations' proposals. Specifically, the president would appoint an advisory committee made up of the NRA leadership and military officials with a mission to "recommend plans for the enlargement of the National Rifle Association." This committee would partner with the NRA to organize shooting competitions for the National Guard and draft-age civilians; through this program, participants would "purchase arms and ammunition at cost." The NRA would essentially act as a monopoly intermediary, since rifle clubs and individuals would have to be affiliated with the association if they wanted access to free or at-cost federal surplus materiel.[24]

Making military education into a sport required a significant investment from the federal government. Drawing on the Swiss model, the NRA advocated for funding a network of local ranges that would be privately held and managed, outfitted with appropriate targets and staffed with expert shooting instructors. The NRA would provide the specifications for the ranges and train the instructors. The federal government would subsidize the project and provide guns and ammunition at cost. The militiamen and civilians fit for service would be organized in "shooting societies" or "rifle clubs" that would include members based on competition qualification. Even though Switzerland had instituted conscription, the NRA insisted that the Swiss model fostered "voluntary firing." In the NRA's view, "no more useful expenditure of money for our national defence [sic] could be made" than to support rifle practice.[25] Its vision was that competition and sportsmanship would "claim the attention of the country" and "[awaken] public interest." In turn, public engagement would "make the development of this military sport, which is really military instruction, more general."[26]

In short, by incentivizing participation in shooting sports, the government would be developing virtuous citizen-soldiers at a low cost.

The government's investment and subsidy of privately owned and operated clubs and their manager and coordinator (the NRA) would not only ensure proper training for the National Guard, but generate interest in shooting among men who were not part of the volunteer militia. Such clubs could be established in local communities, schools, and colleges to encourage young boys' and men's involvement in rifle sports and to instill the value of martial republican citizenship early on.

The development of shooting skills among the broader male public would, in turn, ensure that a large proportion of the military-age population would be familiar with a critical skill needed in modern warfare: marksmanship. In the case of a major war, the government could mobilize and draft this dormant reserve (the "unorganized militia"), which would already have many of the technical and moral skills required to succeed as a soldier. This plan preserved the spirit of the Constitution. It "made all citizens liable for service in the militia, which encourages the handling and carrying of arms by establishing the right of every citizen to do so." At the same time, it went beyond the limitations of the National Guard by inducing through sportsmanship "all citizens fit for active service . . . to qualify for this important attribute of a good soldier."[27]

The NGA proposed legislation to Congress and the president which contained many of the same elements—again revealing the close cooperation and ideological agreement among these actors. Ignoring other military training models, the National Guard focused on rifle practice. The plan made federal funding conditional on states' establishing shooting ranges for the Guard and the public to use. Federal funding would also go toward monetary prizes for individual and team competitions, on the belief that such rewards would incentivize National Guardsmen to master marksmanship, generate public interest in shooting, and inspire recruits to the Guards.[28]

The NRA's fingerprints could be detected in the recommendations issued from within the federal government—more evidence of their shared ideological commitments. Secretary Root commissioned Col. William C. Sanger, the Inspector General of the New York National Guard, to produce a study describing how Germany, Switzerland, and Great Britain organized and trained their military reserves. The choice of models mirrors those offered by the NRA and the NGA. The study would identify the most critical issues the Department should tackle and the best practices that should be applied. Sanger's report was infused with the spirit of martial republicanism, praising the virtue of the citizen-soldiers. "We know that our greatest safeguard against disaster and our greatest help to a position of influence and power will be found in the virtue of our people, in their love of right and their hate of wrong, combined with vigor of mind and body," Sanger affirmed. Despite the dismal performance of the volunteers in the Spanish-American War, which the report discusses in detail, Sanger insisted that "we always have been and always shall be largely dependent upon our citizen-soldiers to fight our battles, and the splendid qualities shown in all our wars by our citizen-soldiers only emphasize what we have always known—that an effective militia is a force of the greatest value."[29]

The Sanger report mirrored the ideological commitments of the NRA and the NGA. Consistent with late-nineteenth-century republicanism, it stressed voluntarism and rejected conscription. It also rejected a large standing army and extolled the virtues of the citizen-soldier. The report stressed that "the people should and will demand the privilege of fighting for their country if it is attacked." Yet they could refuse to volunteer for service if participation in the Guard was inconsistent with American men's social and ideological expectations. Therefore, if the federal government wanted robust militia participation, it should give in to the demands of the NGA and preserve citizen-soldiers' republican independence—especially elected officers and no duty to serve outside the state.[30] Not surprisingly, Sanger too found the solution to the Guard's problems in privately organized marksmanship practice and the establishment of private and state shooting ranges.[31]

With strong support from President Roosevelt and his secretary of war, Congress passed the Dick Act in 1903, which federalized the National Guard, making it the country's reserve corps and providing funding for its training. The Guard's elevated status was signaled in how its affairs came to be managed by the War Department. The Dick Act created a new Militia Division within the Adjutant General's Office of the War Department, removing National Guard affairs from the "Miscellaneous Division" to which it had previously been relegated. James Parker, the assistant adjutant general heading the Militia Division, shared the NRA's goals. Among his top priorities was to improve rifle practice for the National Guard and the (White) male citizenry at large. "Rifle ranges also are needed, not only for the National Guard but also for the citizen population," Parker wrote. "To shoot well is a large part of the education of the soldier, and if the Government can arouse such an interest in shooting in not only the organized but the unorganized militia, then our male population shall be familiar with the accurate use of the rifle."[32]

The law fulfilled the National Guard's and the NRA's expectations in creating the Civilian Marksmanship Program (CMP) and the National Board for the Promotion of Rifle Practice (NBPRP). Both were institutionally housed within the War Department's Militia Division. These institutions were designed to establish a federally funded national program to train the National Guard and encourage citizens to engage in shooting sports. Following the Swiss model, the NBPRP directed the NRA to be the national supervisor of rifle clubs and rifle practice—thus endowing the group with a "semi-official status."[33]

A subsequent law, P.L. 149 of 1905, provided that the Army would sell surplus firearms and ammunition at cost through the CMP to rifle clubs that met the specifications of the NBPRP. Such clubs were also allowed to compete at government-subsidized rates in national matches at Camp Perry. A key specification for CMP was that clubs be affiliated with the NRA. Within five years, Congress amended the law to provide free materiel to NRA-affiliated rifle clubs and individual rifle club members. In 1912, Congress started to provide direct funding to annual NRA competitions and asked the Army to provide 1,000 troops as free labor to help administer the matches. In the 1920s, the association, with help from the National Guard, was able to push through Congress a bill that prohibited the War Department from zeroing out, reallocating, or reducing the appropriation to the NBPRP without Congressional approval—a testament to its growing political power over both parties, neither of which could afford to alienate the country's soldiers.[34]

These laws were a boon for the association. Not only did they provide stable long-term funding for its programs, but, as envisioned by the group, they increased the legitimacy of the NRA by formally linking it to the national defense establishment. Rifle practice as a military and social engagement now had the imprimatur of the federal government. However, for the NRA, the new legislation's most beneficial provision was the de facto recognition of the organization's monopoly over civilian rifle practice. The legislation specified that granting rifle clubs access to free and at-cost materiel required that recipient clubs comply with NBPRP rules. Given the close institutional ties between the Board and the association, it is not surprising that the NBPRP required that all rifle clubs seeking government support must be affiliated with the NRA. A further amendment enacted in 1924 stipulated that both clubs *and* individuals receiving firearms through the program had to be members of the NRA—a restriction that remained in place until 1968. As late as 1968, the *Congressional Quarterly* noted that the CMP requirements benefited the organization, even as the country was going through turbulent times. According to the report, in 1967, after the Detroit riots, "400 members of the Detroit police force were required to pay $5 membership fee to the NRA before they could purchase [government] surplus carbines for use in riot control."[35]

As the NRA itself notes, "the immediate effect of th[ese] law[s] was to approve and lend the support of the federal government to the principles and program of the National Rifle Association. . . . Until given the support of federal recognition . . . [the NRA] had operated under severe difficulties. Here, indeed, was an important milestone in the proud role the National Rifle Association was destined to play."[36] Henceforth, with such incentives, the civilian membership of the organization could only grow, with little investment on the part of the NRA.

NRA membership also came to symbolize more than good shooting skills. It became a symbol of good citizenship, what today the association calls "the good guy with a gun." Incentivizing civilians to own firearms meant that more firearms were available for sports and criminal purposes. At a time when computerized criminal records were unavailable and sharing information across jurisdictions was incredibly challenging, how were authorities to know if a gun owner was an upstanding citizen or a criminal? More specifically, for the Directorate of Civilian Marksmanship (DCM), how could the US Army determine whether surplus military weapons and ammunition went into the hands of criminals? Government authorities had to rely in large part on the NRA's membership recruitment system, which rested on extant members vouching for new applicants and on ideologically driven confidence in the organization itself. The idea was that since the original members of the association were upstanding citizens—members of the National Guard and the broader social and political establishment—any person they recommended would also share these characteristics. A reputable citizen, a true gentleman, would not recommend an anarchist or a criminal as a member of the organization. Therefore, the members themselves were responsible for patrolling the organization's boundaries.

The CMP did keep records on the clubs and individuals who purchased or borrowed arms through the program. In an emergency, it reserved the right to recall weapons on loan.[37] However, the NRA did the initial "vetting," allowing citizens access to the CMP program by offering them membership. From the standpoint of the US government, an NRA membership card—that is, membership in a private organization—constituted evidence of good citizenship, to the degree that this person could be entrusted with a government-provided firearm and that they could be exempted from gun control legislation, such as state or local licensing and registration. This is the origin of the NRA's contemporary distinction between a "good guy with a gun" and "a bad guy with a gun." An NRA member had the government imprimatur of being a "good guy with a gun." Early gun regulations, such as the 1926 Uniform Firearms Act (UFA), a model state legislation, validated that contention.[38]

Through the 1950s, the association's fortunes continued to be tied to the federal government and the War Department's annual appropriations for matches and materiel. External events, such as economic recession, war, and changes in War Department leadership, could influence funding for the NBPRP and the CMP and thus affect the NRA's budget. The NRA had to rely on its relationships within Congress, the National Guard, and the Militia Bureau of the War Department to obtain some relief from one year to the next.

It is not an exaggeration to say that there was no daylight between the NRA, the NGA, and the federal authorities responsible for civilian marksmanship for the first half of the twentieth century. In 1908, Brigadier General James A. Drain visited several states to promote marksmanship. General Drain carried the official title of NRA President and Chief of Ordnance of Washington State, President of the National Militia Board, Chairman of the Executive Committee of the NGA, and President of the NBPRP.[39] Such was the interconnectedness between the association and military authorities that the NRA and the National Guard literally spoke with one voice in Congress. During the 1934 hearings on the National Firearms Act (NFA), General Reckord testified before the House Ways and Means Committee as a representative of the National Guard in his role as the adjutant general of the Maryland National Guard. However, in the Senate, he testified as the representative of the NRA. The committee noted this dual role, but they did not seem to view it as a conflict of interest.[40]

Given these ties to the defense establishment, it is no surprise that the *Congressional Quarterly*, as late as 1968, noted that "the NRA gains some of its strength from its close ties with the Pentagon." Despite the cancellation of federal subsidies for the 1967 National Rifle Matches, a sore point for the association, the group's ties with the military establishment remained robust. As the report noted, the NRA's then executive vice president, Franklin L. Orth, used to be deputy assistant secretary of the Army and a member of the "Subversive Activities Control Board"—a committee tasked with the investigation of Communist activities in American society, including among Black civil rights groups. Furthermore, many CMP former directors who retired from the Army were invited to be "on the NRA payroll." The report also noted that a key NRA power source was its monopoly over the CMP. "A 1903 law," the report said, "gives the Pentagon only two ways to rid itself of surplus firearms and ammunition. It can sell the surplus for scrap. Or it can sell it to NRA members at a bargain price."[41]

CULTIVATING THE CIVILIAN MARKET
IN PARTNERSHIP WITH GOVERNMENT

Despite its success, the association was still smarting from the failure of its New York State venture, which faced political opposition from the governor and ended in bankruptcy. That experience forced the NRA to recognize that while a close relationship with Washington was beneficial, overdependence on government was perilous. Military technology and theory changed, and so did government leaders and their ideologies and priorities. At a time when the emphasis was on centralization, professionalization, and growth of the military branches, the NRA recognized that it was dangerous to tie its fate too closely to the National Guard and the Army.[42]

The CMP provided an avenue for the association to maintain independence by focusing on the "unorganized militia," or the male population outside the National Guard. This untapped market was large and lucrative: "there were hundreds of thousands [of potential members] scattered in small organizations and as individuals across the United States." CMP beneficiaries had *no* obligation to the military or the National Guard. They did not have to engage in any form of military preparedness other than rifle practice. Their only obligation was to pay their NRA dues. This "unorganized militia" became the foundation for the association's loyal mass membership and political power well into the twenty-first century.[43]

Police departments represented another lucrative market opportunity for the association. The 1920s was a decade of rising social violence. Armed bank and mail robberies had become so frequent that state and local governments encouraged vigilante groups to act as police auxiliaries. Robberies on trains carrying mail occurred so often that all 10,000 railway mail police officers were armed. Yet police departments hired officers based on physical size and patronage; shooting skills were not a criterion for the job. As police departments started to arm officers, the NRA discovered an untapped new market. Through the 1920s, NRA membership among police officers increased exponentially as the association developed specialized police training and convinced departments to offer bonuses to officers who qualified as marksmen. In the 1930s, as the country faced successive waves of strikes, riots, and other forms of unrest amid the Great Depression, the NRA further cultivated its relationship with police by publishing extensive articles on how police officers should use chemical weapons when breaking up social unrest.[44]

During the two world wars, the Army's demand for soldiers significantly elevated the NRA's reputation and power and showcased its commitment to martial republicanism. Not only did many in its leadership and staff return to active duty as officers and serve with distinction during World Wars I and II, but the association worked with the War Department on war preparedness. During World War II, the group trained more than 160,000 draft-age civilians to meet the Army's infantry rifleman standards. The association also worked with state governments to train civilians for Home Defense: armed auxiliaries who secured arms production facilities and government buildings. After the emergency evacuation at Dunkirk forced British forces to leave their arms behind, the NRA organized a drive among its civilian members to collect and donate firearms to the United Kingdom for home front defense.[45]

After World War II, interest in shooting and hunting among returning soldiers increased exponentially, and so did the association's ties to the civilian market. The NRA developed specialized course offerings, such as shotgun shooting for hunters, gun safety instruction, and conservation programs. It admitted hunters to membership for the first time in 1946; until then, membership had been confined to military and civilian marksmen. By the 1950s, the association's programming included divisions for high-power rifles, small-bore rifles, pistols and revolvers, junior and collegiate, gun collectors, hunting and conservation, shotguns, and international competitions. As America entered an era of peace and prosperity, the NRA's focus shifted from war to sports and leisure in service to military preparedness.[46]

Although the association developed various programs through the 1960s, it continued to understand its mission as military preparedness. It viewed itself as a partner of the US government, not an antagonist. "With Congressional approval, our government helps the NRA's rifle clubs with the loan of rifles and the issue of ammunition and equipment. So, you see, the business of a free, armed citizenry is a joint ideal, shared by the National Rifle Association and Uncle Sam," declared *The American Rifleman*.[47] A 1950 cartoon published in the magazine shows the NRA in a trusting and cooperative relationship with the government (fig. 5.1).

The association, depicted as a young White man in a black suit and bowtie, was the White salesman and promoter of rifle practice and ascriptive martial republican ideology to the male public. The NRA was to train America's men in the moral and technical skills required for military service through sports.[48] Figure 5.2 outlines the evolution of the NRA in the context of government policy change. The lighter boxes represent NRA actions, and the darker boxes what is happening at the federal level. The arrows at the top of the figure show the two periods in the evolution of the relationship between the group and the government. During the first era

Figure 5.1 Uncle Sam and the NRA, *The American Rifleman*, March 1950, 33.

the NRA viewed itself as a government defender, and during the second as a government antagonist.

During the nineteenth century, the group had its sights on becoming a marksmanship trainer for the National Guards. However, with the federalization of the National Guards in 1903 and the US Army assuming responsibility for training the militia, the NRA became the federal government's partner in inculcating patriotic spirit in the country's White civilian men of draft age. During the era of mass mobilization, from World War I to Vietnam, the NRA worked with the federal government in promoting marksmanship and military preparedness. However, as the era of mass mobilization ended in the 1960s and the federal government gave in to pressures on gun control, the relationship between the NRA and the defense establishment started to fray. As I discuss later on, this opened the door for the politicization of the organization and its eventual transformation from an association of loyal citizen-soldiers fighting external enemies on the side

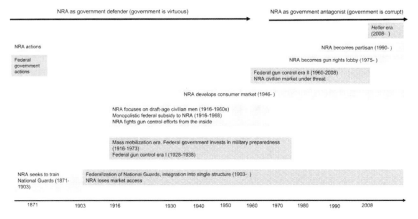

Figure 5.2 Political evolution of the NRA from government
defender to government antagonist (1871–2022).

of government authority to one of citizen-soldiers fighting "corruption"
within government.

The NRA's political activism and government opposition bore fruit in
the twenty-first century. First, the group was incorporated into the Republican Party, and its absolutist views on gun rights came to be part of the
party platform and messaging, even in an era of increased mass shootings
and gun violence. Second, in the 2008 *District of Columbia v. Heller* decision, the Supreme Court recognized an individual right to bear arms for
self-defense and revolution. Through the 2010 *McDonald v. Chicago* decision, the individual right to own firearms applies to the states. In June 2022,
in *New York State Rifle & Pistol Association, Inc. v. Bruen*, the Court struck
down a New York State law that required applicants for concealed carry
permits to provide a "proper cause" that went beyond a desire for safety.
The decision extended the individual right to bear arms—including concealed weapons—beyond the home to public spaces.

LIMITED MILITARY USE

In much the same way that the enrolled militia of the Revolution failed
to meet the demands of late-eighteenth-century wars, the NRA's riflemen did not meet the needs of the twentieth-century military. The idea
of marksmanship as central to military strategy was part of a doctrine that
emerged from the American Civil War and an era when military innovation came from the private sector. Individual inventors pushed their ideas
to the Army. The citizen-marksman model combined eighteenth-century

ideology and nineteenth-century military experience. Its political success depended on late-nineteenth-century political opportunity structures that incentivized individuals or groups to act as political entrepreneurs, promoting military technology to the armed forces.

As the historian Barton Hacker has argued, technological innovation in the military was driven by industry from the Industrial Revolution to World War I. During this period, the military could not pursue military innovation systematically due to its smaller size and the federal government's limited financial bandwidth (before the federal income tax amendment). As General Wingate's example illustrates, scientific advancement in military technology emerged from individual craftsmen and amateur scientists who then approached political leaders and the military to sell their innovations. Because innovation was in the hands of entrepreneurs with various skill levels and political contacts, military planners had little control over the process. Furthermore, they could not accurately judge the usefulness or effectiveness of these new products. Worse, since innovations did not build on each other in a controlled and organized fashion, technologies were not seamlessly integrated into existing military systems. Essentially, the military was forced to pick and choose from what was available rather than pursue a program of research and development based on its own assessment of needs.

But the dream of training a million men as reserve citizen-soldiers was more an ideologically driven fantasy than a reality.[49] By the third decade of the twentieth century, the military theory on which the NRA based its marksmanship program had become obsolete, made irrelevant by the evolution of military technology. Airplanes and armored vehicles, not to mention today's computer systems, nuclear weapons, and unmanned drones, radically changed how wars are fought. However, much like militarily unsuitable but politically useful nineteenth-century volunteer militia, these programs attracted powerful political support because they represented the dominant (in defense and partisan circles) ascriptive republican ideology. They remained in the federal budget for almost a century.

The mismatch of needs, desires, and available products that could not be easily interwoven into existing strategy and operations led to "a catastrophe almost beyond comprehension."[50] Unlike in the Civil War, where armies marched across terrain, World War I forced troops into trenches because mechanization prevented movement. Machine guns, chemical weapons, and—to a lesser degree—air strikes combined to produce thousands of daily casualties, even absent offensive moves. The modern army needed solutions to logistical problems: motorized transport, armored fighting vehicles, and aircraft were the promise of the future. The early-twentieth-century military demanded methods for bringing endless supplies to immense armies; chemical weapons did not help the military address these critical problems.[51] Neither did rifle practice.

The lesson of World War I, and even more so of World War II, was that the military needed to assume control of the process of technological innovation and harness it to fulfill its vision of the war of the future—it needed central planning. New doctrines of airpower and mechanization provided the basis for retooling operations, tactics, and military organization—theories that competed with ascriptive republican perspectives. As the twentieth century progressed, it became clear that wars were no longer to be fought by large civilian armies of infantry riflemen; the war of the future would be won by technology.

Nuclear weapons and applied electronics completely revolutionized war theory, doctrine, and operations. Twenty-first-century wars rely on the disruption of the enemy's electronic and electrical systems, air surveillance, drones, and remote-controlled air attacks. The Vietnam War, the last war to use many infantrymen, notwithstanding, by the end of World War II military leaders recognized that the era of the rifleman—the virtuous citizen-soldier marching on—was irrevocably gone, and programs training civilians in marksmanship were all but irrelevant to modern warfare.[52]

By 1933, critics of the citizen-soldier model started to argue that government-funded shooting programs had no military value because "few soldiers will ever be sent on the modern field of battle again . . . to fire .30 caliber bullets at the enemy." On the eve of America's entry into World War II, the NRA found itself fighting against new theories that prioritized technology, logistics, and communications over marksmanship. Confident in their republican assumptions, its leaders continued to insist on the superiority of marksmanship as a core focus of military defense, even attributing the highly mechanized German Army's success to foot soldiers. At the association's 1940 annual meeting, leaders discussed the German attack on Poland. In an event that included the assistant secretary of war, the assistant secretary of commerce, United States senators, several congressmen, Army Chief of Staff General George C. Marshall, and many other top military officers, the attendees pointed out that "while the aviation and mechanized forces of the German Army received most of the newspaper credit for the swift success of the German forces, it was the efficiency of the German Infantryman, the foot soldier with his rifle, which set the stage for the operations of the more spectacular units." Col. Church had exhibited similar admiration for the German riflemen in 1914.[53]

After World War II, the political climate continued to shift, and martial republicanism was no longer the dominant model for the organization of the country's military forces. Despite the NRA's insistence that there was military value in the Civilian Marksmanship Program, political leaders continued to cast serious doubt on the program's utility and even its security. An independent evaluation of the NBPRP programs commissioned by Congress in 1965 found them lacking. According to the report, only 3 percent of military recruits had prior experience with the CMP program. Furthermore, many of the people who participated in CMP did not meet the criteria for military service. The vast majority of those who participated in the marksmanship programs in the 1960s did not volunteer for military service.[54] Clearly, most shooters engaged with marksmanship for sport, and as much as they appreciated free or discounted federal weapons, they had no intention of joining the Army.

Even worse, reports surfaced in the early 1960s that members of anti-government extremist organizations had joined the NRA and, through their rifle club memberships, accessed government-provided weapons and ammunition. Robert DePugh, leader of the Minutemen, an anti-Communist militant organization, bragged that many members of his group were NRA and rifle club members and that he was an NRA life member.[55] During the same period, a report by the Anti-Defamation League (ADL) identified cases of Ku Klux Klan groups forming rifle clubs, inviting men as young as seventeen to join, and using the clubs to evade gun control laws, much like the nineteenth-century Klan evaded Reconstruction-era prohibitions. The goal of these groups was to attack Black communities and civil rights movement participants.[56] In response to these claims, Congress commissioned an independent study. The study was authorized under Title VI of the Civil Rights Act of 1964, which prohibits educational organizations that receive federal funding from discriminating based on race and ethnicity.[57]

In 1979, a gun control organization filed a lawsuit against the Department of Defense claiming that the DCM programs were discriminatory because they required Americans to become NRA members to access government benefits (i.e., discounted weapons and ammunition). The court agreed, ordering the government to make the program available to all Americans. However, DCM/CMP beneficiaries still had to be members of a DCM-affiliated gun club, and most such clubs were NRA affiliates.[58]

The GAO report did not focus on discrimination. Instead, it implied that the NRA's gatekeeping system was sorely lacking. The study recommended that the Army develop better methods of accountability and control over the program and assume direct responsibility for performing background checks on individuals and club officials affiliated with the DCM. It further recommended that rifle club officers should be fingerprinted, and their fingerprints submitted to police authorities. Although it extolled the mission and goals of the DCM, the study pointed out the program's limited efficacy in translating members into military recruits.[59] In a confrontational hearing in the Senate, Franklin Orth, the NRA's leader, argued that oaths of loyalty and referrals notwithstanding, the NRA could not just expel members, even if they sought to overthrow the government. For the NRA, expulsion required an indictment.[60]

The General Accounting Office (GAO) was tasked with evaluating the NBPRP's programs again in 1991. Its conclusions echoed the same points made by experts in 1933—almost sixty years earlier. "Military Preparedness: Army's Civilian Marksmanship Is of Limited Use" was the title of the report, which went on to say that despite significant changes in the US military, the program had changed little since its inception in the 1920s. Furthermore, the program was not aligned with the Army's objectives and mission, and the number of recruits the Army got through the program was minuscule. Essentially, in the name of republican ideology, the US Army was subsidizing a civilian hobby.[61]

The Civilian Marksmanship Program continues to exist today. Since 1996 it is "self-funded," meaning that rather than receiving a direct federal appropriation, the program covers its administrative costs through army materiel sale to individuals and rifle clubs. The NRA is not involved in its administration, nor is it any longer a monopoly beneficiary, but the group does support its continuation, and benefits from CMP ads in its magazines.[62]

Military usefulness notwithstanding, the NRA's shooting programs had attracted a faithful group of participants by the 1920s. Shooting and hunting had become popular sports for men and many women by the late nineteenth century. As other beneficiaries of government largesse and subsidies have done at various points during the twentieth century, civilian rifle clubs, veterans' associations, police groups, and militia associations banded together to protect the programs. As Robert Wohlforth, a critic of the militia, acknowledged in the 1930s, such programs persisted largely because of the political power of these organized and politically active constituents, who were represented in Congressional hearings by veterans' groups and the NRA. By the 1930s, the NRA was a politically powerful mass membership organization.[63]

LEADERSHIP EVOLUTION

According to the officially sanctioned NRA narrative, the transformation of the organization from a group that sought to compromise with government to an absolutist political advocacy organization was initiated by the grassroots membership. Ordinary members, angered by the association's weak response to the 1968 Gun Control Act, turned out at the polls to punish legislators who put their gun rights in jeopardy, and in doing so sent a strong signal to the group's leadership about the importance of lobbying and "the danger of compromise."[64] However, the transition was more likely instigated by changes in leadership than by radicalism among followers. In fact, the NRA itself credits Rep. John Dingell (D-MI) and two professional lobbyists with introducing a resolution in the 1973 annual convention to create a committee focused on structuring the association's lobbying activities and spearheading the effort to create a lobbying arm for the organization. The Nixon administration's gun control proposals targeting handgun ownership gave such efforts a necessary boost. In 1974, the NRA Board approved a no-compromise resolution, pledging to fight "any proposed legislation . . . which is directed against the inanimate firearm rather than against the criminal misuse of firearms."[65]

Following the establishment of the Institute for Legislative Action (ILA) in 1975, hard-liners sought to create a parallel, independent line of authority to challenge the NRA's leadership from within. ILA principals such as Harlon Carter believed that the association had tried to restore its tattered public image by tacitly withdrawing from gun control politics. Hard-liners thought that the leadership accepted compromises (such as the Gun Control Act of 1968) and focused on sports and recreation instead of the right to bear arms. The ILA hired the trusted Reagan pollster Richard Wirthlin and the conservative direct-mail pioneer Richard Viguerie to help the group develop a political communication strategy centered on "no compromise" on gun rights. The ILA began to produce its own biweekly newsletter, independent of the NRA. At the same time, ILA leaders worked at the state level to organize activist grassroots organizations.[66]

The evolution of the group's leadership reflects the transformation of the NRA from a military organization to a civilian recreation-focused group and, later, to a political activist organization. The membership list of the organization constitutes jealously guarded information that neither researchers nor the general public can access. However, the membership of its Board of Directors has always been public information. For many years, *The American Rifleman* published biographical sketches of candidates for the Board. An examination of the Board's membership can provide clues about the changes in the organization over time.

Before World War II, the NRA's Board of Directors was dominated by active-duty and retired military officers from federal and state forces. These individuals had strong ties to the defense establishment and were primarily concerned with the role of marksmanship in American defense policy.

After the war, however, the organization took on a civilian character. More civilian (White) men (and a minuscule number of women) took on leadership roles. These individuals steered the organization in a new direction, seeking to cultivate activities of interest to the civilian market while preserving the NRA's relationship to the DCM and the defense establishment as part of America's military preparedness system. These men were accomplished professionals—engineers, lawyers, businessmen—deeply involved in the civic life of their communities. For most, firearms were tools of recreation for shooting and hunting. Very few were farmers or ranchers, and equally few were professionally engaged with guns (e.g., as gunsmiths or working for gun manufacturers).

The organization's leadership changed again after the 1977 "Revolt at Cincinnati," which brought to the helm political hard-liners concerned with gun rights and gun policy exclusively.[67] At that point the leadership had already transitioned to mostly civilians, with only a few active-duty military members. The enactment of the GCA (1968) alienated and radicalized a portion of key stakeholders. Combined with changes to the DCM programs in the late 1960s that ended the NRA's monopoly, this made it easier for the organization to transition to an outsider politics model. The new leadership consisted almost exclusively of political activists who prioritized pro-gun legislation and the Second Amendment.

Every year, the organization elects about a third of its Board to serve three-year terms. The American Rifleman provides short biographies for all candidates. In the 1920s and 1930s, the lists included the person's military rank, state of origin (which for National Guard officers showed their association with that state's militia organization), and for civilians, their occupation (e.g., assistant secretary of war). This practice continued through the early 2000s.[68]

As of the 1950s, the biography included occupation and the type of firearms activity the individual engaged in. During this period, candidates did not mention any political involvement on behalf of firearms. For example, in 1954, the future NRA President and 1977 "revolt" leader Harlon B. Carter's biography noted: "Chief, U.S. Border Patrol of the Immigration and Naturalization Service. Member, NRA Board of Directors and Member NRA Protest Committee. Nationally known pistol and high-power rifle competitor. Interested in firearms training. Author of many articles on shooting."[69]

By the late 1970s, candidates included extensive information on service activism, both with firearms and, more broadly (for some), with political activism. As of the 1980s, most candidates emphasized their political activism and their service to the NRA and local firearms organizations. Many also emphasized their success in recruiting new activists to the cause. Some did not even mention their occupation or any other demographic information—only their political credentials. By 1984, Lou Benton's biography stated that the candidate was "Chairman Audit, Chairman Grants-in-Aid, and member Range Development Committees. Professional engineer. . . . A hunter and competitive shooter. . . . While Chairman of NJ Citizens Committee, coordinated sportsmen, collectors, NRA clubs, dealers and private police in the fight against gun registration, financing and carrying the case to the U.S. Supreme Court. Currently advocating gun owners civil rights including public land access, and state preemption of firearms control assuring our right to own, carry, and use guns as guaranteed by the State Constitution and the Bill of Rights."[70] In the 1990s, candidates routinely included general political statements in their biographies, such as: "Firm believer in America, Constitution, the Second Amendment, and gun ownership," or "believes NRA's top priority is defending Second Amendment, developing more effective grassroots organization."[71]

By the beginning of the twenty-first century, the magazine reverted to publishing only candidates' names and state affiliations, not their biographies. Presumably, the biographical information was communicated to voting members in separate mailings or via the NRA's website. I did not have access to archived NRA website information, but various online sources allowed me to gather basic background information about these candidates.[72]

How these candidates characterized themselves and what they prioritized is a key clue to how the NRA leadership changed from a military organization to a sports and civil defense group to a political lobbying group. I sought to document the transformation of the organization from a military to a partisan/political group by examining the biographies of Board candidates. I sampled one year from each decade since the 1920s to code. I assume that the profiles of the candidates the organization put forward for Board membership did not vary systematically from year to year. For example, I do not expect that one year includes only men and the next only women. Therefore, selecting one year per decade allows me to document changes in the Board's makeup even if I do not capture the slight variations that may have occurred from one year to the next.

Using the biographies and, for twenty-first-century candidates, information from online sources, I coded each candidate in terms of the following characteristics: 1) gender; 2) state of origin; and 3) military experience (active or former officer, war veteran). I also created categories for their employment: 1) lawyer; 2) government official (elected; worked for an agency; law enforcement); 3) farmer or rancher; 4) business directly

related to guns (e.g., guns dealer, sports shop owner/operator, gun manu-
facturer); and 5) other business or professional occupation. The first two
employment groups are of interest because they have the knowledge and
resources to influence politics. For the years where biographical statements
were available, I also coded the candidates in terms of whether or not they
mentioned politics ("political advocacy"), whether they prioritized gun
politics over such other issues as shooting sports, conservation, or military
preparedness, whether politics was mentioned before characteristics like
their employment record ("priority"), and whether they asserted an absolutist position on firearms ("no compromise").

In the post–World War II bios, not all individuals report their employment status or their experience as a war veteran (military officers typically
mentioned their title). These choices are meaningful because they suggest
what information people thought was important for the voting members to
have. It is thus telling that none of the candidates in the 1950s and 1960s reported war veteran status even though it is highly likely that many of them
served during World War II. Similarly, it is noteworthy that many candidates in the 1980s and 1990s did not report their employment or profession, likely thinking it less relevant than their status as political advocates
and their political commitment to gun rights. These trends attest to the
changing character of the organization leadership, from a group of military
officers to a group of professionals engaged with marksmanship, and finally
to a group of political activists.

As figure 5.3 shows, up until World War II three-quarters of the leadership came from the military officers' rank, even as the organization made
active efforts to recruit civilians.[73] During World War II, the makeup of the
candidates shifted, with only a thin majority of Board candidates (53 percent) being officers. This is likely both because of the NRA's active efforts to
recruit civilians and because many officers were at the war front in 1944. By
the 1950s the Board consisted primarily of civilians, and only 5 percent of
candidates reported a military rank. The representation of military officers
on the Board continued to be low in 1964 (12 percent) and 1974 (8 percent),
but increased somewhat in 1984 (17 percent) and 1994 (18 percent). Importantly, in 1984 and 1994, a number of the civilian candidates reported military service in war (24 percent and 18 percent, respectively), both World
War II and Vietnam. In 2004, only 9 percent of the candidates appear to
have been military officers.

The data clearly show that the organization's leadership became civilian-
dominated in the 1950s. The variation in the proportion of Board candidates reporting their status as businesspeople or professionals varies across
the decades, either because people did not report their occupation or

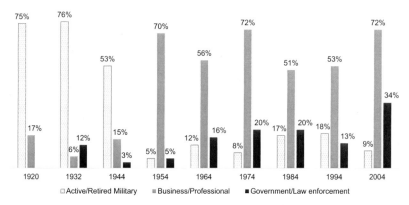

Figure 5.3 Evolution of NRA Board of Directors membership (1920–2004).

because they reported being retired. Relatedly, by the twenty-first century, several people on the NRA Board were celebrities affiliated with sports, the entertainment industry, and Hollywood, such as the basketball player Karl Malone, the NFL football player Dave Butz, the singer Ted Nugent, and the actors Tom Selleck and Susan Howard.

The figure also shows the proportion of the NRA Board candidates in each sampled year who worked for the government in some capacity other than the military. This category includes elected officials, agency personnel (typically, people who worked in state environmental agencies and park service agencies), and police and law enforcement. Given the small numbers for each group within the government category, it was not meaningful to separate them out. However, over time, this group came to be dominated by elected officials at the state and federal levels. The data show that as of the 1970s, the proportion of Board nominees who came from within partisan politics or law enforcement increased. In 1974, 20 percent of Board candidates had a government affiliation (other than military), while in 2004 that figure was 34 percent.

It is also important to note that the number of lawyers among Board candidates increased markedly over time. In 1974, 4 percent of candidates were lawyers; by 2004, 31 percent listed law as their profession. Many of these attorneys worked specifically on gun issues and received referrals from the NRA. This is suggestive of the symbiotic relationships that characterized the NRA leadership as it transformed into a political advocacy organization.

I also assessed the proportion of Board candidates each year from 1944 to 1994 who mentioned political involvement and advocacy engagement. This is meaningful for the post–World War II era when candidate bios are provided. In the 1950s and 1960s, political advocacy was mentioned only by a small minority of candidates, mostly by pointing out their service to the NRA's legislative affairs committees or identifying themselves as lobbyists. This changed substantially after the 1977 "Revolt at Cincinnati." By 1984, 82 percent of candidates explicitly identified as political advocates. Many candidates prioritized advocacy by mentioning it first, before other things, including their service positions or their employment. The proportion who identified as political advocates climbed to 87 percent in 1994.

Overall, the trends suggest that within a century, the organization's leadership moved away from the nonpartisan military and into the hands of civilians, partisan elected officials, and lobbyists dedicated to the cause of individual gun rights. In the process, the character of the organization changed. The organization was politically freed from its moorings in the professionalized, nonpartisan federal military establishment, and this allowed the group to transform from federal government "insider" to "outsider." By freeing itself from the strictures of the defense establishment, the NRA could afford to become a vocal critic of government.

The change in leadership translated very quickly into a new focus for the organization, a change that was signaled in the group's mission statement. By January 1978, the NRA was no longer the promoter of "social welfare and public safety, law and order, and national defense" as it had been for decades.[74] Instead, it was "the foremost guardian of the second amendment," which the association interpreted as a guarantee of an individual right of citizens to own firearms for sport, protection, and resisting government tyranny. By the 1990s, gone were the loyalty oaths and referral requirements. The references to national defense, preparedness, and government subsidies through the DCM also disappeared from NRA membership ads. "The NRA," stated the magazine, "[is] the foremost guardian of the traditional American right to 'keep and bear arms,' [and] believes every law-abiding citizen is entitled to the ownership and legal use of firearms, and that every reputable gun owner should be an NRA Member." A revised version of its traditional statement of purpose, emphasizing the use of arms for "pleasure and protection," was moved from prominence to the back pages of the publication.[75] By 1984, the mission statement had been further amended to explain that the NRA's main purpose was "to protect and defend the Constitution of the United States, especially with reference to the right of the citizen to acquire, possess, transport, carry, transfer ownership of and enjoy the right to use arms."[76] The group was no longer a quasi-governmental, military organization nor a government defender. It had become a government antagonist, political advocacy outfit dedicated to a single cause: gun rights. Within a decade, the group had become an integral part of the Republican Party, and it had set its sights on the federal government.

CHAPTER 6

An Organization of White Men

The state militia system was in disarray for most of the nineteenth century. From early on, military commanders recognized that citizen-soldiers who did not receive professional training, and were more interested in weapons and appearances than in soldiering, did not make for very good soldiers in battle. Yet, attempts to professionalize and reform the militia fell flat because citizen-soldiers had significant political capital and represented a substantial portion of the voting base. The militia acted as vote-aggregators and enforcers for political parties. Parties also recruited militia officers for local and state political office. Not surprisingly, the performance of the militia (National Guards) in the Civil War left a lot to be desired.

As I discussed in chapter 5, the NRA was founded after the Civil War by two Union officers, Col. William C. Church and Gen. George Wingate, as a military/patriotic organization with a mission to improve the marksmanship skills of the militia. Their goal was to improve the military preparedness of the state forces and draft-age civilians. At that time, the people who were eligible for the NRA's services were predominantly White men. Black men typically served in noncombat roles, and women—with few exceptions—were thought to have no role on the battlefield.

But it is not in irony that *NRA: An American Legend* describes the group as "diverse." This characterization may be a puzzling choice for any audience who understands diversity from the perspective of demographic characteristics like gender, race, or ethnicity. Indeed, the organization has a very different understanding of diversity, which it pursued doggedly to expand its market: diversity in weapons and weapons usage. The NRA has been very proud to have developed various sports and events, expanded the number and type of firearms used for competitions, provided services to hunters, and diversified its portfolio. Diversity—in weapons—came to the NRA lexicon long before the association became a gun rights group.[1]

When it comes to demographic makeup, the NRA was founded as an organization of White men with differing interests in firearms. The group mirrored the upper echelons of the military in its makeup and ideology. Given its origins in the officer corps of the citizen soldiery of the Civil War era, in the first several decades of its existence the group drew members from the military and often socially elite backgrounds. White men dominated the NRA leadership and membership, and participants in sponsored events were overwhelmingly White men. As in the militia musters of the early nineteenth century, African Americans and White women were a rarity as participants at NRA shooting competitions. When they were present, White women were in the audience cheering on their husbands and sons, while African Americans were most likely there as cleaners and servers.

The focus on White men has continued throughout the organization's history. The NRA's membership records are private and inaccessible. However, my analysis of the pictures of individuals that graced the cover of its magazines, *The American Rifleman* (1940–2020) and *America's 1st Freedom* (2001–2018) documents how rare has been the presence of White women and any people of color. Even in an era when minorities and women have achieved positions of prominence in politics, even among conservatives, such political figures are unlikely to grace the cover of NRA publications. The same is the case for the inner pages. My analysis of the pictorial content of *The American Rifleman* from 1960 to 2018 and *America's 1st Freedom* from 2000 to 2017 shows that pictures of White men predominate, while pictures of non-White people are exceedingly rare.

RACE IN NRA HISTORY

Since the early 2000s, the NRA has branded itself as the oldest and largest civil rights organization in the world.[2] In this story, which pits good and bad guys with guns against each other, the Ku Klux Klan was the nation's first "domestic terrorist organization" and the first "gun control organization."[3] The Klan's goal was "to undo the results of the Civil War by keeping blacks in a state of de facto slavery."[4] Here the Klan exists outside of any institutional context—the state, whether in the form of the law, law enforcement, or the justice system, is conspicuous in its absence. As the political theorist Corey Robin has argued in a different context, the NRA's Reconstruction and Jim Crow South—not to mention the country's other regions—is "Mad Max" territory where man kills man unconstrained by any moral or legal authority. This is not the South of Ida B. Wells, where lynchings were tacitly if not openly supported by "respectable" Whites, often in positions of authority, who justified such actions under the fig leaf of alleged Black rapes of White women.[5]

Opposite the Klan stood the NRA, a group "founded by Union officers who aimed to protect American liberty." According to this myth, the NRA was an egalitarian and inclusive organization. A key goal of its principals was to "prove to the world that free, armed black Americans possess the character, courage, and skill not only to be entitled to full legal civil rights but to be fully accepted in every social sphere."[6] According to the NRA leader Wayne LaPierre, "the NRA broke the 'color line' long before integration. Long before there were African American major league baseball or football players, there were tens of thousands of African American NRA members."[7] In other words, the modern NRA looks back and discovers an NRA that was at the forefront of racial integration in the depths of Jim Crow America. In some ways, it is as if the NRA was the Union Army itself.

This story is pure propaganda. The NRA was a product of the post-Reconstruction era—born out of the Union Army and committed to the Union, but without any commitment to abolition or Black civil rights. If anything, its principals viewed African Americans in stereotypically negative terms and were as impatient with Black demands for political rights as most White elites of the era—including military elites.[8] Far from championing Black political rights, the NRA and its leaders placed Confederate generals such as Robert E. Lee on an equal footing with Lincoln as "national heroes" and men of "respectability, courage, and unselfish patriotism."[9]

Pharcellus Church, the father of the NRA founder Col. William C. Church, was a Congregationalist minister and author. Rev. Church was sympathetic to abolitionism and a critic of the fugitive slave law of 1850.[10] But abolitionist politics was not his intellectual focus. Church's main concern was improving the finances of the Baptist Church by encouraging the benevolence of congregants.[11] Slavery concerned him primarily because it caused a rift within the transatlantic Evangelical Alliance, making his plans for establishing fundraising systems more challenging.[12]

Political rights for Black people and women were not among Col. Church's social causes. According to his biographer, although Church came to adulthood at the center of abolitionist activism in Boston, he did not approve of the movement. "A genuine colored man was something of a rarity," concluded the Colonel. For the conservative Church, attempts by "noisy advocates of emancipation" to swarm the local courthouse to free captured fugitives were inconsistent with the rule of law and should be discouraged.[13] In fact, William Church's position on abolitionism has more in common with the twentieth-century "law and order" ideology used to suppress Black activism than with civil rights advocacy. Col. Church was not a supporter of women's emancipation or the suffragist movement, either, as he confessed in an editorial essay for *The Galaxy*.[14]

Col. Church was a fervent believer in the Union, and before the war his preoccupation was with the preservation of the United States—"he never discussed the problem of the Negro," asserted his biographer.[15] During the war, Church rebuffed calls to publish articles against slavery and in favor of the recruitment of Black soldiers in the popular and influential *Army & Navy Journal* he edited. Yet, a year after the Emancipation Proclamation, he printed a short item that described the 20th Regiment United States Colored Troops as "Black warriors."[16] In 1886, he even asked that words such as "n*****" be banned from the Army's vocabulary. After the conclusion of the Civil War, he doubled down on his beliefs about slavery. "Slavery now is buried in a grave as deep as the grave of John Brown, whom, with short-[sighted] frenzy . . . [officials hanged] under State law against inciting insurrection, instead of under the greater laws of the Union which he had equally violated," Church wrote. In other words, John Brown's attack on Harper's Ferry in the name of abolition should have been punished with death. However, allowing the national government to try and convict Brown might have produced a sectional rapprochement, as the North would be complicit.[17]

After the Civil War, Church supported sectional reconciliation and the incorporation of former Confederates into Union institutions.[18] The sectional reconciliationist perspective as it developed after Reconstruction was heavily influenced by Southern sensibilities and especially by the "Lost Cause" narrative. It positioned the South as an honor-bound society of cavaliers and dames fighting for local democratic rights against a ruthless, inhuman, industrial North. The perceived urgent need to overcome the trauma of the Civil War and Reconstruction and reestablish the Union incentivized Northern and Southern elites to find common ground—a way to understand the experience that was agreeable to both sides. According to the historian David Blight, the myth of the "soldier's faith" became a cornerstone of reconciliation. This myth asserted that regardless of the cause they fought for, soldiers on both sides were valorous and deserved to be honored equally for their service. Reconciliation allowed the South to maintain the false premise that it fought for the principle of democratic self-governance or "states' rights" rather than for the preservation of slavery.[19]

The reconciliationist mind frame, especially the myth of the "soldier's faith," facilitated the NRA's overtures more broadly to Confederate officers and Southerners. Given its national ambitions, the association quickly invited Confederate leaders like General P. T. Beauregard, the commander who attacked Fort Sumter, and Major General Dabney Maury to be on the Board as founding members. In the early years, NRA matches were populated primarily by Northern rifle clubs and National Guard militia companies. Even after Reconstruction and into the early twentieth century,

White Southern members and teams were a rarity, possibly because of the cost associated with attending matches in New York and sectional animosity. However, by the early twentieth century, the NRA could claim clubs in all sections.[20]

At the same time, reconciliation enabled the North to sideline and suppress demands for Black political rights in the name of sectional unity—including demands for equality within the military services. By the turn of the century, the response to war trauma had become the triumphant resurgence of White supremacist "redemption."[21] Less than two decades later, President Woodrow Wilson—an admirer of the Confederacy—ordered the strict segregation of the federal workforce.

In the *Army & Navy Journal*, Church did not directly address slavery or Black voting rights. However, he did discuss Black rights in the context of Army service. His perspective would not place him in the civil rights pantheon. According to Church, White people believed that with the conclusion of the Civil War and Reconstruction, "great work was done," and they were "inclined to rest." The freeing of the slaves was as far as Col. Church was willing to go. However, Black advocates proposed that with "the physical freedom of the black man secured; it is now [time] to give him political freedom." The abolition of slavery had encouraged "the partisans of the African race" to "trumpet forth that their task is not yet accomplished." These claims presented a serious problem, according to Col. Church. If republican ideology was followed to its logical conclusion, Church warned, then Black soldiers—thirsty for recognition and equal political rights—would not accept being limited to labor service in the military. If Black men became voters, elected officials would have to address their other demands—including expectations to serve as equals in the military. Satisfying Black thirst for rights, "tickling Sambo's fancy, or his shins," was shrewd electoral politics, in Church's judgment. For office-seekers, "a vote is a vote"—but what could be the implications of such a strategy, Church asked? If Black men were to be elected to "civic office and honor," wouldn't "Sambo's" next step be a demand for "military rank and honor"?[22] The article's tone clarifies that the prospect of Black combat soldiers and officers was far from a welcome eventuality for Col. Church.

Fifty years later, the tone of the magazine had not changed. A 1918 article in Church's journal showed what White officers and the rank and file thought of Black soldiers. According to the piece, Black soldiers were incapable of understanding military hierarchy, believing that the highest rank in the service was that of "Sergeant." "Shu', cap'n," a Black soldier says. "I des a callin' you dat. I know you ain't no sah-junt, but hit do look lack'd d'big fokes up at Wash'n'ton would make a nice un a man as what you is a sah-junt." Another man is quoted as saying, "De boss man got two chickens on his shoulduhs."[23] As we will see, similar themes emerge from the NRA's *The American Rifleman.*

The NRA bylaws did not have race or gender stipulations, which the association has proudly presented as evidence of its "color blind" philosophy.[24] But given the organization's purpose and institutional connections, the NRA couldn't have, nor did it need such restrictions. The NRA was essentially a federal military contractor following federal rules. The federal government and the states no longer barred African American men from military service, but they did not encourage it, either. As discussed in earlier chapters, the US Army maintained a minimal number of segregated, under-resourced African American units. Most Black militia units were disbanded after the Dick Act as states declined to fund them. By the 1930s, even New York, a state with a long history of Black militia companies, maintained only one African American regiment. Local civilian rifle clubs could and did have racial criteria for membership.

As was typical of fraternal associations of this era, the NRA required sponsorship for new members by an existing member in good standing—a requirement that persisted through the 1960s. This stipulation was meant to ensure the membership's racial, class, and ideological purity: the men who were admitted to NRA rifle clubs were to be "reputable citizens," that is, White middle- and upper-middle-class individuals. In all likelihood, the few clubs that did include African American members were segregated Black rifle clubs such as the Circle X Club of Washington, DC. In any event, the NRA did not maintain records on its members' race and could not specify how many Black members it had, beyond saying that the number was very small—certainly not "tens of thousands," as LaPierre claimed. In 1964, at the height of the civil rights movement, press reports suggested there were sixteen Black rifle clubs across the country.[25] By contrast, there were thousands of White rifle clubs during this period.

NRA championships involved elite teams of officers rather than the rank and file; Black soldiers had few opportunities to participate in matches or the organization more broadly. There were very few Black Army regiments to begin with, and the Army did not train them as marksmen. It is thus no surprise that newspaper accounts suggest that African American participation in military shooting matches was rare. In fact, the national press covered two such cases in the first half of the twentieth century: the Army sent two Blacks and one Puerto Rican soldier to compete at the NRA's national matches at Sea Girt in 1906. In 1931, the Hawaiian National Guard team, which included Japanese, Chinese, and indigenous-heritage soldiers, caught the eye of the *New York Times* reporter writing on the national matches at Camp Perry.[26]

Black volunteers at the state level did participate in annual military training, however, and in some cases they participated in local or regional National Guard shooting competitions. Various state newspapers report African American soldiers participating and winning state or regional National Guard competitions. However, there is no other mention in the press that I could find of Black shooters at NRA-sponsored matches during the Jim Crow era. Where they existed, Black troops were primarily relegated to the back of parades and musters. They were designated for labor duty in war, as they were not viewed as fit for combat and certainly not for elite combat roles such as sharpshooting. White political and military leaders believed it neither necessary nor desirable for Black troops to bear arms or to participate in marksmanship practice.[27] Through the first half of the twentieth century, Black National Guard units, in states where they existed, were segregated in their annual training, typically following the White units, so many of their events involved Black troops exclusively. States invested very little in Black National Guard units, so it is unlikely that authorities would sponsor them to attend marksmanship competitions. From the Southern states' perspective, segregated local musters and parades within Black spaces were sufficient to quell Black demands and Northern criticism without incurring White anger. In any event, most Black volunteer companies were dismantled after 1903 with the federalization of the militia.[28]

GENDER IN NRA HISTORY

In much the same way that it did not have race restrictions, the NRA did not have gender stipulations in its bylaws. This lack of restrictions did not mean much in the context of the early twentieth century, except to twenty-first-century commentators and audiences who seek to create a usable history of the association consistent with today's egalitarian sensibilities. Neither the association nor its military sponsors ever thought that women would seek to become NRA members or event competitors. As the historian Laura Bowder shows, several late-nineteenth-century upper-class women did shoot. Hunting was a fashionable and appropriate sport for elite White women, and gun manufacturers even sought to develop firearms appropriate for women to use. Magazine ads from the era depict fashionably dressed women and even young girls with hunting rifles,[29] though these depictions are a far cry from the citizen-soldier model promoted for men. This continues to this day: rarely if ever are women portrayed as soldiers.

Until the 1960s, women were ubiquitous as audience members at NRA-sponsored championships, but were rarely present as shooters. Events organized exclusively for women were not part of the championship events. For example, at its early matches at Creedmoor, the NRA "entertained the ladies" by organizing amateur target-shooting events for them. Women were far more likely to be found at the "Ladies Luncheon" the NRA hosted for its leaders' spouses than at the range. In general, women's presence at such events was meant to add to men's enjoyment. As *Forest and Stream* magazine noted in 1910, "every day during the matches, hundreds of ladies lend their presence to make the scene interesting and agreeable."[30] As a member's spouse noted in 1951, "the convention was a huge success as far as the ladies were concerned. I particularly liked the luncheons being for men and women together—it made for better mixing." These comments suggest that other events were gender-segregated.[31]

NRA bylaws did not restrict participation to men, not because the organization was egalitarian, but because the idea of a woman rifleman was outside the leadership's worldview—especially since most NRA leaders came from the national and state military. After all, in its earliest reports, the association noted that its goal was to afford the opportunity to "the male citizen fit for military service [to receive] at least part of the training which is necessary for war."[32] Through World War II, they wanted to train citizen-soldiers and "riflemen," not hunters; women were neither citizens (in terms of political rights, not until 1920) nor soldiers. Neither the Army nor the National Guard recruited women in their combat units, so military teams by definition did not include women.

As a result, the few women who competed in NRA-sponsored championships were civilians who challenged the established norms. Some were performers who worked fairs, in the vein of Annie Oakley; others were university students who became interested in shooting sports and forced their way onto all-male teams. Many came from families where hunting and shooting were part of the culture. The women who participated in formal competitions against men were few and far between. They included: Elizabeth ("Plinky") Servaty-Toepperwein, who competed in the 1906 Annual Matches; Gloria Jacobs, a world champion in pistol shooting, of whom gun ads said, "this little lady can handle a Colt like nobody's business";[33] and skeet shooting champion Alice Bull, who in 1949 became the first woman on the NRA Board of Directors and in the 1970s served on the NBPRP.[34] Elsewhere, women champions were described as "attractive"—an adjective never used to describe men.[35] According to one 1953 column, women shooters were "fugitives from the bridge club" and "among the smartest looking. . . . Each is a living example of what the well-dressed woman pistol shot is wearing this season."[36] Neither "citizen" nor "soldier," the idle, upper-middle-class homemaker was the NRA's woman of the era.

An apt illustration of the disconnect between the NRA's ascriptive republican ideology and women's participation in shooting sports is the case of the first woman ever to compete in an NRA-sponsored match: the aforementioned "Plinky" Servaty-Toepperwein. *NRA: An American Legend* dedicated an entire page titled "Breaking the Gender Barrier" to Toepperwein, complete with a large photograph. The association presents Plinky as a prime example of the group's gender-egalitarian roots and inclusivity. But in reality, she is the exception that proves the rule.

In 1906, Mrs. Toepperwein, a professional shooting performer working in county fairs with her husband Adolph, applied to compete in an NRA-sponsored civilian match. Although the organizers initially sought to exclude her, the bylaws did not have a gender requirement for participation. Not only did Mrs. Toepperwein participate in the match; she qualified for a medal. Her victory created significant confusion for the association and the War Department, highlighting that neither had expected women to compete. Specifically, competition rules stipulated that all those who met qualification standards would have their names sent to the War Department as potential candidates for the National Guard. This was because both the NRA and the military authorities viewed these matches as recruitment opportunities for the services. Yet only men were eligible to volunteer for the militia or the Army. As the *Trenton Times* noted, "authorities are puzzled what to do in the case of Mrs. Toepperwein."[37] Needless to say, a citizen-soldier she did not become.

RACE AND GENDER IN *THE AMERICAN RIFLEMAN*

In the NRA universe, minority men and especially African Americans are exceedingly rare. So are women—even White women. Non-White women are practically nonexistent. The magazine is not meant for them, and that is evident in the pictorial content and the content of the articles. I coded the cover art of 953 issues of *The American Rifleman* spanning the period from 1940 to 2020.[38] I also coded the covers of *America's 1st Freedom* from its first circulation in 2000 to 2019. The cover of the magazine showcases what the publication is about and invites readers to open it up and explore. Therefore, what is on the cover is highly suggestive of the organization's identity and intended readership.

A total of 356 covers of *The American Rifleman* (37 percent) included pictures of people. Most of the other covers just showed firearms. Especially in the new century, most covers have displayed the latest handguns and assault rifles. A similar proportion of *America's 1st Freedom* (38 percent) covers include pictures or cartoons of people. For *The American Rifleman*, most of the covers that displayed people depicted archetypal NRA members: soldiers, hunters, and sportsmen. Some covers are intergenerational, depicting fathers (or grandfathers) hunting or shooting with their sons or grandsons. There are little Boy Scouts in the woods. Some covers portray gun professionals, such as gunsmiths. There are also plenty of historical figures that the NRA venerates: George Washington, Thomas Jefferson, Theodore Roosevelt, Ulysses Grant, and other presidents have graced many a cover. The images of American presidents, both historical (e.g., Thomas Jefferson, Theodore Roosevelt) and contemporary (e.g., Ronald Reagan, who is featured on the cover three times, twice with NRA leaders; or more recently, Donald Trump), serve to create cognitive and affective bridges between notions of male political authority, power, republican citizenship, and the NRA.

Some covers have a political focus; this is especially the case since the 1990s. Political portraits include both NRA leaders such as Wayne LaPierre or Charlton Heston, and NRA foes such as various Democratic elected officials. Typical of emotional appeals, the NRA uses positive depictions of in-group leaders to inspire and generate enthusiasm, and negative portrayals of its "enemies" to activate threat and anger and to encourage political action. Most *America's 1st Freedom* covers are explicitly political, portraying either the NRA's supporters or its foes. Supporters are depicted positively, in good lighting. Foes typically look angry, threatening, or hysterical. Red or dark filters are often applied to the foes' pictures to make them look scarier.

A staggering 86 percent of *The American Rifleman* covers that show people are pictures of White men. Only 17 convers (5 percent) show non-White men. These include two covers showing Native American chiefs in traditional headgear. The first ever picture of a Black man on the cover is a Vietnam soldier in May 1985. Then in September 1997, a Black boy is included in an ensemble picture of kids surrounding Charlton Heston. Not until November 2006 did *The American Rifleman* feature a Black politician on its cover: a portrait of ranking Democratic Representative John Conyers along with pictures of then House Minority Leader Nancy Pelosi, Senator Ted Kennedy, and Senator Hillary Clinton. During the Obama years, the magazine featured the country's first Black president on its cover six times. All six show Obama angry or scowling, projecting negative emotions. Figure 6.1a shows the number of covers in each decade that depict White or non-White men in *The American Rifleman*. Figure 6.1b contains

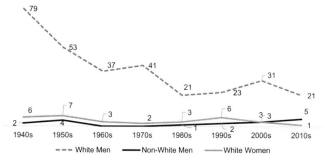

Figure 6.1a *The American Rifleman* covers per decade depicting White men, non-White men, or White women (1940–2020).

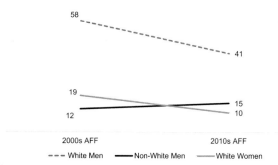

Figure 6.1b *America's 1st Freedom* covers per decade depicting White men, non-White men, or White women (2001–2018).

the same information for *America's 1st Freedom*. The number of covers depicting White men declined significantly after the 1950s, but this was not because the magazine used pictures of other groups. Especially in the last two decades, it simply switched to pictures of firearms. The number of covers in each decade that showed non-White men is negligible.

More *America's 1st Freedom* covers than those of *The American Rifleman* show non-White men. Specifically, of those covers that include pictures or caricatures of people, 62 percent show White men and 17 percent show non-White men. During the first decade of the magazine's publication, there were 12 covers that depicted non-White men. Between 2010 and 2018, there were 15 such covers. Overall, for every 4 covers showing the picture of a White man, there is 1 showing a non-White man.

There is also more differentiation in positive and negative depictions of both non-White and White men. This differentiation aligns with the person's position on gun rights. The non-White men who are depicted in positive light on these covers are NRA supporters: Sheriff David Clarke, the gun activist Colion Noir, the civil rights activist Roy Innis (an NRA Board member), or Otis McDonald, the gun owner defendant in the Supreme Court case that bears his name. Interestingly, Colion Noir is referenced as "urban gun enthusiast," which suggests the conflation of urban and Black.[39] I did not locate any White NRA supporters described as "urban." Other pictures are typically of non-White police officers. Most negative depictions of non-White individuals are of President Obama and other Black Democrats, such as Conyers or Eric Holder. These men are typically shown scowling and angry. These data are suggestive about the identity of the organization and its audience, and reflect how the NRA sees itself and the kind of image it seeks to project to the world.

Between 1940 and 2020, White women have been on the cover of *The American Rifleman* a total of 31 times, or 6 percent of the total (fig. 6.1a). During this entire period, only two covers have included non-White women. In the 1940s, the cover included female hunters and shooters. In the 1960s, the three covers that showed women include a shooting champion who was also a nurse in the Air Force,[40] an unnamed White woman attending an exhibit at the NRA annual meetings, and a teenage skeet champion.[41] In the 1970s, there were two covers, one depicting the "Ladies at Camp Perry," all-female shooting teams participating in the championships, and another showing a collegiate champion. Three covers in the 1980s included women; two of them showed the American 1984 Olympic shooting medalists, men and women, one of them at the Games and the other at the White House. The third was of a woman shooting champion.[42]

The presence of women on the cover of the magazine changed qualitatively and quantitatively in the 1990s as the NRA shifted its dominant focus to partisan politics. One cover, in March 1997, continued the tradition of showcasing women shooting champions. A July 1997 cover depicted the NRA's new leadership, photographed in the shadow of the Capitol building; the six-person team includes four White men and two White women. However, the remaining covers convey direct political messaging.[43]

In April 1993, the magazine cover featured a picture of a racially diverse set of gun owners, both men and women, draped in the American flag and portrayed in the shadow of the iconic colonial minuteman. The image draws on martial republican ideology, linking the NRA's past and present. The picture suggests that the organization's members, who now come from all groups, continue the tradition of the citizen-soldier, and thus have a duty to remain vigilant against political corruption. A similar point is conveyed in the September 1997 cover. The image features then NRA Vice President Charlton Heston surrounded by a racially diverse group of young children, including two girls, under the caption: "Are Gun Rights Lost on

Our Kids?" The description of the cover picture notes: "will you let the Bill of Rights and our legacy of Freedom be squandered or will you stand shoulder to shoulder with NRA First Vice President Charlton Heston . . . to preserve it?" As in the earlier cover, the organization draws on republican themes to suggest that NRA members are the guardians of American values and freedom, and they have a duty to preserve "gun rights," a constitutive part of American citizenship, for the benefit of the next generation.[44]

The two remaining covers that depict women are explicitly partisan and visually underscore that women who oppose the NRA are a serious threat to the organization and to good citizenship. In October 1993, as Congress debated gun control legislation, the NRA's publication featured a black cover, a blood-red font, and distorted, unflattering, angry, and somewhat threatening pictures of six political opponents: Attorney General Janet Reno, the gun control activist Sarah Brady, FBI Director Louis Freeh, Rep. Chuck Schumer (D-NY), and Senator Howard Metzenbaum (D-OH), surrounding the picture of President Bill Clinton. "We warned you that they are coming, and they are here," proclaims the title. A few months later, in January 1994, another overwhelming cover features color-highlighted cutouts of newspaper lead articles about gun control superimposed on a picture of Hillary Clinton. The preposterous title reads: "Hillary's Plan to Fund Healthcare: Tax Guns."[45]

In the first eighteen years of the twenty-first century, *The American Rifleman* featured women on the cover only four times. One is a return to the magazine's early themes of sports, and it features a White father with his three children, two girls and one boy, all in camouflage and holding shotguns. But even in this more old-fashioned depiction the caption is political: "put a little freedom under their tree," the title reads. A second is a picture of NRA Vice President Sandy Forman, pistol in hand. The only other portrayal is explicitly political. Preparing NRA members to vote in the 2006 midterm elections, the November issue is once again the black background with four angry, distorted pictures of Democratic leaders: Senator Ted Kennedy (D-MA) and Rep. John Conyers (D-MI), bookended by pictures of a very angry Hillary Clinton and a vexed Nancy Pelosi. The caption reads: "Election Day 2006: This is the opportunity we've been waiting for, [says] Sarah Brady."[46] In November 2018, the cover is the Statue of Liberty under water under the title: "Your vote is all that prevents the socialist wave."

As the analysis of *The American Rifleman*'s covers suggests, the NRA did not consider women part of its core audience. Women were featured on covers as athletes and shooting champions. But the citizen-soldier of the NRA's worldview has never been a woman. The sole female military officer to have graced the cover between 1960 and 2018, Air Force Lt. Gail Liberty, was depicted in her role as a shooting champion—a sportswoman in a competition setting—not in her political role as an Air Force medical officer serving her country.[47] Even as women became an ever-larger proportion of the armed forces, the NRA never shifted its perspective to include them in its world.

In the two instances where women are portrayed in a political context, one a cover of adults in 1993 and the other of kids in 1997, women are not the protagonists. They are part of an assemblage added in an ascriptive republican context meant to apply to men. In the few covers—all since the 1990s—where women are depicted in an explicitly political role, as legislators or policy advocates (as in the case of Sarah Brady or Hillary Clinton who did not hold elected office at the time of either of the covers that featured her), they are the villains and not the heroes. These women represent political corruption, the antithesis of virtue. They are said to be motivated by private gain, and to be acting against the best interests of the Republic, seeking to curtail the citizens' liberty. But even in this context, except for the one depiction of Hillary in the 1990s, women are not the protagonists. They are part of a cast of foes, the "anti-gunners."

The covers of *America's 1st Freedom* suggest a similar pattern. The ratio of men to women on the cover is better than it is in *The American Rifleman* (about 4 to 1). However, an overwhelming number of these depictions are of female politicians who oppose gun rights. These include several pictures of Hillary Clinton, Nancy Pelosi, and Dianne Feinstein. Most of these portrayals are stereotypically negative. The women are portrayed as hysterical: mouths open, eyes bulging—a far cry from the rational commonsensical republican citizen-soldier. It is noteworthy that in the twenty-first century especially, the NRA did not lack prominent pro-gun politicians: Sarah Palin, Joni Ernst, Marsha Blackburn, and a host of Congressional candidates (such as Lauren Boebert and Marjorie Taylor Greene) in recent cycles have supported gun rights. In fact, because of the partisan realignment that has taken place in the political elites and the electorate, and the resulting partisan polarization, it is virtually impossible for a Republican—man or woman—who does not express support for gun rights to be elected today. Sarah Palin, an NRA life member and a famously armed "mama bear" who shot deer from helicopters, never graced the cover of either magazine. Yet, according to the NRA, Palin had "star power" and her speech accepting her nomination as candidate for vice president attracted more viewers than Barack Obama's acceptance speech (which is not true).[48] The pro-gun woman that *America's 1st Freedom* has featured twice on the cover is NRA spokeswoman Dana Loesch, looking defiant.

Interestingly, *America's 1st Freedom* has featured non-White women on the cover. However, these are meant to be warnings: a Black gun-owning single mother imprisoned in New Jersey, allegedly because of her gun;[49] a Black reporter who allegedly lost her job because she criticized a superior who supported gun control; or a starving African woman, victim of civil war and genocide on that continent.[50] These stories seek to blend two NRA narratives that have become more prominent in the twenty-first century: women as victims of social violence and crime, and gun rights as "civil rights." I will address both in more detail in a later chapter.

The cover of the magazine is the most prominent signal to the audience about the organization's identity. However, it could be that the NRA reserves internal content for non-White audiences. Regardless of what is reflected on the cover, the pages of the publication may tell a different story. I address this by counting the number of the pictures (photographs, sketches, or cartoons) of White and non-White men and women in the magazine itself (figs. 6.2a and b).

My collection includes all issues of *The American Rifleman* from January 1960 to December 2018. For each issue of this magazine, I have retained articles that have political content or discuss the organization itself. I did not include in my collection pages that had technical articles about guns, gun ads, or classified ads. As a result, the measure undercounts the number of pictures of White men. For each issue, I created a standardized measure by dividing the number of relevant pictures by the number of pages included in my collection for that issue. I have also copied all *America's 1st Freedom* issues from 2001 to 2017 in their entirety. I created per-page averages for each year and for each decade. Figure 6.2 shows the per-page average number of pictures of White men, White women, and non-White people for

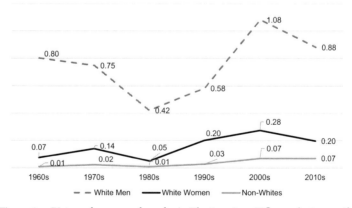

Figure 6.2a Pictures by race and gender in *The American Rifleman* (1960–2018).

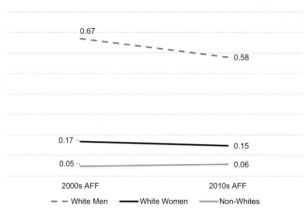

Figure 6.2b Pictures by race and gender in *America's 1st Freedom* (2001–2017).

each decade. In the 1960s and 1970s, White men are depicted on four out of every five pages in *The American Rifleman*. The number drops to about every other page in the 1980s and 1990s, but it climbs to almost one per page in the 2000s and 2010s. By contrast, White women were a rare sight from the 1960s through the 1980s. Pictures of White women increased to about one every five pages in the 1990s and have remained at this higher level since. Finally, my measure suggests that pictures of non-White people have been very rare across this period. The pattern is similar for *America's 1st Freedom*: pictures of White men appear on every other page, while White women appear once every six pages. Non-White people are rare even in recent years (fig. 6.2b).

It is not only in pictures that the NRA projects its ascriptive republican ideology. As I will discuss in chapters 7 and 8, the narratives it uses to describe the political world—its virtuous riflemen and the corrupt extremists and criminals—betray the racialized and gendered lenses through which the association perceives the world.

[CHAPTER 7]

Political Virtue

As I outlined in chapter 1, ascriptive republican narratives are based on the related notion pairs of political virtue/corruption and freedom/slavery. I identify three interrelated ascriptive republican narratives in the American experience: the early Republic narrative, the post–Civil War narrative, and the late-twentieth-century modern NRA narrative. All three associate the bearing of arms and political participation with political virtue. Yet they differ in how they define the agents of virtue, their main traits, and their goals. They also differ in whether they view the possession of firearms as *instrumental* for virtue because arms facilitate military preparedness, or as *intrinsic* to virtue in that material possession itself is evidence of a virtuous citizen. These differences reflect the NRA's ideological adaptation to a new political and institutional environment.

Political virtue was associated with mandatory military service in the early Republic. The bearing of arms was thought to encourage the development of political virtue and men's desire for freedom. Early Americans associated volunteer service in a standing army with corruption because, to them, soldiers who fought wars for pay had no allegiance to the Republic. However, by the time of the Civil War, American military institutions had recognized the inefficiency of conscription and had transitioned to voluntarism. In response, republican ideology had come to redefine voluntarism as politically virtuous. Now it was the possession of arms and marksmanship training in private life rather than military service alone that facilitated the development of political virtue as it morally and physically prepared men to volunteer for service.

By 1871, when William C. Church and George Wingate signed the NRA's incorporation documents, Americans had accepted that conscription was not an effective way to organize the country's defensive forces, and state militia had long since turned to volunteers. Military theory had changed as well. The lesson of the Civil War was that aimed fire—marksmanship—

was an essential skill for modern soldiers. The emphasis on marksmanship over team skills fit well with the NRA's new voluntaristic republican model. As a result, the symbol of political virtue was no longer the conscript militiaman—the colonial citizen-soldier—but the "riflemen." Riflemen were an elite group of soldiers. Not just any enlisted man could achieve that distinction. At the same time, riflemen could be draft-age civilians who developed the skills necessary for political virtue in the private domain. Therefore, the NRA narrative decoupled political virtue from military service and situated its origins in the private rather than the public realm. Engagement with arms was a prerequisite for the development of political virtue. Still, this engagement could occur in the hunt or at the range, providing for the family rather than necessarily serving the state. Even if the virtuous rifleman was not a soldier, he was committed to defending constituted authority—he was a government man.

In addition to military institutions, the post–Civil War era brought fundamental changes to American politics and society. As the ink was drying on the NRA's incorporation, Congress was engaged in Radical Reconstruction, a project meant to recognize formerly enslaved people's social and political equality in the South and assist in their integration into American society. At the same time, Southern apologists were beginning a project to transform the memory of the Civil War and forge sectional reconciliation on a foundation of White supremacy. Military leaders from both sides played a key role in sectional reconciliation. As a product of the military establishment, the NRA supported this project by inviting Southern military leaders to its Board of Directors. At a time when African American men were admitted into military service (albeit not in combat units), the elite "rifleman" served to redraw the boundaries of political virtue in the narrative to exclude Black soldiers.

In the late twentieth century, after the NRA severed its ties to the federal government and lost its federal subsidy and exclusive access to free or discounted firearms and ammunition, the group's orientation changed, and so did its ascriptive republican narrative. No longer tethered to military preparedness, the NRA focused on the consumer market. As a result, it pursued a new definition of the virtuous citizen. The new citizen-soldier was neither the colonial minuteman nor the rifleman. In the contemporary narrative, the NRA assigns political virtue to all citizens committed to the cause of gun rights; gun owners—regardless of skill—are the vanguard of the virtuous. Ironically, more than half of gun owners admit to very little knowledge of firearms but that is no barrier for the NRA.[1] Military service or preparedness is no longer deemed necessary for the development of

TABLE 7.1. Virtue Ascriptive Republican Narratives

	Sources of Virtue	Agents of Virtue	Traits of the Virtuous
Republicanism of the Early Republic	Mandatory military training (public domain) (arms *instrumental*)	Citizen-soldiers	Dedication to the common good Common sense (reason) Moral and martial readiness
Early NRA Republicanism (1871–1960s)	Rifle training as a sport (private domain) Volunteer military service (arms *instrumental*)	Riflemen	Dedication to the common good Common sense (reason) Moral and martial readiness Political readiness
Late NRA Republicanism (1990s–present)	Political activism on behalf of gun rights and gun ownership (arms *intrinsic*)	Gun owners	Dedication to gun rights (stand-in for common good) Common sense (reason) Political readiness

political virtue. Instead, the act of purchasing and owning a firearm and active political support for gun rights are sufficient to confer political virtue on a citizen and make him "a good guy with a gun." In this sense, firearms have become *intrinsic* to virtue rather than instruments for the development of political virtue. Table 7.1 tracks the evolution of political virtue across the three ascriptive republican narratives.

FROM CITIZEN-SOLDIER TO RIFLEMAN

American republican tracts of the Revolutionary era attributed virtue to the citizen-soldier because he prepared for war in times of peace. The citizen-soldier had a civic obligation to serve the country at arms and to engage in regular military training to prepare for war in times of peace. Military preparedness was essential for the development of political virtue because it cultivated personality traits necessary for both war and politics. Through training at arms, the citizen-soldier developed discipline, independence, and cold reason or "common sense," all of which helped him be a good soldier in war and recognize and defend the public good in politics. Through training at arms, (White) Americans remained a free people.

The early NRA narrative placed the "rifleman" rather than the "citizen-soldier" at the center of its republican vision of politics. Although both constructions relate to the military, the two are not the same. Traditionally, military forces were separated into infantry, artillery, cavalry, and armored forces. Infantry forces were divided into heavy infantry (heavily armed and armored soldiers who fought in line formation) and light infantry (or "rifle-men" who fought in looser formation). After the Napoleonic Wars, the light infantry became popular as more accurate and easier-to-use firearms entered the market.[2] These "riflemen" were elite units—similar to what today we call "special forces"—as they required specialized and intensive marksmanship training. They were expert marksmen who could take out enemy targets from long distances.

The revolutionary citizen-soldier ideal was a relatively more egalitarian and inclusive construct than the "rifleman" because it potentially included all White male citizens even as it excluded all women and Black men. In this narrative, the development of political virtue was not tied to rank or position within the military; it was one's level of preparedness and one's willingness to sacrifice his life that determined his political virtue and thus his fitness for political rights. White men who were excluded from political membership but who served the country in war could and did employ the citizen-soldier ideal to justify their claims to political inclusion. African American men also used their service in war to argue that they deserved political rights.

The early NRA narrative limited political virtue and thus moral deservingness for citizenship to only "riflemen." Through the trope of the rifleman, the NRA attempted to redefine and reclaim for White men the definition of the politically virtuous citizen, which was threatened by the Reconstruction Amendments. The image of the rifleman operated as a racialized trope that invoked middle-class White male respectability. By linking political virtue exclusively with expert marksmanship—a skill that was not emphasized in the training of most soldiers and was available to few Black recruits—and de-emphasizing all other aspects of military training, the association in effect claimed that riflemen were more virtuous or more likely to develop virtue than other soldiers. Thus, the riflemen's political preferences should be given greater weight.

According to *The American Rifleman*, "it is, of course, generally recognized that the man with the rifle is still the deciding element [in war]"—the truly virtuous man.[3] No other soldier could "supersede the group of good marksmen trained not to dwell upon the aim—capable of that almost instantaneous cooperation between hand and eye which is, in point of fact, the secret of success."[4] No support personnel, no truck driver, cook, or logistics expert—jobs that African American soldiers may have had—could ever qualify as a "rifleman." It was America's riflemen, not other soldiers or citizens, who had "steady hands" with firearms and politics. They were "willing to sacrifice personal fortunes," "give their lives," and even be slandered by "political enemies" in service to the Republic.[5]

FROM RIFLEMAN TO GUN OWNER

As the NRA changed from a political insider to a partisan outsider organization committed to the cause of elevating gun rights to "America's 1st Freedom," its definition of the virtuous citizen also changed to accommodate the new conditions. Through the 1960s, the virtuous citizens consisted of the "riflemen"—men who engaged in private-domain gun training, shooting sports, and hunting. Through such activities, they developed the technical skills, discipline, independence, and patriotism to be ready for military service when the country demanded their sacrifice. However, several developments, both within the NRA and within American politics and society more broadly, contributed to a redefinition of the class of virtuous citizens.

The 1977 "Cincinnati Revolt"—the hard-liner takeover of the NRA—accelerated a process that began in the 1960s and culminated in the 1990s. The association severed its links with the US military establishment and the federal government in terms of leadership and finances. The era of mass military mobilization ended with Vietnam. Military technology, political experience, and ideology made mass military commitments undesirable. America's military entanglements also indirectly contributed to the shift in the narrative from military preparedness to political vigilance. Much as World War II elevated the American GI to a hero on the side of democracy, the war in Vietnam dimmed the luster of "the rifleman," as many civilians and veterans became disillusioned with the mission and the way the US government handled the conflict.[6] The end of the Cold War in the late 1980s produced a generalized euphoria and a broad consensus that liberal democracy had won the day.[7] At the end of history, there was less need for "riflemen," or so it seemed.

In the last quarter of the twentieth century, militarism and mass mobilization ended, but violent crime rose. Civilians were more likely to be attracted to firearms as a means of self-defense than for reasons of military preparedness. These developments meant that the NRA came to think of its audience primarily as "citizen-protectors,"[8] defenders of the family and the community from crime, rather than as citizen-soldiers committed to military readiness. This change in focus freed the association from the construct of the rifleman as soldier-in-waiting and enabled it to reach out to the broader public based on nonmilitary appeals and without the restriction of referrals and loyalty pledges. By 2000, a credit card was the only precondition for membership. As the organization liberalized its membership criteria, it also opened the narrative boundaries of membership in the category of virtuous citizen.

The gun owner became the NRA's new citizen-soldier. The consumer act of legally purchasing a firearm was now sufficient to elevate individuals to enlightened armed citizens. "NRA members are *consumers*, whether they are collectors, shooters, hunters, competitors, or simply purchase a firearm for defense of their homes," asserted *NRA: An American Legend*.[9] Gun purchasers, using their credit card at Walmart—not riflemen trained at the range—were the new virtuous citizen-soldiers defending American democratic principles. They "were the catalyst," the "heart" of "a reborn" movement whose main goal was to expand the ranks of gun owners by preventing government regulation of the sale and purchase of the vast majority of firearms.[10] The NRA became "the leaders of our freedom movement" who helped "millions of gun owners across the nation ma[ke] their voices heard," and in the process "changed the history and course of the nation." These gun owners had "shake[n] off the ancient yoke of vassals and serfs" and asserted their rights against politically corrupt elites.[11]

The contemporary gun rights narrative has decoupled gun ownership from military service and any form of formal firearms training, including safe handling practices. In this view, government-mandated safety training is an unnecessary burden, comparable to government-compelled speech. Mandatory safety training is harmful because it has the "potential to disenfranchise citizens from a civil right, which the Constitution guarantees 'shall not be infringed.'" Citizens may be forced to "spend money and time" that "they may not have . . . to exercise a right." Gun safety training is tantamount to requiring "a class in civics and current events before being licensed to vote"—an onerous requirement that harkens back to discriminatory literacy tests.[12]

Thus, no training of any kind is necessary to join the virtuous. In fact, the association strongly resisted legislation that would require gun purchasers to learn how to use and store their firearms or would mandate safe storage practices.[13] In the NRA's view, responsible citizens could determine for themselves what practices were better suited to their needs. Furthermore, a loaded weapon could be a better choice when facing an intruder, even for children.[14] According to the NRA's Wayne LaPierre, security devices could create a moral hazard, since they could make parents less vigilant and less willing to model proper gun behavior for their kids. Additionally, he argued, "While people with a headache usually have some margin of time to struggle with the top of the aspirin bottle, people confronting a burglar cannot request a time-out. In short, the federal government has not yet been able to persuade the 'National Association of Home Burglars' to sign a side agreement giving an extra five minutes warning to victims—time for residents to remove trigger locks."[15] Epidemiological studies suggest that many gun owners, including parents of young children, may have internalized this laissez-faire approach to gun safety to great human cost.[16] The contemporary virtuous, it seems, no longer need to spend time at the range. Time spent at the gun dealer is sufficient.

DECOUPLING POLITICAL VIRTUE
FROM MILITARY SERVICE

Unlike the narrative of the early Republic, which associated political virtue with participation in military service, the NRA narrative hinged political virtue on skill as a rifle shooter. This association of patriotism with marksmanship decoupled political virtue from military service altogether, and its reimagining of the source of political virtue allowed the NRA to stretch and shrink the boundaries of virtue simultaneously in racialized directions.

A "rifleman" was not necessarily a serviceman in the NRA's world. As long as they were proficient marksmen, *civilian* men (not women) also qualified as "riflemen" from the NRA's standpoint, and so could be counted as virtuous citizens. Therefore, military service was not necessary for the development of political virtue. According to the group, marksmanship alone—not other forms of military training, as was the case with the republicanism of the Revolution—was primarily responsible for developing self-discipline, independence, bravery, and unemotional reason: the traits that led citizens to recognize the public good and commit to it.[17]

Political virtue could be developed through training in marksmanship as a civilian, even by men who never enlisted. Target shooting fostered "the habits of self-discipline, initiative, and attention to detail," which were the foundation of good citizenship.[18] Shooting instilled dispassionate reason, which was necessary to the soldier and the political member—the citizen. Shooters learned to calmly evaluate prevailing conditions and estimate risks, costs, and benefits before they pulled the trigger. Shooting "molds people into better sportsmen and better citizens."[19] Thus civilian shooters and especially the association's members were among the country's most virtuous men. These men would make virtuous soldiers if the country called on them.

Military service was also not sufficient for the development of patriotism. Marksmanship, not soldiering, was the critical determinant of political virtue, but not every soldier was a marksman. Servicemen in positions that did not require marksmanship did not necessarily become as virtuous as riflemen, in either war or politics. Mastering military technology was insufficient to instill political virtue in "Johnny Jones," the average citizen-soldier.[20] Even infantry tactics that required firearms, but taught line formation and "firepower" (massed fire), were suspect in their ability to instill political virtue. "Heart and ability" had to be complemented by skill "on the range or in the hunting field."[21] Only a "beautiful, precise human machine," an expert rifleman, could achieve the polity's objectives in war and peace.[22]

Men who lacked shooting experience as citizens were unlikely to make disciplined and virtuous soldiers. Bad shooters were likely to engage in "disorderly practices." Across all cases of "drunkenness" and AWOL soldiers he came across, one Army officer told *The American Rifleman*, "not one of the men . . . has been a good rifle shot nor was at all interested in rifle shooting."[23] Such poorly trained recruits were a danger to themselves and the nation, unlikely to "live long enough" to learn "the true capabilities of his rifle and its value when properly used."[24]

Even in World War II, the association doubled down on its ideology. Military technology had changed radically by 1940, and so had the organization of the American forces. But the NRA continued to insist that both war and politics needed civilian marksmen. Rather than a relic of the nineteenth century, the organization posited that marksmanship was vital, as it changed "the outcome of wars."[25] The idea that war would be decided by technological advantage and logistics—operations that necessitate teamwork and skills—was "absurd" to *The American Rifleman*. "Fire-superiority depend[s] upon a rifle that is inherently accurate, handled by a man who has been thoroughly trained in the principles of accurate individual marksmanship," the association assured its members.[26] "Rifle training," the NRA asserted, "is more important than ever . . . not only from the military angle but from the standpoint of good citizenship in peace as well as war."[27] To the NRA and its network of rifle clubs fell "the responsibility of giving Johnny Jones, the grocer's clerk, about to be a soldier, a real chance [to become] a first-class fighting man."[28]

Through the decoupling of military service and political virtue, the NRA created four groups of people. First were military-trained marksmen—a group consisting almost exclusively of White men—who were virtuous but few, since the military didn't emphasize marksmanship for all classes of soldiers. Second were civilian marksmen—an equally White category—who would be counted on to join the military in times of war and were numerous and virtuous.[29] The third group, soldiers who were not marksmen—a category that included most African Americans in the services—could be virtuous, but their patriotism as reflected in their rifle skills was not of the caliber of the marksman. Some were not virtuous at all, and their behavior veered toward criminality.[30] Finally, the general population included people who were not engaged in shooting sports and whose political virtue varied. A cartoon from the December 1944 issue of *The American Rifleman*

"Sho', Sarge, Ah tol' dem strangers Ah's wuhkin' on a secret weapon. Tol' 'em de gawds own truff, too! Dis baby sho' is a mystery t' me!"

Figure 7.1 Black men in the military, *The American Rifleman*, December 1944, 15.

(fig. 7.1) depicts how the NRA perceived Black soldiers: uncouth, unintelligent, and incapable of learning how to shoot a rifle. In other words, they were thought to be incapable of developing political virtue. "Dis baby [the rifle] sho' is a mystery t' me," says the Black soldier to his White superior, using a derogatorily stereotypical Black Southern dialect.

FIREARMS IN THE PRIVATE DOMAIN AS A SOURCE OF VIRTUE

The NRA rejected the early American republican notion that political virtue developed through military service, suggesting that such service was neither necessary nor sufficient to instill patriotism in men. "Intimacy" with firearms is what contributed to political virtue. Most men developed this familiarity in the nonpolitical, private sphere. Early Americans did not win their independence and organize a democratic society because they developed political virtue through conscript service. Instead, they were virtuous because they were intimately acquainted with firearms through private pursuits.[31]

The NRA insisted that people learn to use and appreciate arms as tools of everyday life. The knowledge to handle them properly and the skill to use them efficiently were "part of everyone's upbringing."[32] America's men used firearms to feed and protect their families and to shoot for recreation and sport in their private lives. Hunting for food or trade instilled independence and self-reliance. At the same time, shooting for sport enhanced a man's ability to protect his family from harm and fostered a sense of social responsibility to others. Both activities taught discipline and unemotional, rational thought—or common sense. By encouraging these traits in men, these activities imparted political virtue.

The Revolution "was won by the gun in the home and the ability of the homeowner to use it."[33] These "ordinary citizens" had "an intimate knowledge of firearms gained through the use of personal weapons," but they were not "soldiers by profession," only "from necessity."[34] In this myth, revolutionary militiamen were neither conscripts nor members of the standing army. They were volunteers who decided to serve when the country needed them. Similarly, in the NRA's narrative, the West was won not because of the involvement of the US Army,[35] but because of the White man's facility with the rifle, his ability to deliver "strong medicine" and "kill Indians like there would be no tomorrow." The orchestrated campaign to exterminate the buffalo brought "the Redman to heel." As *The American Rifleman* tells the story, after one such demonstration of skill and prowess with rifles, Indians returned to their village and, in submission, "respectfully raised a U.S. flag that had been given to them."[36]

Ignoring the long history of conscription in colonial America and the early Republic, the NRA insisted that the heroes of the Revolution were "hunters" first and then "soldiers." This myth contradicts historical reality on multiple levels. First, it suggests that the colonial militiamen were generally effective and capable soldiers, which they were not—complaints by numerous military commanders attest to that fact. Second, it elevates marksmanship to the primary skill revolutionary soldiers and Western expeditionary forces needed, when military commanders of the era stressed massed fire. "Musketry was instrumental in forging a new nation," *The American Rifleman* insisted.[37] Yet historians argue that muskets were not very accurate and complex to reload, and that hitting targets was more chance than skill.[38] Third, it intimates that the Patriots developed their technical skills exclusively in the private realm of providing for the family, not in service to the state.[39] Finally, the narrative suggests that facility with civilian-use firearms translated into expertise with military firearms, which, according to historians, does not appear to be the case.[40]

Historians paint a different, more complicated picture of the prevalence and use of firearms in colonial America. England sent both soldiers and military arms and supplies to ensure the colonies' success in early colonial settlements. However, as colonies became established and the threat from Native tribes seeking to preserve their lands declined, fewer people came to own firearms, and very few owned military-quality weapons. By the Revolution, firearm ownership in the colonies had declined even further, though it continued to be much higher than in England.[41] These accounts are consistent with the ridicule of colonial and early American conscript forces, who mustered with brooms because they could not afford to own military weapons. Adeptness with firearms usage, even with civilian weapons, was not necessarily high. Historians have documented numerous firearms accidents and misfirings in colonial America and the early Republic. Such mishaps occurred largely because firearms were not accurate and their owners did not adequately maintain them, as well as because those who wielded them were not adequately trained in their use—not far from contemporary reality.[42]

THE "US" THAT WAS THE MILITIA

The NRA elaborated a romanticized myth about the social composition of the militia. "Back then, the militia was—us. The militia was your average citizens standing together with their firearms to defend their country from all enemies," *The American Rifleman* tells us.[43] But who, exactly, is "us"? Who are these average citizens? In answering that question, the NRA draws on two different stereotypes associated with White men: the respectable, middle-class professional of suburban spaces and the cowboy or woodsman of rural America. The first stereotype associated political virtue with middle-class thrift, industriousness, and independence, implicitly asserting that Black men, considered lazy, unintelligent, and dependent, could not develop political virtue. The second stereotype drew on the trope of "Manifest Destiny," rejecting Native Americans' political claims and portraying them as savages who had no place in the body politic of the Republic.[44] At the same time, both images invoke their racial opposite: the poor, urban, dependent, violent, and lazy Black man.

The militiamen came from America's urban working and middle classes in one version of the NRA's myth. They were "farmers, mechanics, shipwrights, lawyers, students and teachers, shopkeepers and blacksmiths."[45] In a more contemporary rendition, the virtuous citizen gun owners consisted of "the police, the firemen, the construction workers, the truck drivers, the heavy equipment operators."[46] These middle-class men used firearms for hunting, sport, and personal security, and they developed independence, discipline, and common sense through these pursuits—the building blocks of political virtue.[47]

NRA: An American Legend, written in 2002, claimed that these independent, self-sufficient, middle-class, "average" men formed a political society of equals in a land that "had yet no titles, so a man without a peerage [i.e., a title of nobility] was able to own his own land." These independent and self-sufficient men could "pursue their own dreams" and "thrived according to their abilities and their effort."[48] And because of the way they pursued their dreams of success, these men learned how to use firearms and thus how to be good citizens who recognized and protected the public good. This idealized account of American society in the early Republic not only dismisses the role of formal institutions such as the militia and the US Army in establishing law and order; it seems also to have completely erased Native Americans from the terrain, asserting that Western lands had no owners and no claims on them. Free and enslaved Black people are also absent. Their service in the Revolution is never acknowledged, and the existence of slavery is never recognized. The NRA's America appears as a political entity to consist exclusively of White men—despite the group's claim of being the oldest civil rights organization in the land.

These myths of origin are inconsistent with historical evidence. As discussed in chapter 3, colonial militiamen were White men who came from larger towns and cities because—except for Southern slave patrols—only larger organized settlements could afford a security and defense budget. Even in those settlements, the budgeted expenditures were insufficient. Given the high cost of procuring weapons, communities privatized the responsibility to buy firearms to individuals, but with limited success. This system contributed significantly to the inefficiency and ineffectiveness of the citizen-soldier model. Still, larger settlements, such as New England towns, were far more likely than rural and frontier outposts to have the organizational and fiscal capacity to provide collective security to citizens. Frontier towns often depended on the US Army, the Regulars, for security and government functions.[49]

According to the historians Richard Uviller and William G. Merkel, military censuses from the early Republic showed that in New England, which was urban by the era's standards, much of the militia (sometimes even 100 percent) owned their mandated arms and maintained them in good working order. However, data from frontier states show that few militiamen owned guns, and in some cases states didn't even seem to have a militia force. Between 1820 and 1830, the proportion of militiamen who reported owning serviceable military firearms declined from 50 percent to 32 percent, suggesting that the enrolled militia system had all but collapsed.[50]

Furthermore, NRA membership advertisements reinforced the association between middle-class White males and the ideal of the virtuous citizen-soldier. In 1957, *The American Rifleman* published advertisements for membership in the NRA addressed to "your fellow sportsman." The text and the accompanying sketches are very explicit about who would make a good rifleman and NRA member. The group identified "farmers, lawyers, mechanics, physicians, merchants, conservationists, executives, [and] members of the armed services and law enforcement" as the types of people who should seek membership. The sketches reinforce these class specifications, but they also reveal the gender and race of the welcome recruit: a White man (fig. 7.2).

A decade later, the Browning Firearms Company advertised its new product, the Browning Superposed rifle, in the NRA's magazine (fig. 7.3).

Figure 7.2 NRA membership application ad, *The American Rifleman*, July 1957, 12.

Figure 7.3 Browning Superposed Rifle ad, *The American Rifleman*, August 1967.

The ad claimed that the rifle "is desired by . . . a broad cross-section of American Sportsmen. . . . The truth of the matter is, just about anybody who enjoys the sport of hunting or target shooting can hardly afford not to own a Browning Superposed." The image associated with the text illustrated this "just about anybody" as imagined by the company. Not one of the people were of color.

This "broad cross-section," which is also presumably *The American Rifleman*'s core audience, includes twenty-five White individuals. Most appear from their dress to be middle-class—the NRA's "reputable citizen." Three of the twenty-five are women: two appear to be housewives, and one is dressed as a nurse. Among the men, six wear uniforms. The picture includes a police officer, a fireman, a soldier, and a sailor, typical of the NRA's traditional pre–World War II audience. Non-uniformed classes are also represented: two bespectacled men in suits carrying briefcases—probably meant to signal White-collar occupations such as lawyer. One suited gentleman in a bowler hat, reminiscent of John Steed from the popular 1960s British show *The Avengers*, carries a black umbrella in one hand and a long gun in the other. Other men appear to symbolize farmers, and one man appears to be a tradesman carrying a toolbox. Diverse as this target audience may have been in terms of class, the picture suggests that as late as the 1960s, the NRA's law-abiding "rifleman" was a White man.

Figure 7.4 Army National Guard ad, *The American Rifleman*, July 1958, 102.

And it was not only gun manufacturers who targeted the White middle-class male with ads on the pages of *The American Rifleman*. Advertisements the US Army placed in the magazine focused on the same demographic. A 1958 ad sought to recruit for the Army National Guard (fig. 7.4). Ten years after the official integration of the services, it depicted a smiling, clean-cut, White young man—a picture that evokes middle-class White respectability—as the "citizen-soldier." By placing this ad in the magazine, the Army thought it addressed a White middle-class audience.

This stereotypical image of gun owners as staunchly middle-class, respectable (White) men persisted in the twenty-first century. An article in 2002 set out to dispel what the author considered prevalent media-promoted myths about gun owners. Gun owners were "bland, basic and middle-of-the-road. . . . One is a doctor. Another is a retired police detective. Two are in advertising and public relations; one is a house painter, another has a construction business, and all of them make a relatively good living."[51]

URBAN AND RURAL: RACIALIZED
CONTRADICTIONS OF VIRTUE

The NRA narrative contains significant contradictions reflective of White society more broadly. Even as it embraced middle-class White professionals, the NRA decried urbanization and life in urban spaces—often associated with Blackness—as the source of political corruption.[52] *The American Rifleman* argued that commercialization and the comforts of city life weakened the independent spirit of America's (White) men.[53] "The Industrial Revolution ... was beginning to replace this self-sufficient jack-of-all-trades [i.e., the rifleman] with classes of specialists, whose talents and training did not adapt them to military life."[54] "Urban centers and gentrified rural enclaves of well-off city dwellers" were "invading and displacing rural culture."[55] Increased industrialization, congestion, and work specialization— what modernity called "civilization"—contributed to a decline in martial and political virtue, according to the group. The "great leaders of America and of the world [had] been men whose roots lay in the soil," but urban Americans lacked the "greatness" of this earlier generation, including their "common sense."[56]

The narrative went on to say that urban life led to complacency, crime, and moral dependency—traits stereotypically associated with Black people.[57] Urbanization led people to "lose sight of the basic values of individual rights" and disrespect "human dignity and freedom of the individual."[58] Modern-day youth raised in cities "spent their lives on city streets and automobiles and seldom if ever [saw] the country." This stunted their "mental attitudes," which required "years of environment and training" to develop.[59] Never mind that colonial militia were urban institutions; for the NRA, urbanites could not understand the moral importance of firearms nor their centrality to physical safety and protection. "Urbanites have got smog on the brain," sneered an NRA member.[60] Military officers quipped that "only the country boys" (White men) could shoot. "City boys [i.e., Black men and immigrants] ... were woefully off," making them a menace in war. "I'd hate to have some of these birds supporting me during an advance. They'd be apt to drop their rounds on our own troops," an officer opined.[61]

Even in the new century these stereotypes persisted, albeit in a more adversarial tone. Urbanites are characterized by "almost complete dependence upon and full delegation of responsibility to others for one's safety and well-being. This is a new concept in our history, but one familiar to European serf descendants."[62] "Our teeming cities ... create many of the social problems for which we out here in the gun-owning sticks get blamed," claimed *America's 1st Freedom* in 2002. In some "inner-city areas . . . the thought of a young man with a gun gives me cold chills."[63]

The changing demographics of the American population, especially the large-scale, undesirable immigration from "countries where the possession and use of firearms by the public was actively discouraged," were also cited as contributing to the loss of martial spirit and political virtue. The manly, self-reliant, gun-toting frontiersman of the Revolution had become a shopkeeper with a foreign accent.[64] Because of their socialization and upbringing, which did not include firearms, immigrants were not prepared for the duties of political membership in the Republic. Immigration and urbanization, both processes associated with non-White groups (eastern and southern Europeans were not considered White in the early twentieth century),[65] went hand in hand with social groups that accepted "the invasion of individual rights" in exchange for "the comforts of government protection."[66] Urban dwellers were also expected to be more prone to crime, agitation, and political violence. Consistent with social theory of the era, the NRA perceived social disturbances, looting, and rioting as diseases of urban life, and implicitly of Black (and immigrant) men. Thus, it was the duty of (White) "riflemen" to serve as law enforcement auxiliaries to prevent political violence by urbanites.[67]

As an alternative to the urbanized and complacent city folk, the NRA offered a second portrayal of the virtuous rifleman—that of the "woodsman." Written in the twentieth century and imbued with implicit associations between Blackness and urban spaces, the NRA's story reimagined the revolutionary militiamen. The inspiration for these revised revolutionary heroes most likely came from popular novels of the era, but schoolbooks of the early twentieth century also reflected these myths.[68] Consistent with "manifest destiny" mythology, such accounts whitewashed settlers' violence against Native tribes, presenting it as heroic resistance against savagery.[69] These Revolutionaries were frontiersmen "dressed in buckskin or fringed homespun" and living on remote farms and in isolated settlements. These remote settlements were inhabited by "scattered frontiersmen" who always faced danger and "fought as individuals or small groups."[70] They spent months at a time traveling "in total wilderness." These virtuous men "built a nation" with "only rifle, powder and ball, knife, hatchet, and blanket," things that they could "easily carry on their backs."[71] School textbooks of the era offered a similar account. For example, West's 1913 textbook portrayed settlers as armed only with their personal weapons, "ax and rifle (in the use of which weapons they have never been equaled)" and "unorganized and uncaptained." These rugged men "subdue[d] a continent" and spread democracy, capitalism, and the Protestant ethic of hard work and independence across the land.[72]

The American Rifleman hosted stories about rugged "woodsmen" who chose to live in remote cabins far from urban settlements and depended on their rifles for food and protection from menacing, "savage" Indians and bandits.[73] Proximity to other people was cause for despair for the NRA's rural rifleman. The only thing that "caused the woodsman anxiety" was creeping urbanization, "the disconcerting frequency with which he passed cabins along the trail." Seeing places that had "an urban character" made the woodsman "feel sort of mournful and apprehensive," as urbanization signaled the decline of political virtue.[74]

Overall, the emphasis on the use of firearms in the private domain served to strengthen the association between arms, political virtue, and racialized tropes associated with geography and space. Whether a respectable middle-class city dweller or a fearless rural woodsman, the NRA's citizen-soldier was a White man who developed his commitment to the public good through hunting, shooting, and protecting private property. Other racial groups, the narrative implied, did not engage in this virtuous form of firearms use. Blacks used firearms to commit crimes, resist constituted authority, or project an image of violence and promiscuity.[75] Native Americans used knives and tomahawks to hunt and kill, but firearms to attack settlers seeking to bring Christianity and democracy to the West. Indians were "a lazy lot" who viewed firearms as currency and thus could not appreciate their political power or use them effectively in war.[76] These groups lacked commitment to the public good and the Republic, and they could not be considered virtuous citizens.

THE ROLE OF CHOICE

Another key difference between classical and NRA ascriptive republican narratives centers on the role of choice—specifically, choosing to serve in the military (or to own firearms, in the later narrative). Republican narratives of the Revolution feared that centralization of military power in the hands of one leader, combined with a professional army, would lead to tyranny. Political leaders had incentives to subvert the public good and pursue private gain; a professional army that remained active in times of peace and answerable only to its paymaster was a threat to the Republic. Thus, republicans emphasized that citizens had a *duty* to be prepared for war in times of peace as a counterweight to potential elite corruption. Through military service, citizens developed a commitment to the public good and thus recognized corrupt intent in political leaders. This idea of duty was institutionalized in the form of conscription. Since citizen-soldiers were not volunteers, they were obligated as citizens to serve as soldiers in peace and war.

By the late nineteenth century, classical republican beliefs that the Army and the militia were two rival forces in the polity and that a large professional army could be inimical to democracy had fallen by the wayside. Through the travails of the Civil War and the strengthening of federal government institutions, the country had developed a national political ideology, one that combined White supremacy with democratic electoral institutions and economic liberalism. Especially after the debacle of mobilization in the Spanish-American War (1897), and with World War I on the horizon, most Americans did not object to the professionalization and strengthening of the federal armed forces.

On the contrary, by the second decade of the twentieth century, many Americans—especially elites within the military establishment—believed that the winds of war blowing over Europe made it necessary to increase the size and improve the training of all US forces. In the NRA narrative of the first half of the twentieth century, the US Army ("professionals") and the militia/National Guard ("citizen-soldiers") were complementary. They represented two parts of the national defense system. What differentiated the two was not their nature, but their area of authority. The US Army was responsible for foreign wars and defense against external enemies, but its domestic role was minimal. The militia supplemented the US Army in foreign campaigns as needed, but their primary role was domestic. As late as 1964, the NRA attributed America's military might to the "citizen-soldier standing ready at the side of the professional soldier."[77]

In this narrative, the government did not have a duty to mandate service in war or peace. Americans were too autonomous and "impatient" a people for the government to force them into military service.[78] Men who grew up in the right environment, who were taught at a young age to be hardworking and self-sufficient, and who grew up using firearms for food and recreation were expected to *choose* to become civilian riflemen.[79] These men would hone the skill of marksmanship as civilians and develop political virtue along with it. If war came and the country needed their service, these virtuous civilian marksmen would volunteer to serve. Thus, unlike the republicanism of the early Republic, early NRA republicanism insisted on voluntarism rather than conscription.

The state did not have to force citizens to serve because those citizens who engaged with arms in their daily lives and practiced marksmanship at the range already had the political virtue required to volunteer for service in times of national need. The NRA was critical of the Wilson administration's decision to institute a draft in 1917, maintaining that "whether the ends either of military necessity or justice are to be served by such a course [the Selective Service Act] is problematical." Justice required that the riflemen be given "a chance to gratify their patriotic desires" before other—less skilled and less virtuous—men were called to active service via the draft.[80] During both world wars, the association insisted that there were plenty of men, many trained in marksmanship through civilian rifle clubs, who "will flock to the colors." These men were "inspired by an Ideal" that made them willing to give "their time, energies, and sustenance" in support of their beliefs "without regard for immediate personal gain."[81]

In this revisionist republican worldview, the primary responsibility of a republican state was to encourage citizens to use arms in the private domain by giving them easy access to firearms and shooting training. Subsidies for rifle clubs and removal of gun ownership restrictions were central to attracting volunteer citizen-soldiers. If modern citizens had easy access to firearms, they would develop the moral and technical skills required of the citizen-solider. These citizens who used firearms for safety, sport, and subsistence would find it easy and desirable to make "the abrupt transition from civilian to military life." Given this intimacy with firearms, the transition was nothing more than symbolic. Sports shooters became a professional soldier's equal "by sticking cockades in their hats, picking up muskets or rifles, and mustering on the village green."[82] It is ironic how closely this phrase parallels Frederick Douglass's exhortations during the Civil War.

For the NRA, conscription was not only unnecessary and unproductive; it was also a hallmark of tyranny. Conscription was associated with military weakness and likely, if not inevitable, defeat on the battlefield. In this version of the republican myth, authoritarian regimes banned individual gun ownership but recruited large conscript armies. Restrictions on individual gun ownership contributed to political corruption because the citizens had neither the means to develop political virtue nor the ability to resist a tyrant. Private gun ownership is why America's riflemen had an advantage: because "accurate aim rifle fire" delivered by "competent" men "overcame the advantages in numbers of enemy troops" who lacked the same tradition in musketry.[83]

In one sense, the NRA narrative flipped on its head the role of conscription and voluntarism prescribed by the early American republican narrative. In this new myth, state-mandated service (instead of voluntarism) was ethically problematic because it did not contribute to the development of political virtue. Conscription is why tyrannical states were destined to lose in war: they forced their men to serve rather than encouraging choice and marksmanship, which fostered the development of political virtue in private life. Conscript soldiers in authoritarian societies received technical training at arms, a militaristic practice sometimes admired by NRA principals. Yet, a dearth of tradition in personal gun ownership and the use of firearms in daily life meant that these men lacked the independence and political virtue required of riflemen.[84]

Tyrannical governments could train their armies in warfare technology, but they could not instill the political virtue required to win battles and be republican citizens—especially in countries populated by non-White people.[85] According to *The American Rifleman*'s overtly racist argument, conscription in Japan had existed for 1,000 years, which explained why "the Army has always ruled Japan." As a result, the Japanese regime was declared "an unparalleled background for modern totalitarianism"; "little yellow men of the Pacific have [always] existed under a military dictatorship," making them incapable of political virtue and republican citizenship.[86] It didn't help the Japanese case that they were "never a nation of rifle shooters, [and] they consider[ed] the bayonet the most essential part of the weapon they carry."[87]

Only in the last year of World War II did the NRA support conscription—even over the objections of many in armed forces leadership.[88] The sheer destruction the war wrought on the European continent brought home the realization that "power is the only thing that seems to count." Europe experienced the results of political corruption. The only way to avoid a similar fate was for the US to embrace mandatory military service.[89] For *The American Rifleman*, the United States needed universal military service, not voluntarism or a system that allowed for civic alternatives. Echoing early American republican themes, the magazine asserted that "a true democracy" rested on "compulsory military service." And nothing in the "history of democracy" or "the history of America" suggested that such a practice might be "undemocratic" or "un-American." Democratic principle, noted the magazine, requires that "every citizen who wishes to enjoy the privileges of a democracy" must be willing to serve at arms, not as "bricklayers, foresters, government clerks, dam builders, or canal diggers."[90] The Founders would have approved.

The "facts," according to *The American Rifleman*, were that "every successful democracy in history" required universal military service and that democratic "degeneration" happened when citizens were unwilling to serve and approved of their replacement by "substitutes" such as "professional soldiers." Furthermore, in a statement that today's NRA would completely disavow, the magazine argued that conscription was part and parcel of the American political tradition. As encoded in the Second Amendment, Americans' right to bear arms was meant to ensure proper military training for all (male) citizens. According to *The American Rifleman*, "to ensure the right of the State to demand universal military service of its citizens [is why] the Second Amendment went into the Bill of Rights: 'The right of the citizen to possess and bear arms not be infringed!'"[91] However, this enthusiastic support for conscription did not last; soon after the war, the NRA returned to advocating the voluntary model based on sportsmen who prepare for war through shooting competitions and marksmanship training. By August 1945, as soldiers began to return from the war front, *The American Rifleman* shifted its focus from universal service to programs meant to attract men returning from war to shooting and hunting.[92]

As discussed in earlier chapters, the "choice" to be virtuous was associated with race in American ascriptive republicanism. White people "chose" the path of liberty and armed defense of the Republic, while Black men "chose" slavery and dependency. This theme of choice remains an important component of expressions of racial prejudice even today. Specifically, modern narratives, including modern gun rights narratives,[93] depict Black people as having "chosen" the route of criminality and state dependency (welfare) over hard work and independence, the hallmarks of republican citizenship.[94] The "choice" to become a rifleman and to pursue marksmanship draws on these same pervasive themes. In this myth, neither political virtue nor corruption is an innate characteristic of individuals or groups; rather, it is the outcome of people's choices. Choosing marksmanship maximizes the distance between the virtuous (White) rifleman who, through sport, prepares to sacrifice his life for the nation, and the Black man, the criminal and perpetual supplicant to the state for protection, help, and support.

"COMMON SENSE"

Like classical republicanism, the NRA positioned moral independence—rationality, or as the NRA deemed it, "common sense"—as central to virtue. Virtuous citizens in the Republic had to exercise reason. An enlightened public was crucial for a democratic form of government. "No other system of government depends so much upon an informed citizenry," the group counseled in 1964.[95] An "informed public" could be an "effective deterrent" to political corruption because informed citizens would recognize political actions that deviated from the public good—and would raise the alarm.

In this myth, "common sense" was not innate but cultivated. More so than other citizens, shooters developed the detached rationality required for constructive political engagement. From early on, marksmen were trained to control their emotions on the range, as emotionalism harmed performance in competition. Emotions such as anxiety could cause a rifle-man to feel that "he is not himself" and cause his muscles to tense up, with consequences for his performance. Therefore, riflemen were trained to control their emotions and not give in to fear, panic, or any "overwhelm-ing sense of inferiority" that could accompany anxiety.[96] This training on the range paid dividends in politics: riflemen were no more governed by "emotional reaction" or "misinformation" in their response to politics than they were when pulling the trigger.[97] Thus, riflemen more than others had the "common sense" and virtue required to discern friend from foe.[98]

Rational thinking was grounded in being informed about relevant politi-cal concerns from trusted sources that spoke the truth. In turn, rational cit-izens could discern the difference between the truth and propaganda from "fifth columnists" or "special interests."[99] "Public opinion . . . when based on true facts and sound reason, is a source of strength for our nation," the NRA declared in 1960.[100] Gun owners "value facts more than opinions and [demand] thoughtful debate rather than 'spin,'" asserted Heston, four de-cades later.[101] Gun rights supporters didn't make political debate "personal," responding to politics in "childish" ways, unlike their opponents.[102] Solving social problems required that "our efforts be based on reason and knowl-edge, not on emotions or misinformation."[103] The politically educated pub-lic understood what is in the public interest and could "see through the aims and devices of those who are attempting to manipulate public opin-ion for selfish interests."[104] One could not help but wonder how this NRA would feel about the raw emotional appeals of today's organization.

Consistent with republican ideology, the NRA believed that citizens' natural rights came with "certain obligations which must be fulfilled in ap-plying that right."[105] According to *The American Rifleman*, "the freedoms and liberties that our society provides also impose a number of responsibil-ities." For citizens to "discharge their responsibilities capably," accurate in-formation was vital.[106] The riflemen, "as thinking citizens," were obliged to have an understanding "of the problems that proposed gun laws [create]."[107] Therefore, virtuous citizens, such as the riflemen, had a moral responsibil-ity to be politically engaged. The virtuous riflemen were duty-bound to use reason and seek "true facts" over propaganda.[108] A cartoon in the February 1953 issue of *The American Rifleman* emphasized the importance of political engagement for the "legitimate sportsman" (fig. 7.5). A bespectacled White man behind a dais, representing "the law," reminds the youthful "legitimate sportsman" who appears in front of him with a shotgun that it is the politi-cal branch and not the courts who determine gun laws, thus it is the gun

Figure 7.5 "The Gun Law Problem," *The American Rifleman*, February 1953, 46.

owner's vote that can influence political outcomes. The law is just a neutral arbiter—another deeply ironic conservative myth, especially on the heels of the *Bruen* decision.

As rational republican citizens, the riflemen had to be politically engaged, not just informed. According to the NRA, gun control advocates had an advantage because they "spread their doctrines" through the press and sought to "educate the public to their point of view."[109] Thus the riflemen had a social responsibility to be politically engaged and disseminate relevant information to protect the public good. They had a duty to contact their representatives to ensure that they possessed the "true facts" about the damage firearms legislation could cause to the Republic. They had to evaluate the opposition in an "unprejudiced" way, and they had an obligation to vote against elected officials who threatened the public good by supporting gun restrictions.[110]

Lack of political engagement among the riflemen could have major social and political consequences. If uninformed and emotional citizens pressured elected officials to enact legislation that threatened the public good, the citizens, not legislators, were to blame. Following the republican script, the association warned that when the public and especially the riflemen were indifferent or silent "before the threat of disarmament by persons with other interests," then "the ultimate responsibility for bad firearms laws cannot rest with those who make the laws."[111] The riflemen had a duty to protect private gun ownership through political engagement, and their failure to do so would be evidence of poor citizenship.

Starting in the 1940s, the NRA sought to "educate" members on gun policy issues and communication with elected officials. As editor-in-chief, C. B. Lister initiated a monthly column, "What Lawmakers Are Doing," which provided information on gun-related bills in state legislatures along with the NRA's evaluation of those bills. In later years, the NRA labeled its legislative news service "Modern Sentry Duty," evoking republican themes of armed vigilance and protection. *The American Rifleman* also published columns advising members how to write letters to elected officials and local newspapers.[112]

Going back to the republican narratives of the Revolutionary era, "common sense" or rationality has always been gendered and racialized— exclusively associated with the White, male citizen-soldier. Women were not entrusted with the responsibilities of republican citizenship because their emotionalism could lead them to consequential misjudgments in politics. Their inability to control their fear made them unsuitable for war, as well. Similarly, Black people were viewed as emotional individuals whom enemies of the republic could easily manipulate.

The NRA adapted classical republican narratives of virtue to meet the political and ideological context first of the late nineteenth century, and then the late twentieth century. Conscription and the carrying of arms in service to the country were replaced as sources of political virtue by voluntarism and private-domain uses of arms. In the context of private engagement with firearms, (White) men developed the independence, common sense, and discipline required of the virtuous citizen. These qualities they carried with them to the battlefield and the polls. The NRA's rifleman, who replaced the citizen-soldier as the embodiment of virtue, was an elitist and racialized construction. The riflemen were portrayed as (White) men engaged in urban, middle-class occupations but imagined as the product of the rural countryside away from the laxity and corruption of the (Black) inner city.

Through the 1960s, the NRA presented its riflemen as defenders of public authority. They were citizen-soldiers and police auxiliaries who used their private-domain-honed skills to protect the nation and public order. Stories in *The American Rifleman* taught NRA members about military tactics and riot control strategies along with hierarchical ideas about what it means to be a good American. These narratives privileged Whiteness, nativity, and middle-class respectability. Since the 1970s, after it lost its government subsidies, the NRA has developed a new understanding of the rifleman. The new virtuous citizen is the gun owner. The consumer act of buying a firearm and a commitment to gun rights is necessary and sufficient for political virtue.

Over the same period, the group's position on the federal government changed. For more than a century, the NRA benefited from federal largesse. During the era of mass mobilization, the NRA believed that the federal government-protected political liberty, and the association was its foot soldier. But after the era of mass mobilization ended, the NRA and the defense establishment parted ways, and the federal government embraced gun control as a solution to rising crime, the group's view of Washington changed. No longer was the government the virtuous representative of the republican citizenry; instead, it was a corrupt elite hostile to republican virtue.

[CHAPTER 8]

Political Corruption

The NRA narratives are not only about the politically virtuous rifleman. The group also has a story about who is corrupt and an enemy of the Republic, and why. Much like other republican narratives, the NRA myth offers an account of the agents of corruption, as well as their traits, goals, and political behaviors. In the republican narrative prevalent during the early Republic, the primary agent of corruption was the standing army. Professional soldiers worked for pay, not for country and glory, and thus they were happy to do the bidding of their paymaster. By contrast, citizen-soldiers fought wars not for personal gain but for the public good—to protect the Republic. The presence of professional soldiers was a double threat. Not only could they turn against democratic institutions; their presence was a disincentive for citizens to train at arms. Since training at arms was the primary source of virtue, a republic that maintained a standing army was in danger not only of disloyal professional soldiers taking over the government, but of unvirtuous citizens unable to recognize and fight the threat.

By the late nineteenth century, when the NRA was founded, Americans had developed a new consensus on the sources of republican virtue and corruption. Conscription was no longer viewed as necessary or sufficient for developing valor. Instead, voluntarism—the *choice* to develop martial skills, become a "rifleman," and serve in war—was a superior process for cultivating political virtue. Professional soldiers and volunteer National Guards were no longer at opposite ends of the virtue-corruption continuum; they were equally virtuous agents of the Republic, complementing each other.

In the early NRA narrative, the threat to the Republic came primarily from civil society, outside government institutions. America was in danger from groups who viewed gun control as a means to social and political change (that is, the overthrow of capitalism and American democracy), citizens who were well-meaning but misunderstood the role of firearms in society, and a few self-seeking politicians and government bureaucrats. Criminals were also a threat, not only to individual safety but—because crime incen-

tivized calls for gun control and liberal calls to rehabilitation over punishment—to democratic institutions.[1] The opposition, warned the NRA, could
be "sincere but ignorant of the facts, insincere and politically motivated, or
working for personal gain."[2] The "fanatics" and "extremists"—the socialists,
the Communists, and the civil rights activists of the twentieth century—
wanted a means to confiscate private guns and disempower the people,
weakening democracy. In both political practice and public discourse, these
groups were essentially interchangeable. Political authorities and federal
law enforcement saw little difference between Communism and civil rights
activism, treating both as threats to the American political system.[3] These
categories have been and continue to be implicitly racialized. "Do-gooders"
is another group the NRA identifies as a threat to political virtue. The do-
gooder is a well-meaning citizen who reacts emotionally and lacks the cold
reason and common sense required for political judgments. (This is a heavily
gendered category.) Table 8.1 shows show the similarities and differences in
the conceptualization of political corruption across the three eras.

Politicians and law enforcement were also suspected of political corruption. Depending on their position on gun ownership and gun control,
elected officials and unelected "bureaucrats"—a category which in early decades included police authorities—could be fanatics or corrupt self-seekers,
and thus a threat. Members of law enforcement could be corrupt bureaucrats who supported gun control because it made their work easier and who
did not consider the effect of gun restrictions on the people's political virtue.
More recently, as the NRA has brought many rank-and-file officers and even
police leaders to its corner, in part through its marksmanship training programs for police,[4] its view of police has become much friendlier. In the modern NRA narrative, political elites who support gun control are the epitome
of political corruption, intent on destroying democracy. Since the 1990s,
the partisan realignment has brought most gun-control-supporting politicians into the Democratic Party. As a result, it is primarily the Democrats
that the NRA associates with political corruption and tyranny.

THE DO-GOODER

The "do-gooder" is the sincere person who "literally would not harm even
a germ-laden fly."[5] Do-gooders are enablers more than they are corrupt actors. Do-gooders lack political virtue not because of malice and ill intent,
but because of misinformation and lack of political acuity. The do-gooder
doesn't understand guns and is falsely convinced that gun control would
reduce crime and social disturbances. Such fears are "dangerous," and
people like this "should never be involved in setting gun politics." Gun ac-

TABLE 8.1. Corruption in Ascriptive Republican Narratives

	Source of Corruption in Citizens	Agents of Corruption	Traits of Corruption
Republicanism of the Early Republic	No military training Unwillingness to die for the country	Standing army and its elite paymasters	Military service for pay Seeking personal gain Emotionalism
Early NRA Republicanism (1871–1960s)	No rifle training Unwillingness to die for the country	*Non-system actors*: Fanatics/extremists (e.g., Communists, civil rights groups) Do-gooders Criminals *System actors*: Police and politicians supporting gun control	Emotionalism Opposition to established authority
Late NRA Republicanism (1990s–present)	No gun ownership Unwillingness to promote gun rights	*Systemic actors and their societal allies pursuing progressive social change*: Progressive social movements (e.g., BLM) Politicians supporting gun control Government agencies (CDC, ATF, FBI) "Globalists" The UN The "mainstream" media	Emotionalism Opposition to established group privileges (gun ownership)

tivists have even coined a psychological condition for the do-gooder: she is a "hoplophobe," a person characterized by an "irrational or morbid" fear of guns. Even a medical doctor has weighed in on the "diagnosis."[6]

Many citizens who don't own guns fall in the category of the uninformed do-gooder, who lacks reason and "common sense." In republican narratives, dispassionate reason is central to identifying and defending the public good. These citizens can't discern "true facts" from "propaganda," making them vulnerable to misinformation.[7] Such people are "brainwashed by dishonest politicians and lying media members who want you to believe their false narrative."[8]

A lack of common sense also makes do-gooders prone to emotionalism. Rumors and fearmongering, like those surrounding "fifth columnists" in World War II, during the Cold War, and around the political assassinations and race riots of the 1960s, activate do-gooders' "unreasoning instinct to soothe our fears." In turn, this lack of common sense leads to a "senseless and shameful torrent of anti-gun hysteria."[9] This lack of reason made people overreact and focus on the weapon that killed John F. Kennedy rather than the man who pulled the trigger. The response to the assassination was "a highly emotionalized reaction to the weapon with which the terrible deed was performed," the organization determined. It "was hysterical in nature."[10] Such "sensational news blind[ed] people to the true facts."[11]

The NRA attributed the passage of the 1968 Gun Control Act (GCA) to emotionalism among legislators pushed by do-gooder constituents. Congress was "dazed by several tragic assassinations," and the result was that emotions rather than cold reason prevailed among legislators.[12] Cities, too, became infected with "neuroticism" and the advocacy of "very emotional people," resulting in gun control ordinances.[13] The daily and "hysterical" reporting of murders by the media and supporters of gun restrictions contributed to the rise of anti-gun politics.[14] Anxious do-gooders respond reflexively to social problems with demands for new laws, but being "hoplophobes" they lack knowledge and understanding of existing legislation.[15] In turn, this "hysteria" has led do-gooders to support restrictions on the fundamental rights of citizens. Since external stimuli such as crime or assassinations guide the do-gooder's response, the danger is that such people would support more extreme forms of restrictions. Over time, this could destroy democracy.[16]

Although do-gooders do not understand the importance to freedom of firearms, as voters they have a public voice, making them exceedingly dangerous. "Year after year, well-intentioned, but frequently ill-informed do-gooders prevail upon their elected representatives to 'do something' about armed crime, juvenile delinquency, and gun accidents. Then a flood of severe firearms control proposals are introduced."[17] A cartoon published in the November 1967 issue of *The American Rifleman* shows how the NRA imagined its adversaries: all were portrayed as men, even though the "do-gooder" appears feminized (fig. 8.1).

Figure 8.1 "The Faces of the Opposition," *The American Rifleman*, November 1967, 18.

According to the NRA's ascriptive republican narrative, women are often among these do-gooders. Since their role is confined to the domestic sphere, women are not typically conceived as "riflemen"—citizen-soldiers—or criminals or extremists. Women are wives and mothers, operating primarily in the private domain and thus often uninformed about political issues. Although the world of the riflemen had no political role for women, in America after 1920 women have been voters who contact legislators about issues. This was a thorny problem for citizen-soldiers and the NRA because, as voters, women could influence policy and the future of the Republic in ways inconsistent with the public good. *The American Rifleman* complained about women's naiveté and political meddlesomeness. Many women "think they know more about the requirements of a *military* training program than do the men" of the profession, the group protested.[18]

The concerns about women's misguided political activism on behalf of gun control persisted into the 1950s and 1960s. Women, driven by emotionalism, made the wrong causal inferences with grave political consequences, *The American Rifleman* warned. "A women's group holds a meeting at which Mrs. Brown tearfully tells the tale of how her son was injured while he and a companion toyed with a loaded gun. Therefore, guns are bad, and something should be done. . . . [E]very member of the group writes to her representative. The lawmaker, faced with a hundred letters from voting women, is not apt to disregard them."[19] "Sobsisters (male and female) emote[d] in certain ladies' journals over [crime]," while "neurotic 'moms' and the tender-minded of both sexes" were captured by "get rid of guns hysteria," declared *Guns* magazine in 1960.[20]

A 1953 cartoon depicts a White, respectable, middle-class woman in a hat and high heels as the naïve do-gooder whose political activism in support of gun control leads to the empowerment of the "criminal element," hiding behind her in the picture, and the destruction of the "legitimate sportsman," the virtuous citizen-soldier. The "good gun laws" are marginalized in a corner, unable to help (fig. 8.2).[21] The solution was to provide proper political education to women to make them good "republican mothers"—a responsibility that fell to fathers and husbands. Given the role of women as voters, the NRA advised its readers to "open the eyes of the mothers" by bringing them into contact with gun culture through shooting programs for their children.[22]

More recent depictions continue to be based on gendered stereotypes. For example, according to Charlton Heston, those who "parrot what's politically correct" in the media, including gun control narratives, were "bubbly but brainless twenty-five-year-old TV reporters." These women "cock[ed] [their] lovely head" and "squint[ed] in pained empathy," ostensibly not realizing that they were doing the bidding of corrupt political elites.[23]

Figure 8.2 "The Gun Law Problem," *The American Rifleman*, February 1953, 17.

THE FANATIC

A different threat to the Republic is the fanatic. The fanatics have made up their minds against guns, and they are not amenable to argument or reason. The fanatics are not necessarily "corrupt" in republican terms, as their goal is not personal gain and power. But their inability to seek out "true facts," coupled with their political activism, make them dangerous nonetheless. Their singlemindedness, and the fact that they "have hypnotized themselves into believing" that gun control will reduce crime, make them irrational enablers of political corruption.[24] In that sense, they are as hysterical in their reactions as the do-gooders. They are "ready to doom whatever they dislike," regardless of the consequences to the country.[25] "Uninformed and biased" fanatics "blam[e] firearms rather than people for crimes, suicides, and accidental shootings."[26] They make politics personal, "grow[ing] childish in the process." When debating issues, they digress to "a name-calling contest."[27] Fanatics are engaged in "an all-out scorched-earth campaign" whose main goals is not to change policy but "to destroy the one group that's strong enough to stand up for the Second Amendment."[28]

What often motivates the fanatics is a deep mistrust of the American citizen coupled with an unreasoned faith in government. This dichotomy was further accentuated as the NRA moved from a government defender to a government antagonist in the 1980s and 1990s. From this perspective, anti-gun fanatics fear democracy and embrace elitism, doubting the virtue of the "riflemen" while blindly following government bureaucrats. Anti-gunners "mistrust their fellow Americans—their honesty, intentions, and self-control."[29] Support for gun control is thus synonymous with "believing that [the] people cannot be trusted."[30] Fanatics "[sought] to change society to fit their desired model."³¹ This model consists of increased regulatory requirements, creating a "government bureaucracy dedicated to slowly poisoning the historic American" tradition.³²

Fanatics refuse to acknowledge that for a republic to remain healthy, the people should be responsible for "disciplin[ing] ourselves as free men . . . working and fighting for our . . . security." If the state came to have exclusive responsibility for security, then the people would become enslaved, "disciplined by harder men," and they would find themselves "working and fighting to provide opportunity and security for . . . [their] masters."³³ Fanatics put "small town ideas in the class of things to be sneered at," not realizing the detrimental effect of their ideas on American political culture and institutions.³⁴

The assassinations and riots and the spike in violent crime during the 1960s emboldened the fanatics and provided the rationalization for their hysteria. "The professional anti-gun bigots have had a golden opportunity to promote their singular mania," complained the association.³⁵ In the NRA's telling of the story, the fanatics view the world as a Manichean struggle between an absolute good (a world without guns) and an absolute evil (private gun ownership). These "extreme reactions" can exacerbate division and disunity, leading to incivility. In the process, the riflemen, "our finest citizens," are socially victimized. The possessors of "true facts" are "subjected to ridicule and misunderstanding . . . classified by some as members of the lunatic fringe of society."³⁶

Fanatics led the charge in the culture wars of the 1980s and 1990s, using race and gender as weapons to neutralize and silence virtuous gun owners. Instead of protecting "simple truths" in domains such as "traditional male/female relationships, traditional families, immigration . . . traditional moral and sexual practices, and . . . firearm ownership," fanatics distorted reality and "fragmented" American "mainstream culture."³⁷ These fanatical anti-gunners "hate guns and people who own them" so much that the NRA developed a pseudo-psychological category for them to add to "hoplophobia." According to one article, "leftists and so-called progressives," especially in the media, suffered from "NRA Derangement Syndrome—a type of hysteria."³⁸

Contemporary NRA principals present themselves as color-blind egalitarians—if not outright civil rights leaders—whose main concern was the preservation of what they increasingly called the "civil rights" of America's gun owners. It was anti-gun fanatics who held little respect for traditional values passed down through American history by the nation's European founders, anti-gun fanatics who sought to brand the NRA and its supporters as bigots living in states where people were "lynch-dragged behind a pickup truck" and as "right-wing extremists" who "blew up a federal office building."[39] Corrupt and fanatical anti-gunners "are telling America you're a paranoid, bloodthirsty, bigot who wants to punish churches, bribe judges, and terrorists, arm snipers and sell criminals machine guns to kill cops," stated a 2004 NRA political advertisement in *America's 1st Freedom*.[40] According to the group, it was these corrupt anti-gun elites who sought to establish divisions in the population and "by virtue of descent or skin color or religious distinction or physical prowess or code of conduct [deem] some superior to others."[41] In essence, according to the NRA, anti-gunners exploited gender and race to sow division and generate support for a cause meant to shift the balance of power from citizens to the select few. For these fanatical elites, guns were a pretext: "it's not guns they hate," stated NRA leader Wayne LaPierre, "it's each one of us having the temerity to exercise our Constitutional rights to pursue Liberty."[42]

George Soros, a Jewish financier and philanthropist, has been the NRA's top exemplar of a politically corrupt fanatic. In the late 1990s, the Soros-endowed Center of Crime, Communities, and Culture donated $300,000 in support of *Hamilton v. Accu-Tek*. This was one in a series of civil cases against gun manufacturers in which gun control proponents argued that manufacturers and retailers were liable for instances of gun crime.[43] There is little evidence that Soros or his foundation has had much direct involvement in the gun debates. The foundation's records show contributions to gun control causes totaling $3 million. Most of that money was given to the Funders' Collaborative for Gun Violence Prevention between 1999 and 2002. The most recent contribution was a small amount in the wake of the Newtown, Connecticut mass shooting.[44]

His modest role in gun control politics notwithstanding, to the NRA Soros is the prime example of a corrupt fanatic. A hypocrite, the "unspeakably wealthy" Soros has preached in favor of reducing the financial influence of the rich in politics, but at the same time he has used his wealth and that of "leftist plutocrats" to promote his self-interest and power.[45] The group has ignored that Soros is a Holocaust survivor who has fought against Communism and in support of ordered liberty and regulated capitalism. Instead, the NRA claims that he has held "the peculiar view" that "our free economy is a more potent threat than Communism or Nazism," but all the while he has been financing American elections.[46]

In this narrative, Soros's primary goal is to "control the White House, the U.S. Senate, and the Supreme Court," according to *America's 1st Freedom*. He is "the sugar daddy funding countless front groups."[47] In furtherance of this goal, he "imported to these shores" bad actors with the expertise to subvert the Constitution—such as "the woman most responsible for

Figure 8.3 "George Soros' Hypocrisy," *The American Rifleman*, April 2004, 16.

the confiscatory long-gun ban in Australia."[48] Gun control is a key component of Soros's plan "to diminish, weaken and subjugate the United States
as a world player, to erode our sovereignty, and to domestically erase the
dominant traditional values of the American people."[49]

Drawing on age-old anti-Semitic tropes, such as those expounded by
the infamous *Protocols of the Elders of Zion*, the NRA has warned that
Soros is a modern version of King George III, thirsty for tyranny and
empire.[50] In 2004 he was depicted entirely in black, with a pronounced
nose and a pile of (gold) coins underneath (fig. 8.3). "You can expect
the United Nations to take over American gun rights," the NRA warned
in 2004. George Soros's plan "for a global gun ban [is] being railroaded
through the U.N."[51] The group has charged that Soros has used a secretive "underground" campaign. Previewing the "illegal voter" charges of
the Trump era, as early as 2004 NRA leader LaPierre argued that "while
parts of the Soros Billionaire Club's machine are highly visible," this secret
and implicitly illicit campaign aims to "register millions of voters" in support of Democratic gun control candidates.[52] This was an effort to "Buy
Back America"[53] by "drown[ing] out the voice of the average voter of average means."[54]

Not surprisingly, the NRA fiercely rejected the premise that its exclusive and uncompromising stance on gun rights—especially as it developed
after the 1977 "Cincinnati Revolt" that brought hard-liners to power in the

organization—was itself a mark of fanaticism. Instead, it took such claims by its opponents as evidence that the riflemen, the exemplars of common sense and good citizenship, were derided and marginalized, opening up the Republic to mortal threats. As a cartoon published in 1974 suggests, the riflemen persisted and towered over the fanatics—portrayed here as bespectacled men in suits, possibly signaling bureaucrats, or journalists— who seemed perplexed by the ineffectiveness of their efforts to destroy him (fig. 8.4).

Some fanatics work in the media, which amplifies their reach and ability to influence uninformed and emotional citizens. "False and misleading statements by a few publicity-hungry individuals are being exploited by some newspaper reporters in search of sensationalism," the NRA warned.[55] Media reporting on guns consists of "vehement diatribes" often "reek[ing] of [anti-gun] bigotry and parochial thinking." Stories about guns are "libelous," containing "false information."[56]

Fanatics in the media are especially dangerous because of their ability to reach many uninformed citizens and spread "propaganda" while at the same time blocking the rifleman's access to media to express his views on the importance of firearms. According to the NRA's critique of the media, "[modern] communications are more efficient," but that also means that the media can carry "insidious propaganda" and "disseminate [it] over the world." The association, the victim of this libel, does not have the same access to disseminate its counternarrative. "The reverse flow of truth" is more

"We keep telling him he's dead, but he won't lie down."

Figure 8.4 *The American Rifleman*, September 1974, 22.

limited, as it "reaches wherever we have the intelligence and initiative to send it."[57] The result is an imbalance of power between the virtuous and the corrupt that favors the wicked.

This was the professed reason why the NRA started its new magazine, *America's 1st Freedom*, in 2000. Meant to be sold in public outlets to the general public, and not just NRA members, the magazine was developed because the association realized that "it is no longer reasonable to think the national media will fairly report the gun debate." According to the group, "the majority of mainstream media" was complicit in the effort "to strip away our constitutionally guaranteed firearms rights," and as a result they distorted or ignored the NRA's perspective. The new magazine aimed at "report[ing] the news from the perspective of the concerned, law-abiding gun owner."[58]

THE EXTREMIST

Perhaps the most acute political threat came from "extremists"—a racialized political construct. Unlike "the riflemen," who were promoters and protectors of government institutions, "extremists" were foreign and domestic political outsiders hostile to American democracy. Some were "fifth columnists"—that is, Americans operating within the United States as spies and agitators on behalf of foreign adversaries. Concern about "fifth columnists" was especially high during World War II and the early Cold War. Others were "socialists" and "Communists"—individuals who rejected democracy. African Americans, who often reached out to internal and external progressive groups, from abolitionists (in the antebellum era) to socialists (in the twentieth century) to social welfarist anti-gunners, could also be viewed as "fifth columnists" (though as I noted in an earlier chapter, the magazine does not explicitly discuss Black politics in any context).

Extremists use violence to create fear and discord within the United States for the purpose of imposing political change. In the NRA's narrative, extremists pursue regime change incrementally. First, they use violence— both crime and political agitation—to provoke fear in the naïve and uninformed American public. Policies that incentivized criminals, such as lax sentencing and gun control, are central to the extremist agenda. Second, they use propaganda, seeking to attribute the incidence of violence to private firearms ownership. According to the NRA, "the real Fifth Columnist" doesn't simply stage an armed attack. "His weapon is the speaker's rostrum, the printing press, the cleverly manufactured and carefully placed bomb."[59] In this view, Communists, "fifth columnists," student radicals, laborites, and Black militants (and possibly the contemporary Black Lives

Matter movement) have used social disorder, riots, bombings, and strikes to disrupt American democracy—not to critique its flaws and expand its reach.

The goal of extremist groups is to take political power away from the virtuous citizens and subvert the Republic. Through violence and propaganda, extremists aim to induce the American public to accept strict gun regulation, especially gun registration—a policy with deep roots in American legal and political tradition. Once these ideological enemies succeed in taking over the government, a gun registry would make it easy for them to identify, locate, and disarm the riflemen. After confiscation, extremists could impose "any form of dictatorship."[60] Thus confiscation is "a prime essential to a successful invasion of our democratic rights," not just "our native soil." In this view, the registration of firearms "has always been a prerequisite to conquest by foreign or domestic dictators."[61] According to Wayne LaPierre, "history proves it [that] in every nation where the scourge of socialism rises to power, its citizens are repressed." What accompanies repression is confiscation: "their firearms are taken."[62] This is why the right to bear arms is "America's First Freedom": without the ability to use force in defense of democratic rights, the right to vote and to select one's political leaders is bound to be lost.

A variety of sources, stories, and cautionary tales were put forth as "proof" that extremists had American democracy in their sights. In 1967, *The American Rifleman* asserted that the "Communist Rules of Revolution," a "fake or real" document that Allied Forces purportedly found in Germany in 1919, "came painfully close" to the NRA's warnings about the enemy within. According to the "Rules," fifth columnists would seek to get gun registration laws enacted and then use the registry to confiscate the firearms and disarm the citizens.[63] Domestic Communists had orchestrated an attack on civilian marksmanship programs and private gun ownership, the group warned. "Police registration of civilian arms which inevitably leads to confiscation abetted the rise of Fascism, Nazism, and Communism."[64] More recently, the NRA has been asserting that "closet Socialists" in the Democratic Party leadership are determined to "turn our country into an unrecognizable socialist nation, devoid of the basic freedoms that the Founders enshrined in the Constitution."[65] A cartoon from the November 1974 issue of the magazine makes the connection clear for the audience: the radicals are using naïve gun control supporters, especially in the press, to dig the grave of gun rights. But that is only the first step; their ultimate goal is the destruction of democracy, signified here by the First Amendment—the right to assemble, vote, and freely express one's political opinions (fig. 8.5).[66]

"Always glad to help. By the way, who is the other grave for?"

Figure 8.5 "Gun Control and the News Media," *The American Rifleman*, November 1974, 42.

An establishment association of law-abiding riflemen, the NRA has been concerned about extremists' effect on republican institutions and culture—the American way of life. Extremists are "determined to destroy what we know and treasure as the American way of life," *The American Rifleman* explained.[67] In countries opposing the United States, the NRA has warned, civilian gun ownership was a highly regulated "privilege" afforded by the police based on political criteria. Communist and fascist regimes keep firearms from "politically unreliable people."[68]

The Holocaust, Black slavery, and a variety of other cases of extreme political oppression, dehumanization, and genocide have been introduced as evidence of the relationship between disarmament and tyranny.[69] Gun registration and licensing are the hallmarks of a "police state."[70] From this perspective, there is little difference between Chicago's gun control laws and the "18th and 19th centuries' 'slave codes' and 'black codes' that prohibited African Americans from being armed."[71] American extremists aspire to bring a similar system to the United States. They would disarm the riflemen through registration and confiscation and erode political virtue from within. Without firearms, law-abiding citizens would not be able to resist tyranny. "Sooner or later, a people without arms, or the knowledge of the use of arms, becomes a slave people," the magazine warned.[72] In this sense, slavery is a choice, not a coercive imposition by an outside authority.

In the early NRA narrative, when the organization was an insider political player closely aligned with the federal government, "extremists" were people outside government. These people were ideologically opposed to the American political system and sought to eradicate American democratic institutions. In later NRA narratives, developed after the NRA lost its institutional ties to the federal government and strengthened its relationship with the Republican Party, becoming part of the New Right coalition, the category of extremists swelled to include a variety of institutional players who were viewed as a threat to gun rights. Thus, as of the 1970s, the politically corrupt adversaries of the NRA and the virtuous gun owners included certain government agencies such as the Bureau of Alcohol, Tobacco, and Firearms (BATF),[73] the Internal Revenue Service (IRS),[74] the Federal Bureau of Investigation (FBI), international organizations such as the United Nations (UN),[75] and elected officials, primarily on the political left and within the Democratic Party.

LAW ENFORCEMENT

Over the years, the NRA has expressed great ambivalence about police and law enforcement more broadly. The patterns of NRA ambivalence are tied to specific contexts and underscore the racialized nature of its ascriptive republican narrative. Following the ascriptive republican script, the association has portrayed law enforcers as both heroic defenders of (White) citizens against (Black) violent criminals, and as tyrannical abusers of (White) law-abiding gun owners' civil liberties. Law enforcers have been both the perpetrators of anti-White racism and the targets of such bias.

Ironically, when removed from the context, certain NRA grievances are almost indistinguishable from those of the Black Panther Party in the 1960s, or Black Lives Matter (BLM) today. The NRA has accused law enforcement of ignoring due process rules and violating the rights of citizens, invading their private spaces without proper cause and authorization, and even fabricating evidence to entrap innocent gun owners. However, the organization's critique of policing practices has focused exclusively on

White victims—people whom the association viewed as "law-abiding gun owners." The NRA has been conspicuously circumspect in cases where law enforcement erroneously targeted and even killed Black people, even law-abiding gun owners.[76] Not only has the organization not actively defended such victims of police brutality; it has exploited such cases to levy charges of reverse racism against minority political actors, from President Obama to BLM.[77]

On the one hand, the organization has portrayed police officers as heroes who put their lives on the line to help citizens by catching violent criminals. According to the organization, "heroic" officers "bravely ran toward danger" to defend civilians, and as such they deserved honor and respect.[78] Police have also been depicted as defenders of civil liberties, even when protests targeted police behavior. They have been there to defend "our God-given freedom to assemble and speak and peacefully protest—to protest, even, against those who protect [i.e., the police] our ability to do so safely."[79] Such was its faith in police as agents of protection that the NRA even suggested that the solution to the problem of mass shootings in schools would be to ensure that all schools hire armed police.[80]

The group's relationship with law enforcement is not limited to a shared worldview that valorizes legal gun ownership and gun rights. The NRA has been instrumental in training police officers in weapons use. Over the years, police departments represented a substantial revenue source for the organization and its member rifle clubs. The association's magazines have hosted articles of interest to police officers, special columns titled "Police News," features by law enforcement leaders such as FBI Director J. Edgar Hoover, and technical pieces on police revolvers. The NRA has also sponsored police shooting matches.[81] Police officers have been featured in NRA membership ads as prototypical of the kind of respectable White man who should seek to be a member.[82] Since the NRA does not release its membership lists, there is no way to ascertain how many police officers are NRA members, but given the organization's long-standing involvement in police firearms training, there is good reason to expect that the number is not trivial.

On the other hand, the association has viewed police as being of limited use, inadequate and under-resourced. It has also disapproved of how city police have backed gun regulation, which the NRA associated with political corruption. In this view, the role of the police is not to prevent crime but rather to respond to it after the fact. "Law-enforcement officers cannot at all times be where they are needed to protect life or property in danger of serious violation," the NRA warned.[83] It is not their "job," and they "cannot protect you."[84] According to the group, "law enforcement exists to apprehend lawbreakers." People were "told to dial 9-1-1 when danger is lurking." Citizens were "led to believe that authorities will arrive . . . and diffuse the situation," which the NRA judged to be "shameful propaganda that costs innocent lives."[85] Only virtuous citizens could prevent crimes by being vigilant and armed, ready to deter a criminal. Underscoring the belief that police forces are inadequate, some NRA commentators suggested that the government should subsidize mandatory weapons training for all school-age children so that they can be responsible for their own safety—precisely because police could not be there in case of a mass shooting.[86]

Besides inadequacy, corruption and abuse of power were central concerns for the NRA. During much of the twentieth century, police officials and especially police chiefs in large cities supported gun control.[87] From the NRA's vantage point, police support for gun control signaled political corruption. Police were lazy and crooked bureaucrats. They primarily cared about their own convenience, not citizens' rights. As one NRA member put it, "the police are a political force."[88] In a critique that few today would associate with the NRA, the organization claimed that officers' main concern was to protect "the policeman's job by complying with the wishes of the dominant political machine."[89]

In a commentary that would strike many as quite ironic in the era of BLM and the concerns that movement has raised about police abuse of power, the NRA frequently complained that law enforcement agents were brutish and corrupt and should not be trusted. As early as the 1940s, the group noted that the police officer did not view himself as "the employee of the citizenry. Instead, he views his job as that of a shepherd watching over a flock—half sheep and half wolves in sheep's clothing." Because of this mentality, police harbored "eternal suspicion," believing that citizens lacked honesty and were "too dumb" to protect themselves.[90] Unlike criminals, "the average policeman is grossly, notoriously—and in some cases even criminally—ignorant" about the use of firearms, opined *The American Rifleman*.[91] The typical police officer "is the last man in the world who should be entrusted with a weapon and a blanket permission to use it," let alone speak with authority on gun control laws.[92]

Gun registration laws were "immediately useful to the police," enabling their political corruption. Such laws gave officers an easy tool to arrest and convict criminals without proving their involvement in serious crimes, "since most of them [the criminals] possessed pistols, and all had 'dangerous weapons' in their homes."[93] However, given that criminals were intimately familiar with firearms' use, the only thing accomplished by "disarm[ing] the citizenry [through gun control was] to remove the one obstacle in the way of the lawbreaker's enjoyment of absolute license."[94] In short, the police put their own security ahead of citizens' safety and well-being and marketed it as righteousness.

It was not only police complaisance and corruption that were a problem for the Republic. With rising crime, the disarming of citizens would necessitate an exponential increase in the size of police forces. This had implications for the health of democratic politics. Drawing on republican themes, the association warned that such an increase would create "the most enormous 'standing army' of police ever seen in the free world."[95] Echoing modern BLM narratives, the association claimed that the potential for political corruption and abuse of power among police was significant. The future of the Republic was in peril if an "omnipresent and omnipotent police . . . benignly look[ed] after the welfare of the citizenry," warned *The American Rifleman*.[96]

The NRA's ambivalence toward law enforcement continued through the 1990s and even into the twenty-first century. In fact, as the NRA became more partisan and more deeply integrated into the conservative movement, its attacks on the legitimacy of police authorities and especially federal law enforcement agencies increased, though peaks tended to track election cycles. The NRA leader Wayne LaPierre warned that law enforcement lacked courage and political virtue, and as a result they pursued action that was easy over tasks that involved risk. "Since it is already illegal for criminals to purchase and possess even one gun, why limit the number of guns or types of guns honest people can own? The answer: arresting violent criminals is dangerous, but arresting nice, peaceable citizens is safe."[97] Therefore, to sustain their image and earn public trust, police sought to criminalize and arrest the "law-abiding" gun owner who presented no social danger, rather than risking their lives in pursuit of "real" criminals. Gun control laws thus gave "jack-booted government thugs more power to take away our constitutional rights, break in our doors, seize our guns, destroy our property, and even injure or kill us."[98]

A cartoon published in the February 1994 issue of *The American Rifleman* is evidence of the association's views of the federal government as bloated, incompetent, and an obstacle. Then-Attorney General Janet Reno is depicted as an enormous, imposing, ape-like figure, with President Clinton hiding behind her like a child (fig. 8.6). She is not an authority figure; she is a caricature of authority—an impostor. This sexist depiction rejects the notion of female authority as legitimate and at the same time infantilizes Clinton, seeking to reinforce the idea that he lacks "common sense" and political responsibility. Reno was working on Clinton's "national gun licensing and registration scheme," the magazine warned. Not only would this plan create another "bloated government bureaucracy," but since

*r you, of
als

Action Team. Call 70:
267-1175 and get a
early warning o
threats to you
rights.

neral Janet Reno
·ban crowd are working out details of
tional gun licensing and registration scheme.

Figure 8.6 "The Clinton Gun Card," *The American Rifleman*, February 1994, 49.

"criminals won't bother with long lines and filling out forms," it is the law-abiding gun owner who may end up in prison.[99] The cartoon is also a prime exemplar of the NRA's sexism: the government here is depicted as an obstreperous, unattractive woman. Gone are the days when the government took the form of Uncle Sam or a respectable White man in suit and tie.

The NRA has continued to issue warnings that federal law enforcement agencies—especially the Bureau of Alcohol, Tobacco, and Firearms (BATF), the agency tasked with licensing gun dealers and investigating certain types of gun law violations—are corrupt and incompetent. According to LaPierre, BATF agents "behave like street thugs." They use their authority "to persecute and entrap citizens who have done nothing wrong and would never contemplate doing anything wrong . . . they manufacture a case."[100]

The claims of federal law enforcement corruption focused on the BATF continued well into the twenty-first century and intensified during the Obama era. Between 2006 and 2011, BATF agents in Arizona staged what came to be known as "Operation Fast and Furious." The agency allowed licensed gun dealers to sell firearms to suspected "straw buyers" so that the BATF could track the guns and build cases against gun traffickers operating between the US and Mexico. The operation became public after a firearm tracked by BATF was found at the scene of the murder of a US Border Patrol officer. Subsequent Congressional investigations revealed that guns used in the BATF operation had been linked to 150 murders in Mexico.[101]

Although "Operation Fast and Furious" was initiated during the Bush administration, for NRA leader Wayne LaPierre it became an indictment of the "rogue U.S. Department of Justice headed by President Barack Obama's Attorney General, Eric Holder." LaPierre argued that "Fast and Furious" was proof that there was "a regime that destroy[ed] the rule of law" and the "Department of Justice [had] become a political operative of the White House," refusing to fulfill "its duty to enforce the law." In this context, "our liberties cannot long survive," and as a result, "there is no justice in America."[102] The NRA's president, James Porter, asserted that "lawlessness is everywhere in the Obama regime," which was characterized by widespread "abuse of power." "The Obama/Clinton regime did extraordinary damage to our liberty over eight years," the association claimed in a 2017 postmortem. "Think of the Justice Department's top-to-bottom corruption, such as the 'Fast and Furious' government-sanctioned, gun-running operation." "For Obama, 'rule of law' is merely his political silly-putty," declared LaPierre.[103] Without any evidence, the group claimed that the operation was really the first step to a gun control law banning semiautomatic weapons.[104]

RACE AND THE NRA'S CRITIQUE OF LAW ENFORCEMENT

The NRA has used race as an implicit critique of *both* law enforcement and its critics—but in all cases, the message rejects claims of structural racism that victimizes Black people, instead focusing on asserted anti-White racism and discrimination or perceived assertion of Black privilege. In these narratives, the racial context matters as it contributes to whether the police or their target represents "the good guy with a gun." The organization has been a firm critic of police and federal law enforcement treatment of certain White gun owners who were harmed by inept police raids—and such criticism was warranted. However, the group's criticism was selective and disproportionate. The NRA has emphasized cases involving White gun owners, even suppressing disconcerting facts to present these gun owners in as positive a light as possible, to accentuate the magnitude of the injustice done to them by law enforcement. At the same time, it has not been equally vocal about cases of African American gun owners who became victims of police brutality. It has also emphasized evidence of misconduct by Black victims—implicitly or explicitly branding them as criminals—to justify its reticence and to avoid criticizing police behavior. In some cases, the NRA has even exploited prominent cases of police brutality against Black people to claim anti-White and anti-police racism on the part of its political opponents—especially Black politicians such as President Obama and Eric Holder.

The earliest NRA defense of a White gun owner who fell victim to police misconduct was in the 1970s, as the organization was transitioning from military preparedness advocacy to civilian gun rights lobbying. In the 1971 case of Ken Ballew, a botched federal raid in a Maryland home, the association approvingly quoted Rep. Charlie Dingell's charge that "this kind of storm-trooper exercise may have been commendable in Nazi Germany, but it . . . is intolerable here."[105] In response to two other botched federal operations in the early 1990s, one in Ruby Ridge, Idaho, and the second in Waco, Texas, Wayne LaPierre repeated similar charges, calling federal law enforcement "jackbooted thugs."[106] In a letter sent to gun control supporters in Congress, the NRA leader claimed that "federal agents wearing Nazi bucket helmets and black storm trooper uniforms [attacked] law-abiding citizens."[107]

In the 1992 Ruby Ridge case, federal law enforcement sought to pressure a White separatist, Randy Weaver, to become an informant in their operation against the Aryan Nations, a violent White supremacist organization headquartered in Idaho. The operation to arrest Weaver on gun charges at his remote home was poorly planned and based on faulty intelligence. In a shoot-out, Weaver's wife and son were killed, along with a federal agent.[108] The NRA published extensive articles on the case both in 1993 and after the US Senate conducted hearings in 1996. The association expressed righteous outrage on behalf of the Weaver family. "BATF entrapment led to the violent deaths of three people," *The American Rifleman* warned.[109] The operation was based on "setups, lies, and blunders by federal police agencies. . . . What happened to Randy Weaver can happen to anybody in this country," the group warned. The NRA emphasized that the FBI "tampered with evidence" and did not follow the protocol that required agents to use deadly force only if they were faced with "death or grievous harm." Instead,

FBI snipers were issued "a license to kill."[110] From the association's perspective, federal law enforcement "had committed the murder [but were] not charged."[111] The association also approvingly repeated criticism by Sen. Dianne Feinstein (D-CA) about the militarization of this federal operation. "This is deeply troubling . . . that's the sort of ninja-clad, military-style, Vietnam-jungle style law enforcement methodology" that is unsuitable for "a domestic law enforcement" agency, the Senator was reported as saying.[112]

Race played a role in the NRA's coverage of the story, which was consistent with the group's implicit position that government officials engaged in anti-White practices. Some NRA principals were very vocal in their beliefs that "a form of reverse discrimination" had been taking place and "the average White man has been the object of ridicule, a social obstructionist considered suspect, while other races are exalted." In this view, "the majority," that is, "the White, middle-class, hard-working, law-abiding, church-going . . . gun-owning mainstream," was increasingly made to feel that they have no place in contemporary America, ignored by "political schemers."[113] In his commentary on Ruby Ridge, Wayne LaPierre picked up on this theme of anti-White discrimination, albeit in a more subtle tone. Not only was the NRA outraged on behalf of the Weaver family; LaPierre even suggested racial bias on the part of the federal government. In his view, what "made Randy Weaver an ideal target" was "his unorthodox religious and political views. . . . He was a White separatist." His ideology notwithstanding, LaPierre suggested, Weaver was just an ordinary gun owner—a good guy with a gun. Yet "the feds painted Weaver as racist, as anti-Semitic, as a criminal." The government used character assassination against a law-abiding gun owner, "but they had to entrap him into his only crime, altering two guns."[114]

The association's reporting on another major botched operation by federal law enforcement followed a script like the Ruby Ridge account. In April 1993, a shoot-out, followed by a tear gas attack and a fire, concluded a fifty-one-day siege of the Branch Davidian compound in Waco, Texas. The operation led to the deaths of 75 civilians. The Branch Davidians were a religious group led by David Koresh, who presented himself as a prophet. In early 1993, credible allegations surfaced that Koresh had sexually abused children in the compound.[115] Additionally, the group was suspected of illegally amassing firearms and ammunition.[116]

On the one hand, the NRA—sounding much like twenty-first-century police detractors such as BLM—criticized the militarization of the federal response to civilians and called for "thorough and independent investigation" of federal law enforcement practices, raising serious questions about the use of tanks and incendiary devices by federal agents. "Why did BATF choose to assemble 100 agents—masked and in black flak jackets, crawling on the roof . . . shooting through windows?" the association asked. This was "a savage display of the government's brute force," *The American Rifleman* concluded.[117] Such a critique bears similarities to contemporary BLM criticism of police militarization and training.[118]

On the other hand, the association sought to downplay the serious claims of child sexual abuse and other crimes that contributed to the operation, in order to support the message of "this could happen to you, virtuous rifleman." According to *The American Rifleman*, the federal government lied when it alleged that "babies were being beaten [in Waco]" as an excuse for the raid. The magazine also implied that Koresh was a law-abiding gun owner who had checked in with local authorities about his firearms.[119] Even a year later, then NRA President Robert Corbin continued to minimize the government's concerns. "Was it worth 83 avoidable deaths and millions of dollars to enforce a gun law?" he mused.[120] Overall, this coverage gives the impression that federal law enforcement had no legitimate reason to initiate an investigation of the Branch Davidians. From this perspective, the whole case boiled down to using trivial legal reasoning ("enforce a gun law") to victimize law-abiding citizens. And, despite what the NRA determined to be a minor offense, the government chose the most aggressive strategy available—one that led to a massacre. Essentially, the association argued, people died so that the government could look tough on guns for the benefit of a naïve and irrational partisan audience.

In both the Ruby Ridge and the Waco cases, it was not just the government's methods, but also its *motivation* that the association sought to impugn. For the NRA, these investigations were a harbinger of the tyrannical methods the government would use to enforce the assault weapons ban, which was then being debated in Congress. Completely stripped of legal and social context, Waco constituted a "horror story of snooping, persecution and violence against American citizens." The NRA's opponents planned to use the ban to "terrorize the public by demonizing a non-existent threat, then 'rescue' them with needless but dramatic action." The case offered a lesson in the Democratic-controlled government's political corruption and hypocrisy—"part of our freedom died in that firestorm."[121] Adding (racially tinged) insult to injury, according to the NRA, the Clinton Department of Justice expended resources on these operations, while "terrorists training for Sept. 11 were attending flight school [in Florida.]"[122] Real violent criminals were going about their business while the government was busy harassing regular, law-abiding citizens for no other reason than that they owned a firearm, the association implied.

Ironically, the most persistent claims that the government has used allegations of minor offenses to persecute innocent civilians have been issued by African American activists, whose voices are entirely missing from the NRA narratives. Since the nineteenth century, Black political activists have documented cases of violence against Black bodies committed by or sanctioned by law enforcement and White elected officials.[123] In the 1960s, in response to persistent police harassment and violence committed against African Americans in the city of Oakland, California, the Black Panther Party (BPP) sought to exercise their right to carry firearms publicly as a display of power and resistance.[124] In recent years, the issue of police brutality against people of color has featured prominently on the national political agenda following killings by police that were caught on camera or otherwise publicized. The BLM movement has made the complete overhaul of policing in America central to its social justice agenda. Activists believe that police brutality is a problem that cannot be addressed administratively, and they seek to reconceptualize policing by demilitarizing, disarming, and even disbanding police departments.[125]

Despite the sharp criticism of abusive methods used by law enforcement, the NRA has generally been silent when it comes to police brutality targeting African Americans and other people of color. From the perspective of the NRA, Black claims of police brutality constitute anti-police bias and implicit, if not explicit, anti-White bias.[126] Going back to the 1970s, the NRA has categorically rejected any similarity between its agenda and that of the BPP. According to the organization, the two groups differ in methods, goals, and character. For the NRA, the BPP was a "political organization," while it saw itself as "non-political and non-partisan." For the NRA, efforts by a minority group to advance racial justice by pointing out the weaknesses of the American political system were inherently divisive and racist. Thus, the BPP was a "racist" group of "militants" who were actively anti-authority and specifically anti-police. They were extremists who "publish[ed] pamphlets on how to assault the police" and embraced "violence to revolutionize America for their own ends," whereas the NRA itself was a nonpartisan, apolitical group "of sportsmen" whose claims thus transcended politics. The association maintained a policy of color-blindness linked to support for duly constituted authority. The group made "no race distinction, and its membership is open to all reputable Americans who pay allegiance to our country." Unlike the BPP, which aimed to use violence to achieve its ends, the National Rifle Association promoted a political right to own firearms but sought "to preserve America by peaceful means for the sake of all good Americans."[127]

Given the NRA's view on race and racial issues, it is not surprising that military-style police raids against Black armed civilians did not receive the attention and criticism of the NRA. In the 1980s, the group was silent when the city of Philadelphia bombed the residence of the Black revolutionary MOVE group, often associated with the Black Panthers.[128] The bombing resulted in the deaths of eleven people, including five children. The fire destroyed an entire city block in a thriving, middle-class Black neighborhood, a block that was never restored.[129] The MOVE case bore many parallels to the Waco raid: a local government used military tactics against armed civilians, the key complaint against whom could be boiled down to their ideology and their bearing of arms. The NRA never asked if achieving the government's goal was worth the deaths of a dozen (Black) people, including children, or if it was appropriate for a democratically elected government to bomb its own citizens.

Even less normatively complex cases of law enforcement abuse against Black citizens were met with silence. On July 6, 2016, Philando Castile, an African American, was pulled over by police. A licensed gun carrier, Castile disclosed to the officer that he had a firearm in his glove compartment. Even though Castile attempted to comply with the officer's instructions, the officer shot Castile several times.[130] The NRA remained silent on the case even as a mass protest was organized in Minneapolis. In its press release, posted on its Facebook page, the group stated that "the nation's largest and oldest civil rights organization" was troubled by the events in Minnesota and urged that the case be "thoroughly investigated." However, unlike in the cases of Ruby Ridge and Waco, the group insisted that it was not appropriate "to comment while the investigation is ongoing."[131] Dana Loesch, an NRA spokeswoman, characterized the situation as "a terrible tragedy that could have been avoided." In this view, this was not a case of government abuse and tyranny, but a tragic accident or a misunderstanding—primarily on the part of Castile. "I've been pulled over while carrying, and I had out my permit before the officer got to the car. There is a reason they teach this in classes," Loesch went on to say. "This is why we have things like NRA carry guard . . . to reach out to the citizens to go over what to do during stops like this."[132] Unlike in the case of Waco, where the NRA went out of its way to massage the portrayal of David Koresh, in the Castile case the victim's alleged misdemeanor was reason enough for the association to distance itself from him. Castile was not "a lawful carrier" of a firearm, Loesch noted, because there was evidence of marijuana in his car.[133]

America's 1st Freedom, an NRA publication dedicated exclusively to politics, mentioned Castile only once in 2016—to support claims of reverse racism. On July 7, 2016, BLM activists organized a protest in Dallas, Texas, responding to the Castile shooting and similar shootings by police. An African American gunman shot and killed five police officers during the protest and injured nine others. In a lengthy article titled "An Attack on Our Cops Is an Attack on Us," the NRA decried the "heinous ambush attack on police," which it described as "racially motivated." It also used the opportunity to attack President Obama for his criticism of police shootings of Black men, further emphasizing the theme of reverse racism. "Just a few hours before the Dallas ambush, President Barack Obama used the recent police killings of two black men, Alton Sterling in Baton Rouge, La., and Philando Castile in Falcon Heights, Minn., to return to a familiar refrain," the magazine noted. "Even before the facts were clear, Obama used those cases to assert that such incidents are 'symptomatic of a broader set of racial disparities that exist in our criminal justice system.'" Such expressions of race-based grievance coming from the White House, the NRA warned, led to a mentality of believing the police were "guilty until proven innocent." In a complete reversal of its stance in the 1990s, now the NRA accused the president of being "quick to second guess police," and "publicly attack them and assume the worst about their motives."[134]

The group's response to the Breonna Taylor case provides further evidence of how the NRA employs race in its police virtue and corruption narratives. On March 13, 2020, three White plainclothes police officers tasked with investigating drug crimes forced entry into a Louisville, Kentucky apartment. Two African Americans, a man and a woman—Kenneth Walker and Breonna Taylor—were in the apartment, sleeping. Walker later claimed that he did not hear the police officers announcing themselves and thought they were intruders. In a scene not very different from Ruby Ridge three decades earlier, Walker fired at one of the officers in fear for his life. The officers blindly returned fire, killing Taylor and endangering residents in the neighboring apartment. A subsequent investigation showed that police violated procedures in serving the warrant, and one officer was charged with wanton endangerment.[135] Although this case bears striking similarities to the botched Ballew and Weaver raids, the NRA remained silent. No accusations of tyranny and corruption were ever levied against the Louisville police department, and the group did not issue warnings that this could happen to any law-abiding gun owner. The former NRA spokeswoman Dana Loesch offered a muted personal (and thus unofficial) response to the Breonna Taylor case. "Question—how loud did the officers announce themselves?" Loesch asked. "You can proudly support law enforcement and also show great concern for the question mark being drawn over self-defense in this country—and this is where I am."[136]

CHAPTER 9

The NRA's Theory of Democracy

In the ascriptive republican narrative of the American Revolution, the White male citizen-soldiers embodied the Republic and were the primary defenders of constituted authority. Ascriptive republican ideology understands citizenship in terms of military service and political participation. Their service and sacrifice made citizen-soldiers virtuous and thus in a position to objectively evaluate political leaders and their commitment to the public good. When leaders promoted the interests of the Republic, the citizen-soldiers stood on their side—they defended constituted authority. But when the leaders betrayed the public good, the citizen-soldiers could revolt in defense of democratic institutions. In the early American republican narrative, a key indicator that political corruption had seeped into the Republic was the presence of a "standing army" of paid soldiers whose allegiance was to the rulers. With the abandonment of conscription after the Civil War, the establishment of a volunteer National Guard and the federalization of state forces, the professional army ceased being a negative moral marker for the health of the Republic.

As I have argued, the NRA follows the same ascriptive republican narrative, but instead of conscription it emphasizes as sources of virtue first voluntarism and military preparedness in the private domain, and more recently gun ownership and gun rights activism. This redefinition of political virtue has wholly decoupled the concept from military service and the public good, ideas central to early republicanism. Similarly, since the moral significance of a volunteer army has changed, the NRA has judged political corruption using gun policy as the primary metric. Governments that institute gun control are undemocratic and corrupt, and their policies undermine institutions and open the door to tyranny.

Widespread gun ownership among citizens is viewed as a "check" on political corruption because "political power grows out of the barrel of a gun."[1] Gun ownership by citizen-consumers becomes the "great equalizer" between the ruled and their rulers. Even if the government is more powerful and better equipped in terms of firearms, an armed citizenry can still act as a "deterrent" to would-be tyrants because it increases the costs of oppression.[2] In this view, the only way to ensure that elected officials shall comply with the electorate's expectations is if politicians know that their lives depend on it. The US Supreme Court in its *Heller* decision endorsed a version of this theory.[3]

The NRA's theory of democracy, which has become known as insurrectionism, is a modern-day version of republican ideology, and as such it shares with early American republicanism a deep pessimism about the vulnerability of democratic institutions. Yet it has hollowed out republicanism's moral commitments. This theory suggests that the rulers are not part of the ruled but a differentiated entity of "others" who are tempted to abuse their role as trustees of the public will. An elected government can become the enemy of the people by directly oppressing its citizens or empowering one group of citizens (e.g., partisan or racial) to suppress another group. Armed with a teleological understanding of history, proponents of insurrectionism warn that gun regulation is a slippery slope leading to state empowerment and corruption. Even if tyranny has not arrived yet, absent an armed citizenry, it is bound to happen at some indeterminate point in the future.[4]

The NRA's ascriptive republican theory of democracy has not changed in more than a century. What has changed is the organization's relationship with the federal government. As I showed in chapter 5, through the 1960s the NRA was deeply integrated into the American military establishment and a recipient of federal subsidies in support of military preparedness through marksmanship. Although gun control appeared on the federal agenda in the 1930s, the NRA could hardly afford to antagonize its benefactors directly, and it may have even agreed with some gun regulations that did not interfere with the cultivation of civilian marksmanship. During this period, the organization was an establishment man, a *defender* of constituted authority. However, this changed in the 1960s. Rising crime and political violence combined with the empowerment of minority groups led the federal government to pursue gun control legislation aggressively. At the same time, the era of mass mobilization and military preparedness ended. The NRA also lost its monopoly access to the Directorate of Civilian Marksmanship/Civilian Marksmanship Program (DCM/CMP) and, with it, its insider status. Now the most promising market for the group was the civilian consumer market, which was threatened by gun control. These changes turned the organization into an *insurrectionist*: a vocal critic of federal authorities. For the NRA, government efforts to enact gun restrictions meant one thing: elected officials were corrupt and a threat to American democracy. This process came as a response to federal action, not changes to the NRA's fundamental ideological commitments.

The NRA's theory of democracy, shared in part by today's US Supreme Court, betrays deep contradictions. First, decoupling political virtue from service and linking it to the consumer act of gun ownership destabilizes the moral foundations of the underlying republican narrative. Second, defining democracy in terms of marksmanship skills and then private gun owner-ship creates logical fallacies and moral traps that are highlighted below. Fi-nally, the way the organization uses the "equalizer" logic to justify the need for women to be armed compared to how the same theme is used in dis-cussions of racial and ethnic minorities—especially African Americans and Jews—betrays the deeply ascriptive assumptions of the NRA's worldview. The story selectively points to slavery and genocide as evidence that the absence of civilian gun ownership rights inevitably leads to the worst kind of tyranny. However, it never explains why American White women who were never statutorily excluded from civilian gun ownership were never-theless excluded from both dimensions of republican citizenship—political rights until 1920 and military service until 1948 (and recall that they were included in combat units only in 2015).

THE RIFLEMEN AS DEFENDERS OF GOVERNMENT AUTHORITY

The NRA was born out of the nineteenth-century military establishment. From early on, its leadership consisted of government men—individuals with a position in the military or the government and with deep loyalty to ascriptive republican ideology as embodied by American institutions. Not surprisingly, the early NRA narrative presented the group and its rifle-men as *defenders* and *extensions* of civil authority. Rifle shooting was not merely a sport; it was training in defense against domestic and foreign enemies. "Behind the fun of competitive shooting," *The American Rifle-man* explained in 1950, "the rifleman and pistoleer know that there lies the grim purpose of providing protection against enemies within and without our borders."[5] NRA members "steadfastly adhered to the full principle of Americanism," declared the group in 1967. As part of that commitment, the association "cooperate[d] closely with appropriate Federal and State agencies including the FBI and State adjutants general."[6]

Loyalty to institutions was not simply a symbolic or rhetorical concern for the association. Monopolistic access to DCM/CMP resources pre-sented the realistic possibility (indeed, the reality) that enemies of the Re-public or plain criminals could get access to military-owned weapons and ammunition. Such an event could lead to significant political embarrassment for the US military and the federal government. The NRA guarded against this eventuality in two ways: by maintaining a closed membership through referrals (which allowed it to exclude undesirable groups, even without official exclusions in the bylaws), and by requiring loyalty oaths. In an era when fears about "enemies within" and "Fifth Columnists" were heightened, the association took steps to ensure—on paper—its members' support for government institutions. Starting in 1940, due to "nationwide concern about so-called Fifth Column activities," the Executive Committee required all members to swear "an oath of allegiance."[7] The typical membership oath specified that new members must have a clean criminal record and that they not be involved with any organization that "has as any part of its program the attempt to overthrow the government of the United States by force or violence." Closed membership helped the group patrol the boundaries of identity and maintain social and ideological homogeneity within the organization. The NRA dropped the oath requirement in the 1990s.

Furthermore, NRA members had an obligation to proclaim their patriotism in substantive terms and help fight the enemy within. Echoing early martial republican themes centered on self-sacrifice, the NRA insisted on the virtue of taxes and volunteer military service—as they sustained national defense. "Every citizen who enjoys the protection of a free government owes a portion of his property and of his personal service to the defense of that government," counseled the magazine.[8] The protection and benefits those members received from the government created obligations of reciprocity. Members owed their support because they received "government assistance–issued guns and ammunition by joining the organization."[9] "Fight the 5th Column Trap to Disarm Americans!" proclaimed one membership ad underneath a sketch of the Minuteman.[10]

The riflemen also had an obligation to provide domestic law enforcement support "for auxiliary police duty in maintaining order, preventing looting, and re-establishing public morale following [natural disasters]."[11] In the era of social change, the riflemen represented authority against progressive social movements. In the post–World War II era, the association envisioned that "millions" of law-abiding riflemen, no longer needed by the military, would "serve in home guard units."[12] According to the NRA, club members were "more adequately trained, and [had] more experience with small arms" than law enforcement officers. This training made them well suited to civil defense tasks such as "the prevention of looting, maintenance of order, and local riot control."[13] Never did the NRA envision its members as the perpetrators of an anti-government riot. Consequently, many articles written by "Generals," "Major Generals," "Captains," and other officers of rank instructed NRA members on several aspects of domestic defense and preparedness. In that sense, the magazine served as a tool for political indoctrination into the ideology and practice of the loyal armed citizen. Even J. Edgar Hoover, director of the FBI, wrote an article on arms training within the Bureau.[14] NRA members also read accounts of specific battles, stories that emphasized dominant American (White) ideologies without question or criticism. If there was ever any critical or evaluative content, it was reserved for the technical characteristics of specific firearms, not politics.

For most of the twentieth century, there was no shortage of enemies for the riflemen to guard against. Domestic and foreign enemies such as the Germans, "the Japs,"[15] and later the Russians lurked in the Republic. Extremists, Communists, and "fifth columnists" presented physical and ideological threats to the American system of government—threats that required the riflemen's vigilance.[16] Even anti-Communist groups met with NRA criticism because of their paramilitary tactics and anti-government ideology. During this period of social upheaval, some extremist right-wing groups organized paramilitary units, purportedly to defend the country from Communism.[17] Although sympathetic to anti-Communism and the goals of these armed paramilitary groups, the association reaffirmed its establishment credentials by disassociating itself from non-government-sanctioned groups. In an editorial, it cautioned that while these groups were "patriotic Americans," what they were doing "is not good because it is being done outside the sphere of constituted authority."[18]

This statement sounds ironic in 2023 after armed groups invaded the state capitol in Michigan in 2020 and after the January 6, 2021, attack by militia and White nationalist groups on the US Capitol, not to mention the August 2022 attacks against FBI offices in the aftermath of the FBI search of Donald Trump's Florida home. The NRA has said precious little to condemn these events, while some commentators believe the group to be morally complicit in them.[19] But in the 1960s, the group was adamant that individual citizens and groups of civilians could not unilaterally form paramilitary units, nor did they have the moral or political authority to determine whether a threat existed and how to respond to it. The legal authority to assess threats and marshal defensive capabilities belonged to duly elected authorities and their chosen agents. "Non-military civil defense capabilities at the state and local level must be developed within the framework of [the] existing government."[20] In other words, according to the NRA, armed citizen groups had no independent authority to use force. Armed civilians could engage in domestic policing, but they had to be mobilized and directed by government authority, not the Proud Boys, for their actions to be legitimate.

What distinguished the riflemen from many other citizens was their commitment to the law. In this republican narrative, abiding by the law is a much broader idea than refraining from crime. It is a concept linked to militarized forms of civic engagement and voluntarism in defense of constituted authority. The riflemen were "law-abiding" in that they were committed in word and deed to the "public good" in the form of military preparedness and civil defense. As such, the rifleman accepted the authority of the government to establish and enforce laws. During a century when progressive social movements spearheaded by women, African Americans, and immigrant workers fought to expand the boundaries of ascriptive republican ideology through wartime service and peacetime activism and mobilization, the riflemen stood on the side of authority, serving the established ideology of White male supremacy.

THE TIGHTROPE OF GUN CONTROL

The organization's central focus through the 1960s was military preparedness through marksmanship, not partisan politics and gun control. For almost the first century of its history, so limited was the NRA's focus on gun control policy relative to national defense and preparedness through sportsmanship that in its 1967 "autobiographical" book, the group spent one chapter (twelve pages, or 4 percent) on its involvement with anti–gun control political advocacy. By contrast, in 2002, when a second volume was released, 50 percent of the book's content was dedicated to gun control politics.[21] Times had changed.

The NRA's first foray into gun control politics came with the enactment of the 1911 Sullivan Gun Law (NY)—the same law the Supreme Court struck down in June 2022 in *Bruen*. Mobilized by increased violent crime and political violence, including an assassination attempt against New York City Mayor William Gaynor, State Senator Tim Sullivan introduced legislation requiring licenses to possess small concealable arms. In modern parlance, the Sullivan Act was a "may issue" rather than "shall issue" law: the issuance of licenses was at the discretion of the police. The purpose of the Act was to provide New York City authorities with tools to fight organized crime and (according to the NRA) threaten the enemies of Tammany Hall.[22] For the group, the law was a threat to military preparedness. Citizens needed a license to practice marksmanship with pistols, since they had to transport their weapons outside the home. The association believed that licenses and restrictions acted as a disincentive for men to engage with firearms sports.

This lack of firearms training made for substandard soldiers in war and naïve, irrational citizens in peace.

New York's Sullivan Law was the earliest, most prominent, and longest-lasting piece of handgun licensing legislation, but not the only one. Within a decade, several other states followed suit. Massachusetts emulated the example of New York, while Arkansas went so far as to require registration of all already owned and new revolvers. Michigan also required handgun registration. North Carolina sought to make it illegal for any person to receive a pistol through the mail without displaying a legal pistol permit. The first federal law regulating the interstate sale of pistols through the US mail was enacted in 1927 to reinforce state statutes requiring a license to purchase pistols. The law did not regulate private shipping companies, only the US Postal Service; therefore its reach and effectiveness were limited.[23]

These developments meant that the NRA had to walk a tightrope. On the one hand, gun control laws could threaten the organization's business model—with financial and political implications. When civilians who were attracted to marksmanship because they enjoyed shooting with handguns rather than rifles did not have the option to own and carry such firearms, that limited the NRA's potential reach and market opportunities. Just as importantly, it limited the pool of trained civilians who could be tapped to serve. On the other hand, the NRA styled itself as a military organization and cultivated a close relationship with the federal government. Openly criticizing efforts to control certain types of firearms would not win the association points when violent crime and "civil disorder" were rising.

There is evidence that through the 1930s, the NRA was genuinely or at least strategically supportive of regulating weapons that could be considered dangerous, and made clear distinctions between firearms suitable for shooting and hunting and weapons of limited use for sports. For example, as late as 1937, the association agreed that certain types of revolvers, such as the .44 Magnum, were not suitable for sportsmen's use, and belonged in "a freak" class of weapons whose use should be restricted to specially trained police officers. According to *The American Rifleman*, "the gun performs no practical function for the sportsman which cannot be [performed] as well or better by arms of standard type . . . it is impossible to defend the Magnum against legislation which would have the practical effect of limiting its sale to agents of the Federal, State, and local police."[24] This position is a far cry from the group's current absolutist stance.

The earliest gun control law supported by the NRA was the Uniform Firearm Act (UFA). Promoted as an alternative to New York's Sullivan Law (1911), the UFA sought to regulate firearms at the point of sale and penalize gun use by criminals. First, the UFA required weapons dealers to be licensed and to maintain a record of purchase for all sales of pistols. The Act also sought to regulate the secondary market in handguns by forbidding pawnshops to sell pistols and by making it a crime to alter the serial number on handguns. Second, the UFA prohibited the ownership of handguns by people convicted of violent crimes, and increased the maximum penalties for violent crimes committed with firearms. Third, it instituted a forty-eight-hour waiting period for handgun purchases meant to discourage the purchase of pistols in the heat of the moment and thus to prevent crimes of passion. After all, if guns were to be used primarily for military preparedness, waiting forty-eight hours to get one was not a major handicap. Finally, consistent with the ideology of the era that the carry of concealed weapons was neither noble nor manly, the Act prohibited concealed carry and created a presumption of intent to commit a violent crime from illegally carrying a pistol.[25]

At the same time, through the UFA, the NRA sought to carve out exemptions for its members in ways that could strengthen its position in the market. Thus, the UFA contained specific exemptions from the pistol carry prohibitions specifically for NRA members. Section 6 of the Act referenced the DCM/CMP program without actually mentioning it, and specified that "the regularly enrolled members of any organization duly authorized to purchase or receive such weapons from the United States or this state" were exempt from licensing requirements, "provided such members are at or are going to or from their places of assembly or target practice." Since the UFA was adopted partially or entirely by several states and the District of Columbia, adopting this type of provision guaranteed that the NRA would maintain a monopoly on civilian marksmanship.[26]

This type of legislation established two classes of Americans, occupying opposite ends of the social deservingness scale. On the one hand, criminals were banned from legal ownership of concealable weapons, and if an individual with a criminal record were found with a handgun on their person, the law presumed an intention to commit a crime. On the other hand, an individual who was a member of an NBPRP-affiliated (i.e., NRA-affiliated) club was afforded the presumption of being a citizen-soldier—a good guy with a gun. Thus, in many jurisdictions, paid membership in the NRA and acceptance of the organization's republican-inspired pledge determined whether citizens needed to secure a pistol license from state authorities or were part of the select category that did not need such a permit.

The first time the NRA went on the record against a federal gun control law was in 1934, when Congress held hearings on the National Firearms Act (NFA). The act taxed manufacturers, importers, and dealers of firearms, and created categories of banned weapons. Possession and sale of banned weapons such as machine guns and sawed-off shotguns, along with mufflers and silencers, was prohibited and required special license and registration with the US Department of the Treasury. The act also required registration for the carry of concealed weapons. Efforts by the Roosevelt administration to include a handgun registration provision in the NFA were defeated in the House of Representatives. Stand-alone bills on handgun registration also failed.

Four years later, the Federal Firearms Act of 1938 (FFA), written with the help of the NRA, sought to dilute registration requirements, and instead focused on manufacturers, dealers, and criminals. The FFA required the registration and licensing of firearms manufacturers and dealers and mandated gun dealers to maintain customer records for six years. It also defined the categories of people who were barred from purchasing firearms, specifically those who had been convicted of violent crime or were fugitives from justice. The law suffered from several deficiencies. First, dealers were barred from "knowingly" selling or transferring firearms to felons, but they were not required to ask for positive proof of identification, thus diluting the law's effectiveness. Second, low entry costs for dealers and limited enforcement coupled with the almost unrestricted capability to ship weapons through the mail system created incentives for individuals to register as dealers to circumvent the law. Third, buyers from states that required licensing were incentivized to buy firearms in states that did not require such licenses, giving false address information which dealers had little incentive to verify. Finally, the Treasury made no effort to police dealer record-keeping. This lack of enforcement, coupled with no requirements (until 1958) to have and record firearms' serial numbers, made the practice of using dealers to control illicit firearms traffic ineffective. Between 1938 and 1968, no dealer was charged with violating the act.[27] Importantly, the law specified that civilian members of the NRA who received firearms and ammunition through the CMP did not have to be licensed for that purpose.[28]

Not only did NRA officials testify in Congress against the NFA; the association also sent out mailings to mobilize its members against the bill. Even though the group opposed the law, it took pains not to criticize public officials and politicize its opposition (unlike the modern NRA). In the 1930s, the relationship between the NRA and the military establishment, especially the National Guard, remained politically robust. Given this close relationship with the military, it is not surprising that even though the NRA begrudgingly accepted laws requiring federal licenses for gun manufacturers and dealers, the organization pushed to place the responsibility for such licensing in the hands of the Department of War rather than the Department of Commerce. Drawing on republican ideology, the NRA reasoned that the regulation of firearms in the country was primarily an issue of national defense, as the overarching objective was not to regulate a commercially available product that was implicated in crimes, as the Roosevelt administration perceived it, but to "[see] that the citizens of the country are qualified as marksmen."[29]

FROM GOVERNMENT DEFENDER TO INSURRECTIONIST

By the 1960s, the orientation of the federal government had been slowly changing for almost twenty years. Harry Truman integrated the armed forces in 1948—for African Americans and women. The US Supreme Court ordered the integration of schools in 1954. The doctrine of "separate but equal" that had propped up the Jim Crow regime was coming to an end. In 1964 and 1965, the Johnson administration shepherded the Voting Rights and Civil Rights Acts through Congress, recognizing African Americans as equal political members.

The turbulence of the 1960s was coupled with a rise in political and social violence. It was not only violent crime that increased at a sharp pace. The third Klan, which emerged in the 1960s (the first Klan operated in the 1860s and 1870s, and the second in the 1920s), and other racist groups lynched civil rights supporters. Political figures, Black and White, progressive and conservative, were assassinated. The Vietnam War, slow racial progress, and ongoing police violence contributed to the riots erupting in cities across the nation. The increased violence intensified calls for effective regulation of the civilian firearms market. After all, President John F. Kennedy had been assassinated with a rifle purchased through mail order.

The enactment of the Gun Control Act of 1968, which followed investigations of the CMP and coincided with the federal government severing ties with the NRA, catalyzed the political radicalization of the NRA. Senator Thomas J. Dodd's (D-CT) efforts to strip the organization of its tax-exempt status and force it to register as a lobbying group further intensified the rift between Congress and the NRA.[30] The group was no longer a government insider. This process culminated in the 1977 "Revolt in Cincinnati," which spearheaded a change in bylaws that catapulted the Second Amendment to the top of the group's agenda. Untethered from its military connections, the NRA was now free to become an "insurrectionist" organization—a force hostile to government actors the association perceived as a danger to its ascriptive republican worldview.

"Insurrection," or the right to rebel against tyranny, is part and parcel of the republican ideology of the American Revolution. After all, this ideology was developed in Revolutionary-era pamphlets to motivate the colonists to rise against the King. Once the Revolution was over, the citizen-soldiers pledged their allegiance to the newly constituted democratic government and crushed rebellions by White citizens and enslaved Black people alike. They became government defenders—establishment men.

The republican-inspired idea that the right to bear arms as enshrined in the US Constitution is a right with political relevance outside of formal institutional structures such as the state militia, emerged in the 1980s in the form of "insurrectionist" theory. By 2022, it became the official position of the US Supreme Court. Already by 1978, the NRA's mission had changed from promoting the "social welfare and public safety, law and order, and national defense" to being "the foremost guardian of the second amendment." The emphasis on the Second Amendment as a right in the political (defense against tyranny), not just the social (self-defense against crime), domain started to appear everywhere—in NRA narratives, law review articles,[31] Congressional debates,[32] and campaign talking points.[33] As early as 1982, NRA hard-liners wanted to frame the debate surrounding California's Proposition 15, a measure requiring registration of handguns, in terms of the Second Amendment and people's need to be armed against government tyranny.[34]

In 1989, the republican-grounded notion that individual gun ownership is linked to political rights exploded into the mainstream when the progressive law scholar Sanford Levinson challenged the traditional explanations of the Second Amendment's legal meaning. Republicanism had "unexpected, even embarrassing" implications for our understanding of gun rights, claimed Levinson in his famous critique. American republicanism, developed long before the emergence of modern bureaucratic states, had no room for the Weberian conception of the state as "the repository of the monopoly of the legitimate means of violence." Instead, the republican origins of the Second Amendment indicate that "just as ordinary citizens should participate actively in governmental decision making through offering their own deliberative insights, rather than be confined to casting ballots . . . so should ordinary citizens participate in the process of law enforcement and defense of liberty."[35] In short, citizens had a right to the bullet when the ballot was not available or sufficient. Civilian gun ownership rights secured access to the bullet.

In the 1980s and 1990s, several NRA-affiliated scholars developed the "insurrectionist theory." The building blocks of this ideology were already present in NRA narratives as far back as the 1930s. However, these legal scholars dressed the argument with historical and legal details and focused primarily on the US Constitution. This theory presented the Second Amendment as the ultimate guarantee of republican citizenship: "the 1st

Freedom" or the "great equalizer," as the NRA calls it.[36] Drawing on republican themes, these authors warn that political elites are always tempted by power and personal gain. In this narrative, the world consists of two contrasted groups: the people and the elites. Much like the standing army of yore, the elites are not "of" the people—at least not the way modern democracy expects them to be—and do not always act in the people's best interest. They do not necessarily share "the people's" values. The elites' primary motivation is not simply personal enrichment, but cultural change that can help entrench them in power. Therefore, the elites are independent moral entities with their own interests. These independent-acting elites need systemic incentives not to exploit the asymmetries of principal/agent relationships. Only if there is a credible threat that "the people" may use violence against them will elites toe the line.

The association argues that the intended goal of the elites is to induce dependency in the people by changing the country's cultural norms. Dependency takes two forms in the corrupt Republic. First, due to gun control, "the people" cannot defend themselves against crime and violence. This weakness makes them dependent on elites for physical security, weakening their republican spirit. Instead of expecting citizens to cultivate personal responsibility and the martial skills necessary to defend the Republic, the state uses its agents to provide collective security, limiting citizens' incentives to develop political virtue. Second, redistributive policies create additional dependency by tying recipients more closely to elite patrons and discouraging personal responsibility and autonomy.[37] By inducing dependency, and by the elites controlling the means of violence, "the people" become weak and subordinated, unable to defend the nation against tyranny. Without private firearm ownership, "the people" are vulnerable to the worst depravities known to humanity—from slavery to genocide.[38] Some NRA-affiliated authors even quote Mao approvingly and without irony, saying "political power grows out of the barrel of a gun," and therefore, so does democracy.[39]

Insurrectionist conceptions of politics view government not as the agent of the people but as an existential threat to political rights. In this model, the rights of both majorities and minorities can be endangered by corrupt and arbitrary government action. People in positions of authority have a persistent incentive to augment their power at the expense of citizens. Neither norms nor laws, not the courts nor the political process, can prevent a political leader from becoming a dictator. Bureaucrats, elected officials, and judges (especially those from the opposing political party) cannot be trusted to uphold democracy and justice. The temptation of power is too much for them to resist. The rule of law persists only when its enforcers know that violations could cost them their lives at the hands of an armed public.[40]

Gun rights activists and publications that promote those rights envisioned firearms ownership as "the great equalizer"—the primary way to level the playing field between the government and its people. As early as 1959, *Guns* magazine summarized this argument as follows: "if everyone has [guns], then a ballot becomes not only possible but inevitable. If only a few have them, a dictatorship becomes tempting and inexorable. . . . The freedom of [a] republic is directly proportional to the dispersal of the arms in the nation. The more general that dispersal and ownership, the more general the freedom."[41]

In this narrative, the consumer act of gun ownership, stripped of any link to military service or even preparedness, is the foundation of democratic politics—what Charlton Heston called the "first freedom."[42] If classical republicanism assumed two coequal pillars—military service and political participation—as grounding the Republic, contemporary NRA ideology argues that a single pillar—gun ownership—is the fountain of political virtue and safeguards all rights, including the right to political participation and voting. The "insurrectionist theory" of gun rights posits that American citizens, in their capacity as individuals, have a right to keep and publicly carry arms, openly or concealed, both for preemptive self-defense and as a deterrent to government tyranny.[43] Gun activists insist that what is at stake in the debate is not simply people's ability to "shoot ducks" (that is, to own arms for recreation). Instead, this is a fight to protect a political right of democracy, a "guarantee that Americans will always have the right and means to protect themselves from criminals, despots, and international terrorists."[44]

The US Supreme Court has put the stamp of legitimacy on insurrectionist ideology. In its 2008 *Heller* decision, the Court reversed 150 years of precedent and delivered to Americans an individual right to own a firearm for home self-defense. The decision relied on NRA-supported historical analysis that most academic historians have condemned as selective and inaccurate.[45] In 2022, the Court extended the individual right to bear arms to include public carry of concealed firearms. The Court also discarded the notion that the government's interest in public safety is relevant when courts evaluate Second Amendment cases.[46] Only history and tradition are relevant in evaluating the constitutionality of gun laws: "The government must demonstrate that the regulation is consistent with this nation's historical tradition of firearm regulation."[47] Tradition is never defined in the opinion. And only laws in existence at the time of the Second Amendment's ratification (1791) or the Reconstruction Amendments (1868)—and only if widely prevalent in the states rather than the Western territories—count as "history" henceforth.[48]

Although the *Heller* decision specified the locus of the right as the home, not the public square, Justice Scalia's majority opinion validated social and *political* motivations for gun ownership, effectively linking gun ownership to political grievances and virulent mistrust in institutions. In a nod to the NRA's ideology, the decision affirmed that the individual's right to bear arms protects one from a tyrannical government. According to Scalia, "when the able-bodied *men* of a nation are *trained* in arms and *organized*, they are better able to resist tyranny" (emphasis added).[49]

Insurrectionism strips republicanism of its moral foundations, and thus makes it a hollow democratic principle. Instead of a theory that associates political virtue with service to the public good, insurrectionist ideology offers a romanticized, profoundly ahistorical view of gun owners and their revolutionary heroes as "rugged individualists" whose only master was their innate sense of patriotism. These men are bound by no collective understanding of the public good and only answer to their individual conscience. This moral independence, exemplified by gun ownership rather than armed service, empowers citizens to resist tyranny.[50] Insurrectionist theory is fundamentally opposed to contemporary Weberian understandings of the state. Instead, it argues that both the state and the individual citizen have the moral authority to use violence for political ends.[51] In an era when equality—variously defined—has become a primary political objective, the slogan "great equalizer" has the power to attract and motivate many people.

This is evident in Scalia's *Heller* decision as well. The Court envisions people in their capacity as individuals, not as members of an organized polity with explicit rights and obligations, who on their own initiative train in arms and organize militias to resist tyranny. Yet, the idea that citizens would use productive time to train in arms and organize militia units to act as a check on government is antithetical to Lockean liberalism, which expected the state to provide security through professional forces.[52] The Court talks of training at arms, ignoring the fact that training requirements were historically associated with military units—enrolled and volunteer. States authorized the creation of military units and set training standards. As I discussed in chapter 3, military training was a state obligation, and when states neglected this duty, the citizens' facility with arms declined and citizen-soldiers performed terribly on the battlefield. Today, in Texas, civilian gun owners are required to complete four hours of classwork and two hours at a range before they are licensed to carry.[53] Not surprisingly, industry data show that more than half of all gun owners consider themselves relatively ignorant about guns—a reality that mirrors America's historical experience.[54] However, that is not sufficient for Justice Alito to consider statistics on the 45,000 gun deaths that occur each year "relevant" to the discussion of a right to bear arms.[55] Many gun rights activists echo this position when they argue that gun deaths are the price Americans must pay for freedom.[56]

Relatedly, these individual gun owners, who at most have received a few hours of training, are expected to be the bulwark against a government that owns tanks, military planes, and nuclear weapons. However, the opinion is clear that citizens are barred from owning "dangerous" or "unusual" weapons, which include those owned by the US Army. As other scholars have argued, this raises the question of how one can expect these undertrained freedom fighters to have a chance against the American Goliath. If citizens were to be an effective check on the government, shouldn't they have access to the same weapons?[57] Indeed, in the context of the eighteenth century, citizen-soldiers were expected to own the same military equipment they used in battle. If we are to reason by historical analogy, this suggests that members of the general public should be permitted to own modern military weapons. Otherwise, what is left is performance politics and citizens menacing individual political actors and each other in the name of whatever set of values they view as un-American.

Another key element in the NRA insurrectionist narrative is that the "people" are homogenous and united—they have the same preferences and interests. Therefore, the preferences of individuals can be aggregated and translated into the public will. Individuals and groups who do not share the "people's" interests, cultural values, and ideology are excluded from the category. Including these others would require recognition that there is no consensus vision of American politics. "People" is in the association's rhetoric frequently substituted for gun owners or NRA members—the vanguard of the virtuous. This interchangeable use of the term reinforces the notion that conservative White men represent the prototypical member of the American nation, and it is their preferences that constitute the national consensus. As one reader put it, "ours is supposed to be a government of, by and for the people. . . . I know I speak for the majority of the uncorrupted [people] when I say we need a senator who is Second Amendment friendly."[58]

The *Heller* decision also betrays ascriptive assumptions not dissimilar to those of the NRA, even as it seeks to bolster its claims to racial egalitarianism. As the Founders understood it, the peoplehood of the era included only White men. Instead of acknowledging this historical fact, the opinion imposes a modern liberal perspective on the Revolution-era militia. It claims that the enrolled state militia organized by the UMA to counter the standing army were themselves a "select militia" (i.e., a standing army) "of the sort the Stuart kings found useful" because only White men rather than men of all races were included. Why would the Founders address their concerns about a "select militia" by establishing another "select militia"? And where is the evidence that a "militia of the whole"—the "people's militia"— was expected to include free Black men, a group that did not qualify as citizens? Yet this exclusion of Black men becomes a key rationale for impugning the federal government, characterizing it as potentially tyrannical: according to the Court, if the federal government had the authority to specify who was eligible for militia duty, then it could use ascriptive criteria to exclude people selectively from such service and thus from gun ownership—as it did in 1792.[59]

While Scalia redefines the militia to suit contemporary color-blind rhetoric and commitments, he also envisions armed *men* ("able-bodied men," to be exact), but not women, to be "better able to resist tyranny." Even in the twenty-first century, the Court harkens back to an ascriptive republican understanding of peoplehood and embraces a gendered vision of armed citizenship. Women today may have gained entry to combat units, but that is not how the Court imagines martial citizenship. This argument does not seem to bother the other justices who joined the opinion. Much like the NRA, the Court seems to equate the modern freedom-fighting citizen with the mythical (White male) minuteman, and not with the many women soldiers who have served the country.

What is more, the Court's argument betrays the uneasy fit between liberal theory's individual citizen and its imaginary vision of the organized and trained defenders of a nation. Ascriptive republican ideology developed during the Revolution included a theory of peoplehood. It explained what kind of people could develop into virtuous defenders of the nation— "republican machines."[60] In republican terms, it was the body of the citizens who could decide when a government was tyrannical; that is why the capacity for armed resistance was needed. A commitment to the common good, expressed as training for battle in times of peace, qualified these citizens to make such determinations. Yet individuals or groups of armed men who expressed political grievances with arms—such as Shays's men or the Whiskey Rebellion participants—were not celebrated as resisters to tyranny; instead they were punished as insurrectionists.

But what constitutes the Court's "nation"? What theory explains why any single modern gun owner or group of gun owners would have the authority to make such a determination and wage armed opposition to the government? The Court's statement implies an idea of peoplehood—and an ascriptive one at that. It is "the able-bodied men" in their *collective* capacity as citizens "of the nation" who are authorized to decide on the government's character. Yet there seem to be no operative criteria other than gender in defining the nation. What determines "a legitimate" fight against tyranny rather than an insurrection? How many and what kind of participants does it take? The participants in the January 6 attack on the US Capitol believed they were fighting for such a legitimate cause, but that is not how the Department of Justice understood these events.

Although the *Bruen* decision does not discuss the armed citizen's right to revolution, its endorsement of an individual right to bring firearms into the public square makes the *Heller* discussion of revolution acutely relevant. According to the *Bruen* decision, "the Second Amendment guarantees an individual right to possess and carry weapons in case of confrontation, and confrontation can surely take place outside the home."[61] However, what constitutes a threat is a subjective assessment. Earlier American laws and traditions required people to retreat from dangerous situations and only use violence as a last resort. Stand your ground laws made the duty to retreat obsolete and opened the door to vigilantism. As we witnessed in 2020 in Kenosha, Wisconsin, people who seek confrontation can find it—with deadly consequences.

The NRA's insurrectionism rejects the notion of a pluralistic society where there isn't a stable majority. The NRA's "majority" is pitted against an "elite," which is, by definition, a small group. Ironically, the NRA prided itself on the "elite" status of its riflemen through the 1960s, but after it lost its ties to the government it shed the elite self-characterization as well. The polarized majority-elite construction does not address what happens in a society with multiple power centers and diverse constituencies where everyone is armed. Guns in the hands of a minority do not necessarily protect them from an armed majority. In a world where everyone is armed, the armed majority will not necessarily be deterred into treating an armed minority with respect. Nor are individual members of a minority group safe from ethnic violence if they are armed. When people become fanatical enough and threatened enough to attack FBI offices and the US Capitol— both protected by trained and armed security forces—what will stop them from attacking armed citizens if they view them as an ideological threat? The NRA and even the US Supreme Court fail to accept what Martin Luther King Jr. understood too well: the rule of law, and not unrestricted possession of firearms, creates safety and cooperation. Citizens' rights are secure only when democratic institutions give fair representation to all groups and the justice system is (and is accepted as) fair and impartial.

For the NRA, the basis of "the people's" consensus is their veneration of the original social compact. Depending on whom you ask, these principles are found in the US Constitution, the English Bill of Rights, or the mythical ancient English Constitution.[62] This is not unlike recent Supreme Court decisions that seem to move the goalposts of historical relevance. In turn, these consensus principles can be reduced to two things: free political expression and the right to bear arms. The rest of the US Bill of Rights rarely makes its existence known in this narrative universe. Although in the US Constitution freedom of speech is listed before the right to bear arms, for the NRA gun ownership is "the 1st Freedom," because without it the people cannot protect free expression or the franchise.[63]

In the NRA world, the law and constitutional rights are not culturally determined constructs, but objective quantities that stand outside historical time and are juxtaposed to "culture." Cultural values vary across groups and eras. Culture can be contested. However, the Constitution cannot be contested, nor is it subject to legal and political interpretation, as it forms the bedrock consensus of the political community itself.[64] Some even place the right to own arms in a mythical prepolitical "state of nature."[65] Treating the Constitution as concrete and uncontestable or situating rights in a prepolitical world enables the NRA to divorce law from politics. If there is a single interpretation of the Constitution, political problems arise when political elites ignore constitutional principles in favor of "cultural values."[66] Of course, sustaining this construction requires NRA principals to ignore that the Constitution sanctioned slavery, and that for centuries, White freedom coexisted materially and ideologically with Black bondage.[67] It was not anonymous and amorphous "cultural elites" or the hated "Klan," but the federal Constitution, that recognized enslaved Black people as three-fifths of a person. Similarly, state constitutions, not a faceless elite, recognized republican political rights only for White men. In the traditional military meaning of the term, the political right of Black men to bear arms remained proscribed until World War II—with the NRA's tacit blessing.

THE PROBLEM OF DEMOCRACY

Another critical problem in the NRA's argument is that the organization equates democracy with gun ownership. This discussion is essential and needs to be taken seriously, because the NRA's argument has found its way into scholarly publications, elite messaging, and public discourse. As Matthew Lacombe has demonstrated, NRA arguments spread quickly among the faithful and the Republican Party. Since the NRA has become a central pillar of conservative politics in recent years, its access and sway have increased.[68] Exposing the motivated logic of the argument is thus crucial, for normative and scholarly reasons.

Modern political science defines democracy in terms of institutions: the presence of free elections, freedom of speech and the press, party competition, and respect for minority rights are all elements of democratic systems.[69] In the NRA narrative, political power and democracy flow out of the barrel of a gun. As a result, the single criterion for political virtue for the citizen and the regime is private gun ownership. Conversely, gun control is evidence of a tyrannical political system and an enslaved, dependent populace. The conceptual limitations of equating democracy with private gun ownership and citizen militarism become visible when we consider the various countries the NRA has used to illustrate its warnings.

The American Rifleman had an easy explanation for the Italian defeat by Greece in 1941. The "truth" of the Greek victory was "that the Italians don't know how to shoot!" Italian soldiers were inferior shots because they were not raised with firearms in the home. Italy was a dictatorship, and as such, it was fearful of its citizens and did not trust them with privately owned firearms. "Ownership of firearms in Italy . . . long has been a privilege to be extended only to those politically satisfactory to the police or military." The result was that the average Italian man lacked political virtue: he was a weak citizen and a terrible soldier. Italy's defeat in the war constituted "irrefutable evidence that the political control of firearms, as in Italy, damages the fighting morale of a people."[70]

Should we infer from this that the 1941 Greek victory was due to Greece's superior soldiers? Did its people have strong "fighting morale"? Given its victory against Italy, should we conclude that Greece was a republic? At the time, Greece was ruled by a Fascist military dictatorship quite similar to the Italian regime. Only months after its victory against the Italians, the Greek Army surrendered to the German Army. What does the German victory over Greece tell us about either country's political regime or the political virtue of their citizens?

The case of Germany further illustrates the logical inconsistencies in the NRA's argument linking private gun ownership, marksmanship, and democracy. Since the nineteenth century, NRA principals viewed the German Army as a model of military preparedness. Germany's male citizens were required to serve in the military and received extensive marksmanship training. The German infantry was so well trained that on the eve of World War I, none other than the NRA co-founder Col. William C. Church expressed great admiration for German riflemen, urging the United States to consider conscription and mandatory training in shooting.[71]

NRA principals continued to express great admiration for German marksmen in World War II. In fact, during the 1940 NRA annual convention, participants were convinced that Germany's success in Poland was attributable to "the efficiency of the German Infantryman, the foot soldier with his rifle." Although he did not receive "newspaper credit," the German rifleman, "not the aviation and mechanized forces," was responsible for the "more spectacular" operations of the campaign, meeting participants concluded.[72] What does the superior performance of the German marksmen tell us about the character of the German regime? Shouldn't a regime whose men are so well trained in shooting that the NRA recognizes their superior performance be classified as democratic? If marksmanship skills did not confer political virtue, and we were thus prohibited from equating skill with democracy, where does democracy spring from?

Perhaps it is the confluence of two conditions that produce democracy. For democracy to emerge, a state should encourage the development of marksmanship through voluntary military service and private ownership. Unlike the republican narrative of the Revolution, which found political virtue in compulsory military service, the NRA's republican narrative recognized voluntary engagement with arms as the source of political virtue and thus of democracy. Perhaps German men were great soldiers, but because their training was not voluntary, they were not good citizens, and therefore their regime was not democratic. However, if that were the case, where does Britain, with its all-volunteer army, rank relative to Germany?

Britain had a volunteer army and it strictly regulated gun ownership going back to the early twentieth century. British men lacked the benefit of the compulsory arms training that the Germans had. They also had no opportunity to develop "fighting morale" or political virtue, because private gun ownership was highly regulated. The NRA frequently brought up the country's stringent gun laws during World War II and later as a warning. For example, in 1941, the group warned that Britain, an ally and a democracy, urgently needed civilian "riflemen and pistoleers" after the defeat of the British Expeditionary Forces at Dunkirk. The British were "facing the German Army in which every man from infantryman to the truck driver has been taught small-arms marksmanship."[73] How could Britain be classified as a democracy under such conditions? How are we to think about the character of the British regime, a polity that restricted civilian gun ownership, relative to the character of the German regime that trained all its men in marksmanship? If there is "irrefutable evidence," as the NRA claimed, that absence of private gun ownership and civilian training in marksmanship "damages the fighting morale of people,"[74] sapping their political virtue, do we conclude that the German people were more virtuous than the

British? *The American Rifleman* emphasized the peril that Britain experienced in World War II due to the absence of trained civilian marksmen: Britain came close to losing its independence and democratic institutions due to its gun control policies. However, the NRA did not explain why British democratic institutions persisted after World War II, or why they existed before the war.

Russia presented an even more complicated case for the NRA's argument. First, NRA authors made comparisons that made it difficult to sustain the logic that private gun ownership led to superior marksmanship, which led to democracy. Before 1917, Russia was an absolute monarchy. After the Russian revolution, the Soviet Union came to be controlled by the Communist Party. In an early article, *The American Rifleman* condemned the Soviet regime as a totalitarian system based on its stringent restrictions on civilian gun ownership. But the same article noted that "during the Tsar's reign in Russia everybody had the right to possess hunting firearms."[75] Assuming that this claim was correct, if an absolute monarchy allowed private firearms ownership, what does that imply about the character of that regime? If the defining characteristic of democratic freedom is private gun ownership, then an absolute monarchy has a greater affinity to a democracy than does a Communist state, or at least we can expect its people to be more virtuous than those of a Communist regime.

Not only is the comparison between Tsarist Russia and the Soviet Union problematic in its conclusion; the NRA's discussion of the Soviet Union itself is equally confusing when addressed using the organization's theory. In 1927, the Soviets established the Ossviachim, a program whose aims were not unlike the NRA's.[76] This program was a private-public partnership between civilian shooting clubs and the state, focused on instructing civilians in marksmanship.[77] During World War II, as the United States and the Soviet Union became reluctant allies in the fight against the Axis, the NRA's stance toward the Communist regime softened. The magazine expressed admiration for the Ossviachim, attributing Russian military success to civilian marksmanship programs or "lifelong training as sniper[s]" that Russians provided to "whole sections of the population." So great was the "Russian system of snipers" that it put to shame "the German imitation."[78]

Russian armies of the Tsarist past had sought to instill fear in their adversaries through "secrecy" and "mystery," but they were exposed as "paper dragons" when "action has shed harsh light upon them." Thus, the Tsarist armies lacked well-trained marksmen, but the Soviet soldiers were better prepared because the "first principle of Communism demanded complete militarization."[79] Consistent with the NRA's republican theory, an absolute monarchy cannot develop an effective rifleman; but the publication also suggested that the Tsarist regime was more democratic than the Communist system because, under the Tsar, people freely owned firearms. Communism was tyranny, but how can this argument be sustained if the Soviet riflemen were "the brave men dying on the Russian steppes"?[80] Surely, if the Soviets trained civilians in marksmanship and had programs similar to the NRA's, then their regime developed political virtue in its citizens.

Perhaps, then, the problem was not with the availability of private arms or civilian marksmanship programs. According to *The American Rifleman*, the Soviet Union required licensing and registration of all private firearms. The regime used political criteria to allocate licenses, giving preferential treatment to members of the Communist Party. Thus, the issue lay with the selective right to own private arms. A democratic country did not use political criteria in determining who gets to own firearms. A democracy did not distinguish between citizens when it came to rights. Russia was "a tyrannical government of the communists" that allowed "only the communists [to] have the right to possess firearms," while "all the hunting [was] controlled and exploited by the state."[81] The lesson from the USSR was that as "the Red Tide moved over Europe," Moscow would suppress democracy the same way it did within Russia itself. The Communist government would "abolish those shooting clubs it could not control." America was about to experience the same wave of restrictions, leading to "the infiltration or abolishment of [American rifle] clubs and the breaking up of the National Rifle Association if they [internal enemies] cannot control it."[82]

From this vantage point, the undemocratic nature of the regime is evident not in the quality of marksmanship among the citizens but in the criteria the regime used to determine which citizens deserved a "right to bear arms." According to the NRA, when authorities use "political" criteria to exclude people from the rights of citizenship (defined in terms of access to firearms), then the regime is corrupt and undemocratic. Corrupt police in American cities allocated licenses based on loyalty to the political machine.[83] Corrupt Communist leaders in the USSR allocated licenses based on loyalty to the Party.

But if democracy is defined as the *universal* allocation of gun rights, what does that mean for the United States? The US has always used political criteria for private gun ownership. Free and enslaved African Americans were excluded from the right to own firearms or to serve in the military. This exclusion was political, and was enshrined in the country's laws and constitutions. It was based on an ideology that did not recognize African Americans as suitable for the duties and privileges of political membership. Loyalty oaths and exclusion of immigrants were other political criteria of exclusion. For most of the country's history, women were excluded from both dimensions of political membership. Therefore, either US institutions have not been democratic, or certain groups do not count in the category of "the people."

Of course, the NRA's argument that private gun ownership and democracy are linked causally is not based on any systematic analysis—it is propaganda. Furthermore, in its current form, which insists on ownership rather than military service or preparedness, the argument lacks a moral foundation, as it equates a consumer choice with political virtue at both the individual and the regime level. Since the early twentieth century, the organization has cherry-picked cases that fit into its ideology while ignoring the wealth of cases that do not. In social science terms, the NRA commits the error of selecting on the dependent variable.

THE PROBLEM OF GENDER

The application of insurrectionist theory to gender further illuminates the logical inconsistencies in the NRA's argument, highlighting the group's ascriptive ideological assumptions. The NRA's democracy narrative never addresses the political exclusion of women—and there is a reason for that. The political exclusion of women does not fit neatly into the NRA's ascriptive republican framework. American martial republicanism equates men, manhood, and political membership. In this construction, men can have claims to citizenship and can defend those claims at arms. Therefore, ascriptive republican narratives are intersectional: they elevate White men to citizenship but exclude others based on race and gender. White women were excluded from bearing arms in the republican meaning of the term, but not from gun ownership. White women have always had access to firearms for social purposes such as hunting or protection.[84] As we saw earlier, the NRA allowed women shooters in its competitions. Gun manufacturers advertised firearms to women—even in the pages of *The American Rifleman*. If what generates a voice in politics is access to firearms, White women surely should have had political rights from early on.

If White women had access to the "great equalizer," why did they not have political rights? Why did it take until 1920 for women to gain the franchise? After the American Revolution, why did coverture strengthen rather than weaken in the United States?[85] Conversely, given that women did not have the political right to bear arms but did have access to firearms, why did they not use their "second amendment remedies"—in contemporary parlance—to gain political liberty? The NRA does not even pose this question, because this question exists outside of its ascriptive republican worldview.

The NRA is not silent about women; it just does not place them in a political context. In the late twentieth century, as the NRA sought to expand the civilian gun market, it courted women heavily. The "great equalizer" became a device to explain why women should be armed. Women and men differ in physical strength, the argument goes. In a world where some men are predators, women are unsafe. "We know there are predators out there. . . . The number of sex offenders living within three miles of your house or campus, it's eye-opening."[86] Violent spouses and partners exist, and they harm and even kill women.[87] These bad guys, by definition, lack virtue. "Criminals are not looking for a fair fight. . . . They are cowardly and prey on . . . easy targets."[88] The causes of gendered violence are not relevant to the "great equalizer" argument. Ascriptive republicanism ascribes corruption to human nature, not to social conditions. For the most part, NRA commentators are not interested in any social causes of violent behavior, because all that matters is that "bad guys with guns" (and bad guys more broadly) exist in society. When the NRA discusses causes of violence, it focuses on private-domain factors and individual behaviors such as the consumption of violent movies, rap music, and video games. The lack of personal responsibility in men (especially Black men) allows for such behaviors to develop. Irresponsible men pose a threat to individual women.[89]

The state's role in this context is to deter would-be criminals through excessive punishment. Because perpetrators are motivated exclusively by pleasure and pain, the more costly the state makes crime, the fewer men will engage in criminal behavior. However, policing is not an effective deterrent to crime because the police cannot be everywhere at once. At best, the police shall investigate crime and arrest offenders. The state thus cannot prevent crimes such as rape or domestic violence.[90]

In this world where the government is powerless to effectively protect its citizens from crime, it is up to each person to protect themselves. Yet individuals do not have the same physical strength, and thus fights between two people are not equal. Women are weak and vulnerable, unlikely to overcome a stronger male attacker. Firearms, though, can change the power dynamics, making women equal to men and able to defend themselves from physical attack.[91] The "private ownership of firearms" is "the great equalizer against violence from all quarters."[92] Firearms "give at-risk women a fighting chance," when otherwise they would be "defenseless against male attackers."[93] A staged picture from 1967 (fig. 9.1) shows how the NRA understood gun ownership among women—as a means of self-defense against men. The caption reads: "Though this scene of a housewife repelling an armed criminal was posed, it depicts accurately what takes place in scores of homes each day."[94]

NRA women do not reject feminism, but their understanding of the

Figure 9.1 Housewife defends baby, *The American Rifleman*, May 1967.

term is very different from what we encounter among progressive women. In this world, feminism is about empowering women to assume personal responsibility for their safety and that of their children. Feminism does not mean leveling the playing field in politics or the job market. It is not about "equal success." Instead, feminism is about equalizing the playing field between the female victim and her physically superior attacker.[95] Without the "great equalizer," gender relations in the domestic sphere would "unavoidabl[y]" revert to "the rules of the Stone Age," with "many women [becoming] defenseless against male attackers."[96]

From this vantage point, political actors' refusal to enable women to be armed is "sexist." Far from pursuing policies of gender equality, progressive women politicians such as Hillary Clinton want to "take power away from women" and reinforce gender inequality in individual security and women's ability to "defend themselves and their families."[97] Therefore, the "war on women"—a slogan used frequently by progressive women activists—is not a conflict over the role of women in the economy, society, and politics. The war on women is not about reproductive rights and women's ability to make choices about abortion. Instead, there is a war on women's right to assume responsibility for their own self-defense: the "right to choose" to carry a firearm—to be "equipped with a great equalizer"—in school, work, and public places where women may be vulnerable to male attackers. And this war is waged by progressive women politicians and their allies. It is these women who have betrayed their sex for political power.[98] These hypocritical women politicians pay lip service to a "woman's right to choose," while denying women the right to choose armed self-reliance.[99]

There are indirect political implications to women's inequality in the domain of self-defense. A woman's public- and private-domain virtue is tied to her ability to provide security to herself and her children. The women themselves should develop the skills and cool reason to protect their safety. Consistent with republican themes, elected officials who deny women the means to be personally responsible for their safety are politically corrupt. "President Obama, [Hillary] Clinton, and their tyrannical peers" encourage victims to be dependent on the state rather than self-sufficient and independent. "They need victims reliant on government to save them, not survivors who have learned they must save themselves."[100]

In this view, the real "war on women" is waged in government efforts to deprive them of the independent capacity to protect themselves with firearms.[101] If women are dependent on government for their security, then they cannot be autonomous, rational citizens, but only political subjects. According to NRA writers, "It's ironic that the ones who want to free us from the mandates of men suddenly want us to relinquish our protection to them." "Those claiming to champion a woman's independence and dignity" instead of encouraging women to carry a firearm counsel women that in a case of assault, they should use passive means of defense, such as "claim[ing] to have a disease or be menstruating."[102]

The analysis of how gender is used and silenced in NRA narratives exposes the deep contradictions within the narrative. The absence of a political dimension of gender and the relegation of women to the social domain is evidence of the ascriptive republican assumptions embedded in the "great equalizer" argument. Women's equality is only a concern in the social domain, not the political, because women rarely exist as political agents in the narrative. Conversely, race has an exclusively political purpose in the NRA cautionary tale.

THE PROBLEM OF RACE

Along with gender, race is the central organizing principle of American politics. Ascriptive republican beliefs rest at the intersection of Whiteness and male virtue. Beliefs about Black people and the meaning of racial equality structure partisanship,[103] polarization,[104] policy preferences,[105] and trust in institutions.[106] Race is a crucial concept for the political dimension of the NRA's "great equalizer" argument. Oppression based on race is a central justification for the "insurrectionist" logic and a means to establish the group's racial egalitarian credentials.

It is no accident that since 1990 the group has branded itself "the nation's oldest and largest *civil rights* organization," claiming to defend citizens' most critical right.[107] Slavery and violence against African Americans have become significant themes in the NRA's narrative, used to justify a political right to arms and a right to insurrection. In a smattering of articles, the association has showcased African American civil rights activists— figures that today's culture has accepted as "heroes"—who owned and used firearms to defend themselves against slavery and the Klan. From Frederick Douglass and Harriet Tubman to Rosa Parks and the Deacons of Defense, the NRA points out people who carried firearms for self-defense against racist attacks.[108]

Some have even portrayed the NRA as a proponent of slave emancipation and Black civil rights. In this view, "the history of the [NRA] has a special meaning for [Black people]. At a time when recently freed slaves were transitioning to being American citizens, they came under assault.... When faced with the threats, coercion, intimidation, and, yes, violence of an organization called the Ku Klux Klan, it was the NRA that stood with and defended the [gun] rights of blacks."[109]

Some observers explained the NRA's enthusiasm for civil rights as a ploy to engage more African Americans with firearms.[110] However, a more likely explanation is that the organization's claimed "civil rights" credentials appeal to a racially conservative White audience committed to an ascriptive republican ideology. By employing the concept of "civil rights" and introducing stories about individual activists who used firearms to protect themselves from the Klan, the NRA brandishes its affirmed egalitarian commitments and its position as a supporter of color-blindness. At the same time, the group validates ascriptive republican beliefs and White racial grievances that the "good guys with a gun" are being unfairly disarmed and disempowered by a corrupt political elite.

Understanding the function of "civil rights" claims in the NRA worldview requires a brief explanation of the difference between civil rights and civil liberties. "Civil liberties" refers to constitutional guarantees—such as the freedom of speech or the right to a trial by jury—that government cannot limit without a solid justification. Conversely, civil rights relate to political equality across all citizens, regardless of their demographic characteristics. In this case, the role of government is to actively protect classes of people from discrimination or injury that is the result of a person's membership in a particular group. Before the Supreme Court's decision in *Heller*, gun rights advocates framed the right to bear arms primarily as a civil liberty. However, in the aftermath of *Heller* and especially after the *McDonald v. Chicago* decision, gun rights proponents have switched gears, framing the issue as a civil right.[111] The NRA has strategically used the term "civil rights" since the 1980s because it is conceptually linked with group-based discrimination, and this may license a White audience to express race-based grievances in implicit ways.

Civil rights organizations zero in on discrimination based on a person's membership in a discrete social group. The underlying concern for these organizations is that group-based discrimination creates social and political inequalities, promoting a hierarchical society. The NRA is not concerned with gender and racial inequality and how to fix it—historically or contemporarily. The NRA did not advocate desegregation within its main area of influence—the military. Col. Church stood opposed to racial equality within the armed services—he never even considered women soldiers.[112] In a century of publishing first *Arms & the Man* and then *The American Rifleman*, seldom did the organization showcase the service of Black men in the armed forces,[113] nor did it pay any attention to their demands for integration and advancement in the ranks. Black people, including Black soldiers, are simply absent from the magazine. Women are present only as victims of violence, not as citizens.

Through the 1960s, the term "civil rights" in *The American Rifleman* is found in the context of "civil disturbances" and "riots."[114] Even in this era, the concern was with the impact of civil rights marches on the rights of gun owners—White men. As one article put it, civil rights were the "great moral and social issue" of the era, but "unfortunately, firearms and reputable firearms owners are being harmed" by it.[115] Thus from very early on, the NRA perceived civil rights and gun rights in opposition to each other. During "the educational [*sic*] integration crisis in the South, 12,000 U.S. Army Regulars were ordered to special duty." What happens if the National Guard is not available to help in "sudden blaze-ups of civic disorder?" the NRA asked in 1967. Its solution was to activate "home guards" and citizens' "auxiliary police organizations" as "potential community stabilizer[s]." Never mind a century-long history of such organizations using arms to protect White supremacy—in 1967, the organization had no doubts of its members' "support of law and order." As "a civilian member of the posse comitatus [*sic*] or as one of the unorganized militia," the rifleman could prove "essential" to quell the violence brought on by civil rights.[116]

This discourse avoids making any moral commitment to racial equality—you can read the term "great moral issue" in any way you choose. This ambiguity helps the organization preserve its egalitarian self-image without meaningfully engaging with the structural problems associated with racism.[117] At the same time, the NRA validates White grievance. By invoking "civil rights," the association claims that gun owners and gun rights advocates—a predominantly White male group—are a distinct social group that experiences discrimination by social and governmental actors because of who they are.[118] Therefore, gun owners should be free to express their political grievances openly, the same way that African Americans claim protection from discriminatory treatment.

The term "civil rights," in reference to gun owners, entered the NRA lingo in 1978 when the group founded the NRA Civil Rights Legal Defense Fund. This fund was meant not to assist in civil rights cases (i.e., cases about group-based discrimination), but to provide legal services to gun owners challenging gun control laws. Neal Knox, an NRA leader, equated racism and gun control in his testimony before Congress in 1979. "I submit to you that there is no qualitative difference between a judge who is prejudiced against blacks and one who is prejudiced against gun owners," said Knox. "The very nature of prejudice is the same."[119] Speaking for the NRA, John Aquillino was more blunt: "gun owners are the new n***** of society," he declared.[120] Similarly, Charlton Heston leveraged his participation in the 1963 March on Washington to criticize African Americans for moral failings and to complain that White, male, Christian gun owners are persecuted and socially diminished by gun control–promoting political elites.[121] These civil rights stories enable the group's primarily White male audience to accept with little pushback the profoundly reactionary idea that in a democracy, political violence against elected officials is a fundamental right of aggrieved groups of citizens.[122] This narrative has made a deep impact among White Americans. It is telling that the 2021 YouGov survey shows that among White people, the belief that Whites face discrimination is strongly correlated with the belief that gun owners face discrimination ($r = 0.76$). It suggests that there is a strong link between White grievances and those associated with identification as gun owners.

The "civil rights" narrative allows the NRA to sympathize with uncontroversial, consensus race politics themes like the rejection of Klan violence. Yet the NRA's Black civil rights groups and leaders have no depth and are treated as interchangeable. They are helpful only as gun owners who carry firearms for self-defense. What is left unsaid is the fundamental critique of American institutions that Black demand for arms entails. Frederick Douglass found nobility in arms because the inclusion of African Americans in military service was a step toward political equality.[123] W. E. B. DuBois urged Black men to "close ranks" and volunteer in World War I for the same reason.[124] Malcolm X, Robert Williams, and the Black Panthers used the idea of armed defense to highlight the failure of the rule of law in American democracy. Their objective was not an armed society that substitutes gun ownership for justice, the objective of the NRA—it was political equality.[125] As Williams put it, "there is no law here. There is no need to take the White attackers to the courts because they will go free." In this context of lawlessness and structural injustice, then, "it is necessary for us to kill. We must be willing to kill."[126]

The NRA's approbation of gun carry among Black civil rights leaders does not mean that the organization approved of the aims of the Black struggle or the Black critique of systemic racism. In 1970, when Black revolutionary groups made the argument that Blacks need the bullet if their rights are to be respected, an argument that is not very different from the NRA's "great equalizer" theory, the NRA branded the Black Panthers a "racist . . . activist, political organization," "consisting of militants" who advocated for political violence "to revolutionize America for their own ends."[127]

The NRA's argument relies on discrete, one-off examples to make overly broad generalizations—a logical fallacy. Specifically, the authors leverage examples of individual members of a group who successfully resisted coercion by members of a different group to make inferences at the societal level. According to this logic, Rosa Parks carried a firearm for protection while organizing Black women in the South. Rosa Parks evaded severe harm at the hands of the Klan. Therefore, gun carry is a generally successful strategy at the group level. This argument ignores the fact that there are many Black disarmament and lynching cases for every case of successful armed self-defense.[128]

In this view, it is better if both the Klan (the "bad" guys) and civil rights activists (the "good" guys) have weapons, since we cannot trust the state to be a fair arbiter and side with the angels every time, or even to be there to help at all. The underlying argument boils down to "if only [oppressed group of choice] had guns," they would not have suffered political disfranchisement and abuse. If only they had firearms, others in society and politics would have feared them and thus respected them more. Yet it is up to group members to determine their status as oppressed. Ironically, Supreme Court Justice Clarence Thomas appears to subscribe to this view of private gun ownership as well.[129] Only the barrel of a gun and the destructive power implicit in arms can ensure that citizens receive the respect they deserve from other citizens and the state. The bullet, not the ballot, is the anchor of democracy.[130] The argument ignores that the Klan formed *in response to* Black men in the South bearing arms. The presence of armed Black men in a position of political authority—a violation of ascriptive republican ideology—motivated White "rifle clubs" to become guerrilla units.[131]

The "civil rights" narrative serves another political purpose. The NRA and its supporters use Black people's arguments for armed defense to impugn their political opponents. They argue that gun control is a racist idea, and therefore gun control supporters are racists. Since contemporary Democrats support gun control, they become implicitly racist by association. The underlying assumption is that if the Klan and the Democrats both support gun control, and the Klan was racist, then the Democratic Party today is also racist. According to the group, those "in the far left" are "hijacking Black lives" and "sweeping black and Hispanic Americans along in their anti-freedom wave." They do so by supporting gun control laws that are "deeply rooted in racism."[132] In the 2022 election cycle, one Black Republican candidate openly made this connection in a campaign ad. The TV ad shows hooded Klan members invading his yard. The candidate brandishes his assault rifle and says, "when this rifle is the only thing standing in between your family and a dozen angry Democrats in Klan hoods, you just might need that semi-automatic." The article in the far-right website "the Blaze" carries the title: "Watch: Black GOP Candidate Wields AR-15 to Defend Home from Ku Klux Klan Democrats in Viral Ad: 'Make Rifles Great Again.'"[133]

The NRA condemns slavery and Jim Crow, yet it is careful not to ascribe political responsibility for these systems to White Americans or the American political system. When systemic failure is mentioned, it is almost in passing, without explanation or condemnation.[134] The political actor most frequently referenced in the narrative is the Klan, described as a "terrorist organization" and a "gun control" organization. The articles provide no additional information on the history, role, motivations, and social/political embeddedness of the Klan. It does not mention, for example, that prominent local White citizens—politicians, judges, and law enforcers—were members of the organization. Yet the stories never raise the question of why virtuous armed White citizens did not come to the aid of their Black neighbors, and why they did not rise up against a tyrannical state that imposed such indignities on many people.

The Holocaust offers another cautionary tale with a similar narrative structure and psychological function. As with the Klan, there is broad agreement among Americans that the Nazis were evildoers. Very few people today want to be associated with Nazism. In this narrative, the Nazis are also presented as gun controllers who confiscated all the guns in Jewish hands. They disempowered the Jews, making it easier to send six million people to their deaths.[135] As with civil rights, the NRA made virtually no mention of the Holocaust from the 1940s to the 1980s—evidence that racial prejudice was not a concern for the organization.[136]

In his 1993 book, the NRA leader Wayne LaPierre used the Nazi example to claim that registration of firearms always leads to confiscation and then to potential genocide. "Ultimately, registration will let the government know who owns guns and what guns they own. History provides the outcome: confiscation. And a people disarmed is a people in danger. In Germany, firearm registration helped lead to the [H]olocaust. . . . The German police state tactics left its citizens, especially Jews, defenseless against tyranny and the wanton slaughter of a whole segment of its population."[137]

Similarly, for Heston, laws requiring the registration of firearms and the licensing of gun owners are equivalent to "Jews forced to wear . . . yellow stars." The purpose of gun control is to mark gun owners as "inferior, unwanted, [and] ridiculed"—to mark them as second-class citizens.[138] Heston is not alone in asserting the links between gun control and the Holocaust. "[D]on't tell me that gun control is always progressive . . . and that governments of all kind should always be trusted, or that guns should only be in the hands of the police or military. All of those clichés, I think, are refuted by this history [of the Holocaust]," the gun rights activist and legal scholar Stephen Halbrook is quoted as saying.[139]

"What Made the Nazi Holocaust Possible? Gun Control," asserted a different article. "If not for gun control, Hitler would not have been able to murder 21 million people," proclaimed another piece, published in the conservative *National Review*.[140] Historians have "documented most everything about" Kristallnacht, except "what made it so easy to attack the defenseless Jews without fear of resistance. Their guns were registered and, thus, easily confiscated," claim NRA-aligned authors. In this oversimplified telling of the history of the Holocaust, the democratically elected government that preceded Hitler had enacted a gun registration law. "The government gullibly neglected to consider that only law-abiding citizens would register, while political extremists and criminals would not," suggests this warning to modern-day "law-abiding" gun owners.[141] In another article, David Kopel claims that "the real story" of the Warsaw ghetto uprising in Poland was that the resistance "was greatly weakened by the gun confiscation the Nazis had imposed after conquering" the country in 1939.[142] Yet Halbrook and LaPierre never ask why the German citizens whose guns were not confiscated did not help their Jewish neighbors against the Nazi state. If private gun ownership is the hallmark of virtue, why were the Ger-

man people, who retained the right to own guns and even received marksmanship training, complicit in the Holocaust?

There is no doubt that the Holocaust constitutes one of history's most
horrific events. The Holocaust, much like American slavery and the extermination of Native Americans, demonstrates the power of dehumanizing
ideologies.[143] As in the United States, ideology determined who constituted
a virtuous member of the polity in Germany. German society was deeply
polarized ideologically between the extreme Left and Right during the
Weimar years. Rival gangs affiliated with each side waged violent battles
in the streets. The *Bruen* decision has made this predicament much more
likely for the United States. In this environment, and with political moderates more suspicious of the Left than of the Right, democratic institutions
could not persist. Through institutional maneuvers, Hitler's National Socialists succeeded in getting into power.[144]

Nazi ideology designated virtuous citizenship based on blood ties and
ideology. Ethnic Germans who conformed to the regime's ideology were
recognized as law-abiding citizens, and they retained their nominal rights.
Jews, Gypsies, Communists, and gay people—individuals outside the circle
of ethnicity and ideology—were excluded from citizenship rights. Years before the 1938 pogrom, the Nazis passed legislation that excluded Jews from
civil service, law, medicine, and higher education. The Nuremberg Laws of
1935 prohibited intermarriage between Jews and Germans. Such individuals were subjected to intense surveillance by regime agents and compliant
citizens alike.[145]

Laws enacted early in the Nazi regime normalized and encouraged anti-
Semitism, prejudice, and race-based violence. Ideologically committed
members of the Nazi Party were responsible for most of the atrocities attributed to the regime. But ordinary people engaged in overtly discriminatory and even violent acts because they were told that it was the right
thing to do and that they were protecting their families, communities, and
the nation from an existential threat. After the humiliating defeat in World
War I, and in the wake of the punitiveness of the Treaty of Versailles, many
German people shared a vision of a homogenous national community that
would be restored to its previous glory. The regime used this vision, paired
with penalties and surveillance, to incentivize German people to identify
with the Nazi group and its ideology, rewarding acts of violence as acts
of virtue.[146]

The NRA's simplistic stories completely ignore the role of political
structures, ideologies, and identities. They refuse to acknowledge that minority groups in America and elsewhere have not been extended citizen-

ship rights—such as armed service and the vote—because they were not viewed as members of the polity by the dominant majority group, not the other way around. State inclusion of a group into military service is recognition of group members as equal citizens. As discussed in earlier chapters, neither women, nor African Americans, nor Native Americans were seen as citizens in the context of ascriptive republican ideology, which was the foundation and justification for their differential treatment. Neither were Jews, Gypsies, or gays in Nazi Germany, which fostered an ideology that combined social Darwinism and racism, not unlike the one that prevailed in the United States in the late nineteenth and early twentieth century.

Gun rights activists do not study history—they use it to create a usable past that resonates with contemporary sensibilities. Thus, history operates in the NRA narrative as a warning to White men: if these minority groups were disarmed and mistreated, this is a likely future for White men/gun owners if they do not resist gun control. Cultural elites first disempowered Black people and Jews by taking away their right to own firearms; subsequently, they reduced them to perpetual slavery or killed them. Even after slavery ended, these elites treated Black people as second-class citizens through segregation. Modern-day gun control is equated with "a badge of slavery,"[147] "black codes,"[148] and "enslavement."[149]

Going back to the 1950s, studies of norms show that authority figures' behavior critically influences prejudice and discrimination in the general public. First, we model our behavior after that of trusted elites.[150] Second, we tend to comply with the directives of authority. Many of us may accept this idea without much resistance when trusted elites tell us that violence is necessary for our group's preservation.[151] Peer pressure from our friends, neighbors, and society more broadly contributes to our conformity with social norms.[152]

In a contested and polarized environment characterized by ideologies that emphasize "us versus them" stories, the level of in-group threat may be so high that we are likely to dismiss even dissent from within our group. For example, Republican voters have been steadfast in their support of Donald Trump despite two impeachments, countless scandals, and his supporters' attack on the US Capitol. Two prominent Republicans who criticized Trump—Mitt Romney and Liz Cheney—lost support among the Republican electorate, and Cheney lost her position in leadership within the Party and her seat in the House of Representatives. It seems that neither the voters nor the Republican leaders are open to in-group dissent.[153]

Political exclusion is unrelated to gun control laws. Both liberal democracies and authoritarian regimes have established gun control measures.

Both types of regimes have survived long periods with strict control of private gun ownership. Very few contemporary polities have laissez-faire gun ownership regimes.[154] As Max Weber and many before him have argued, state monopoly over the legitimate use of force fosters regime stability, but it is not related to regime character. We cannot look at gun control policies alone and predict a political regime's current or future character. Instead, as Reconstruction and the Weimar Republic demonstrated, a state that cannot control violence and thus allows rival groups within society to challenge its political legitimacy with force cannot stay democratic for long.

∴

Part Three

ASCRIPTIVE REPUBLICANISM IN CONTEMPORARY WHITE PUBLIC OPINION

∴

CHAPTER 10

Ascriptive Republicanism and White Gun Attitudes Today

So far, I have argued that White Americans' love affair with firearms is an expression of a worldview whose roots can be found in the American Revolution and the institutions set up during the early Republic. An ideology or worldview is a system of interrelated beliefs that are not necessarily fully coherent, empirical, or provable but consciously or unconsciously guide people's attitudes and behavior. Political ideologies explain and justify how the political world should be organized and how power relationships should be structured. They provide the rationale for assignments of political membership and penalties of political deviance. In short, a political worldview is the pictures we have in our minds of how our political world works, along with the rationalizations—the narratives and stories—for why it should be so.[1]

The founding generation was influenced by martial republican ideology, which argued that democracy depends on the political virtue of citizens to survive. In turn, political virtue is not an innate trait but a quality that the people must cultivate. In this view, citizens become virtuous if they commit themselves to military preparedness in peacetime so that they are ready to defend the Republic in times of danger. Moral independence and commitment to the public good enable citizens to recognize and combat political corruption. Republican ideology understood corruption as pursuing individual interests at the expense of the public good—what today we may call "special interests." As a result, republicans were highly suspicious of political leaders who cultivated independent sources of power, especially democratically unaccountable standing armies.

This American republican ideology was ascriptive: it associated political virtue with White men and recognized only them as political members. Black people were thought to have chosen dependency and slavery over independence and virtue. As a result, they were not suitable for political decisions in a republic. Women were also unsuitable for citizenship because they lacked the physical prowess and cold reason required for training at arms. They could use firearms in the private realm for sport and protection, but not in war. Women were only suitable for republican motherhood: through modesty and chastity, they could raise virtuous sons. Adherents to the modern version of this ideology are suspicious of social groups they perceive as "dependent" on government—such as African Americans or welfare mothers.

This ideology was etched into American political institutions and especially the military. Early laws and state constitutions both reflected and reinforced ascriptive republican beliefs. White men alone were mandated to serve in the state militia, and militia enrollment was a condition for voting rights in many states. Although African Americans of both sexes and White women have served in every American war, this service did not receive equal official recognition, as it was inconsistent with the dominant ascriptive republican paradigm. Not until 1948 did African American men become fully integrated into military institutions. Women were admitted to combat units in 2015—although they too were officially integrated into the services in 1948.

The NRA, a product of the post–Civil War state militias (the National Guards), carried ascriptive martial republicanism into the twenty-first century. The modern NRA links not military service, but gun ownership and political activism on behalf of gun rights, with political virtue and decries gun control as a form of political corruption meant to disempower and weaken citizens relative to ruling elites. It depicts gun control supporters as either naïve do-gooders who don't realize the political ramifications of their policy advocacy or corrupt enemies of the Republic who seek to destroy democratic institutions exemplified by gun rights. These ideas shape the NRA's theory of democracy.

The progressive movements of the post–World War II era—such as the civil rights and feminist movements—relied on a different ideology of democratic membership, which combined political inclusion of previously excluded groups, respect for cultural and social minorities, and civic engagement. This inclusive republicanism, with deep roots in the Black struggle for civil rights dating back to abolitionism, rejected militarized forms of political expression and membership in favor of nonviolent forms of civil disobedience.[2]

How commonly held among white Americans is ascriptive martial republicanism? Does this admixture of martial and ascriptive beliefs add up to a political ideology—an interrelated system of ideas—or are they unconnected to each other? Is ascriptive martial republicanism a worldview prevalent only among gun owners and NRA sympathizers, or is it more broadly shared? Is it a distinct ideology from inclusive forms of republicanism? Do beliefs aligned with inclusive civic republicanism display some internal coherence as well? And what is the relationship between ascriptive republicanism and inclusive civic republican ideology? Finally, what are the political implications of support for ascriptive republican ideology? Do people who embrace this ideology harbor suspicions of America's democratic institutions, and are they more open to militarized politics and political violence—seeing themselves as insurrectionists as the NRA does?

I set out to answer these questions using a new public opinion survey conducted in 2021. The survey draws on work by the political psychologists Deborah Schildkraut[3] and Elizabeth Theiss-Morse.[4] In it, I ask White Americans what traits and behaviors they view as important for making one a "true American." The list of items is designed to align with ideas essential to ascriptive martial republicanism and more inclusive and civic-participatory forms of the ideology.

THE 2021 YOUGOV SURVEY

In May-June 2021, YouGov fielded a nationally representative survey of 1,000 non-Hispanic White respondents. The interview had a median length of twelve minutes. The survey respondents match the distribution of demographic and other characteristics of the White American population. Details on the survey methodology are in the online appendix to this chapter.[5]

In 2004, Schildkraut developed a survey asking Americans how important are various ascriptive traits and behaviors in making one a "true" American. These traits included being of European ancestry, being Christian, and being born in the United States. Respondents were also asked whether behaviors such as pursuing opportunity through hard work, respecting American institutions and laws, letting people say what they want no matter how much you disagree, volunteering in the community, and voting in elections, among others, were important in making someone a "true" American. This battery included ascriptive traits, civic behaviors, and commitments to multiculturalism, but not items related to gender beliefs or martial commitments—ideas central to ascriptive republicanism.[6]

The 2021 YouGov survey included thirteen items from Schildkraut's battery (table 10.1, in bold) and an additional eleven items that I designed and pretested. These items include four statements related to ascriptive beliefs, four related to martial republican beliefs, and three that stress inclusivity and nonviolence. Descriptive analysis shows that behaviors consistent

TABLE 10.1. Importance for Being a "True" American (2021 YouGov Survey)

		Very Important	Somewhat Important	Somewhat Unimportant	Very Unimportant
Ascriptive	**Being born in America**	25%	23%	22%	29%
	Being Christian	19%	13%	18%	50%
	Having European ancestors	5%	8%	22%	65%
	Living in rural America	11%	17%	26%	47%
	Becoming wealthy	4%	14%	32%	50%
	Listening to her father or husband (women)	11%	21%	19%	48%
	Being the provider for his wife and children (men)	36%	28%	15%	23%
Martial Republicanism	Serving in the military	19%	34%	25%	23%
	Volunteering to help the police in cases of emergency	30%	39%	17%	14%
	Not relying on the police to protect oneself and others	17%	28%	28%	27%
	Owning and carrying firearms	24%	19%	18%	39%
Liberalism	**Not relying on the government to get by**	44%	22%	17%	16%
	Pursuing opportunity through hard work	59%	29%	8%	4%
	Letting other people say what they want, no matter how much you disagree with them	56%	31%	9%	5%
	Ensuring that every citizen gets to vote, even if they do not support the same party	80%	14%	3%	2%
Civic Republicanism	**Volunteering in the community**	24%	46%	23%	7%
	Respecting America's institutions and laws	71%	22%	5%	2%
	Voting in elections	70%	20%	7%	3%

		Very Important	Somewhat Important	Somewhat Unimportant	Very Unimportant
	Commitment to resolving political differences exclusively through peaceful means	57%	30%	8%	4%
	Thinking of oneself as American	61%	27%	8%	4%
	Feeling American	51%	31%	11%	6%
Multiculturalism	**Seeing people of all backgrounds as American**	68%	23%	5%	4%
	Respecting the culture and traditions of other groups	59%	31%	6%	4%
	Actively supporting the rights of racial minorities	42%	32%	15%	11%

Note: The survey includes 1,000 non-Hispanic White respondents. Percentages are based on weighted data. The items from Schildkraut's survey are in bold.

with civic republican ideas of political virtue and membership are central to contemporary white Americans' definition of American citizenship—or being a "true" American. An overwhelming majority of White Americans support civic republican principles. These findings are consistent with Schildkraut's work from two decades ago, attesting to the resilience of these ideas in American political culture. Most White Americans also embrace multiculturalist principles, such as respect for other cultures and support for minority rights, while relatively fewer—but by no means a negligible number—characterize ascriptive traits as central to being a "true" American.

As table 10.1 shows, traditional gender roles top the list of ascriptive traits. Specifically, 64 percent of White Americans think that for men, being "providers" in the family is an important characteristic of being a "true" American ("very or somewhat" important), while 32 percent believe that a "true" American woman should "listen to her father or husband." Furthermore, 48 percent of White Americans believe that being born in America is an important element of being a "true" American, while 32 percent believe that being Christian is important. More than a fourth (28 percent) of respondents valorize life in rural America as indicative of "true" American-ness, and 18 percent say that becoming wealthy is also such a marker. Only a minority (13 percent) identify White European ancestry as important for "true" Americanism.

Support for behaviors central to martial republicanism is also relatively high. A majority (53 percent) of White Americans associate "true" Ameri-canism with military service, while 69 percent say that volunteering to help the police is important, and 45 percent think that "true" Americans do not rely on the police to protect themselves and others. According to 43 per-cent of Whites, owning and carrying firearms is also an important sign of being a "true" American.

I used a statistical procedure called factor analysis to test whether White Americans' responses to ascriptive and martial statements are statistically interrelated, indicating that they are part of the same underlying world-view. I looked for evidence that the same might be true for civic republi-can beliefs. I expected that these two groups of items would be internally positively related, but negatively related to the other set. Table 10.2 shows the results of the factor analysis. The highlighted items in each column "fit" together in statistical terms.[7] Consistent with my expectations, the seven ascriptive items and three of the four martial republican items fit together as part of a single ideological system. The idea that people should not be dependent on government to get by—a concept often associated with lib-eralism but integral to republicanism—is consistent with ascriptive martial republican ideology.[8]

Three items that emphasize peaceful political and social participation correlate with three other items emphasizing multiculturalism. These items form a single underlying construct I have labeled *inclusive civic republican-ism* (ICR). The idea of equal access to the vote—a concept key to both lib-eral and civic republican ideology—is also a constitutive part of ICR. These findings are consistent with Schildkraut's previous work and my expecta-tion that an ideology counter to ascriptive republicanism, the result of the progressive mobilizations of the 1960s and 1970s, is also prevalent among White Americans.

Another item of note is that most of the statements that are positively correlated with AMR are *negatively* correlated with ICR, and vice versa. These negative correlations suggest that people do not typically hold both ideologies concurrently and with the same intensity. Correlation analysis based on two additive indices I created shows that AMR and ICR are nega-tively correlated ($r = -0.10$). If I remove from each index the items that show a weak positive correlation with the other index, the negative cor-

TABLE 10.2. Factor Analysis Results (2021 YouGov Survey)

		Ascriptive Martial Republicanism (AMR)	Inclusive Civic Republicanism (ICR)
Ascriptive	Born in America	0.513	−0.247
	Being Christian	0.699	−0.077
	Being of European ancestry	0.658	−0.050
	Living in rural America	0.752	−0.073
	Listening to one's father (women)	0.699	−0.147
	Being a provider (men)	0.632	−0.114
	Being wealthy	0.632	−0.016
Martial Republicanism	Serving in the military	0.595	0.073
	Not relying on the police to protect oneself and others	0.433	0.025
	Owning and carrying firearms	0.667	−0.153
Liberalism	Not relying on government to get by	0.516	−0.123
	Ensuring that every citizen gets to vote, even if they do not support the same party	−0.129	0.629
Civic Republicanism	Volunteering in the community	0.332	0.473
	Voting in elections	0.031	0.484
	Commitment to resolving political differences exclusively through peaceful means	0.050	0.487
Multiculturalism	Seeing people of all backgrounds as American	−0.230	0.656
	Respecting the culture and traditions of other groups	−0.160	0.680
	Actively supporting the rights of racial minorities	−0.140	0.650

Based on 1,000 non-Hispanic White respondents.

relation between AMR and ICR climbs to −0.25. Reliability analyses show that additive indices based on the two sets of statements are internally consistent (alpha$_{AMR}$ = 0.86; alpha$_{ICR}$ = 0.80).[9] ICR is significantly more prevalent than AMR: 79 percent of Whites embrace inclusive civic republicanism, while only 40 percent support ascriptive martial republicanism.[10] It seems that in contemporary America, ICR is the dominant White ideology,

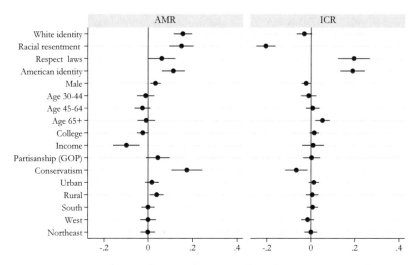

Figure 10.1 Predictors of support for AMR and ICR (2021 YouGov survey).
Note: OLS models with non-Hispanic White respondents; data are weighted.
Variables are recoded on 0–1 scales. Robust standard errors.

but a substantial number of White Americans are committed to an ascriptive republican worldview.

Not surprisingly, AMR and ICR have very different predictors (fig. 10.1).[11] The models are also of different strengths: the first model explains more than 50 percent, whereas the second predicts 31 percent of the total variance. Both White identity (a measure of in-group attachment) and racial resentment (which measures negative beliefs about African Americans) are strong positive predictors of AMR but negative predictors of ICR.[12] These findings are consistent with my contention that ascriptive republicanism is an ideology that valorizes White patriarchal supremacy and implicitly, if not explicitly, views African Americans and women as political inferiors. By contrast, ICR rejects these notions, embracing ideals of multiculturalism instead. American identity and respect for laws correlate positively with both ideologies, suggesting that those who identify with either of the two ideologies also have strong emotional ties to expressive Americanism ("American identity") as measured herein. Men are more likely than women to support AMR, and the opposite is the case for ICR. Identifying as a Republican or a conservative is also positively correlated with AMR. This is consistent with recent studies emphasizing the alignment of ascriptive and partisan identities because of the partisan realignment.[13] However, partisanship does not affect support for ICR, while conservatism is negatively correlated with support for inclusive republicanism. College-educated and higher-income people are less likely to support AMR, while rural Whites are more likely to embrace the ideology. However, education, income, and geography are not significant predictors of support for ICR, evidence that the ideology has broad social appeal in the White population.

GUN OWNERSHIP AND GOVERNMENT-PROTECTED RIGHTS

Given the strong correlation between the ascriptive traits in the AMR index and the "own and carry firearms" item, it is safe to expect that AMR should be a statistically significant correlate of gun ownership. But is that the case even after controlling for other known correlations, such as criminal victimization, partisanship, ideology, and racial resentment?[14] And what should we expect the relationship between ICR and gun ownership to be? On the one hand, peaceful political engagement is central to ICR; on the other, the ICR items correlate positively (albeit very weakly) with "volunteering to serve in the military." There is also evidence that men more than women own guns. Yet could it be that the interaction between AMR and gender is behind higher gun ownership among men?

I specified linear probability models that include known predictors of gun ownership, such as experience with criminal victimization, racial attitudes, partisanship, ideology, and various demographics (table 10.3). All variables are coded on 0–1 scales consistent with the nature of the original variable so that the coefficients are directly comparable. As you may recall, the AMR measure includes an item that specifically asks about the importance of gun ownership for being a "true" American. Including this item in the independent variable would create circularity problems. As a result, the AMR measure does not include this item for all subsequent analyses in chapters 10 and 11.[15]

Table 10.3 shows the results of a linear probability model predicting whether or not there is a gun in the respondent's home. A second model predicts whether the respondent is a gun owner. As the models show, even after controlling for known predictors of gun ownership, AMR is a significant positive predictor of having a gun in the home and being a gun owner. When AMR is included in the model, partisanship and ideology are no longer statistically significant. Furthermore, models for men and women show that the effect of AMR on having a gun in the home and individual gun ownership is statistically significant only among men, not women. The coefficient for men is substantively large. This finding is consistent with my contention that AMR valorizes male-dominated forms of political membership and is thus more influential among White men. ICR does not have a statistically significant effect in any of the models. This means that high

TABLE 10.3. Linear Probability Models of Gun Ownership (2021 YouGov Survey)

	Gun in Home	Gun in Home (Men)	Gun in Home (Women)	Gun Owner	Gun Owner (Men)	Gun Owner (Women)
	B/SE	B/SE	B/SE	B/SE	B/SE	B/SE
AMR	0.193 *	0.298 **	0.057	0.288 ***	0.352 ***	0.147
	(0.10)	(0.14)	(0.14)	(0.09)	(0.13)	(0.12)
ICR	−0.173	−0.205	−0.103	−0.087	−0.062	−0.068
	(0.11)	(0.15)	(0.16)	(0.10)	(0.15)	(0.14)
White identity	−0.135 **	−0.183 **	−0.072	−0.171 ***	0.132 *	−0.192 ***
	(0.05)	(0.08)	(0.08)	(0.05)	(0.08)	(0.06)
Racial resentment	0.075	0.157	0.015	0.12 *	0.196	0.059
	(0.08)	(0.12)	(0.10)	(0.07)	(0.12)	(0.08)
Respect laws	0.016	−0.002	0.055	0.074	0.038	0.095
	(0.08)	(0.12)	(0.11)	(0.07)	(0.11)	(0.07)
American identity	0.132 **	0.008	0.237 **	0.065	−0.04	0.196 ***
	(0.07)	(0.10)	(0.09)	(0.06)	(0.09)	(0.07)
Intercept	0.096	0.286 *	−0.068	−0.133	−0.045	−0.086
	(0.11)	(0.15)	(0.15)	(0.10)	(0.14)	(0.13)
N	978	478	500	978	478	500
Adj. R²	0.12	0.111	0.122	0.142	0.128	0.097
F	7.549	4.648	5.290	7.640	4.800	2.634

Notes: *p<0.1; **p<0.05; ***p<0.001. Data are weighted. Robust standard errors in parentheses. Non-Hispanic Whites only. All variables are recoded on 0–1 scales. Controls include: partisanship, ideology, fear of crime, criminal victimization, gender, age, income, education, region, urban, rural.

and low ICR scorers are equally likely to own firearms. It is possible that even though adherents to inclusive republican ideology own firearms, they do not associate them with political membership. For example, high ICR scorers may be hunters or competitive shooters, but—I claim—they are not likely to embrace insurrectionist ideas.

I set out to investigate whether White Americans have different understandings of firearms due to how strongly they embrace AMR and, secondarily, ICR. I do this by analyzing a series of survey items related to the political importance people assign to firearms. The survey asked respondents to rank order five government-protected rights in importance. These rights include the right to bear arms, the right to vote, freedom of speech, freedom from discrimination, and the right to protest. This question explores how much value or importance White Americans place on gun rights, not absolutely but relative to other essential rights. This question allows me to get to the issue of the primacy of gun rights over the franchise. Recall that the NRA insurrectionist narrative posits that absent the right to bear arms, the right to vote is vulnerable to political corruption. Therefore, in this view, gun rights represent the "1st freedom" and should be valued above the right to vote.[16]

Figure 10.2 shows the ranking of the right to bear arms and the right to vote for all respondents and for high and low AMR scorers (divided at the mean). As the data show, White Americans are divided on gun rights: 40 percent prioritize the right to bear arms, while 49 percent rank it at the bottom. This division reflects differences in ideological commitments between AMR levels. First, 61 percent of AMR high scorers prioritize the right to bear arms, whereas only 16 percent of low scorers do so. In the case of the right to vote, only 32 percent of high AMR scorers rank voting rights as Top-2, compared to 62 percent of low AMR scorers.

Multivariate regression models confirm that controlling for other expected predictors of support for the right to bear arms, such as racial resentment, partisanship, and ideology, those who score higher on AMR are more likely to prioritize the right to bear arms and less likely to prioritize the right to vote (fig. 10.3). In both cases, the effect of AMR is quite sizable: those at the high end of the AMR scale rank the right to bear arms 19 percentage points (ppts) higher than those at the bottom of the scale. Similarly, higher AMR scorers rank the right to vote 18ppts *lower* than low AMR scorers. ICR is negatively correlated with the right to bear arms. High ICR respondents place arms 26ppts lower than do low ICR Whites. A test of coefficients confirms that the effect of ICR on the ranking of gun rights is substantively larger than that of AMR (p < 0.001). The effect of ICR on the right to vote is not significant when controlling for other factors.[17] What is

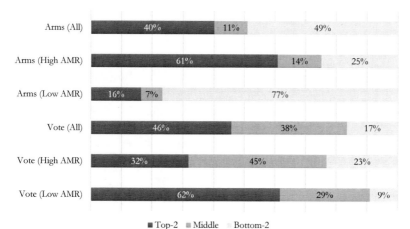

Figure 10.2 Ranking of right to bear arms and right to vote (2021 YouGov survey).

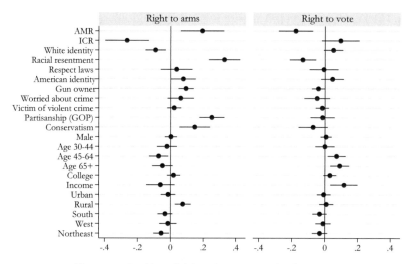

Figure 10.3 Ranking of right to bear arms and right to vote,
OLS models (2021 YouGov survey).
Note: All variables are recoded on 0–1 scales. Data are weighted. Non-Hispanic Whites only. Robust standard errors.

more, interaction models show that the effect of AMR is not conditional on either gun ownership or strength of identification with the NRA. These beliefs are broadly shared beyond the gun owner universe.[18]

FIREARMS FOR PROTECTION AND POLITICAL POWER

I expect that adherents to ascriptive republican ideology not only value gun rights more than other people, but have a distinct understanding of the role of firearms in American society. This understanding is centered on politics, not protection from crime. The NRA narrative about the role of guns in society has changed since the early twenty-first century. After the federal government severed its ties with the NRA and the era of mass mobilization came to an end with the conclusion of the Vietnam War, the association emphasized civilian gun ownership for in-home self-defense and protection. But that is no longer the case. In the twenty-first century the NRA narrative changed, emphasizing a political right to own firearms as a bulwark against government corruption.

Public opinion has also changed. In 1999, the Pew Research Center reported that about half of gun owners (49 percent) reported owning a gun to hunt. Only 26 percent said they owned guns for protection. By 2013, these proportions had reversed: 48 percent said they owned guns for protection and 32 percent said their guns were for hunting. Five years later, in 2017, 67 percent of gun owners said they owned a gun for protection.[19] Other surveys have also shown that in recent years people offer explicitly political reasons for owning a gun. For example, a 2015 YouGov survey showed that 17 percent of gun owners said they own a gun because it is their "second amendment right" and another 9 percent said they own firearms as protection against the government.[20] I expect that AMR high scorers should be more likely to perceive guns in political terms as protection against the government.

The survey included two items that measured beliefs about the purpose of firearms. Both are measured on five-point agree/disagree scales. These items read: 1) people own guns to protect themselves and others from crime; and 2) the government is so powerful that people need guns to protect themselves from it. Figure 10.4a shows the level of agreement with each item for all Whites and high and low AMR scorers. First, two-thirds of Whites (68 percent) agree that people own guns to protect themselves from crime. This result tracks with previous poll results. As expected, this belief is overwhelmingly supported by high AMR scorers (82 percent) but less so (52 percent) among low AMR scorers. Second, 40 percent of Whites agree that people need firearms to protect themselves against the government. This finding indicates that insurrectionist narratives have taken root in the minds of a substantial minority of White Americans. This belief is twice as prevalent among high AMR respondents (54 percent) than among low AMR respondents (24 percent). Insurrectionism, then, has found more support among high AMR Whites than among low AMR Whites.

Multivariate regressions predicting agreement with each of these beliefs

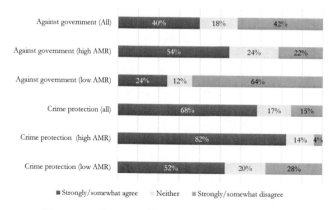

Figure 10.4a Purpose of firearms (2021 YouGov survey).

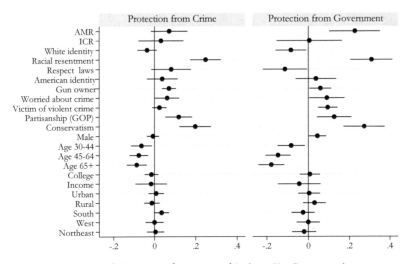

Figure 10.4b Purposes of gun ownership (2021 YouGov survey).
Note: OLS models with non-Hispanic White respondents; data are weighted. Variables are recoded on 0–1 scales. Robust standard errors.

are presented in figure 10.4b. As the results show, AMR is positive but not statistically significant in the "protection from crime" model. When other predictors are considered, high and low AMR Whites are equally likely to believe that people own guns for self-defense. This is also true for ICR. Consistent with other analyses, my data show that support for the self-defense narrative is more prevalent among those who score high on racial resentment, Republicans, and conservatives, and lower among older people.[21]

The same is not the case for beliefs that people need guns to protect themselves against the government. Here, AMR is positive and statistically significant. The size of its effect is similar to racial resentment, partisanship, and conservatism and larger than gun ownership. These results suggest that Whites who embrace ascriptive republican ideology are more likely to view gun ownership in the context of politics—as a check on government overreach and corruption. Supplemental analyses show that this belief is equally spread among gun owners and those who don't own firearms. The same is true for NRA identifiers and those who don't identify with the group.[22] These findings suggest that such beliefs have penetrated beyond the immediate sphere of gun culture. The interaction between AMR and partisanship or ideology is not statistically significant, indicating that AMR is not differentially activated among Republicans or conservatives. This finding is not very surprising given the extensive—albeit asymmetrical—use of insurrectionist themes in politics by judges and partisan actors.[23]

VIRTUE AND CORRUPTION

The modern NRA's ascriptive republican narrative has elevated gun owner-ship as a consumer act—rather than military preparedness—to a symbol of political virtue. For the association, gun owners are vigilant citizens who seek to protect the Republic from political corruption. In turn, the NRA promotes itself as the leader of the virtuous citizen-soldiers—an organization whose mission is to protect political freedom and democracy as it understands those terms. From early in its history, the NRA portrayed its political opponents either as naïve and irrational citizens incapable of comprehending the damage that gun control can do to democracy or as politically corrupt elites seeking to enhance their own power by depriving citizens of firearms. Do these beliefs about virtue and corruption resonate with the White public, especially high AMR scorers?

The 2021 YouGov survey includes several items designed to tap these be-liefs. I seek to determine the prevalence of beliefs about political virtue that are consonant with NRA narratives. I asked respondents whether "owning a firearm is a sign of good citizenship" and if "the NRA works to promote the public good" (five-point agreement scale). I also asked people how strongly they identify with the organization. Specifically, the item asks: "When you think about the National Rifle Association (NRA), how often do you say 'we' instead of 'they'?" (five-point frequency scale). Three additional ques-tions tap dimensions of political corruption as discussed in NRA narratives. Respondents are asked whether they agree that "gun control advocates are naive do-gooders" and that "gun control advocates are over-emotional and irrational" (five-point agreement scales). These two are combined as an additive scale (a = 0.80). The final item asks to what degree they agree with the statement "globalist bankers and financiers support gun control because they want to increase their power" (five-point agreement scale).

Multivariate analyses presented in table 10.4 show that AMR is a posi-tive and significant predictor of NRA-aligned beliefs about political virtue and corruption. First, AMR is a positive and significant predictor of the be-lief that gun ownership is a sign of good citizenship. The substantive effect of AMR is very large—larger than that of partisanship, ideology, racial re-sentment, and even gun ownership. A shift from the lowest to the highest AMR score corresponds to a 43ppt increase in support for the belief that gun ownership is a sign of good citizenship. By contrast, the effect of par-tisanship is 17ppts and gun ownership 9ppts. Second, high AMR scorers are significantly more likely to believe that the NRA works for the pub-

TABLE 10.4. OLS Models Virtue and Corruption (2021 YouGov Survey)

	Good Citizen	NRA Promotes Public Good	NRA Identifier	Anti-gunners Naïve/ Irrational	Global-ists Seek Power
	B/SE	B/SE	B/SE	B/SE	B/SE
AMR	0.428 ***	0.275 ***	0.308 ***	0.274 ***	0.372 ***
	(0.06)	(0.05)	(0.07)	(0.05)	(0.07)
ICR	−0.113 ***	−0.16 ***	0.045	−0.201 ***	−0.043
	(0.06)	(0.06)	(0.07)	(0.07)	(0.08)
White identity	−0.036	−0.089 ***	0.021	−0.027	−0.100 ***
	(0.03)	(0.06)	(0.07)	(0.07)	(0.08)
Racial resentment	0.165 ***	0.367 ***	0.112 **	0.266 ***	0.236 ***
	(0.04)	(0.04)	(0.05)	(0.04)	(0.05)
Respect laws	−0.094 **	0.067	−0.025	−0.015	0.03
	(0.05)	(0.05)	(0.05)	(0.04)	(0.06)
American identity	0.140 ***	0.101 ***	−0.005	0.12 ***	0.014
	(0.04)	(0.04)	(0.04)	(0.04)	(0.05)
Gun owner	0.092 ***	0.022	0.110 ***	0.028	−0.010
	(0.02)	(0.02)	(0.03)	(0.03)	(0.03)
Worry about crime	0.053	0.002	0.145 ***	0.019	0.144 ***
	(0.04)	(0.03	(0.04)	(0.04)	(0.05)
Victim of crime	0.021	0.028	0.048 *	0.073 ***	0.071 ***
	(0.02)	(0.02)	(0.03)	(0.02)	(0.03)
Partisanship (GOP)	0.170 ***	0.277 ***	0.07	0.125 ***	−0.075 *
	(0.04)	(0.04)	(0.04)	(0.04)	(0.04)
Conservatism	0.170 ***	0.186 ***	0.043	0.085 *	0.103 *
	(0.05)	(0.04)	(0.06)	(0.05)	(0.06)
Intercept	0.069	−0.014	−0.144 **	0.209 ***	0.261 ***
	(0.06)	(0.06)	(0.07)	(0.08)	
N	978	978	978	978	
Adj R²	0.55	0.682	0.244	0.436	0.184
F	79.279	150.43	14.506	36.903	11.648

Notes: *p<0.1; **p<0.05; ***p<0.001. Data are weighted. Robust standard errors in parentheses. All variables are recoded on 0–1 scales. Non-Hispanic Whites only. AMR excludes the gun ownership/carry item. Controls include: gender, age, income, education, region, urban, rural.

lic good than those who score low on the scale. This substantive effect is also very large, on par with partisanship and racial resentment, and larger than ideology.

AMR is also a positive and significant predictor of identifying with the NRA. A change from the lowest to the highest point on the AMR scale corresponds to a 31ppt increase in strength of identification with the NRA. By contrast, the effect of owning a gun on identification with the NRA is only

11ppts. The results are similar for the items measuring political corruption beliefs. AMR is a statistically significant and substantively large predictor of political corruption beliefs prevalent in NRA narratives. These beliefs are that gun control supporters are "naïve and irrational" and that "globalist elites promote gun control to increase their political power." As with earlier models, the substantive effect of AMR is typically larger than that of gun ownership, partisanship, or ideology, and on par with racial resentment.

ICR is negative in four of the five models, but statistically significant in three. Those who score high on ICR are significantly less likely than low ICR scorers to believe that gun ownership is a sign of good citizenship. High ICR scorers are also unlikely to believe that the NRA promotes the public good or that gun control proponents are "naïve and irrational." In other words, high ICR scorers reject many of the NRA's ascriptive republican understandings of political virtue and corruption. However, ICR has no statistically significant effect on identification with the NRA.

Overall, these data suggest that beliefs about political virtue and corruption, drawn from ascriptive republican narratives, are popular among many White Americans, and not only those who own guns. Those who embrace AMR ideology and view political membership in ascriptive and martial terms are also more likely to endorse beliefs that gun ownership signifies good citizenship, and conversely that gun control advocates are irrational and naïve.

BLACK GUN OWNERS: CRIMINALS OR GOOD CITIZENS?

I have argued that ascriptive republican narratives associate political virtue and good citizenship with White gun owners. In early NRA narratives, developed during the Jim Crow era, Black soldiers were viewed as incompetent shooters and thus as incapable of developing the political virtue required of republican citizenship. In later stories, Black people, including gun owners, are implicitly or explicitly linked to dependency, violence, and criminality—they are a danger to the Republic and its citizens.[24] These narratives have been perpetuated by the gun rights movement but are also shared in the broader American culture.[25]

In this section, I focus on two interrelated questions. First, do Whites stereotype White and Black gun owners differently, as I claim to be the case? Do they view White gun owners more frequently as patriotic citizens while they see Black gun owners as criminals? Second, are these negative perceptions of African American gun owners more prevalent among those scoring higher on ascriptive republicanism? Answers to these questions are critical because they go to the nature of structural disadvantage. In essence, if a substantial portion of the White public—including people in authority—buys into ascriptive republican beliefs and associates Black gun ownership with criminality, then African Americans find themselves in the contradictory position where attempts to express their good citizenship through gun ownership are likely to be perceived as a threat by White society and public authority. This misperception can have severe negative consequences for African Americans—as we witnessed in the Philando Castile and Breonna Taylor cases and in the many police shootings of unarmed Black people, and as experiments demonstrate.[26] Ideological commitments to ascriptive republicanism may predispose White citizens and police officers alike to perceive African Americans as likely gun carriers and a threat—even if they do not have a firearm on them. At the same time, citizens and even people in authority may perceive armed White men as upstanding citizens to be trusted as if they were police auxiliaries—this is the lesson from the deadly Kenosha, Wisconsin protests, at least.

I investigate these questions with the help of two survey experiments. The first experiment was conducted between January 27 and January 30, 2017. A sample of 723 self-identified White respondents was drawn from the opt-in panel maintained by the survey company Qualtrics. This is a convenience sample, not a representative sample of the White population. I used gender within age quotas to ensure that the characteristics of those surveyed closely match the general White population. In this 2 × 2 experimental design, respondents were randomly assigned to one of four conditions. Under the guise of evaluating characters for a storyline, respondents were shown the face of either a Black or a White man. The accompanying description either characterized the individual as a gun owner or omitted that information. The names I used for the story were either characteristically African American (DeShawn) or typical White (Sean). The pictures used in the experiment came from the Implicit Association Test (IAT) and have been validated to only capture race and not other characteristics (e.g., class status).[27]

It is important to note that the experiment did not measure implicit attitudes. Instead, it was used as a racial prime. I expect that even though the text did not overtly mention race (i.e., it did not characterize the person as "African American" or "White," nor was the term "race" used in the story), exposure to the picture and the name of the individual should act unconsciously to facilitate the expression of beliefs about race.[28] This process should lead respondents to evaluate the Black individual less positively than the White individual. Figure 10.5 shows the actual prime.

Following exposure to the prime, respondents were asked: "For each of

[**Sean Murphy**] Deshawn Lamar Robinson is 34 years old and lives in a medium sized city. He drives a five year old car. He watches sports on cable TV and plays video games. [**He is a gun owner. He owns handguns and a semi-automatic assault rifle**]. Please specify how likely it is that Deshawn possesses the traits listed on the following page.

Figure 10.5 Experimental design, evaluations of Black and White gun owners (2017 Qualtrics).

the following traits, please specify how likely it is that the man described earlier possesses that trait?" They were then offered a list of fifteen attributes rated on a four-point scale (extremely, very, somewhat, or not at all likely). The list included the following positive traits: loyal citizen, patriotic, taxpayer, hard-working, self-reliant, family man, successful, and churchgoer. These traits are consistent with the positive dimension of American republican ideology—the attributes that define political virtue. The negative traits included: dangerous, angry, involved in crime, welfare recipient, untrustworthy, militant, and gang member. These attributes are consistent with the idea of political corruption and criminality.

A factor analysis shows that the positive ("virtue") and negative ("corruption") items load on two separate dimensions (see online appendix). Next, I created two additive index variables: political virtue (alpha = 0.89) and political corruption (alpha = 0.90). Then, I created a single dependent variable in which I took the difference of the negative traits from the positive traits. This measure ranges from 1 (most positive/virtuous) to −1 (most negative/corrupt). I have labeled this measure "relative virtue." Because this index dependent variable is rather complex, I also show models based on responses to the "loyal citizen" and "involved in crime" ("criminal") items.

Figure 10.6 shows the result of OLS regressions with the treatments as the independent variable. I coded the treatments as a single categorical variable ranging from zero (White man) to three (Black man, gun owner). The first panel shows the effect of the treatments on relative virtue. Compared to respondents exposed to "Sean," the White man, those exposed to "DeShawn," the Black man, evaluated the character as less virtuous (b = −0.066; p < 0.05). The same is true of the White gun owner: he too is seen as less virtuous compared to the White man who does not have a firearm (b = −0.081; p < 0.001). A test of coefficients shows that White respon-

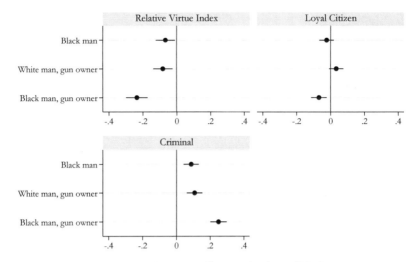

Figure 10.6 Treatment effects, evaluations of Black
and White gun owners (2017 Qualtrics).

Note: OLS regression results, not including demographic controls. Non-Hispanic
Whites only. All variables are recoded on 0–1 scales.

dents assess the Black man and the White male gun owner as equally virtuous. The virtue points a man loses for being Black are equivalent to those
a White man loses for owning firearms. The Black male gun owner (b =
−0.234; p < 0.001) is rated as far less virtuous than any of the other three
men. These results suggest that, on average, White Americans view gun
owners as less virtuous than non–gun owners, but race and gun ownership
are *compounded* in the White mind to create the impression of less virtue.
Therefore, a Black gun owner suffers because of his race *and* his firearm
ownership.

The second panel in figure 10.6 shows the same model using the "loyal
citizen" trait as the dependent variable. The overall picture is very similar.
Here, evaluation of the Black man is not statistically differentiated from that
of the White man: White respondents tend to view both of them equally
as "loyal citizens." Also, respondents are slightly more likely to think of the
White male gun owner as a "loyal citizen," but this effect is not statistically
significant either. The Black male gun owner, however, is significantly less
likely than the control or either of the other two treatments to be considered a "loyal citizen" (b = −0.069; p < 0.001). The effect of race and gun
ownership is compounded for Black men.

The third panel in figure 10.6 shows the same model with "criminal"
as the dependent variable. Not surprisingly, the Black man is more likely
than the White man to be seen as a criminal (b = 0.086; p < 0.001). The

White gun owner is also more likely to be considered a criminal (b = 0.107; p < 0.001). These two effects are statistically similar. These results suggest that, on average, a Black man is as much a criminal as a White man with a gun. However, we see again the compounding effect of race and gun ownership status. The Black male gun owner is significantly more likely to be viewed as a criminal (b = 0.249; p < 0.001) not only relative to the White man, but relative to each of the other treatments.

The first experiment did not speak to any conditional effects of ascriptive republicanism because the experiment did not include the relevant battery of items. A second 2 × 2 experiment was included in a 2021 survey fielded by Lucid. The survey was fielded between November 8 and November 15, 2021, and included 1,205 non-Hispanic White respondents. On average, the interview lasted fifteen minutes.[29] First, respondents were asked the Americanism items. After the battery, the survey included one item that asked: "Most Americans would agree: a [White/Black] man with a gun is most likely to be a [good citizen/violent criminal]." Responses ranged from "very true" to "very false" (four-point scale). Survey participants were randomly assigned to one of the four question versions. This experiment is different from the previous one because no picture or story was used, and respondents were asked to generalize about a group in stereotypical ways. This question format is likely to activate higher levels of social desirability bias. My theory suggests that those at the top end of the AMR scale should agree more strongly with the association of Black gun ownership and criminality and should reject the association of White gun ownership with criminality. The reverse should be the case for high ICR scorers.

Using OLS regression, I first estimate the main effect of the treatment. Support for the statement associating a White gun owner with good citizenship averaged 41 percent. Support for the opposite statement was significantly lower, at 33 percent (p < 0.001). Agreement with the positive statement referencing a Black gun owner was 48 percent—significantly higher than for the White gun owner (p < 0.001). Agreement with the association between Black gun ownership and criminality averaged 37 percent, similar to the base condition (p = 0.253). However, consistent with the earlier example, the Black gun owner is more likely to be viewed as a criminal than is the White gun owner (p = 0.07).[30] The results suggest that the average White respondent—perhaps driven by social desirability— embraces the counter-stereotypical view of Black gun owners as good citizens. At the same time, White ambivalence is evident in that they are also more likely to endorse the criminal stereotype for Black gun owners, but not so much for White gun owners.

Figure 10.7a shows the effect of the interaction between the treatment and ascriptive republicanism on agreement with the characterization. The line that crosses zero represents the effect of the White gun owner as a "good citizen." Relative to the zero line, support for the statement that a White gun owner is a violent criminal declines significantly as a function of AMR. The same is the case for the characterization of the Black gun owner as a "good citizen." By contrast, AMR has no statistically significant effect on White support for the stereotypical perception of a Black gun owner as a criminal. At high levels of AMR, White respondents are as likely to agree with the "good citizen" as they are with the "criminal" characterization of Black gun owners. However, high AMR Whites strongly reject the characterization of White gun owners as "criminals."

As figure 10.7b shows, a different pattern emerges when we examine responses at different levels of ICR. First, as with AMR, ICR has no significant effect on supporting the stereotypical association of Black gun ownership with criminality. However, support for the association between White gun ownership and criminality increases as ICR rises. At the highest levels of ICR, respondents are equally likely to describe the White gun owner as a "good citizen" or a "criminal." Similarly, support for the association between Black gun ownership and good citizenship increases as ICR increases. These patterns are the reverse of what we saw earlier with AMR.

Taken together, the results from these experiments suggest that stereotypical views of White gun owners as "good citizens" and Black gun owners as not so are, in part, driven by a deep commitment to ascriptive republican ideology. For many White Americans, especially those who score high on AMR, the "good guy with a gun" is more likely to be a White man than a Black man, while a Black man with a gun is more likely to be a criminal.

CONCLUSION

Despite the rise of a powerful counter-ideology in the 1960s, ascriptive republicanism continues to motivate many White people and guide how they understand the role of firearms in American society. White Americans who embrace ascriptive republican ideology tend to view gun politics through the same lens as the NRA. High AMR scorers, whether they themselves own firearms or not, are more likely to adopt the association's understanding of political virtue and corruption—ideas that link gun ownership with good citizenship and gun control with irrationality or willful undermining of democratic institutions. They are also more likely to subscribe to racialized understandings of political virtue and corruption: for this group

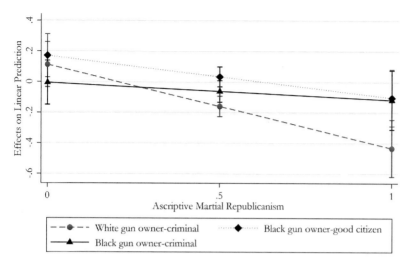

Figure 10.7a Effect of treatment on support of gun owner
characterization by AMR (2021 Lucid).
Note: Model includes demographic controls. All variables are recoded on 0–1 scales.
Non-Hispanic White respondents only.

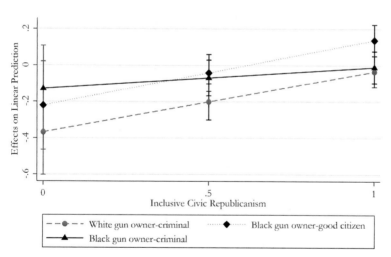

Figure 10.7b Effect of treatment on support for characterization by ICR (2021 Lucid).
Note: Model includes demographic controls. All variables are recoded on 0–1 scales.
Non-Hispanic White respondents only.

of Americans, White gun owners are more likely to be viewed as well-intentioned patriots, but Black people and Black gun owners activate more negative or less positive associations.

"Insurrectionism"—the idea that gun ownership is a political right that enables citizens to limit government abuse and corruption—is also more deeply held among those White Americans who embrace ascriptive republican ideology. There is little doubt in my mind that many if not most of the people who scaled the walls of the Capitol building on January 6, 2021, were guided by ascriptive martial republican understandings of a citizen's duty when the Republic is in danger. They saw themselves as protectors of cherished institutions, not as enemies of democracy. From their point of view, American democracy as they understood it was in danger, and they showed up to defend it. As we are about to see in chapter 11, the effect of ascriptive republicanism does not end with general ideas about the NRA and the meaning of guns in politics. Instead, ascriptive republicanism is implicated in violent radicalization, support for political violence, and support for anti-democratic norms.

CHAPTER 11

From "Stand Your Ground" to "Stand Back and Stand By"

Modern democracy has little room for citizen-initiated political violence—whether as a matter of theory or of practice. As developed in the nineteenth and twentieth centuries, the Weberian state is empowered through popular democratic processes—a process of legitimation—to control the monopoly of the use of physical force within its territory. Enlightenment-era natural law theories recognized limited individual rights to violence (i.e., self-defense) as existing prior to the state or "the social compact," but even these theories enabled the sovereign to impose limits. Weberian theories of the state insist that the state alone makes decisions about who can legitimately use coercive force, when they can do so, and how.[1]

The NRA's theory of democracy draws on very old ideas about virtue and corruption in public life, but it has abandoned critical practices that form the moral foundation of classical republicanism. Insurrectionist theory has decoupled private firearms ownership from military preparedness and service. Instead, it has elevated the consumer act of owning firearms itself into the defining characteristic of political virtue. An armed man is "a good guy," a responsible citizen endowed with the right to determine how to use armed violence—in the private domain and politics. In earlier ascriptive republican narratives—including that of the pre-1960s NRA—gun ownership was *instrumental* to virtue. Today, gun ownership is *intrinsic* to political virtue—it serves to distinguish between the virtuous and the wicked. In the NRA's insurrectionist theory, the gun owners *are* "the people," those responsible for operating as a check and balance against the elites' and their supporters' authoritarian predispositions. In one sense, insurrectionist theory has foisted the "Castle Doctrine," the idea that a man is the king of his home and has a right to protect it with force, on the nation. The new doctrine suggests that the gun owner is also the king of his nation, and his right to self-defense extends to insurrection against established authority. Insurrectionism is a profoundly anti-democratic ideology with deep mistrust of and hostility toward constitutional government, as it rejects the notion that the system of checks and balances embedded in the American constitutional order is sufficient to preserve individual liberty.

Incompatible as it may be with modern democratic practices, the NRA's theory of democracy has assumed a prominent place in American political discourse in recent years. The organization itself has been developing this insurrectionist theory tied to the Second Amendment since at least the 1980s. In addition to writings by NRA-affiliated lawyers, this theory is evident in the writings and speeches of the group's principals.[2] Yet it has been mainly in the twenty-first century that the idea of a right to firearms for political, not private ends has leaped into the broader public discourse. The Supreme Court's decisions in *District of Columbia v. Heller* and *McDonald v. Chicago*, and more recently in *New York State Rifle & Pistol Association, Inc. v. Bruen*, undoubtedly aided this process. The Supreme Court's new composition, combined with minority opinions and justices' commentary, suggests an appetite for much broader and more radical interpretations of the right to bear arms as a political right.[3] The *Bruen* decision established as the primary criterion for determining the constitutionality of gun control legislation whether such a law would have existed at the time of the establishment of the Republic. Given the flawed historical analysis of the decision and the demand to look at a very narrow historical window, legislatures will have a tough time justifying gun control laws.

In recent years, we have seen the language of armed violence invade American politics in unprecedented ways. First, as the relationship between the NRA and the Republican Party became closer in the 1990s, insurrectionist rhetoric was adopted by party principals and candidates. Democrats anxious to win in competitive districts have drawn on insurrectionist themes in recent years. Second, several candidates—Democrats and Republicans—have produced ads in which they hunt or shoot skeet to showcase their gun-friendliness. More famously, several members of the US House of Representatives sent out family Christmas cards with themselves and their underage children holding military-style rifles next to a Christmas tree. Others have filmed themselves assembling military weapons to demonstrate their ease with arms and, by extension, their Second Amendment bona fides. Yet not all such associations are as positive. At least one candidate—a self-styled "conservative patriot"—posed while firing an automatic weapon with words such as "reduce spending" and "defend 2nd amendment" scrolling across the screen. The candidate does not utter any words—the gun does all the work for him. In others, candidates pose with military-style rifles under messages that they "will take back Washington."

Even more influenced by insurrectionism are ads in which candidates aim at or shoot at the "government" (imagined in the form of legislative product), the media (shooting a television), or their opponents. One controversial ad depicts the candidate in a Wild West shoot-out with an actor standing in for his political opponent. The opponent is Senator Mark Kelly, whose wife, Gabby Giffords, was shot by a mass shooter. Candidates have also made calls for people to "use their second amendment remedies,"[4] or "the ammo box,"[5] and for "second amendment people" to stop an opponent.[6] In another ad, a heavily armed candidate breaks into a suburban home to "hunt for RINOs."[7]

What are the consequences for public opinion of this heavily militarized discourse? At a time of heightened partisan polarization and division across identity lines, how do average Americans react when political elites use the language and imaging of military aggression against their opponents? Studies suggest that this climate is not conducive to a healthy democracy. First, there is evidence that this aggressive discourse is contagious—especially on social media. People imitate the behaviors of their favorite elites.[8] Second, studies show that a small minority of Americans, around 7–10 percent, could be vulnerable to violent radicalization. This does not mean that all of them may take up arms against the government of the United States, but a large enough number may behave in aggressive ways that it could threaten democratic norms.[9] For example, we have seen the number of violent threats against elected officials—especially women—increase exponentially in recent years.[10] This level of exposure to violence—even if it does not amount to physical harm—can be very damaging for democratic representation, let alone individual representatives who experience fear and anxiety. The *Bruen* regime which made it exceedingly difficult for states and localities to regulate the public carry of firearms may lead to greater levels of political violence and chilling effects on citizens' public political expression.

In addition, studies show that the current political climate of partisan and racial antagonism may have weakened support for democratic norms in the White public. Partisans are likely to forgive or rationalize their party's candidates who behave in undemocratic ways.[11] Partisans are also more open to causing harm to members of the other party.[12] At the same time, prejudiced Whites are likely to embrace authoritarian leaders and support anti-democratic ideals to ensure the political exclusion of racial "others."[13] Studies underscore that trust in government and belief in the integrity of democratic institutions—such as elections—are entangled with racial prejudice and White grievances.[14]

This chapter aims to assess White Americans' support for militarized policies, political violence, and anti-democratic norms more broadly. Do White Americans support expanded "stand your ground" laws that enable people to shoot protesters? Do they approve of firearms in political protests? Do they agree with the insurrectionist theory that political violence is justified? How many people approach politics instrumentally thinking that the ends justify the means or that what the majority wants should prevail over the rights of minorities? Equally important is evaluating the relationship between ascriptive republicanism and support for anti-democratic norms, policies, and practices, including political violence. I expect that ascriptive republican ideology is a positive predictor of militarism and support of political violence. Furthermore, I expect that the effect of ascriptive republicanism should be conditional on partisanship and identification with the NRA.

MILITARIZED POLICY PREFERENCES

Embracing ascriptive republicanism has implications for support of militaristic public policies—the use of extreme penalties, including vigilantism and armed violence. Starting with Florida in 2005, we have seen the emergence of "stand your ground" regimes in recent years. As of 2021, thirty-six states have enacted some type of "stand your ground" law. These laws moved away from the common law tradition that required a "duty to retreat," instead taking to the public domain the idea that one's home is "their castle," where they have a right to defend themselves with force. Stand your ground laws enable individuals to claim self-defense even in cases of public confrontations where the option to de-escalate was available but not used or when the shooter behaved aggressively. Studies suggest that such laws increase rather than decrease armed violence, since they enable individuals to express aggression rather than call the police.[15]

In recent years, America has experienced a wave of racial justice protests, many in response to police shootings of minorities. Riots and looting followed some protests. At other protests, bands of armed militia groups—mostly White men—claimed to be self-appointed public safety officers working on keeping the peace and protecting public property. In Kenosha, Wisconsin, a seventeen-year-old armed vigilante shot and killed two protesters and wounded a third.[16] In response to protests and counterprotests, some state legislators have argued for expanding "stand your ground" laws to protect citizens shooting at protesters whom they perceive as dangerous to life or property. According to many critics, such laws are designed to chill participation in political protests and incentivize vigilantism.[17] Combined with public carry laws that allow citizens to carry firearms in public spaces either openly or concealed, such proposals—if enacted into law—create significant incentives for violent escalation.

Others have supported the militarization of police forces as a solution to both crime and violent protests. The National Defense Authorization Act of 1990, under the guise of supporting the "War on Drugs," created a program that allows the Army to transfer military materiel to local police departments. As of 2020, more than 8,200 law enforcement agencies partake in this program, contributing to the expansion of police militarization beyond major urban centers to smaller communities and college campuses. Studies indicate that police militarization has contributed to more aggressive tactics and has increased the probability of shootings of civilians without improving public safety outcomes.[18]

I expect that ascriptive republicanism is a positive and statistically significant predictor of White Americans' support for such militarized policies that encourage both vigilantism and police violence. The 2021 YouGov survey included four items related to militarized public policies—three that pertain to legalizing vigilantism and one that pertains to expanding the militarization of police departments at the expense of social services: 1) "Stand your ground laws, under which people who are in a public place and believe that their life or safety is in danger are not expected to retreat but are allowed to kill or injure the person whom they think is threatening them"; 2) "Laws that criminalize protests that take place on a public highway and block traffic"; 3) "Laws that protect citizens who shoot at protesters whom they think are violent and threatening private property"; and 4) "Laws that redirect money from social programs (such as health and education) to purchase military-grade equipment for police departments." All items were scored on four-point support/oppose scales.

In 2019, the *New York Times* published the "1619 Project," an initiative to highlight the integral role of slavery in the American experience and center the contributions of African Americans to the narrative of American history. In essence, the project principals argued that slavery was central to American economic and political development, and that we cannot and should not view slavery as an aberration or a Southern faux pas. This is a position consistent with much of contemporary historical analysis.[19] The project sparked intense debate about how history should be taught to America's schoolchildren. Several states introduced legislation targeting how America's history of racism is taught in classrooms. The laws limit how teachers discuss ideas such as racial privilege, explicit or implicit bias, discrimination, and oppression. Some impose financial penalties on schools that do not comply with these laws. A recent national survey shows that 30 percent of White Americans believe that issues of racial inequality should never be taught in schools. Another 15 percent concede that such issues should be taught only "a little."[20]

In addition to the questions mentioned above, the 2021 YouGov survey included an item asking White Americans about the degree to which they supported "laws that classify as terrorism any activity that promotes ideologies that criticize America's White and European heritage" (four-point scale). This item sought to assess whether White Americans who subscribe to ascriptive republican ideology are willing to penalize critics of racism and White privilege in the same way that laws penalize people who use political violence against civilians.

Figure 11.1 shows the proportion of White Americans who support each of these militarized policy ideas, overall and by one's level of ascriptive republicanism. The results suggest that a substantial number of White Americans are willing to use the tools of the state to harshly penalize people they view as an ideological threat. First, both stand your ground laws (60 percent) and laws that criminalize protests that disrupt traffic (64 percent) are supported by large majorities of White Americans, while about half (49 percent) support laws that would allow vigilantes to shoot protesters with impunity. In all these cases, support is driven primarily by high AMR respondents. Low AMR respondents tend to oppose these policies. Only a fourth of all White Americans (28 percent) support the militarization of police at the expense of social services. A similar proportion (26 percent) support classifying and punishing as "terrorism" ideas that challenge the centrality of America's White European heritage. In these cases, too, we see a strong asymmetry between high and low AMR scorers. Specifically, high AMR scorers are at least four times more likely to support these policy ideas than are low AMR scorers.

The effect of AMR continues to be substantively strong even when we

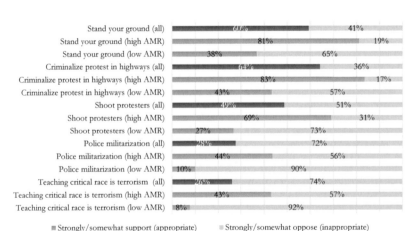

Figure 11.1 Support for militarized policies (2021 YouGov survey).

TABLE 11.1. OLS Models of Support for Militarized Policies (2021 YouGov Survey)

	Stand Your Ground	Immunity for Shooting Protesters	Criminalize Protest	Militarize Police	Classify Critical Ideologies as Terrorism	Appropriate to Bring Guns to Protests
	B/SE	B/SE	B/SE	B/SE	B/SE	B/SE
AMR	0.324 ***	0.309 ***	0.117 *	0.487 ***	0.678 ***	0.211 ***
	(0.06)	(0.07)	(0.06)	(0.07)	(0.07)	(0.07)
ICR	−0.067	−0.244 ***	−0.004	−0.07	−0.11	−0.239 ***
	(0.07)	(0.07)	(0.07)	(0.07)	(0.07)	(0.07)
White identity	−0.065 **	−0.01	0.008	−0.069 *	0.136 ***	−0.029
	(0.03)	(0.04)	(0.03)	(0.04)	(0.04)	(0.04)
Racial resentment	0.327 ***	0.358 ***	0.543 ***	0.153 ***	0.108 **	0.153 ***
	(0.05)	(0.05)	(0.05)	(0.05)	(0.05)	(0.05)
Respect laws	−0.012	0.052	0.158 ***	0.002	0.025	−0.111 **
	(0.05)	(0.05)	(0.05)	(0.05)	(0.04)	(0.05)
American identity	0.137 ***	0.071 *	0.019	0.051	0.039	−0.016
	(0.04)	(0.04)	(0.04)	(0.05)	(0.04)	(0.04)
Gun owner	0.07 ***	0.03	0.012	0.01	−0.01	0.105 ***
	(0.02)	(0.03)	(0.02)	(0.03)	(0.03)	(0.03)
Worry about crime	0.048	0.014	0.05	0.098 **	0.098 **	−0.009
	(0.04)	(0.04)	(0.04)	(0.04)	(0.05)	(0.04)
Victim of crime	0.027	0.036	0.036	−0.027	−0.049 *	0.053 **
	(0.02)	(0.02)	(0.02)	(0.02)	(0.03)	(0.03)
Partisanship (GOP)	0.186 ***	0.186 ***	0.105 **	0.104 ***	0.019	0.057
	(0.04)	(0.05)	(0.04)	(0.04)	(0.04)	(0.04)
Conservatism	0.165 ***	0.144 **	0.136 **	0.115 **	−0.107 *	0.251 ***
	(0.05)	(0.06)	(0.05)	(0.05)	(0.06)	(0.06)
Intercept	0.086	0.101	−0.02	−0.092	0.041	0.254 ***
	(0.06)	(0.07)	(0.07)	(0.06)	(0.06)	(0.07)
N	977	977	977	978	975	978
Adj. R²	0.564	0.525	0.555	0.39	0.351	0.355
F	95.92	73.904	82.415	33.401	21.955	27.412

Notes: *p<0.1; **p<0.05; ***p<0.001. Data are weighted. Robust standard errors in parentheses. All variables are recoded on 0–1 scales. Non-Hispanic Whites only. Controls include: gender, age, education, income, region, urban, rural.

control for other parameters. All five models included in table 11.1 explain a substantial portion of the variance in the data. AMR is positive and statistically significant in all six models, indicating that AMR high scorers are significantly more likely to support this type of policy. Furthermore, the substantive effect of AMR is larger than the effects of partisanship or ideology, and rivals the effect of racial resentment—the three other variables that have statistically significant effects across most if not all models. When racial resentment is excluded from the models, the effect of AMR strengthens substantially. The effect of AMR is strongest when it comes to beliefs that criticism of America's White heritage should be classified as "terrorism" and punished accordingly. Agreement with this proposal among those at the highest levels of AMR is 68ppts higher than for those at the lowest levels of AMR. Similarly, support for immunity for citizens who shoot protesters is 31ppts higher among high AMR scorers relative to low AMR scorers. Even on the very trenchant topic (given *Bruen*) of bringing firearms to political protests, high AMR scorers are 21ppts more supportive than those low on AMR. ICR is negatively correlated with all five dependent variables, but its effect is statistically significant only in one model—vesting with immunity armed citizens who shoot protesters.

GUNS IN POLITICAL SPACES

The proliferation of permissive gun-carrying regimes that enable citizens to bring their firearms outside the home has led to people bringing guns into political spaces. It is now relatively common in many states to see citizens going about their daily activities—shopping, eating at restaurants, or walking down the street—with a firearm visibly strapped on their bodies. For several years, the US has also witnessed gun rights protests where gun owners publicly carry firearms to protest gun control laws. For example, in January 2020, more than 20,000 gun rights activists staged an armed protest in Richmond, Virginia, to register their opposition to proposed gun control legislation in that state. Similar rallies have taken place across the country since at least 2010.[21]

However, in addition to gun rights protests, people have openly carried firearms to other types of political protests in recent years, events unrelated to gun rights. As early as 2009, news articles reported that gun rights activists openly carried assault-style rifles to protests staged outside events headlined by President Obama.[22] That year, as Obama and his surrogates ramped up the effort to pass the Affordable Care Act, the media began to report about people openly carrying firearms at healthcare town halls. Such practices raised concerns in the Secret Service tasked to protect the president and other top government officials. The presence of armed citizens at these political events appeared problematic not only for the security of the president, but because the open carry of firearms "changed the atmosphere surrounding such events. They're intimidating people like it's a Western saloon." Observers feared that the presence of weapons in a heated environment could "turn a verbal clash between demonstrators into a shootout."[23] However, for gun rights supporters, public gun carry is part of their fundamental right to gun ownership, and the public carry of arms in political spaces is a form of symbolic expression of in-group solidarity and ideology.[24]

By 2021, the US had experienced numerous instances of armed violence and intimidation in political spaces. In August 2017, White nationalists organized the violent "Unite the Right" protest in Charlottesville, Virginia. Three years later, news emerged that a group of armed civilians who staged armed protests against public health measures meant to combat COVID-19 had plotted to kill the governor of Michigan. In August 2020, an armed vigilante shot and killed Black Lives Matter protesters in Wisconsin. During the same period, armed groups pressured local governments to enact legislation known as "second amendment sanctuary laws"—largely symbolic ordinances that prohibit the enforcement of existing gun control laws mandating background checks and manner of gun storage, and extreme risk laws permitting the removal of firearms from those who present a risk of harm to themselves or others.[25] The violence culminated in the storming of the US Capitol on January 6, 2021. This event appears to have been organized by armed militia groups such as the Oath Keepers and the Proud Boys—many of whom were devotees of the QAnon conspiracy.

Legal scholars have also become concerned about the implications of carrying firearms in political spaces and what such practices may mean for the free expression of political opinion. For some, the first and second amendments are on a collision course in the middle of the public square. Democratic politics mandates freedom of expression and the ability to cast a vote free of coercion. Timothy Zick, a legal scholar, warns that open carry in political spaces is fundamentally anti-democratic, as it can have a chilling effect on the free expression of political opinion.[26] Citizen participation in public politics—from protests to town hall meetings—may be dampened by the presence of firearms, and the decline may be asymmetric, further exacerbating existing political inequalities in American society.

But little is known about what the public thinks about the presence of armed citizens in political protests. The 2021 YouGov survey asked: "Some people say it is appropriate for citizens to bring their firearms to protests to prevent violence from counter-protesters and agitators. Others say that guns in protests are dangerous. How about you? How appropriate do you think it is for citizens to bring firearms to protests?" (four-point scale). I expect that support for guns in protests will be positively correlated with AMR but negatively correlated with ICR—an anti-militaristic ideology.

People's support for guns in protests may be contextually driven—that is, it may depend on who brings the guns. People may be more open to attending a protest if the organizers are armed. This is because they may feel more secure if people who share their ideology and interests are the ones armed. Conversely, people may be less likely to attend a protest if the counterprotesters bring firearms. I conducted an experiment by randomly splitting the respondents into two groups and asking each group: "How likely would you be to attend a social protest if you knew that [rally organizers with whom you agreed politically had brought firearms/that counterprotesters, that is, people who disagreed with you] came to the same rally and brought firearms?" The purpose of this question was to assess whether the presence of firearms in a public political space, such as a protest, might have chilling effects on people's participation in such events, and if so, whether the chilling effects might be stronger when people are confronted with counterprotesters who are armed. A final question asked gun owners how likely they would be to bring their firearms to a protest.

First, I look at each item descriptively (fig. 11.2a). A quarter (26 percent) of White Americans believe that bringing guns to political protests is appropriate. The vast majority disapprove of the practice. As with militarized policies, there is a significant difference in support between high and low AMR scorers: 37 percent of high AMR scorers think that the presence of guns at protests is appropriate, compared to 13 percent of low AMR scorers. The data are also very revealing when it comes to chilling effects. More than three-fourths of White Americans say they would not attend a protest if the rally organizers or the counterprotesters were armed. The data do suggest differential chilling effects by levels of AMR. Specifically, tolerance of armed protest organizers is higher among high AMR scorers (32 percent)

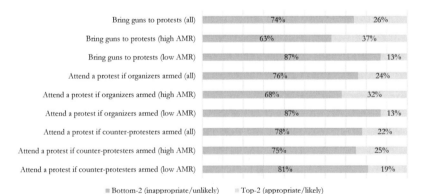

Figure 11.2a Support for guns at protests (2021 YouGov survey).
Note: Model includes demographic controls. All variables are recoded on 0–1 scales. Non-Hispanic Whites only. For full models, see Appendix tables 11.2a and 11.2b.

than low AMR scorers (13 percent). Among high AMR scorers, 25 percent would still attend if the counterprotesters were armed.

A consistent picture emerges from multivariate models (online appendix, table 11.2a). Those who score high on AMR are more likely to believe that bringing firearms to political protests is appropriate (21ppts). Conversely, ICR is a negative and significant predictor of similar magnitude (–24ppts). Only conservative ideology has a similarly large effect (25ppts). It is also important to note that partisanship is not significant in the model.

The split sample structure of the question about likely attendance at a rally where people are armed allows me to test whether chilling effects are stronger when people expect the organizers or counterprotesters to show up armed. More people are willing to attend when the organizers are armed than when the counterprotesters are, but this difference is small (p = 0.089). As AMR increases, so does readiness to attend a rally where the organizers are armed (fig. 11.2b). The interaction between the treatment and ICR is not significant.

The final question asks gun owners if they would bring their firearms to a protest. Interestingly, neither AMR nor ICR influences the likelihood of a gun owner bringing a firearm to a political rally. Men, conservatives, and those who don't think that respect for laws is important show an increased propensity to bring a firearm to a political rally (online appendix, table 11.2a).

Overall, the analysis suggests that a small but sizable minority of White Americans—many more of them high AMR scorers than low AMR scor-

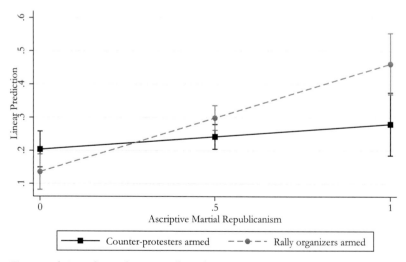

Figure 11.2b Attend armed protest, effect of treatment by AMR (2021 YouGov survey).

ers or high ICR scorers—believe that it is appropriate for citizens to bring firearms to political protests. These White Americans also assert that they would attend such a protest, especially if it is the organizers rather than the counterprotesters who are armed. Yet for most Americans—especially women, older people, and Democrats—guns in protests are unacceptable and intimidating. These chilling effects can have profound consequences for democratic politics (online appendix, table 11.2a). Asymmetries in political participation resulting from the presence of firearms in public spaces can deepen existing inequalities.

Social protest in America is a form of constitutionally protected speech that is a critical foundation of democracy. Studies show that politicians learn about citizens' demands from protest activity and are more likely to respond to these demands.[27] If guns at protests "chill" attendance, that could have implications for democratic responsiveness. If women and Democrats or those who score high on ICR or low on AMR are more likely to be intimidated by firearms and thus less likely to attend protests or public meetings of any kind, their ideological and policy preferences may become less visible—and consequently their elected officials might also be less attentive to these issues. Any group that becomes discouraged from attending political protests because of the presence of guns might find that their voices become muted and their issues less well-represented at all levels of government. That would be a significant loss for American democracy.

VIOLENT RADICALIZATION

The combination of partisan polarization (especially on issues of gun rights), steady increases in the number of guns in civilian hands, and an uptick in violent political rhetoric during both the Obama and Trump presidencies have led to concerns that we may be about to witness significant increases in political violence. Studies of elected officials show that they have experienced more threats of violence in recent years.[28] Public opinion scholars have also reported a high appetite for violence among the public, though it is difficult to estimate what percentage of citizens may become radicalized.[29] My goal here is to estimate whether the potential for radicalization is higher among Whites who score high on AMR than among those with low AMR scores. If so, support for ascriptive republican ideology may contribute to violent radicalization.

The 2021 YouGov survey included three items measuring willingness to support political violence. These items are 1) "we should support organizations that fight for our group's rights, even if they use violence"; 2) "we should participate in public protests against oppression of our group even if such protests may turn violent"; and 3) "we should fight with arms if necessary to protect the rights of our group." The items are adapted from the Radicalism Intention Scale (RIS), a battery used extensively in terrorism research to assess support for political violence.[30] All three were scored on a four-point Likert scale ranging from "strongly support" to "strongly oppose." A factor analysis shows that all three items fall on the same dimension (eigenvalue = 1.45). I created an additive index based on these three items (alpha = 0.75). Another question asks, "how much do you feel it is justified or not justified for people to use violence to pursue their political goals in this country?" This question is scored on a four-point scale ranging from "very justified" to "not at all."

Figure 11.3a shows White Americans' violent radicalization potential for the overall population and by AMR levels. First, it is important to note that only a small minority of White Americans appear to support political violence based on the RIS index. Only 7 percent of people score high on the RIS index, and even among high AMR scorers, only 9 percent appear to have high intent for violence. Similarly, only 9 percent of White Americans believe that political violence may be justified, while the vast majority say it is not justified (fig. 11.3b). These proportions are similar to those reported in other studies. Of course, expressing violent intent in surveys is not a sufficient indicator that an individual will really engage in violence. Many people may be expressing frustration and anger through such answers. However, in a population of 200 million, these numbers are not negligible and should be taken seriously—especially since there is evidence that aggression online can be contagious and can act to motivate and

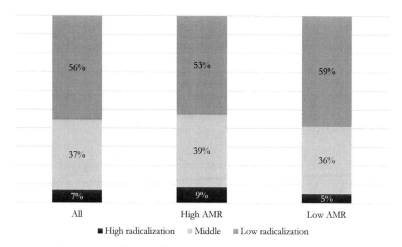

Figure 11.3a Political violent radicalization (2021 YouGov survey).

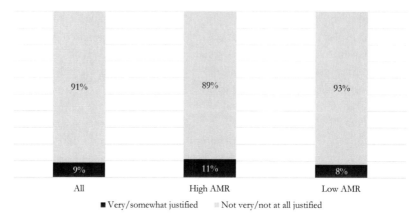

Figure 11.3b Political violence justified (2021 YouGov survey).

radicalize people, and since threats against public officials have increased exponentially.[31]

Multivariate models confirm the centrality of ascriptive republican ideology in radicalization. In both the RIS index and the question about whether political violence is ever justified, AMR is positive and the strongest predictor of support for political violence (37ppts). ICR is negative and significant, but its effect is substantively smaller (−14ppts). By contrast, partisanship and political conservatism are null in both models (fig. 11.3c).

These data suggest that White Americans who view the world through ascriptive republican lenses may be more vulnerable to violent radicalization than other people are. What is more, the data show that the effect of AMR is not conditional on partisanship or conservatism, but rather on gun ownership and identification with the NRA. As a reminder, I measure identification with the NRA through an item that asks, "how often do you say 'we' rather than 'they' when thinking of the NRA?" I ask this of everyone in the sample. Neither gun ownership nor a paid NRA membership is necessary for a person to feel a kinship with the group. As figure 11.3d shows, the effect of AMR on violent radicalization is far stronger among those White Americans who strongly identify with the NRA than among those who do not. The interaction with gun ownership suggests a similar, albeit weaker pattern (fig. 11.3e). These results suggest that ascriptive republican ideology is more persistently activated among White Americans who engage with the gun culture. These individuals are not necessarily gun owners: 20 percent of people who do not own guns report strong identification with the NRA.

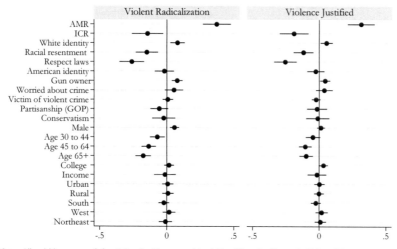

Notes: All variables are re-coded on 0-1 scales. Data are weighted. Non-Hispanic whites only. Robust SEs.

Figure 11.3c Support for political violence (2021 YouGov survey).
Note: All variables are recoded on 0–1 scales. Data are weighted. Non-Hispanic Whites only. Robust standard errors.

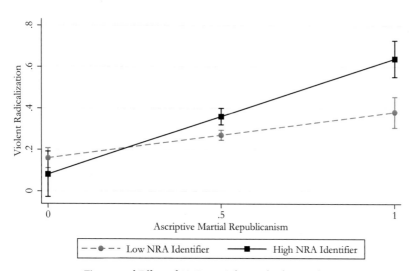

Figure 11.3d Effect of AMR on violent radicalization by
NRA identification (2021 YouGov survey).
Note: Non-Hispanic Whites only. Data are weighted. All variables are recoded on 0–1 scales. For full results, see Appendix table 11.3b.

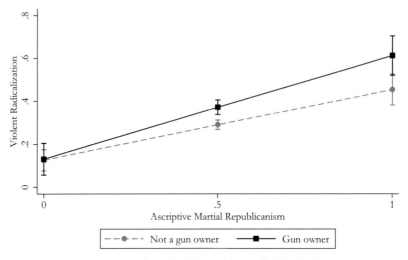

Figure 11.3e Effect of AMR on violent radicalization by
gun owner status (2021 YouGov survey).
Note: Non-Hispanic Whites only. Data are weighted. All variables are recoded on
0–1 scales. Full results are in Appendix table 11.3b.

Overall, the data indicate that a small minority of White Americans, concentrated among gun owners and NRA identifiers who subscribe to ascriptive republicanism, are vulnerable to violent radicalization.

SUPPORT FOR ANTI-DEMOCRATIC NORMS, MOVEMENTS, AND LEADERS

During the Obama era, there emerged greater tolerance of anti-democratic behavior among the public and the elites alike. For example, readers may remember when a Republican Congressman screamed "you lie" at President Obama as the latter formally addressed a joint session of Congress in September 2009. However, many more democratic norms were dispensed with during the Trump administration, as the president called for his opponents to be "locked up," pardoned political supporters convicted of serious offenses, and sought to interfere with the administration of the 2020 election in unprecedented ways.

Recent public opinion studies have implicated both partisan polarization and racial antagonism as critical correlates of citizens' support for anti-democratic norms and behaviors.[32] These findings add to a long and venerable tradition in political science, demonstrating that support for democratic norms is context-dependent and quite malleable.[33] Here, I seek to show that adherence to ascriptive republicanism is a strong predictor of support for anti-democratic norms, movements, and leaders, even when controlling for partisanship, ideology, and prejudice.

The survey included several items assessing people's support for anti-democratic norms, movements, and leaders. Specifically, respondents were asked about their agreement with each of these statements: 1) "The will of the majority should always prevail over the rights of minorities" ("absolute majority rule"); 2) "I don't mind the politician's methods if they get things done" ("ends justify means"); 3) "We should use all available force to maintain law and order" ("extreme force"); 4) "QAnon is a group of patriots dedicated to exposing the corruption of the deep state" ("QAnon"); 5) "Donald Trump was among the country's best presidents" ("Trump best President"). All items were scored on four-point agree/disagree scales. Respondents were also asked whom they voted for in the 2020 election (Biden, Trump, or someone else).

Support for minority rights is a crucial component of democratic politics. A system where a numeric majority can strip minorities of all rights and protections is not a democracy. The country's framers were well aware of the danger of the tyranny of an "overbearing" majority and took many steps to protect minority interests.[34] However, not all contemporary White Americans share these concerns. As figure 11.4a shows, 28 percent of all White Americans endorse absolute majoritarianism. Support is higher among those who score high on AMR (39 percent), but significantly lower among those who score low on AMR (16 percent).

Similarly, institutional constraints are essential in a democratic system. Not all methods of action are legitimate. Even if the goal has merit, illegitimate means can taint the result. For example, killing abortion providers does not add to the legitimacy of the right-to-life movement. Similarly, using procedural maneuvers to invalidate the 2020 election would not have made for a legitimate Republican presidency. However, a third of all White Americans today say that they would be happy not to scrutinize a politician's methods if they "get things done." Essentially, for many White Americans today, the ends justify the means: if undemocratic processes are used to achieve a desirable end, so be it. This sentiment is much more broadly shared (45 percent) by high AMR scorers than by low AMR scorers (21 percent).

Finally, democratic states have the authority and legitimacy to use force to defend the public good—whether in the form of police coercion or military preparedness. However, maintaining public order does not justify nor excuse the use of extreme force—a lesson central to the Black Lives Matter narrative. Democracies have to manage how force is used or risk losing legitimacy. This is why policies that legalize vigilantism constitute a significant threat to democratic politics. Yet most White Americans (52 percent)

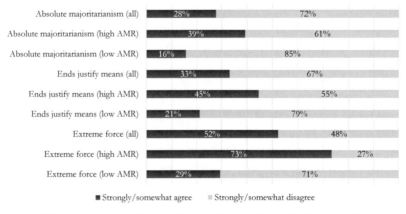

Figure 11.4a Support for anti-democratic norms (2021 YouGov survey).

believe that "we should use all available force to maintain law and order." Once again, we see that a desirable end—public order—appears sufficient to justify using illegitimate means—extreme force. Here we see one of the most dramatic differences between high and low AMR scorers: 73 percent of high AMR respondents, but only 29 percent of low AMR scorers, endorse this position—a 44ppt difference (fig. 11.4a).

QAnon is a conspiracy theory that circulated through social media. QAnon ideas have attracted large numbers of followers, especially among conservatives. Unlike the Tea Party, which stressed limited government and policy priorities consistent with that goal, QAnon stresses suspicion and animosity toward the Democratic Party and its supporters—many of whom are minority group members. Adherents to QAnon believe that a secretive group of satanic pedophiles and cannibals (the "deep state") has taken control of the federal government and the media. Racist and sexist beliefs are also prevalent among QAnon devotees. The group aims to restore legitimacy to the United States government by reinstating Donald Trump as president. Studies show that many QAnon supporters participated in the January 6 riots at the US Capitol.[35] There is no evidence that the NRA supports QAnon. *The American Rifleman* has not referenced the group. However, the NRA and the broader gun rights movement have promoted similar ideas related to sinister globalist elites that seek to harm American democracy. Therefore, it is reasonable to expect that for people who subscribe to ascriptive republicanism, QAnon exemplifies political virtue—that it is a group of patriots. As figure 11.4b shows, 29 percent of White Americans believe that QAnon is "a group of patriots dedicated to exposing the corruption of the deep state." The proportion is much higher among high AMR scorers (46 percent) than among low AMR scorers (12 percent).

The Trump presidency evoked strong emotions on both sides of the political spectrum. Experts have argued that American democracy experienced normative and institutional erosion under Trump for the first time since World War II.[36] Republican support for Trump persisted even as his transgressions against democracy accumulated.[37] Democratic opposition and hostility endured as well. Scholars have offered numerous explanations of what factors contributed to Trump's political appeal. Among these explanations, White anti-Black attitudes and White in-group attachment figured as the most substantiated.[38]

The 2021 YouGov survey included two items that referenced President Trump. First, it asked about vote choice in the 2020 election. Second, it asked respondents whether they agreed that Trump was among the country's best presidents (four-point scale). More than half (53 percent) of White Americans judge Trump among the country's best presidents. This proportion is much higher for high AMR scorers (78 percent) than low AMR scorers (25 percent).

The vote choice question allows me to test whether ideologies of Americanism influenced White Americans' support for Trump in the election. Analyzing presidential vote choice is important because it moves us past the world of gun culture and gun politics. This evaluation of the effect of Americanism on vote choice allows me to link ascriptive republicanism to electoral politics. Among respondents to the vote choice item, I dropped those who said they did not vote or voted for a third-party candidate. I specified the dependent variable so that "1" indicates a vote for Trump

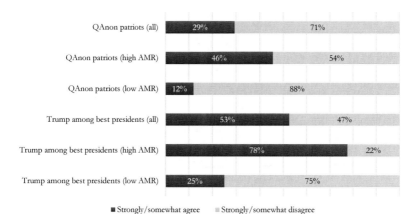

Figure 11.4b Support for anti-democratic movements and leaders (2021 YouGov survey).

and "0" indicates a vote for Biden.[39] The results show that 58 percent of all Whites voted for Trump and 42 percent voted for Biden. These proportions match the national election returns. Not surprisingly, 86 percent of those high on AMR voted for Trump, compared to 29 percent of low AMR scorers.

Table 11.2 shows the results of multivariate regression models for each of these dependent variables. These analyses validate the strength of the corre-

TABLE 11.2. Support for Anti-Democratic Norms, Groups, and Politicians (2021 YouGov Survey)

	Absolute Majority Rule	Use Force to Establish Order	Ends Justify Means	QAnon Patriots	Trump Best President	Voted for Trump in 2020
	B/SE	B/SE	B/SE	B/SE	B/SE	B/SE
AMR	0.372 ***	0.324 ***	0.464 ***	0.391 ***	0.171 ***	0.231 ***
	(0.06)	(0.06)	(0.06)	(0.06)	(0.06)	(0.07)
ICR	−0.132 *	−0.127 *	−0.119	−0.001	−0.045	−0.214 ***
	(0.07)	(0.07)	(0.08)	(0.07)	(0.06)	(0.05)
White identity	0.087 **	0.010	0.084 **	0.059 *	−0.017	−0.071 **
	(0.04)	(0.03)	(0.04)	(0.03)	(0.03)	(0.03)
Racial resentment	0.05	0.191 ***	0.023	0.102 **	0.373 ***	0.316 ***
	(0.05)	(0.05)	(0.05)	(0.05)	(0.05)	(0.05)
Respect laws	0.008	0.164 ***	0.036	−0.056	0.014	0.008
	(0.05)	(0.04)	(0.06)	(0.04)	(0.05)	(0.05)
American identity	−0.051	0.034	−0.039	−0.03	0.059	0.086 **
	(0.04)	(0.04)	(0.05)	(0.04)	(0.04)	(0.04)
Gun owner	−0.02	0.03	−0.01	0.056 **	0.015	−0.014
	(0.03)	(0.02)	(0.03)	(0.03)	(0.02)	(0.02)
Partisanship (GOP)	−0.013	0.045	−0.021	0.10 **	0.452 ***	0.582 ***
	(0.04)	(0.04)	(0.05)	(0.04)	(0.04)	(0.05)
Conservatism	−0.017	0.105 **	−0.128 **	0.179 ***	0.17 ***	0.198 ***
	(0.05)	(0.05)	(0.06)	(0.05)	(0.05)	(0.05)
Intercept	0.27 ***	0.035	0.308 ***	−0.06	−0.213 ***	−0.059
	(0.07)	(0.06)	(0.08)	(0.06)	(0.07)	(0.06)
N	977	978	978	976	978	872
Adj. R^2	0.144	0.433	0.141	0.397	0.722	0.782
F	9.113	59.136	8.602	37.867	325.06	500.64

Notes: *p<0.1; **p<0.05; ***p<0.001. Data are weighted. Robust standard errors in parentheses. All variables are rounded on 0–1 scales. Non-Hispanic Whites only. Controls include: national economic evaluation, personal economic evaluation, fear of crime, gender, age, income, education.

lation between AMR and these beliefs—already apparent from the descriptive analysis—by controlling for other covariates. First, AMR is positive and statistically significant in all six models. Republicanism (partisanship) is significant in only three of the six models. Even ideology is significant in five of the six models. The coefficient for AMR is very large in all models. In the first four models, AMR has the largest substantive effect of all variables in the model. Specifically, a change from the lowest to the highest level of AMR corresponds to an increase of 37ppts in support for absolute majoritarianism, 32ppts in support for the use of extreme force, and 46ppts in beliefs that the ends justify the means. The effect of AMR is surpassed by partisanship and racial resentment only in the two Trump models.[40]

THE JANUARY 6 INSURRECTION

One item in the 2021 YouGov survey specifically referenced the January 6 attack on the US Capitol building by supporters of former president Trump keen on stopping the certification of the results of the 2020 election. Respondents were split among two versions of the item. The first statement said, "the people who participated in the January 6th rallies at the Capitol are patriotic Americans," and the second said, "the people who participated in the January 6th riots at the Capitol are traitors." Respondents were asked for their level of agreement with the statement on a four-point agree/disagree scale.

The two versions correspond to the two primary frames surrounding the January 6 events. Trump and his supporters in the media portrayed the attack on the Capitol as an attempt by honorable and patriotic Americans to protect democratic institutions by exposing a fraudulent election. A year later, Trump supporters even held vigils to honor these "martyrs."[41] The Democrats and many others argued that this was a riot that betrayed American democracy and should be treated as sedition or treason.[42] I expect that more respondents will side with the negative framing of the January 6 events than with the positive framing, but Whites who score high on AMR will push back against the negative framing and embrace the positive characterization. The reverse should be the case for high ICR scorers.

First, 30 percent of White respondents agree with the positive characterization of the January 6 events as "rallies by patriots." Conversely, 53 percent agree that the event was "a riot by traitors." The difference is statistically and substantively significant ($p < 0.001$), underscoring that many White Americans continue to think of the January 6 events as honorable despite the hundred indictments and multiple convictions of participants.

As expected, the interaction between the treatment and AMR is negative and significant, and the one with ICR is positive and significant. As figure 11.5a shows, respondents become significantly more supportive of the positive framing as AMR increases, but they do not push back very much against the negative framing. By contrast, respondents both embrace the negative framing and strongly push back against the positive framing as a function of ICR (fig. 11.5b).

The data also show a significant and positive three-way interaction between the treatment, AMR, and partisanship (b = 0.615; p < 0.01). Figure 11.6a shows the results of the interaction among Democrats. In this group, as AMR increases, support for the positive ("patriot") framing of the January 6 insurrection increases. Conversely, as AMR increases, support for the negative ("traitors") framing declines. Democrats who score at the highest levels of AMR are as likely to support the negative framing as they are the positive one. Although White Democrats have had a very negative view of the insurrection, the data show significant variability in perceptions of the events among these partisans based on their support for ascriptive republican ideology.

A different pattern emerges among Republicans. Here, support for the positive framing increases as AMR increases, but AMR does not affect support for the negative framing (fig. 11.6b).

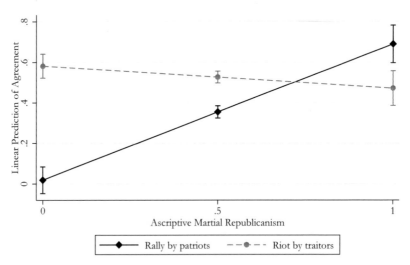

Figure 11.5a Agreement with characterization of January 6 events by AMR (2021 YouGov survey).

Note: Model includes controls. All variables are recoded on 0–1 scales. Data are weighted. Non-Hispanic Whites only. Full results are in Appendix table 11.5.

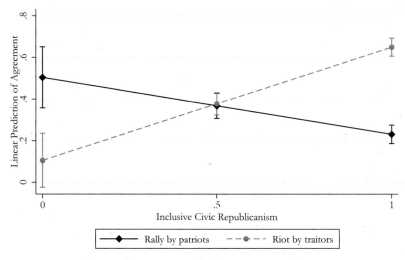

Figure 11.5b Agreement with characterization of January
6 events by ICR (2021 YouGov survey).
Note: Model includes controls. All variables are recoded on 0–1 scales. Data are
weighted. Non-Hispanic Whites only. Full models are in Appendix table 11.5.

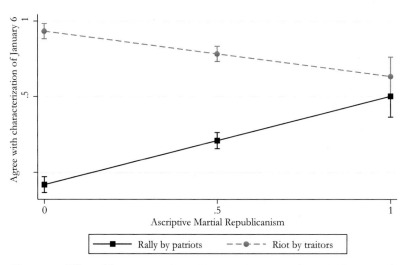

Figure 11.6a Effect of the treatment by AMR among Democrats (2021 YouGov survey).
Note: Non-Hispanic Whites only. Data are weighted. All variables are recoded on
0–1 scales. Full models are in Appendix table 11.6.

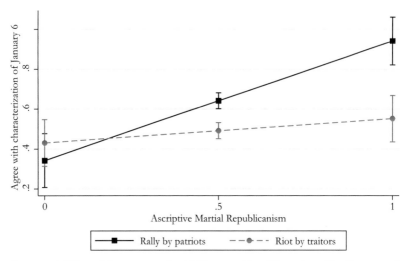

Figure 11.6b Effect of the treatment by AMR among Republicans (2021 YouGov survey). *Note*: Non-Hispanic Whites only. Data are weighted. Variables are recoded on 0–1 scales. Full models are in Appendix table 11.6.

Not surprisingly, given the centrality of ascriptive republicanism in NRA narratives and the close association of the group with the Republican Party, identification with the NRA is also consequential for how White Americans frame the January 6 insurrection. However, the relationship between partisanship and NRA identification is strong but not overwhelming (r = 0.36): not all NRA identifiers are Republicans, and vice versa. The models show a significant three-way interaction between the treatment, ascriptive republicanism, and NRA identification (b = 0.911; p < 0.05).

Specifically, as figure 11.7a shows, among those who identify with the NRA, as ascriptive republicanism increases, so does support for the positive framing of the January 6 events. As is the case for Republicans, among NRA identifiers the effect of AMR in the negative frame is not significant. Among those who do not identify with the NRA, ascriptive republicanism has implications for responses to both treatments. As figure 11.7b shows, Whites who do not identify with the NRA are more likely to endorse the positive framing of January 6 as AMR increases. Conversely, they are less likely to accept the negative framing as a function of AMR.

Overall, the data suggest that ascriptive republicanism colors the way White Americans understand what happened at the US Capitol on January 6. White Republicans and NRA identifiers are more likely to endorse the positive framing of the events as a function of AMR, but ascriptive

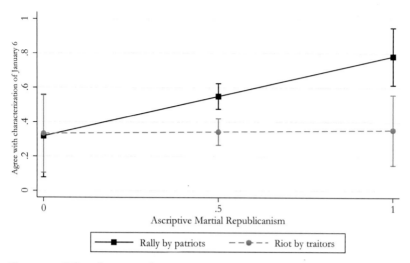

Figure 11.7a Effect of treatment by AMR among NRA identifiers (2021 YouGov survey). *Note*: Non-Hispanic Whites only. Data are weighted. All variables are recoded on 0–1 scales. Full models are in Appendix table 11.7.

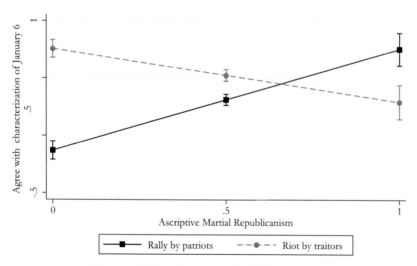

Figure 11.7b Effect of treatment by AMR among non-NRA identifiers (2021 YouGov survey).
Note: Non-Hispanic Whites only. Data are weighted. All variables are recoded on 0–1 scales. Full models are in Appendix table 11.7.

republicanism does not affect how they respond to the negative framing. However, for Democrats and non-NRA-identifiers, AMR influences how they respond to both frames, but in opposite directions.

The effect of ascriptive republicanism on White Americans' behaviors and attitudes does not end with owning firearms, supporting the Second Amendment, and endorsing the NRA. It spills over to support for militarized policies and vigilantism. It influences how White Americans perceive the presence of firearms in political events such as protests—a practice that many critics view as a threat to Americans' freedom of political expression. Ascriptive republican ideology also colors how White Americans interpret the events of January 6, 2021—one of the most significant threats American democracy has faced in recent years. Democrats and those outside of the NRA's orbit are also vulnerable to the effects of this ideology. Although the Democratic Party has condemned the events of January 6, Democratic partisans who embrace ascriptive republican ideology are as likely to agree with a positive framing of the event as "a rally by patriots" as to believe it was a riot.

Democratic Stability in Peril

In recent years, the NRA's luster has diminished. Internal strife, a bankruptcy, a leadership crisis, and a challenge to the organization's 150-year-old charter in New York State have consumed much of the group's time and resources. Its reputation was further tarnished when it became the subject of a US Senate investigation alleging that the group had become a Russian foreign asset, something the Col. Church-era "patriotic organization" would have a hard time processing. The group is still politically powerful, but observers consider its bite less consequential than it was a few years ago, before the Trump era.[1]

Even if the NRA lies wounded on the battlefield of the culture wars, the Supreme Court and the Republican Party have lifted its martial banner. Also, a substantial minority of the American population shares the group's ideology, and their voices are loudly heard at rallies, on right-wing cable programs, and on social media. The NRA's apocalyptic vision of a political world of a weak and unresponsive government, unregulated campaign spending, unencumbered access to the means of violence, unaccountable policing of communities of color, and harsh criminal punishment has come to fruition. The association has won, and now it is obsolete and irrelevant—a victim of its own success.

As I showed in this book, the NRA is the institutional embodiment of a political ideology that emerged during the early Republic. This worldview, which I have called ascriptive republicanism, fused two ideological streams popular at the time of the founding: martial republicanism and White male supremacy. Republicans believed that the virtue required in making decisions for the public good could only be developed through armed service. Only through the selfless act of bearing arms for the Republic could members of the polity become trusted stewards of the public welfare in politics. In the American political tradition, only White men were thought to have the proven moral capacity to develop political virtue and thus to be entrusted with political decision-making. According to this myth, African

Americans had chosen the dependency of slavery over the hardships of freedom, which made them unsuitable for political membership. Similarly, White women were dependent, incapable of "common sense," and physically weak, and therefore not to be entrusted with either armed service or political rights.

Furthermore, ascriptive republicanism was institutionalized in the state militia, an organization set up by the US Constitution and prominently mentioned in the preamble of the Second Amendment. Early US law required all White men of military age to participate in the state militia and furnish their own arms and equipment. State constitutions further linked militia service and political participation by making White men's militia enrollment a condition for voting rights. Although the military efficacy of the state militia was highly contested, the institution persisted for more than a century because it played an important political role. Militia units helped political parties recruit candidates for office, rally voters to the polls, and on many occasions, intimidate the opposition into not voting—or even helped to orchestrate political coups.[2]

The NRA was the creation of Civil War militia officers who recognized the military limitations of the National Guard and sought to improve the quality of training available to citizen-soldiers. The group envisioned a partnership with the federal government to incentivize White young men to take up shooting sports and learn how to be virtuous citizens who would volunteer for military service. This partnership, and the economic incentives that came with it, lasted for more than six decades.

From early on, the organization's theory of democracy was rooted in ascriptive martial republicanism. The NRA believed citizens should train at arms to develop the political virtue required to defend constituted authority and recognize and defeat corruption. In recent decades, after the era of mass mobilization and the draft ended, the NRA focused on the civilian market. As a result, it dropped training as a prerequisite for political virtue. In this new context, the consumer act of purchasing a firearm is, by itself, evidence of good citizenship.

For the first century of its history, the group stood by the federal government, ready to defend national institutions from foreign and domestic foes. Communism, anarchism, and—implicitly—the progressive movements of the 1960s and 1970s were on the list. After its relationship with the government frayed in the 1960s the NRA turned its sights on government. The group portrayed the armed citizens of the late twentieth and the twenty-first century as having the right and, indeed, the obligation to use political violence against a corrupt and tyrannical government. This is the message that came through loud and clear when armed militia groups invaded state legislatures in 2020 to protest public health measures imposed to combat the COVID-19 pandemic. The narrative also emerged on January 6, 2021, in Washington, DC, when a mob of Trump supporters stormed into the US Capitol. These people, as well as those who tried to break into the FBI offices in Ohio in August 2022 and those who concocted a plan to abduct and kill the governor of Michigan, viewed themselves as citizen-soldiers fighting against a corrupt and tyrannical government.

The NRA may have declined in influence, but its worldview has become institutionalized in American law in ways bound to affect American life in its political and social dimensions for many decades to come. In a trio of decisions handed down between 2008 and 2022, the US Supreme Court has vindicated and expanded gun rights, recognizing an individual right to armed self-defense and insurrection.[3] In *District of Columbia v. Heller* (2008), the Court recognized an individual right to civilian gun ownership for self-defense in the home, but also to protect against tyranny. In *McDonald v. Chicago* (2010), the Court determined that not only the federal government, but even states were barred from infringing on Americans' gun ownership rights. In *New York State Rifle & Pistol Association, Inc. v. Bruen* (2022), the Court extended the right to bear arms outside the home into the public domain and determined that only history and tradition, not public safety concerns, should come to bear when courts evaluate the constitutionality of gun regulations. These decisions coincided with other radical institutional changes imposed by the Court, including gutting the Civil Rights Act and especially voting rights protections (*Shelby County v. Holder* [2013]), rejecting the argument that women have an individual right to control reproductive decisions (*Dobbs v. Jackson Women's Health Organization* [2022]), and siding with an individual right to religious expression over the principle of separation of church and state and allowing the institutionalization of prayer in public schools (*Kennedy v. Bremerton School District* [2022]).

In the three gun rights decisions, the most authoritative judicial institution in the world's oldest democracy, the symbol of the rule of law, has told citizens that they cannot and should not trust their democratically elected governments to keep them safe from crime. They are better off carrying firearms wherever they go—never mind that half of all gun owners don't know how to use their weapons. Worse, the Court warns that democratically designed and controlled American political institutions—including the courts—are incapable or unwilling to protect the rule of law. Citizens may need to enforce democracy and public order with bullets, not ballots.

The militaristic ideology of the NRA has infiltrated the public. Hostility against government and politics has increased in recent years, and we now see evidence of people seeking to retreat from political engagement because of the changes in culture and institutions. My data show that the consequences of this new regime are not lost on the American public. The presence of firearms at political events can chill participation. People would rather stay home than risk injury or death when untrained "good guys with guns" come to political rallies and protests. As gun violence spreads to fairs, festivals, and holiday parades, more people may think twice about attending those too. Anecdotal evidence from newspaper stories and my ongoing research suggest that elected officials and their staffers are also impacted by this "new normal." They are more likely to plan events carefully, become less accessible to constituents through electronic forms of communication, and be more vigilant about what issues they talk about in public. From school board members to US Congress members, some carry arms to work or plan to do so. Ironically, in the name of self-defense and individual safety, which now includes public confrontations with no duty to retreat, the Court may be forcing Americans to withdraw from social interactions and destroying the social capital that is considered so central to a stable democratic polity.[4]

The same radical intent is evident in the Republican Party. A new generation of Republican leaders at the national and state levels have turned the party of Lincoln into a party that represents authoritarianism, defiance of norms, the insurgency of White male grievance, citizen militarism, and a Darwinian vision of liberty. Notwithstanding the 2022 federal compromise law that strengthened background checks and "red flag" provisions allowing police to remove guns from people with a documented history of violence, the Republican Party continues to push in the other direction. Republican legislatures have deregulated gun ownership, lifting or lessening various state and local licensing, permitting, and training requirements. Second Amendment sanctuaries have proliferated, challenging federal-local cooperation on gun law enforcement. At the same time, election deniers and Trump supporters continue to harp on militaristic themes and flirt with the promotion of political violence.

A new generation of Republican elected officials and candidates are openly and proudly undermining democratic institutions in the name of ascriptive republican ideologies—White Christian nationalism most prominently. Republicans such as Senator Josh Hawley (R-MO) have lamented the decline of American Christian manhood and put forth an ascriptive republican vision of society.[5] In this premodern world, virtuous citizens resemble "the Roman plebeian who lived by his own labor, [and] who voted without reward according to his own convictions."[6] These virtuous citizens could "share in self-government" because they "discipline[d] [their] passions and sacrifice[d] in the service of others." These men drew on their "masculine virtues" of "courage, independence, and assertiveness" to "stand strong against those who would try to make you dependent on their wealth or influence" and defend the Republic.[7] Others, such as Eric Greitens (R-MO) or Jerone Davison (R-AZ), have adopted aggressive, martial messaging, full of military imagery. In campaign ads, they shoot at "the government," break into homes with military weapons to "hunt RINOs," or shoot at "Democrats" dressed in Klan hoods.[8] The tenor among these Republicans appears to be that institutions that do not represent their brand of ascriptive republicanism should be destroyed because they do not express the party's vision of what America is about.

The institutionalization of ascriptive republicanism in law and politics has crucial implications for the state and the public. The Court's change of course on guns has come at a time of deep partisan polarization in the elite and the public. The partisan sorting has led to the alignment of partisanship, ascriptive identities, and belief systems.[9] The result has been more divisive and emotionally charged politics. For many citizens, political competition has taken on the character of a Manichean fight between good and evil, "us vs. them." At stake are deeply held moral values and visions of peoplehood. As Kari Lake, the Republican candidate for governor of Arizona, said in a recent speech, "It is not just a battle between Republicans and Democrats. This is a battle between freedom and tyranny, between authoritarianism and liberty and between good and evil." Grassroots members of the reactionary Right share this view of American politics.[10]

Goaded by partisan media, especially on the Right, more and more people dehumanize their political opponents and refuse to feel empathy for them.[11] These processes of emotional distancing increase the threat associated with the opposition. At the same time, just as the Court prescribes, few people trust the government to be an effective and neutral arbiter of conflict. Ideological commitments and elite rhetoric have also contributed to a decline in trust in the institutions of democracy—including elections.[12] Ascriptive ideologies and race-based grievances—fomented by political elites and partisan media—undercut public trust.[13] Anecdotal reports suggest that some citizens on the Right no longer believe in democracy, proclaiming that the United States was never meant to be a democratic polity, but instead "a republic." For Republican activists, the United States is "a constitutional republic." "When I hear the word 'democracy,' I think of the democracy of the Democratic Republic of the Congo. That's not us," an Arizona Republican argued, using distinctly racialized tropes.[14] In this way, the Republican base rejects majoritarianism when they believe that they are in the minority. In other instances, as my data show, Whites who embrace ascriptive republicanism approve of a draconian majoritarian politics where minority rights do not count at all. Both themes are deeply threatening to liberal democratic institutions.

As discussed in chapters 9 and 10, White Americans who embrace ascriptive republican ideology are more likely to harbor hostility toward democratic institutions and view political violence as justifiable. Elite endorsement of this militaristic, anti-statist worldview, especially in America's hyper-polarized political context, can strengthen the influence of such ideas on a portion of the public.[15] Increased public support can ensure a vicious cycle because elites are incentivized to double down to meet public demand for militarism.

Experts indicate that at least 344 million firearms are in civilian hands—more guns than there are adult residents, in fact.[16] Yet although the proportion of households that own guns has declined since 1970, the number of firearms in civilian hands has increased. These trends suggest that some people are stockpiling firearms.[17] On average, gun owners own five guns each. No other democracy in the world has so many gun-owning civilians, or so many firearms circulating in the civilian market.[18]

And it is not simply that the stockpile of guns is increasing. Some people in the population are heeding the call and are expecting armed confrontation. As more and more guns become concentrated in the hands of a relatively small portion of the public, many of whom share an ideology, this path can lead to more than performances of armed manhood. It can increase social and political violence and deepen the fracturing of American political life. We witnessed this in Charlottesville, in Kenosha, at the Michigan state capitol, and at the US Capitol. We saw it when a judge's family was shot at their home by a politically motivated assailant and other judicial officials were put under police protection.[19] Most recently, we witnessed it when FBI agents and a judge handling the investigation into Donald Trump's Florida home were put under protection because of death threats from the former president's supporters, while one armed man sought to attack an FBI office in Ohio.[20] The Court and Republican elites are on the path to bringing to life a self-fulfilling prophecy—a dystopian America depleted of social and public trust and reliant on firearms for personal and collective security.

Where are we going from here? What might the future hold? In the long run, careful historical research coupled with innovative arguments may help states and localities carve out more regulatory authority than the *Bruen* opinion seems to allow. What America needs in the years to come is a vocal, forceful public response. We need a social movement that embraces and articulates a demilitarized vision of community and politics along with an inclusive vision of peoplehood. As a long tradition in political science going back to *The Civic Culture* and my data show, such an ideology—what I call inclusive civic republicanism—is also deeply rooted in the American public, and can be a unifying ideology. ICR bridges Americans' deep commitment to their communities and the public good with robust support for multiculturalism and peaceful political activism. This ideological premise can help movement participants articulate a right to feel safe in the home and public spaces while rejecting gun carry, militarization, and political violence. After all, nonviolence is as deeply rooted in the American tradition as gun carry is, and the state must attend to the safety concerns of individuals who are ideologically opposed to carrying firearms in public spaces.

There is no doubt, however, that an effective response will take time, especially given the disarray and lack of effective leadership on the Left and in the center, let alone Republican-orchestrated institutional changes designed to sap much of the other side's political power. The institutional changes imagined by the NRA and ushered in by the Supreme Court will tie the hands of lawmakers in many ways, and for a very long time, making it more difficult for states and localities to find effective solutions to gun violence. Race, rights, and rifles will remain ideologically and politically entangled in American life for a long time.

Acknowledgments

I discovered that to write a book, it takes a village. Actually, it takes two villages. First, there is the intellectual village of all those who came before me, without whose research and insights this book would not have been possible. I have a deep sense of gratitude for the many scholars in political science, history, law, and gun studies whose work provided the building blocks for this edifice. Second, there is the network of professional friends and colleagues who generously supported the project, giving me time and resources. The University of Illinois Chicago (UIC) has been a strong supporter of my work on gun politics. I received generous financial support from three UIC programs: the Chicago Area Study directed by Maria Krysan, the Chancellor's Discovery Fund, and the Office of Social Science Research. UIC's Institute for Research on Race and Public Policy provided me with course releases that helped me secure the time to complete this ambitious project, as well as a sounding board to present earlier versions of the project. I am in their debt. Furthermore, I spent my sabbatical at Northwestern University's Center for the Study of Diversity and Democracy and the Institute for Policy Research. The scholars at both centers have made me feel at home, and I have learned a lot from the many research presentations and mini-conferences organized there. I want to thank Jamie Druckman and Al Tillery for arranging for this opportunity.

Two people deserve my eternal gratitude for their contribution to this project in material ways. Jeff Kopstein was enthusiastic about the project and helped me secure the necessary funds for my survey. Al Tillery also believed in the project and helped me organize a book workshop. I will not forget their support. I am also grateful to Rogers Smith, Kristin Goss, Nathan Kalmoe, and Kimberley Johnson, who gracefully agreed to read the book and provide detailed and very helpful comments.

You all have no idea how nervous I was going into that workshop! In a discipline that continues to prize and build out its compartments even as it hopes and strives for interdisciplinarity and cross-fertilization, I felt a bit like Don Quixote fighting windmills. After all, I am a public opinion scholar producing a book that sought to trace an ideological tradition from the American Revolution to contemporary public opinion. I wanted to embed our understanding of modern gun politics and militarism more broadly in the historical context. My goal was to take history seriously and grapple with it substantively. Some close advisors worried about me not staying in my lane—and I worried, too. I think the most gratifying moment was to hear Rogers Smith say, "Alexandra! Ascriptive republicanism! Of course!" Who knew that an "of course" could be so important in a scholar's life—but trust me, it really is. Equally gratifying have been the several instances of scholars telling me: "I should have known this, but I honestly had no idea!" My ambition is that you, reader, will have the same reaction. Please, don't be shy, either. Email me and let me know.

These are not the only people in my village. There are many. I want to thank Lisa Krissoff Boehm, Chris Mooney, Jane Junn, Lisa Miller, Dan Kelemen, Will Adler, Carl Zimring, Kate Boulay, Greg Jacobson, Brendan Shanahan, EJ Fagan, Jamie Druckman, Mike Neblo, Sara Goodman, and Shanna Pearson-Merkowitz, who read and commented on earlier versions of the book and the book proposal. Their suggestions and advice enriched the project and made me a much better scholar. Cara Wong, Jen Merolla, Loren Collingwood, Dan Slater, and Eric Gonzalez Juenke offered me opportunities to present various versions of this work at their institutions. I am very grateful. Participants at the workshop on the Ethics, Law, and Social Science of Firearms and Self-Defense held at St. Anselm's College offered helpful feedback and support. My CRISS peeps have also provided support and encouragement along the way, and I thank them for that. I could not have done this without Noah Kaplan, who allowed me to vent, challenged my thinking, and checked my statistical analysis. Thank you, my friend!

Evan Ramzipoor, my developmental editor, was fantastic. She helped me tighten the manuscript and put up with me not knowing where to place commas, how to use proper paragraph transitions, and never making up my mind about past or present tense usage. I am sorry, Evan, I still don't know if it is more appropriate to talk about the NRA's ideology in the past or the present tense. Maybe it is my desire to bury it in the past that guides my grammatical choices.

Data collection for this project would not have happened without the help of my undergraduate and graduate students, who photocopied and coded seventy years' worth of issues of *The American Rifleman* and another twenty years of *America's 1st Freedom*. Louise Macaraniag, Andrea Manning, Mary Kettering, Mine Tafolar, Eddie Salinas, Beyza Buyuker, and the indomitable Kyle Pinkerton combed through the pages; counted words, phrases, and pictures; and identified interesting items for me to review. Thank you all—I couldn't have done it without you.

Sara Doskow, my editor at the University of Chicago Press, and her team have been simply wonderful. They have patiently answered a million technical questions, and took my haggling over word counts in good humor. Sara's editorial comments have helped me make important improvements to the manuscript, and I am grateful for her guidance. I am very proud that this book will sit next to the amazing lineup of offerings at UCP!

The four years that it took me to write this book were not easy. I had a difficult pregnancy and an amazing newborn boy who made rightful and joyous demands on my time. The isolation of COVID, not to mention two months of long COVID symptoms, did not help. Family health crises made the whole process even more daunting. I persevered thanks to the love and support of my husband, Steven Corey, my mother-in-law, Lori Corey, and my son's caregiver, Gabriella Rosendo. Gabriella and her entire family became part of our family. Not only did she teach me how to raise my child to be the sweetest and gentlest little boy, but she was there for us at every turn, through thick and thin. I owe her a huge debt of gratitude.

Steven Corey stood by me through every hardship, including the birth of our son (though I think he was ready to bolt from the delivery room!), a major operation, two bouts of COVID, and my mother's unexpected double surgery. He has been there for all my professional ups and downs, sharing with me my joys, my disappointments, and my doubts. As a historian he opened my eyes to the "republican revisionist tradition" in history and introduced me to the works of Edmund Morgan, Bud Bailyn, Linda Kerber, and Gordon Wood—the works that made it all "click" for me. I guess when geeks unite, they combine reading lists!

Last, but not least, I must thank my mother, Dr. Xanthi Pappa, and my sister, Eugenia, who has held the fort in Greece and shouldered significant caregiving and other responsibilities. My mother dreamed of an academic career, but widowhood with two young children made that impossible. Yet even working in a small, under-resourced hospital, she continued to do research and publish in her field. She bequeathed me a love of reading and learning and a drive for excellence. She secretly (actually, not so secretly!) wanted me to be a medical doctor, but she is proud of my achievements even if they don't involve scalpels, only words.

Notes

EPIGRAPH

1. David W. Blight, *Race and Reunion: The Civil War in American Memory* (Cambridge, MA: The Belknap Press of Harvard University Press, 2001), 100.

2. David Zucchino, *Wilmington's Lie: The Murderous Coup of 1898 and the Rise of White Supremacy* (New York: Atlantic Monthly Press, 2020), 190.

INTRODUCTION

1. The book engages with republican theory. When the word "republic" is capitalized, it references the ideal of a democratic participatory state. Small-r republican is a reference to republican theory. References to the Republican Party are capitalized.

2. Charlton Heston, *The Courage to Be Free* (Kansas City, KS: Saudade Press, 2000), ch. 1, 1–7. The book includes a compilation of Heston's various speeches on guns and some added commentary.

3. Heston, *The Courage to Be Free*, 176.

4. Heston, 1–7.

5. Heston.

6. Heston, 176–77.

7. Heston, 101, 118.

8. Heston, 68–69.

9. Heston, 9. In reality, most founders were very young men.

10. Heston, ch. 6.

11. Heston, ch. 1, ch. 5.

12. Heston, ch.1, 1–7; also see: Wayne LaPierre 2014 NRA Convention Address.

13. Jennifer Carlson, "Revisiting the Weberian Presumption: Gun Militarism, Gun Populism, and the Racial Politics of Legitimate Violence in Policing," *American Journal of Sociology* 125, no. 3 (2019): 633–82.

14. Sean P. O'Brien and Donald P. Haider-Markel, "Fueling the Fire: Social and Political Correlates of Citizen Militia Activity," *Social Science Quarterly* 79, no. 2 (1998): 456–65.

15. Philip S. Gorski and Samuel L. Perry, *The Flag and the Cross: White Christian Nationalism and the Threat to American Democracy* (New York: Oxford University Press, 2022).

16. David Zucchino, *Wilmington's Lie: The Murderous Coup of 1898 and the Rise of White Supremacy* (New York: Atlantic Monthly Press, 2020).

17. Philip J. Cook and Kristin A. Goss, *The Gun Debate: What Everyone Needs to Know* (New York: Oxford University Press, 2020), 178–98; Dan M. Kahan et al., "Culture and Identity-Protective Cognition: Explaining the White-Male Effect in Risk Perception," *Journal of Empirical Legal Studies* 4, no. 3 (2007): 465–505; Robert J. Spitzer, *The Politics of Gun Control*, 4th edition (Washington, DC: CQ Press, 2008 [1995]), 17–24; Jennifer Carlson, *Merchants of the Right: Gun Sellers and the Crisis of American Democracy* (Princeton, NJ: Princeton University Press, 2023).

18. Matthew Lacombe, *Firepower: How the NRA Turned Gun Owners into a Political Force* (Princeton, NJ: Princeton University Press, 2021), chs. 3–4.

19. Saul Cornell, *A Well-Regulated Militia: The Founding Fathers and the Origins of Gun Control* (New York: Oxford University Press, 2006); Mark Tunick, "John Locke and the Right to Bear Arms," *History of Political Thought* 35, no. 1 (2014): 50–69; H. Richard Uviller and William G. Merkel, *The Militia and the Right to Arms, or How the Second Amendment Fell Silent* (Durham, NC: Duke University Press, 2003).

20. Anne Schneider and Helen Ingram, "Social Construction of Target Populations: Implications for Politics and Policy," *American Political Science Review* 87, no. 2 (1993): 334–47; Rogers Smith, *Stories of Peoplehood: The Politics and Morals of Political Membership* (New York: Cambridge University Press, 2003); John T. Jost, *A Theory of System Justification* (Cambridge, MA: Harvard University Press, 2020). A competing set of such stories, often proposed by subordinate groups, seek to provide a moral basis for why the existing social structure should be changed. These narratives can seek to redefine the boundaries of social identities and group attributes so that subordinate groups can claim membership (e.g., Black folks are virtuous because they have fought in wars just like White people have); create new superordinate social categories (e.g., American rather than Black or White) that are inclusive of subordinate groups; or change the criteria for moral worth in ways that benefit the subordinate group (e.g., religious values and not secular liberalism should define membership).

21. Sidney Tarrow, *The Language of Contention: Revolutions and Words, 1688–2012* (New York: Cambridge University Press, 2013).

22. Mary Ann Glendon, *Rights Talk: The Impoverishment of Political Discourse* (New York: The Free Press, 1991); Milton Lodge and Charles S. Taber, *The Rationalizing Voter* (New York: Cambridge University Press, 2013); Smith, *Stories of Peoplehood*. For the framing of the Second Amendment as a civil right and an "absolute right," see: Joseph Blocher and Darrell A. H. Miller, *The Positive Second Amendment: Rights, Regulation, and the Future of Heller* (New York: Cambridge University Press, 2018); Timothy Zick, "Framing the Second Amendment: Gun Rights, Civil Rights, and Civil Liberties," *Iowa Law Review* 106 (2020): 229–97.

23. Rogers M. Smith, *Civic Ideals: Conflicting Visions of Citizenship in U.S. History* (New Haven, CT: Yale University Press, 1997). John Locke was not a republican; his theory rejected popular sovereignty in favor of constitutional monarchy which he viewed as better suited for the protection of property rights. See James T. Kloppenberg, *Towards Democracy: The Struggle for Self-Rule in European and American Thought* (New York: Oxford University Press, 2016), 1–20; Edmund S. Morgan, *American Slavery, American Freedom: The Ordeal of Colonial Virginia* (New York: W. W. Norton & Co., 2003 [1975]), 381–82.

24. John Locke, *Two Treatises of Government* (New York: George Routledge and Sons, 1884 [1690]); Adam Smith, *The Wealth of Nations* (London: William Strahan & Thomas Cadell, 1776).

25. LaPierre has been writing a monthly column called "Standing Guard" since 1991.

26. C. B. Lister, "Invasion," *The American Rifleman* 91, no. 2 (1943): 11.

27. Jennifer Carlson, *Citizen-Protectors: The Everyday Politics of Guns in an Age of Decline* (New York: Oxford University Press, 2015); Jennifer Carlson and Kristin A. Goss, "Gendering the Second Amendment," *Law and Contemporary Problems* 80, no. 2 (2017): 103–28; Scott Melzer, *Gun Crusaders: The NRA's Culture War* (New York: New York University Press, 2009); Angela Stroud, "Good Guys with Guns: Hegemonic Masculinity and Concealed Handguns," *Gender & Society* 26, no. 2 (2012): 216–38.

28. Laura Browder, *Her Best Shot: Women and Guns in America* (Chapel Hill: University of North Carolina Press, 2006), ch. 1.

29. Tracy Garnar, Sione Lynn Pili Lister, and Jennifer Carlson, "Whiteness and Impunity: Examining Virginia's Second Amendment Sanctuary Movement," *Sociological Inquiry* 92 (2022): 597–622.

30. Cornell, *A Well-Regulated Militia*; Uviller and Merkel, *The Militia and the Right to Arms*.

31. Colleen E. Terrell, "'Republican Machines': Franklin, Rush, and the Manufacture of Civic Virtue in the Early Republic," *Early American Studies* 1, no. 2 (2003): 110.

32. Bernard Bailyn, *The Ideological Origins of the American Revolution* (Cambridge, MA: The Belknap Press of Harvard University Press, 1992), 55–94; Edmund S. Morgan, "Slavery and Freedom: The American Paradox," *The Journal of American History* 59, no. 1 (1972); Tyler Stovall, *White Freedom: The Racial History of an Idea* (Princeton, NJ: Princeton University Press, 2021), ch. 1, ch. 3; Gordon S. Wood, *The Empire of Liberty: A History of the Early Republic, 1789–1815* (New York: Oxford University Press, 2011), ch. 1.

33. Alexis de Tocqueville, *Democracy in America* (New York: Penguin Books, 2004 [1835]), part III, chs. 23–26.

34. Gabriel Almond and Sidney Verba, *The Civic Culture: Political Attitudes and Democracy in Five Nations* (Princeton, NJ: Princeton University Press, 2015 [1963]). These perspectives also draw on de Tocqueville's account of early American democratic practices.

35. Angela Y. Davis, *Women, Race, and Class* (New York: Random House, 1981); Jake Hodder, "Casting a Black Gandhi: Martin Luther King Jr., American Pacifists and the Global Dynamics of Race," *Journal of American Studies* 55, no. 1 (2021): 48–74; Peniel E. Joseph, *The Sword and the Shield: The Revolutionary Lives of Malcolm X and Martin Luther King, Jr.* (New York: Basic Books, 2020); Anthony C. Siracusa, *Nonviolence before King: The Politics of Being and the Black Freedom Struggle* (Chapel Hill: University of North Carolina Press, 2021).

36. Elizabeth Cobbs, "Fighting on Two Fronts: World War One, Women's Suffrage, and John Pershing's 'Hello Girls,'" *South Central Review* 34, no. 3 (2017):, 31–47, discussing women's service in World War I; Frederick Douglass, "Men of Color, To Arms!" *Douglass' Monthly*, March 21, 1863; Frederick Douglass, *Narrative of the Life of Frederick Douglass* (Boston, MA: Anti-Slavery Office, No. 25 Cornhill, 1845); Linda Kerber, *Women of the Republic: Intellect and Ideology in Revolutionary America* (Chapel Hill: University of North Carolina Press, 1980), arguing that female chastity was central to American republicanism, because modest and chaste mothers raised virtuous sons; Stephanie McCurry, *Women's War: Fighting and Surviving the American Civil War* (Cambridge, MA: Harvard University Press, 2019).

37. A. Leon Higginbotham, *In the Matter of Color: Race and the American Legal Process, the Colonial Period* (New York: Oxford University Press, 1980); Winthrop D.

Jordan, *White over Black: American Attitudes toward the Negro 1550–1812* (Chapel Hill: University of North Carolina Press, 2012 [1969]), 20–24, 50–56, 191–92. All discuss early colonial laws where Christian and White were used interchangeably to describe individuals deserving of political freedom. Race hardened as the determinant of freedom/slavery only after enslaved African people started to convert to Christianity to gain freedom. Also see Ibram X. Kendi, *Stamped from the Beginning: The Definitive History of Racist Ideas in America* (New York: Nation Books, 2016).

38. Smith, *Civic Ideals*, 1–40. Stovall, *White Freedom*, ch. 3.

39. Rogers M. Smith, "Ideas and the Spiral of Politics: The Place of American Political Thought in American Political Development," *American Political Thought* 3, no. 1 (2014): 126–36. Stovall, *White Freedom*, esp. ch. 1, ch. 3.

40. Morgan, "Slavery and Freedom"; Stovall, *White Freedom*, 8–24.

41. Jon Nisbett and Dov Cohen, *Culture of Honor: The Psychology of Violence in the South* (Boulder, CO: Westview Press, 1996), 85.

42. Joanne B. Freeman, *The Field of Blood: Violence in Congress and the Road to Civil War* (New York: Farrar Straus & Giroux, 2018), discussing duels and other forms of interpersonal violence in the halls of Congress, especially in the antebellum era; Jack Kenny Williams, "The Code of Honor in Ante-Bellum South Carolina," *The South Carolina Historical Magazine* 54, no. 3 (1953): 113–28. The first recorded duel in American history took place in Massachusetts in 1621.

43. Williams, "The Code of Honor in Ante-Bellum South Carolina," 113–28; Orlando Patterson, *Slavery and Social Death: A Comparative Study* (Cambridge, MA: Harvard University Press, 2018 [1982]), ch. 3.

44. Douglass, *Narrative of the Life of Frederick Douglass*. See especially the description of Douglass's fight with his master.

45. Carole Emberton, *Beyond Redemption: Race, Violence, and the American South after the Civil War* (Chicago: University of Chicago Press, 2013); Francois Furstenberg, "Beyond Freedom and Slavery: Autonomy, Virtue, and Resistance in Early American Political Discourse," *The Journal of American History* 89, no. 4 (2003): 1295–1330.

46. Bruce A. Glasrud, ed., *Brothers to the Buffalo Soldiers: Perspectives on African-American Militia and Volunteers, 1865–1917* (Columbia: University of Missouri Press, 2011); Benjamin Quarles, *The Negro in the Making of America* (New York: Touchstone, Simon & Schuster, 1996 [1964]).

47. Kerber, *Women of the Republic*, chs. 2–3; Uviller and Merkel, *The Militia and the Right to Arms*, 27 (according to the authors, the phrase to "bear arms" has traditionally been used in military contexts); Wood, *The Empire of Liberty*, 12–14.

48. McCurry, *Women's War*, ch. 1. For a discussion of Black and White female spies from the South and the North, also see: Thavolia Glymph, *The Women's Fight: The Civil War Battles for Home, Freedom, and Nation* (Chapel Hill: University of North Carolina Press, 2020).

49. Service Women's Action Network, *Women in the Military: Where They Stand*, 2019, https://www.servicewomen.org/wp-content/uploads/2019/04/SWAN-Where -we-stand-2019-0416revised.pdf, 2019.

50. Alexander Keyssar, *The Right to Vote: The Contested History of Democracy in the United States* (New York: Basic Books, 2009), ch. 2.

51. NRA, *Americans and Their Guns: The National Rifle Association Story through Nearly a Century of Service to the Nation* (Harrisburg, PA: Stackpole Company, 1967), 10–15.

52. Heston, *The Courage to Be Free*, 46.

53. Uviller and Merkel, *The Militia and the Right to Arms*; Kevin M. Sweeney, "Firearms Ownership and Militias in Seventeenth- and Eighteenth-Century England and America," in *A Right to Bear Arms? The Contested Role of History in Contemporary Debates on the Second Amendment*, ed. Jennifer Tucker, Barton C. Hacker, and Margaret Vining (Washington, DC: Smithsonian Scholarly Press, 2019). In 1862, African American men were included in militia obligations to allow their service in the Civil War. This obligation of male citizens to serve as state soldiers remained federal law until the Dick Act of 1903, when the country formally turned to all-volunteer armed forces.

54. Sweeney, "Firearms Ownership and Militias," 114–15.

55. Harry S. Laver, *Citizens More Than Soldiers: The Kentucky Militia and Society in the Early Republic* (Lincoln: University of Nebraska Press, 2007), ch. 1, ch. 3; Edmund Morgan, *Inventing the People: The Rise of Popular Sovereignty in England and America* (New York: W. W. Norton & Co., 1989), 153–73.

56. Stovall, *White Freedom*, 13.

57. Douglass, "Men of Color, To Arms!"; Kellie Carter Jackson, *Force and Freedom: Black Abolitionists and the Politics of Violence* (Philadelphia: University of Pennsylvania Press, 2019); Peniel E. Joseph, *Waiting 'Til the Midnight Hour* (New York: Henry Holt & Co., 2007); Joseph, *The Sword and the Shield*; Corey Robin, *The Enigma of Clarence Thomas* (New York: Metropolitan Books, 2019); Robert Franklin Williams, *Negroes with Guns* (Detroit, MI: Wayne State University Press, 1998 [1962]).

58. Davis, *Women, Race, and Class*; Martha S. Jones, *Vanguard: How Black Women Broke Barriers, Won the Vote, and Insisted on Equality for All* (New York: Basic Books, 2020), 228–38; Joseph, *The Sword and the Shield*, 241; Martin Luther King Jr., "I Have a Dream," August 28, 1963, http://www.americanrhetoric.com/speeches/mlkihaveadream.htm.

59. Douglass, "Men of Color, To Arms!"; W. E. B. DuBois, "Close Ranks," *The Crisis* 16, no. 3 (1918). On the White reaction, see: C. Irvine Walker, Carolina Rifle Club, Charleston S.C., 1905 [1869], HathiTrust.org, http://hdl.handle.net/2027/wu.89072984933—minutes of the Charleston "Rifle Club" which organized as a paramilitary organization to resist Black authority in the form of Union-organized Black militia. Carole Emberton, "The Limits of Incorporation: Violence, Gun Rights, and Gun Regulation in the Reconstruction South," *Stanford Law and Policy Review* 17 (2006): 618–20.

60. John Hope Franklin, *The Militant South* (Cambridge, MA: The Belknap Press of Harvard University Press, 1956), 98; Ricardo A. Herrera, *For Liberty and the Republic: The American Citizen-Soldier, 1775–1861* (New York: New York University Press, 2015). Also see: Kristin L. Hoganson, *Fighting for American Manhood: How Gender Politics Provoked the Spanish-American and Philippine American Wars* (New Haven, CT: Yale University Press, 1998), 1–15.

61. Glasrud, *Brothers to the Buffalo Soldiers*, Introduction; Bruce A. Glasrud and Michael N. Searles, eds., *Buffalo Soldiers in the West: A Black Soldiers Anthology* (College Station: Texas A&M University Press, 2007). These books discuss the history of the African American volunteer militia companies, and the US Army regiments (Buffalo Soldiers).

62. John Jost and Orsolya Hunyady, "The Psychology of System Justification and the Palliative Function of Ideology," *European Review of Social Psychology* 13, no. 1 (2003): 111–53.

63. Cynthia Greenlee, "How History Textbooks Reflect America's Refusal to Reckon with Slavery," *Vox.com*, August 26, 2019, https://www.vox.com/identities/2019/8/26/20829771/slavery-textbooks-history; Heather Hickman and Brad J. Porfilio, eds., *The New Politics of the Textbook: Problematizing the Portrayal of Marginalized Groups in Textbooks* (Boston, MA: Sense Publishers, 2012); Jonathan Zimmerman, "Brown-ing the American Textbook: History, Psychology, and the Origins of Modern Multiculturalism," *History of Education Quarterly* 44, no. 1 (2004): 46–69.

64. Willis Mason West, *American History and Government* (Boston: Allyn & Bacon, 1913), 146. Also see: NRA, *Americans and Their Guns*, 10–15; Spitzer, *The Politics of Gun Control*, 17–23.

65. William D. Adler, *Engineering Expansion: The U.S. Army and Economic Development, 1787–1860* (Philadelphia: University of Pennsylvania Press, 2021); Michael L. Tate, *The Frontier Army in the Settlement of the West* (Norman: University of Oklahoma Press, 1999). The US Army provided most of the functions of a government on a smaller scale. In addition to protecting settlers from Indian tribes and White marauders, the Army was central to the economic development of the West. It built roads, schools, hospitals, and chapels, dug canals, and provided medicine and poor relief.

66. Mike McIntire, Glenn Thrush, and Eric Lipton, "Gun Sellers' Message to Americans: Man Up," *New York Times*, June 18, 2022, https://www.nytimes.com/2022/06/18/us/firearm-gun-sales.html.

67. Michael Gershon, "Eric Greitens's 'RINO Hunting' Ad Shows the Radicalization Pipeline in the GOP," *Washington Post*, June 23, 2022, https://www.washingtonpost.com/opinions/2022/06/23/eric-greitens-rino-hunting-ad-must-be-rejected/.

68. For recent debates on the teaching of slavery and America's racial history in public schools, see: Alexandra Filindra and Craig Burnett, "Who Should Control Education Policy? White Racial Attitudes and Support for Citizens' Involvement in Education Policymaking" (unpublished manuscript, last updated December 1, 2022, MS Word document).

69. For example, see: "We Believe in America: 2012 Republican Party Platform," August 27, 2012, https://www.presidency.ucsb.edu/documents/2012-republican-party-platform; Alexandra Filindra and Noah J. Kaplan, "The Racialized and Gendered Underpinnings of Second Amendment Meanings in White American Opinion" (unpublished manuscript, last revised September 15, 2022, MS Word document). According to the *New York Times*, early drafts of advertisements for the AR-15 assault rifle had taglines such as "Ice the Perp" or "Save the Hostage," implicitly linking the consumer act of purchasing the weapon with police/military service imagery. See: McIntire, Thrush, and Lipton, "Gun Sellers' Message to Americans."

70. Asawin Suebsang, "'Ignore Guns, Talk Inflation': Memos Show GOP Strategy after the Uvalde Massacre," *Rolling Stone*, June 4, 2022, https://www.rollingstone.com/politics/politics-news/uvalde-gop-trump-guns-strategy-1362970. According to the article, Republican party memos in response to the Uvalde, Texas, school shooting advised candidates to ignore the issue of guns and change the topic to anything else. "'Ignore guns, talk inflation,' one such memo, written for a top-tier GOP Senate candidate, succinctly reads, citing polling data of voter concerns ahead of the critical 2022 midterm elections. Other documents predictably decried liberal desires for 'gun-grabbing' and 'gun confiscation,' and made whataboutism-type references to gun violence in Chicago."

71. NRA-ILA, "Oppose a Ban on Keeping a Firearm Accessible for Self-Defense,"

last accessed June 3, 2022, https://www.nraila.org/campaigns/2019/virginia/
mandatory-firearm-storage. The NRA opposed Virginia's Virginia Code § 18.2-56.2,
which makes it a crime to recklessly leave a loaded, unsecured firearm in a manner that
endangers a child. It also makes it unlawful for a person to authorize a young child to
possess a firearm unless under the direct supervision of an adult. Most recently, Ohio
weakened the training requirements for armed teachers in schools. McIntire, Thrush,
and Lipton, "Gun Sellers' Message to Americans."

72. Hoganson, *Fighting for American Manhood*, 1–15.

73. Furstenberg, "Beyond Freedom and Slavery," 1295–1330; Emberton, "The Limits of Incorporation," 615–34.

74. Morgan, *Inventing the People*, 162.

75. Morgan, 169.

76. Karen L. Cox, *Dixie's Daughters: The United Daughters of the Confederacy and the Preservation of Confederate Culture* (Gainesville: University Press of Florida, 2003), ch. 4.

77. Kirk Savage, *Standing Soldiers, Kneeling Slaves: Race, War, and Monument in Nineteenth-Century America* (Princeton, NJ: Princeton University Press, 1997), ch. 5; Kevin M. Levin, *Searching for Black Confederates: The Civil War's Most Persistent Myth* (Chapel Hill: University of North Carolina Press, 2019).

78. James O. Farmer, "Playing Rebels: Reenactment as Nostalgia and Defense of the Confederacy in the Battle of Aiken," *Southern Cultures* 11, no. 1 (2005): 46–73; Stephen Gapps, "Mobile Monuments: A View of Historical Reenactment and Authenticity from Inside the Costume Cupboard of History," *Rethinking History* 13, no. 3 (2009): 395–409; Tony Horwitz, *Confederates in the Attic: Dispatches from the Unfinished Civil War* (New York: Vintage Books, 1999).

79. Martha Derthick, *The National Guard in Politics* (Cambridge, MA: Harvard University Press, 1965), ch. 1.

80. African Americans have been associated with criminality both historically (see George Fredrickson, *The Black Image in the White Mind: The Debate on Afro-American Character and Destiny, 1817–1914* [New York: Harper and Row, 1971]) and contemporarily (see Mark Peffley and Jon Hurwitz, *Justice in America: The Separate Realities of Blacks and Whites* [New York: Cambridge University Press, 2010]).

81. Joshua Horwitz and Casey Anderson, *Guns, Democracy, and the Insurrectionist Idea* (Ann Arbor: University of Michigan Press, 2009), ch. 6.

82. Deborah J. Schildkraut, *Americanism in the 21st Century* (Cambridge, UK: Cambridge University Press, 2011); Elizabeth Theiss-Morse, *Who Counts as an American? The Boundaries of National Identity* (New York: Cambridge University Press, 2009).

83. Nathan P. Kalmoe and Lilliana Mason, *Radical American Partisanship: Mapping Violent Hostility, Its Causes and the Consequences for Democracy* (Chicago: University of Chicago Press, 2022).

CHAPTER 1

1. Abigail Censky, "Heavily Armed Protesters Gather Again at Michigan Capitol to Decry Stay-at-Home Order," NPR, May 14, 2020, https://www.npr.org/2020/05/14/855918852/heavily-armed-protesters-gather-again-at-michigans-capitol-denouncing-home-order; Orion Rummler and Rebecca Falconer, "In Photos: Groups Protest the Coronavirus Lockdowns Across the U.S.," Axios, May 15, 2020, https://www.axios

.com/coronavirus-protest-social-distancing-1bc7fb5a-b94c-471e-adf2-c50bfad4f242
.html.

2. Maggie Haberman and Luke Broadwater, "Trump Said to Have Reacted Approvingly to Jan. 6 Chants about Hanging Pence," *New York Times*, May 25, 2022, https://
www.nytimes.com/2022/05/25/us/politics/trump-pence-jan-6.html.

3. Eric Maulbetsch, "Boebert: 'Second Amendment Isn't about Hunting, Except
Hunting Tyrants, Maybe,'" *Colorado Times Recorder*, December 31, 2020, https://
coloradotimesrecorder.com/2020/12/boebert-second-amendment-isnt-about
-hunting-except-hunting-tyrants-maybe/33413. Boebert has also argued that the
second amendment is "absolute" and anyone who says otherwise is "a tyrant"; Adam
Staten, "Marjorie Taylor Greene Suggests 'Second Amendment Rights' Should Be
Used against Democrats," *Newsweek*, January 11, 2021, https://www.newsweek.com/
marjorie-taylor-greene-suggests-second-amendment-rights-should-used-against
-democrats-1668286; Sam Stein, "Sharron Angle Floated '2nd Amendment Remedies' as 'Cure' for 'the Harry Reid Problems,'" HuffPost, June 16, 2010, https://www
.huffpost.com/entry/sharron-angle-floated-2nd_n_614003; Steve Benen, "Second
Amendment Remedies, 2014 Style," MSNBC, October 23, 2014, http://www.msnbc
.com/rachel-maddow-show/second-amendment-remedies-2014-style.

4. Michael Gershon, "Eric Greitens's 'RINO Hunting' Ad Shows the Radicalization
Pipeline in the GOP," *Washington Post*, June 23, 2022, https://www.washingtonpost
.com/opinions/2022/06/23/eric-greitens-rino-hunting-ad-must-be-rejected.

5. Nick Corasaniti and Maggie Haberman, "Donald Trump Suggests Second
Amendment People Could Act against Hillary Clinton," *New York Times*, August 9,
2016, https://www.nytimes.com/2016/08/10/us/politics/donald-trump-hillary
-clinton.html.

6. Josh D. Hawley, "Speech at the National Conservatism Conference," July 18, 2019,
https://www.hawley.senate.gov/senator-josh-hawleys-speech-national-conservatism
-conference; Josh D. Hawley, "Keynote Address at the National Conservatism Conference on the Left's Attack on Men in America," November 1, 2021, https://www.hawley
.senate.gov/senator-hawley-delivers-national-conservatism-keynote-lefts-attack-men
-america.

7. District of Columbia v. Heller, 554 U.S. 570 (2008), 24–25.

8. John Locke, *Two Treatises of Government* (New York: George Routledge and
Sons, 1884 [1690]); Mark Tunick, "John Locke and the Right to Bear Arms," *History of
Political Thought* 35, no. 1 (2014): 50–69; Samuel Huntington, *American Politics: The
Promise of Disharmony* (Cambridge, MA: The Belknap Press of Harvard University
Press, 1981).

9. Gabriel Almond and Sidney Verba, *The Civic Culture: Political Attitudes and Democracy in Five Nations* (Princeton, NJ: Princeton University Press, 2015 [1963]).

10. Robert Putnam, *The Upswing: How America Came Together a Century Ago and
How We Can Do It Again* (New York: Simon & Schuster, 2021), chs.1, 5.

11. Niccolo Machiavelli, *Discourses on Livy*, trans. Harvey C. Mansfield and Nathan
Tarkov (Chicago: University of Chicago Press, 1996).

12. James T. Kloppenberg, *Towards Democracy: The Struggle for Self-Rule in European and American Thought* (New York: Oxford University Press, 2016), 1–18; Rogers
Smith, *Stories of Peoplehood: The Politics and Morals of Political Membership* (New
York: Cambridge University Press, 2003).

13. Bernard Bailyn, *The Ideological Origins of the American Revolution* (Cambridge, MA: The Belknap Press of Harvard University Press, 1992), 60.

14. Kloppenberg, *Towards Democracy*, 1–18.

15. Adam Smith, *The Wealth of Nations* (London: William Strahan & Thomas Cadell, 1776).

16. Bailyn, *The Ideological Origins of the American Revolution*; Gordon S. Wood, *The Creation of the American Republic* (New York: W. W. Norton, 1969).

17. In this context, property was understood not simply as real property but more generally as rentier property—see Gordon S. Wood, *The Empire of Liberty: A History of the Early Republic, 1789–1815* (New York: Oxford University Press, 2011).

18. This suggests that the ideologies of modern/hostile racism and modern sexism have republican not liberal roots. For these beliefs see: David O. Sears and P. J. Henry, "The Origins of Symbolic Racism," *Journal of Personality and Social Psychology* 85, no. 2 (2003): 259–75; Janet K. Swim et al., "Sexism and Racism: Old-Fashioned and Modern Prejudices," *Journal of Personality and Social Psychology* 68, no. 2 (1995): 199–204.

19. Wood, *The Creation of the American Republic*, 36–42; Bailyn, *The Ideological Origins of the American Revolution*; James D. Savage, "Corruption and Virtue at the Constitutional Convention," *The Journal of Politics* 56, no. 1 (1994): 174–86. There is significant irony in this elevation of the planters and yeomen into the ideal of virtuous citizenship in the late eighteenth century. Most middling and larger farmers were highly integrated in world commodity markets as American products found their way to Europe. Planters were also highly dependent on British merchant houses for credit, and most were perennially in debt. See: Woody Holton, *Forced Founders: Indians, Debtors, Slaves, and the Making of the American Revolution* (Chapel Hill: University of North Carolina Press, 1999), 1–18. Furthermore, historians have documented that the American Revolution emerged in urban centers not rural communities. See Benjamin L. Carp, *Rebels Rising: Cities and the American Revolution* (New York: Oxford University Press, 2007).

20. For example, see C. B. Lister, "The Most Uncommon Thing," *The American Rifleman* 89, no. 3 (1941): 4; NRA, *Americans and Their Guns: The National Rifle Association Story through Nearly a Century of Service to the Nation* (Harrisburg, PA: Stackpole Company, 1967), 10–19.

21. Bailyn, *The Ideological Origins of the American Revolution*; Edmund Morgan, *Inventing the People: The Rise of Popular Sovereignty in England and America* (New York: W. W. Norton & Co., 1989), ch. 7; Wood, *The Creation of the American Republic*; Gordon S. Wood, *The Idea of America* (New York: Penguin Press, 2011); Gordon S. Wood, *The Radicalism of the American Revolution* (New York: Vintage Books, 2011 [1991]). NRA, *Americans and Their Guns*, 10–19.

22. Morgan, *Inventing the People*; Richard Uviller and William G. Merkel, *The Militia and the Right to Arms, or How the Second Amendment Fell Silent* (Durham, NC: Duke University Press, 2003). According to Bailyn, a deep-seated republican ideology prevented the colonists from interpreting the actions of Parliament during the crisis of the 1760s as a mistake, miscommunication, or even bad faith. Rather, the colonists interpreted the imposed taxes as a concerted, organized, and deliberate attack on liberty both in England and in the colonies. The goal of this conspiracy was to dissolve the English constitution and take away individual rights. These beliefs were especially prevalent among nonconformist churches who suspected that the Church of England planned to set itself up as the official religion, which would lead to both

temporal and spiritual slavery. Bailyn, *The Ideological Origins of the American Revolution*, 95–97.

23. Mirren Gidda, "NRA: Legal Guns Are a 'Great Equalizer' for the Blacks," *Newsweek*, June 1, 2017, http://www.newsweek.com/legal-guns-wisconsin-gun-laws-concealed-carry-permits-second-amendment-nra-619176; Stephen A. Halbrook, "What Made the Nazi Holocaust Possible? Gun Control," *America's 1st Freedom* 15, no. 2 (2014): 72; David Kopel and Richard Griffiths, "Hitler's Control: The Lessons of Nazi History," *National Review*, May 22, 2003, https://www.nationalreview.com/2003/05/hitlers-control-kopel-griffiths/; David Kopel, "Jim Crow and the Racist Roots of Gun Control," *America's 1st Freedom* 11, no. 3 (2011): 42–46.

24. Priya Satia, *Empire of Guns: The Violent Making of the Industrial Revolution* (Palo Alto, CA: Stanford University Press, 2018), chs. 6–7.

25. Bailyn, *The Ideological Origins of the American Revolution*, ch. 4.

26. For example, the British Army used Hessian (German) mercenaries in the American Revolutionary War. For more information on mercenaries in early modern Europe, see: Janice E. Thomson, *Mercenaries, Pirates, and Sovereigns: State-Building and Extraterritorial Violence in Early Modern Europe* (Princeton, NJ: Princeton University Press, 1994). Regimes controlled by the aristocracy or absolutist monarchs often preferred to recruit and pay mercenaries rather than use conscription, which could lead to subjects leveraging military service for political empowerment. See especially: John Ferejohn and Frances McCall Rosenbluth, *Forged through Fire: War, Peace, and the Democratic Bargain* (New York: W. W. Norton & Company, 2017), chs. 1, 12.

27. Machiavelli, *Discourses upon the First Ten Books of Titus Livy*; Bailyn, *The Ideological Origins of the American Revolution*.

28. Robert Dowlut, "Right to Keep and Bear Arms: A Right to Self-Defense against Criminals and Despots," *Stanford Law and Policy Review* 8 (1997): 25–40.

29. British historians argue that this was not meant as a broad right of the people to own firearms, as some have suggested. Rather, continuing concerns about the possible persecution of Protestants in Ireland prompted Parliament to include the provision in the Bill of Rights. For this debate, see Tim Harris, "The Right to Bear Arms in English and Irish Historical Context," in *A Right to Bear Arms? The Contested Role of History in Contemporary Debates on the Second Amendment*, ed. Jennifer Tucker, Barton C. Hacker, and Margaret Vining (Washington, DC: Smithsonian Scholarly Press, 2019); for an opposing view, see Joyce Lee Malcolm, *To Keep and Bear Arms: The Origins of an Anglo-American Right* (Cambridge, MA: Harvard University Press, 1994).

30. Kloppenberg, *Towards Democracy*.

31. According to Edmund Morgan, militia in England were used by both Catholic and Protestant rulers to suppress religious outsiders. Morgan, *Inventing the People*, ch. 7. Also see J. R. Western, *The English Militia in the 18th Century: The Story of a Political Issue, 1660–1802* (London: Gregg Revivals, 1993 [1965]).

32. Bailyn, *The Ideological Origins of the American Revolution*, 127–28.

33. Bailyn, *The Ideological Origins of the American Revolution*. Among the grievances in the Declaration of Independence was that "*he has kept among us, in times of peace, standing armies without the consent of our legislature.*"

34. NRA, *Americans and Their Guns*, 10–19.

35. Lawrence Delbert Cress, *Citizens in Arms: The Army and the Militia in American Society of the War of 1812* (Chapel Hill: University of North Carolina Press, 1982); Bailyn, *The Ideological Origins of the American Revolution*.

36. Francois Furstenberg, "Beyond Freedom and Slavery: Autonomy, Virtue, and Resistance in Early American Political Discourse," *The Journal of American History* 89, no. 4 (2003); Edmund S. Morgan, "Slavery and Freedom: The American Paradox," *The Journal of American History* 59, no. 1 (1972); Tyler Stovall, *White Freedom: The Racial History of an Idea* (Princeton, NJ: Princeton University Press, 2021), chs. 1, 3.

37. Locke, *Two Treatises of Government*; Tunick, "John Locke and the Right to Bear Arms."

38. Josiah Quincy, *An Oration Delivered before the Washington Benevolent Society of Massachusetts, on the Thirtieth Day of April, 1813, Being the Anniversary of the First Inauguration of President Washington* (Boston: Printed by William S. and Henry Spear, 1813), 18, 28. As cited in Furstenberg, "Beyond Freedom and Slavery," 1307.

39. Morgan, "Slavery and Freedom"; Furstenberg, "Beyond Freedom and Slavery"; Stovall, *White Freedom*, 1–15, ch. 2.

40. It is important to note that throughout, and unless otherwise warranted, I use the masculine pronoun in reference to "the citizen." This is done to reinforce the understanding that the American ascriptive republican tradition afforded political rights exclusively to (White) men. Feminine pronouns are used when I make specific reference to women and their political status.

41. Nathan Place, "Marjorie Taylor Greene Mocked for Saying Canada's New Gun Laws Could Spark Russian Invasion," *The Independent*, June 2, 2022, https://www .independent.co.uk/news/world/americas/us-politics/marjorie-taylor-greene-canada -gun-laws-russia-b2092104.html.

42. Lauren Boebert, "Second Amendment," Congresswoman Lauren Boebert, n.d., https://boebert.house.gov/issues/second-amendment; Josh Israel, "Constitutional Rights Are 'Absolute,' Say Republicans Who Want to Gut Voting Rights," *American Independent*, April 9, 2021, https://americanindependent.com/republicans-second -amendment-absolute-biden-gun-control-voting-rights-voter-suppression; Daniel Villareal, "Lauren Boebert Rips Joe Biden over Gun Control Measures: 'Second Amendment Is Absolute,'" *Newsweek*, April 9, 2021, https://www.newsweek.com/ lauren-boebert-rips-joe-biden-over-gun-control-measures-second-amendment -absolute-1582214.

43. Alan Taylor, *The Internal Enemy: Slavery and War in Virginia, 1772–1831* (New York: W. W. Norton & Co., 2014), ch. 1, loc. 328 of 11066, Kindle; Furstenberg, "Beyond Freedom and Slavery," 1301.

44. Bailyn, *The Ideological Origins of the American Revolution*; Cress, *Citizens in Arms*; Morgan, *Inventing the People*; Uviller and Merkel, *The Militia and the Right to Arms*; Carole Emberton, "The Limits of Incorporation: Violence, Gun Rights, and Gun Regulation in the Reconstruction South," *Stanford Law and Policy Review* 17 (2006); Carole Emberton, "'Only Murder Makes Men': Reconsidering the Black Military Experience," *Journal of the Civil War Era* 2, no. 3 (2012): 369–93; Furstenberg, "Beyond Freedom and Slavery"; Stovall, *White Freedom*.

CHAPTER 2

1. Edmund Morgan, *Inventing the People: The Rise of Popular Sovereignty in England and America* (New York: W. W. Norton & Co., 1989), 162.

2. Samuel Huntington, *American Politics: The Promise of Disharmony* (Cambridge, MA: The Belknap Press of Harvard University Press, 1981). Huntington argues that that

American national identity is based not on the valorization of ascriptive traits (such as common ancestors, common experiences, common ethnicity, or common religion) but on a shared allegiance to the principles of liberal democracy which he calls "the American Creed." See his chs.1–2. For a critique, see Rogers M. Smith, *Civic Ideals: Conflicting Visions of Citizenship in U.S. History* (New Haven, CT: Yale University Press, 1997), 26–30.

3. Gabriel Almond and Sidney Verba, *The Civic Culture: Political Attitudes and Democracy in Five Nations* (Princeton, NJ: Princeton University Press, 2015 [1963]).

4. Anna Suranyi, *Indentured Servitude: Unfree Labour and Citizenship in the British Colonies* (Montreal: McGill-Queen's University Press, 2021), ch. 1.

5. Suranyi, *Indentured Servitude*.

6. Steven Joseph Rosswurm, "Arms, Culture, and Class: The Philadelphia Militia and 'Lower Orders' in the American Revolution, 1765–1783" (PhD diss., Northern Illinois University, 1979), 490–97.

7. A. Leon Higginbotham, *In the Matter of Color: Race and the American Legal Process, the Colonial Period* (New York: Oxford University Press, 1980), 54.

8. Alexander Keyssar, *The Right to Vote: The Contested History of Democracy in the United States* (New York: Basic Books, 2009), 14–25.

9. Keyssar, *The Right to Vote*, 12–25; Ricardo A. Herrera, *For Liberty and the Republic: The American Citizen-Soldier, 1775–1861* (New York: New York University Press, 2015), 18, 65–66, 83–86; Robert Reinders, "Militia and Public Order in Nineteenth-Century America," *Journal of American Studies* 11, no. 1 (1977): 87; R. Claire Snyder, *Citizen-Soldiers and Manly Warriors: Military Service and Gender in the Civic Republican Tradition* (New York: Rowan & Littlefield Publishers, 1999), 95–96.

10. Carole Emberton, "The Limits of Incorporation: Violence, Gun Rights, and Gun Regulation in the Reconstruction South," *Stanford Law and Policy Review* 17 (2006); John Hope Franklin, *The Militant South* (Cambridge, MA: The Belknap Press of Harvard University Press, 1956), 188–89; Herrera, *For Liberty and the Republic*, 70.

11. Bertram Wyatt-Brown, *Honor and Violence in the Old South* (New York: Oxford University Press, 1986), 38–39.

12. Morgan, *Inventing the People*, 153–73; Alexandra Filindra, Beyza Buyuker, and Noah J. Kaplan, "Do Perceptions of Ingroup Discrimination Fuel Whites' Mistrust in Government? Insights from the 2012–2020 ANES and a Framing Experiment," *Polity*, November 23, 2022, https://www.journals.uchicago.edu/doi/10.1086/722763.

13. Maureen A. Craig and Jennifer A. Richeson, "Stigma-Based Solidarity: Understanding the Psychological Foundations of Conflict and Coalition among Members of Different Stigmatized Groups," *Current Directions in Psychological Science* 25, no. 1 (2016): 21–27.

14. Edmund S. Morgan, *American Slavery, American Freedom: The Ordeal of Colonial Virginia* (New York: W. W. Norton & Co., 2003 [1975]), 65–66, 326–27.

15. Ariella Gross, *What Blood Won't Tell* (Cambridge, MA: Harvard University Press, 2008), chs. 2–3.

16. B. Keith Payne, "Prejudice and Perception: The Role of Automatic and Controlled Processes in Misperceiving a Weapon," *Journal of Personality and Social Psychology* 81, no. 2 (2001): 181–92; Mark Schaller, Justin H. Park, and Annette Mueller, "Fear of the Dark: Interactive Effects of Beliefs about Danger and Ambient Darkness on Ethnic Stereotypes," *Personality and Social Psychology Bulletin* 29, no. 5 (2003): 637–49.

17. Gross, *What Blood Won't Tell*, 55.

18. Gross, *What Blood Won't Tell*, 55.

19. Francois Furstenberg, "Beyond Freedom and Slavery: Autonomy, Virtue, and Resistance in Early American Political Discourse," *The Journal of American History* 89, no. 4 (2003), 1295–1330; Kenneth S. Greenberg, *Honor and Slavery* (Princeton, NJ: Princeton University Press, 1996), 98.

20. C. S. Cartwright, "Diseases and Peculiarities of the Negro," in *The Industrial Resources etc., of the Southern and Western States*, ed. James Dunwoody and Boronson De Bow (New Orleans: De Bow's Review, 1853), 316; Franklin, *The Militant South*, 84.

21. State v. Mann, 13 NC 263 (1829) established the inferiority of Black people. Black people were viewed as "uneducatable" and "inherently venal." See Higginbotham, *In the Matter of Color*, 10.

22. Furstenberg, "Beyond Freedom and Slavery," 1295–1330.

23. John W. Edmonds, *Reconstruction of the Union, in a Letter to Hon. E. D. Morgan, U.S. Senator from New York, from Judge Edmonds* (New York: American News Co., 1867).

24. Edmonds, *Reconstruction of the Union*, 16.

25. Howard Washington Odum, "Social and Mental Traits of the Negro" (PhD diss., Columbia University, 1910), 343.

26. Gerald Horne, *The Counter-Revolution of 1776: Slave Resistance and the Origins of the United States* (New York: New York University Press, 2014); Micki McElya, *Clinging to Mammy: The Faithful Slave in Twentieth-Century America* (Cambridge, MA: Harvard University Press, 2007); Alan Taylor, *The Internal Enemy: Slavery and War in Virginia, 1772–1831* (New York: W. W. Norton & Co., 2014), ch. 9.

27. Alexis de Tocqueville, *Democracy in America* (New York: Penguin Books, 2004 [1835]), 401. For a discussion of how foreigners approached the contradiction between slavery and republicanism in the US, see Franklin, *The Militant South*.

28. Franklin, *The Militant South*, 18–19, 34, 68.

29. Rogers M. Smith and Desmond King, "Racial Reparations against White Protectionism: America's New Racial Politics," *The Journal of Race, Ethnicity, and Politics* 6, no. 1 (2021): 82–96; Rogers M. Smith and Desmond King, "White Protectionism in America," *Perspectives on Politics* 19, no. 2 (2021): 460–78; Filindra, Buyuker, and Kaplan, "Do Perceptions of Ingroup Discrimination Fuel Whites' Mistrust in Government?"

30. Corey Robin, *The Enigma of Clarence Thomas* (New York: Metropolitan Books, 2019), chs. 8–9.

31. Taylor, *The Internal Enemy*, loc. 162–64, 687–729 of 11066, Kindle.

32. Edward E. Baptist, in *The Half Has Never Been Told: Slavery and the Making of American Capitalism* (New York: Basic Books, 2016), provides a detailed account of the cruelty of American slavery and the complicity of Northern capitalism in sustaining the system. Taylor, *The Internal Enemy*, loc. 162–64 of 11066, Kindle. Rebecca de Schweinitz, "'Loving Hearts' and 'Brave Ones': Slavery, Family, and the Problem of Freedom in Antebellum America," *Slavery & Abolition* (2020): 1–26.

33. John Hope Franklin and Loren Schweninger, *Runaway Slaves: Rebels on the Plantation* (New York: Oxford University Press, 1999); Greenberg, *Honor and Slavery*; Sally E. Hadden, *Slave Patrols: Law and Violence in Virginia and the Carolinas* (Cambridge, MA: Harvard University Press, 2001); Whitney Sewell et al., "Vile Vigilance:

An Integrated Theoretical Framework for Understanding the State of Black Surveillance," *Journal of Human Behavior in the Social Environment* 26, nos. 3–4 (2016): 287–302.

34. Frederick Douglass, *My Bondage, My Freedom* (New York: Miller, Orton & Mulligan, 1855), 65–72; 87–96; Greenberg, *Honor and Slavery*, 41–43; Hadden, *Slave Patrols*, 19; Orlando Patterson, *Slavery and Social Death: A Comparative Study* (Cambridge, MA: Harvard University Press, 2018 [1982]), loc. 116 of 14254, Kindle.

35. Herbert Aptheker, *American Negro Slave Revolts* (New York: International Publishers, 1983 [1949]); Greenberg, *Honor and Slavery*, 33; Hadden, *Slave Patrols*, 126.

36. Greenberg, *Honor and Slavery*, 49.

37. Frederick Douglass, "A Simple Tale of American Slavery," Sheffield *Mercury*, September 12, 1846, https://docsouth.unc.edu/neh/douglass/support5.html; Robert William Fogel and Stanley L. Engerman, *Time on the Cross: The Economics of American Negro Slavery* (New York: W. W. Norton & Co., 1974), 5. Camillia Cowling et al., "Mothering Slaves: Comparative Perspectives on Motherhood, Childlessness, and the Care of Children in Atlantic Slave Societies," *Slavery & Abolition* 38, no. 2 (2017): 225, argue that slaveholders controlled enslaved women's reproduction, in some cases preventing childbearing and in others encouraging and promoting it. Gregory D. Smithers, "American Abolitionism and Slave-Breeding Discourse: A Re-evaluation," *Slavery & Abolition* 33, no. 4 (2012). Smithers discusses the social memory of slave-breeding in African American history and how slaves themselves narrated sexual violence in the context of slavery.

38. Joshua D. Rothman, *The Ledger and the Chain: How Domestic Slave Traders Shaped America* (New York: Basic Books, 2021). The price slave traders asked for such women depended on skin color. Rothman characterizes these practices as "commoditized fantasies of racial and sexual domination" (p. 150). Sex trafficking was a constitutive part of the slave trader's business model; observers characterized slave pens—the buildings that housed slaves for sale—as brothels (p. 152).

39. Hadden, *Slave Patrols*, 131.

40. Douglass, *My Bondage, My Freedom*, 65–72; 87–96.

41. Andrea L. Dennis, "A Snitch in Time: An Historical Sketch of Black Informing during Slavery," *Marquette Law Review* 97, no. 2 (2013): 292. For example, Georgia's laws specified that "Every negro, mulatto, or mustizoe, who shall hereafter give information of the intention of any other slave to poison any person . . . shall, upon conviction of the offender or offenders, be entitled to and receive from the public of this province, a reward of twenty shillings . . . and shall also be exempted from the labor of his or her master on that day."

42. Baptist, *The Half Has Never Been Told*; Terri L. Snyder, *The Power to Die: Slavery and Suicide in British North America* (Chicago: University of Chicago Press, 2015); Sewell et al., "Vile Vigilance."

43. Robert Dowlut, "Right to Keep and Bear Arms: A Right to Self-Defense against Criminals and Despots," *Stanford Law and Policy Review* 8 (1997); Supreme Court Justice Clarence Thomas has endorsed similar beliefs. See Robin, *The Enigma of Clarence Thomas*.

44. Rob Mickey, *Paths Out of Dixie: The Democratization of Authoritarian Enclaves in America* (Princeton, NJ: Princeton University Press, 2015), chs. 1–2.

45. For example, see articles emphasizing that gun control is a "racist" policy pursued by "the Democrats"—David Kopel, "Jim Crow and the Racist Roots of Gun

Control," *America's 1st Freedom* 11, no. 3 (2011): 42-46; Clayton Cramer, "The Racist Roots of Gun Control," *Kansas Journal of Law and Public Policy* 4, no. 2 (1995): 17-26; Ann Coulter, "Negroes with Guns," AnnCoulter.com, April 18, 2012, http://www .anncoulter.com/columns/2012-04-18.html; Greg Pollowitz, "Ann Coulter's (Truthful) Rhetoric on Gun Violence and Race," *National Review*, January 16, 2013, http://www .nationalreview.com/media-blog/337839/ann-coulters-truthful-rhetoric-gun-violence -and-race-greg-pollowitz.

46. Aptheker, *American Negro Slave Revolts*; Eugene D. Genovese, *Roll, Jordan, Roll: The World the Slaves Made* (New York: Vintage, 1976), 587-98; Horne, *The Counter-Revolution of 1776*, chs. 5-6.

47. Richard Bell, "Slave Suicide, Abolition and the Problem of Resistance," *Slavery & Abolition* 33, no. 4 (2012): 525-49; Greenberg, *Honor and Slavery*, 99; James C. Scott, *Weapons of the Weak: Everyday Forms of Peasant Resistance* (New Haven, CT: Yale University Press, 1987).

48. Snyder, *The Power to Die*, 7-22.

49. Stephen Kantrowitz, *More Than Freedom: Fighting for Black Citizenship in a White Republic, 1829-1889* (New York: Penguin Books, 2012), 1-35.

50. See especially the critique of Southern historical revisionism in Genovese, *Roll, Jordan, Roll*, 587-98.

51. Furstenberg, "Beyond Freedom and Slavery," 1318; Tyler Stovall, *White Freedom: The Racial History of an Idea* (Princeton, NJ: Princeton University Press, 2021), ch. 3.

52. Franklin, *The Militant South*, 76.

53. Furstenberg, "Beyond Freedom and Slavery," 1318; Donald R. Hickey, "America's Response to the Slave Revolt in Haiti, 1791-1806," *Journal of the Early Republic* 2, no. 4 (1982): 361-79; Horne, *The Counter-Revolution of 1776*. Jefferson's *Notes on the State of Virginia* (Philadelphia, PA: Printed and sold by Richard and Hall, 1848) provide a detailed and complex account of his beliefs about race and slavery. https://docsouth .unc.edu/southlit/jefferson/jefferson.html.

54. Greenberg, *Honor and Slavery*, 103-4; Furstenberg, "Beyond Freedom and Slavery"; Douglas R. Egerton, *Gabriel's Rebellion: The Virginia Slave Conspiracies of 1800 and 1802* (Chapel Hill: University of North Carolina Press, 1993), 78; Forrest G. Wood, *Black Scare: The Racist Response to Emancipation and Reconstruction* (Berkeley: University of California Press, 1970).

55. Bob Myers, *"Drapetomania": Rebellion, Defiance and Free Black Insanity in the Antebellum United States* (PhD diss., University of California Los Angeles, 2014); Christopher D. E. Willoughby, "Running Away from Drapetomania: Samuel A. Cartwright, Medicine, and Race in the Antebellum South," *Journal of Southern History* 84, no. 3 (2018): 579-614.

56. C. Irvine Walker, Carolina Rifle Club, Charleston S.C., 1905 [1869], HathiTrust .org, 5-6, http://hdl.handle.net/2027/wu.89072984933.

57. Franklin, *The Militant South*, 84; Furstenberg, "Beyond Freedom and Slavery"; Willoughby, "Running Away from Drapetomania"; Greenberg, *Honor and Slavery*; Jenny B. Wahl, "The Jurisprudence of American Slave Sales," *The Journal of Economic History* 56, no. 1 (1996): 143-69.

58. Bernard C. Nalty and Morris J. MacGregor, *Blacks in the Military: Essential Documents* (Wilmington, DE: Scholarly Resources, Inc., 1981); Benjamin Quarles, *The Negro in the Making of America* (New York: Touchstone, Simon & Schuster, 1996 [1964]), 57.

59. Nalty and MacGregor, *Blacks in the Military*; Quarles, *The Negro in the Making of America*.

60. Higginbotham, *In the Matter of Color*, 137.

61. Agenda item, Council of War of the Continental Army, October 8, 1775, Peter Force, American Archives, Series IV, as cited in Nalty and MacGregor, *Blacks in the Military*, 7.

62. Quarles, *The Negro in the Making of America*. A key premise for resisting Black slave enlistments was that slaves could not possibly feel patriotism. This idea continues to be perpetuated up to the modern era. For example, one recent academic analysis noted that "the idea of fighting for an independent United States or for any cause was mostly foreign to black slaves. Other than the feelings of newly arrived slaves from Africa who longed for their former villages and homeland, blacks had no reference to a sense of belonging in their present state. . . . Most blacks had no affinity for their colony or future state, or for national unity." Michael Lee Lanning, "African-Americans and the American Revolution," in *The Routledge Handbook of the History of Race and the American Military*, ed. Geoffrey W. Jensen (New York: Routledge, 2016), 31. For a key counterargument, see Frederick Douglass, "The Meaning of July 4th to the Negro," *Journal of Pan African Studies* 3, no. 5 (2009 [1852]).

63. Quarles, *The Negro in the Making of America*, 59. On Massachusetts policy, see Nalty and MacGregor, *Blacks in the Military*, 9.

64. Quarles, *The Negro in the Making of America*.

65. James Madison to Joseph Jones, November 28, 1780, in William T. Hutchinson and William M. E. Rachal, eds., *The Papers of James Madison* (Chicago: University of Chicago Press, 1962), 2:209, as cited in L. Scott Philyaw, "A Slave for Every Soldier: The Strange History of Virginia's Forgotten Recruitment Act of 1 January 1781," *The Virginia Magazine of History and Biography* 109, no. 4 (2001): 370.

66. Carol Anderson, *The Second: Race and Guns in a Fatally Unequal America* (New York: Bloomsbury, 2021).

67. "Proclamation to the Free Colored Inhabitants of Louisiana," September 21, 1814, *Niles Weekly Register*, December 3, 1814, in *The Negro in the Military Service of the United States, 1639–1886* (Microfilm M858, National Archives, Washington, DC), as cited in Nalty and MacGregor, *Blacks in the Military*, 16.

68. Harold D. Langley, "The Negro in the Navy and Merchant Service, 1789–1860," *The Journal of Negro History* 52, no. 4 (1967): 273–86; Robert E. May, "Invisible Men: Blacks and the U.S. Army in the Mexican War," *Historian* 49, no. 4 (1987): 463–77. For example, Ulysses S. Grant was attended to by Black servants.

69. Nalty and Macgregor, *Blacks in the Military*.

70. William C. Stinchcombe, *The American Revolution and the French Alliance* (Syracuse, NY: Syracuse University Press, 1969).

71. Sanford F. Schram and Richard C. Fording, "Racial Liberalism Resurgent: Connecting Multi-Racial Protests and Electoral Politics Today," *The Journal of Race, Ethnicity, and Politics* 6, no. 1 (2021): 97–119.

72. Quarles, *The Negro in the Making of America*, 31; Taylor, *The Internal Enemy*; Hadden, *Slave Patrols*; Horne, *The Counter-Revolution of 1776*.

73. Joshua Bloom and Waldo E. Martin Jr., *Black against Empire: The History and Politics of the Black Panther Party* (Berkeley: University of California Press, 2016); Peniel E. Joseph, *The Sword and the Shield: The Revolutionary Lives of Malcolm X and Martin Luther King, Jr.* (New York: Basic Books, 2020).

74. Emberton, "The Limits of Incorporation"; Furstenberg, "Beyond Freedom and Slavery"; Stovall, *White Freedom*.

75. Stovall, *White Freedom*.

76. Cameron McWhirter, *Red Summer: The Summer of 1919 and the Awakening of Black America* (New York: Henry Holt & Co., 2011).

77. Glenda Elizabeth Gilmore, *Defying Dixie: The Radical Roots of Civil Rights, 1919–1950* (New York: W. W. Norton & Co., 2009).

78. US Department of Justice, "A Report on the Activities of the Bureau of Investigation of the Department of Justice against Persons Advising Anarchy, Sedition, and the Forcible Overthrow of the Government," submitted to Congress by Attorney General A. Mitchell Palmer, November 15, 1919 (Washington, DC: Government Printing Office, 1919), 101–2; "Indict 105 People in East St. Louis Riot Probe: Wholesale Indictments in Illinois Riot Investigation," *Chicago Defender*, August 18, 1917.

79. David J. Garrow, *The FBI and Martin Luther King, Jr.: From Solo to Memphis* (New York: Open Road, 2015).

80. Joseph, *The Sword and the Shield*.

81. Bloom and Martin, *Black against Empire*.

82. Peniel E. Joseph, *Waiting 'Til the Midnight Hour* (New York: Henry Holt & Co., 2007).

83. Andrew Mark Miller, "GOP Lawmakers Slam 'Marxist' Black Lives Matter for Statement Blaming U.S. for Cuban Unrest," *FoxNews.com*, July 15, 2021, https://www.foxnews.com/politics/gop-lawmakers-slam-marxist-black-lives-matter-for-blaming-u-s-for-cuban-unrest.

84. Benjamin Wallace-Wells, "How a Conservative Activist Invented the Conflict over Critical Race Theory," *The New Yorker*, June 18, 2021, https://www.newyorker.com/news/annals-of-inquiry/how-a-conservative-activist-invented-the-conflict-over-critical-race-theory.

85. Marek D. Steedman, "Resistance, Rebirth, and Redemption: The Rhetoric of White Supremacy in Post–Civil War Louisiana," *Historical Reflections* 35, no. 1 (2009): 101.

86. Snyder, *Citizen-Soldiers and Manly Warriors*.

87. Otis A. Singletary, *Negro Militia and Reconstruction* (Austin: University of Texas Press, 2011 [1957]), ch. 3.

88. On the first Klan, see Allen W. Trelease, *White Terror: The Ku Klux Klan Conspiracy and Southern Reconstruction* (Baton Rouge: Louisiana State University Press, 1971). On the second Klan, see Linda Gordon, *The Second Coming of the KKK: The Ku Klux Klan of the 1920s and the American Political Tradition* (New York: W. W. Norton & Co., 2017). On the third Klan, see David Cunningham, *Klansville, U.S.A: The Rise and Fall of the Civil Rights–Era Ku Klux Klan* (New York: Oxford University Press, 2013).

89. Hadden, *Slave Patrols*, 172.

90. Walker, Carolina Rifle Club, Charleston SC, 7.

91. Otis A. Singletary, "The Texas Militia during Reconstruction," *The Southwestern Historical Quarterly* 60, no. 1 (1956): 26.

92. W. Scott Poole, "Religion, Gender, and the Lost Cause in South Carolina's 1876 Governor's Race: 'Hampton or Hell!,'" *The Journal of Southern History* 68, no. 3 (2002): 573–98.

93. Eric Foner, *The Second Founding: How the Civil War Remade the Constitution* (New York: W. W. Norton & Co., 2019); Trelease, *White Terror*.

94. LeeAnna Keith, *The Colfax Massacre: The Untold Story of Black Power, White Terror, and the Death of Reconstruction* (New York: Oxford University Press, 2008); Walker, Carolina Rifle Club, Charleston SC.

95. Snyder, *Citizen-Soldiers and Manly Warriors*, 95.

96. Walker, Carolina Rifle Club, Charleston SC.

97. William A. Dunning, "Reconstruction, Political and Economic," in *The American Nation: A History*, ed. Albert Bushnell Hart (New York: Harper & Brothers, 1907).

98. Poole, "Religion, Gender, and the Lost Cause"; US Senate Subcommittee on Privileges and Elections, "Report on the Denial of Elective Franchise in South Carolina at the State and National Election of 1876, to Accompany Miscellaneous Document 48," Forty-Fourth Congress, Second Session (Washington, DC: Government Printing Office, 1877), mentioned in Poole, "Religion, Gender, and the Lost Cause."

99. Thomas Holt, *Black over White: Negro Political Leadership in South Carolina during Reconstruction* (Chicago: University of Illinois Press, 1979). The records of the Carolina Rifle Club of Charleston indicate that the group was armed with firearms from the state arsenal, and they remained armed after the election. The Black Adjutant General reported that state arms were in the hands of White rifle clubs, completely undermining the ability of state militia and threatening the government. Jeffery Strickland, "How the Germans Became White Southerners: German Immigrants and African Americans in Charleston, South Carolina, 1860–1880," *Journal of American Ethnic History* 28, no. 1 (2008): 52–69. Strickland describes German rifle club participation in Black political suppression.

100. Walker, Carolina Rifle Club, Charleston SC, 17, 20, 22–23, 51.

101. Emberton, "The Limits of Incorporation"; Carole Emberton, *Beyond Redemption: Race, Violence, and the American South after the Civil War* (Chicago: University of Chicago Press, 2013); Keith, *The Colfax Massacre*. It is also important to note that similar arguments were used by supporters of emancipation and Black political rights who rightly feared that after the withdrawal of the Union Army from the South, Black people would need firearms to defend themselves against White retribution because Southern authorities would not defend them. These arguments are referenced in Justice Thomas's concurring opinion in *McDonald v. City of Chicago*, 561 U.S. 742 (2010).

102. Walker, Carolina Rifle Club, Charleston SC, 19, 47.

103. William Cohen, "Riots, Racism, and Hysteria: The Response of Federal Investigative Officials to the Race Riots of 1919," *The Massachusetts Review* 13, no. 3 (1972); McWhirter, *Red Summer*.

104. McWhirter, *Red Summer*.

105. The Chicago Commission on Race Relations, *The Negro in Chicago: A Study of Race Relations and a Race Riot* (Chicago: University of Chicago Press, 1922), 2.

106. David Zucchino, *Wilmington's Lie: The Murderous Coup of 1898 and the Rise of White Supremacy* (New York: Atlantic Monthly Press, 2020).

107. Allen D. Grimshaw, "Lawlessness and Violence in America and Their Special Manifestations in Changing Negro-White Relationships," *The Journal of Negro History* 44, no. 1 (1959): 52–72; Special Committee Authorized by Congress to Investigate the East St. Louis Riots, H.R. Rep. 1213, vol. 114, (Washington, DC: Government Printing Office, 1918); Chicago Commission on Race Relations, *The Negro in Chicago*; Thurgood Marshall, "The Gestapo in Detroit," *The Crisis* 50, no. 8 (1943); Walter White and Thur-

good Marshall, *What Caused the Detroit Riot?* (Washington, DC: National Association for the Advancement of Colored People, 1943).

108. Stacy St. Clair and Christy Gutowski, "Kenosha Cops Explain Why They Ignored Kyle Rittenhouse's Attempt to Surrender after Shooting," *Chicago Tribune*, November 5, 2021, https://www.chicagotribune.com/news/ct-kyle-rittenhouse-murder -trial-cops-ignore-surrender-20211105-m4n5mmnzjfhqnoadls75q37wdi-story.html.

109. Grimshaw, "Lawlessness and Violence in America," 277. Grimshaw is quoting from an article in *The Outlook*, titled "Racial Tension and Race Riots," *The Outlook* 122 (1919): 533, here p. 277. McWhirter, *Red Summer*, 240.

CHAPTER 3

1. John Hope Franklin, *The Militant South* (Cambridge, MA: The Belknap Press of Harvard University Press, 1956), ch. 9; Edmund Morgan, *Inventing the People: The Rise of Popular Sovereignty in England and America* (New York: W. W. Norton & Co., 1989), ch. 7; Richard Uviller and William G. Merkel, *The Militia and the Right to Arms, or How the Second Amendment Fell Silent* (Durham, NC: Duke University Press, 2003), 123–24.

2. Franklin, *The Militant South*, ch. 9; Walter M. Pratt, *"Tin Soldiers": The Organized Militia and What It Really Is* (Boston: R. G. Badger, 1912); Uviller and Merkel, *The Militia and the Right to Arms*, 59, 65–66.

3. Gordon S. Wood, *The Empire of Liberty: A History of the Early Republic, 1789–1815* (New York: Oxford University Press, 2011), 8–9, ch.3 .

4. Saul Cornell, *A Well-Regulated Militia: The Founding Fathers and the Origins of Gun Control* (New York: Oxford University Press, 2006), ch. 2; Lawrence Delbert Cress, *Citizens in Arms: The Army and the Militia in American Society of the War of 1812* (Chapel Hill: University of North Carolina Press, 1982), 15; Uviller and Merkel, *The Militia and the Right to Arms*, ch. 2.

5. Cress, *Citizens in Arms*, 16–19.

6. Alexander Keyssar, *The Right to Vote: The Contested History of Democracy in the United States* (New York: Basic Books, 2009), 14–25.

7. Keyssar, *The Right to Vote*.

8. Franklin, *The Militant South*, 172.

9. Francis Newton Thorpe, *The Federal and State Constitutions, Colonial Charters, and Other Organic Laws of the State, Territories, and Colonies Now or Heretofore Forming the United States of America* [United States], 59th Cong., 2d sess., HR doc. 357 (Washington, DC: Government Printing Office, 1909), https://catalog.hathitrust.org/ Record/001140815, vol. 4, 235.

10. Thorpe, Vol. 1, 544.

11. Thorpe, Vol. 2, 673.

12. Cress, *Citizens in Arms*, 35–38.

13. Hadden, *Slave Patrols*; Franklin, *The Militant South*, 96–129.

14. Franklin, *The Militant South*, ch. 9.

15. Cress, *Citizens in Arms*; Uviller and Merkel, *The Militia and the Right to Arms*, 118–20; L. Scott Philyaw, "A Slave for Every Soldier: The Strange History of Virginia's Forgotten Recruitment Act of 1 January 1781," *The Virginia Magazine of History and Biography* 109, no. 4 (2001): 369.

16. Kevin M. Sweeney, "Firearms Ownership and Militias in Seventeenth- and Eighteenth-Century England and America," in *A Right to Bear Arms? The Contested*

Role of History in Contemporary Debates on the Second Amendment, ed. Jennifer Tucker, Barton C. Hacker, and Margaret Vining (Washington, DC: Smithsonian Scholarly Press, 2019). According to Sweeney, probate court records show that there was significant variation in private gun ownership both across colonies/states and over time. Individual gun ownership rates appeared to decline by the late eighteenth century, and few people owned military-grade weapons. This explains the great urgency that the revolutionaries were faced with in seeking to equip the Continental Army with suitable muskets.

17. Uviller and Merkel, *The Militia and the Right to Arms*, 113–15, 285–86. According to Uviller and Merkel, "militia members . . . were expected to keep and bear arms necessary for meeting the security needs of the nation, arms falling within certain standards and regular limits defined by Congress. Guns of that sort did not necessarily correspond to each individual's sense of convenience or perceived need to defend himself and family independent of military obligation" (p. 115).

18. Cress, *Citizens in Arms*; A. Leon Higginbotham, *In the Matter of Color: Race and the American Legal Process, the Colonial Period* (New York: Oxford University Press, 1980); R. Claire Snyder, *Citizen-Soldiers and Manly Warriors: Military Service and Gender in the Civic Republican Tradition* (New York: Rowan & Littlefield Publishers, 1999); Alan Taylor, *The Internal Enemy: Slavery and War in Virginia, 1772–1831* (New York: W. W. Norton & Co., 2014); Uviller and Merkel, *The Militia and the Right to Arms*.

19. John W. Chambers, *To Raise an Army: The Draft Comes to Modern America* (New York: Free Press, 1987).

20. Jason Kaufman, "'Americans and Their Guns': Civilian Military Organizations and the Destabilization of American National Security," *Studies in American Political Development* 15, no. 1 (2001): 88–102. According to Kaufman, the lack of training was so severe that militia in Oxford, Massachusetts voted to cancel their annual target practice for fear of public embarrassment (p. 93). Robert Reinders, "Militia and Public Order in Nineteenth-Century America," *Journal of American Studies* 11, no. 1 (1977): 85; William Faulkner, *Requiem for A Nun* (New York: Vintage Books, 2011 [1951]). Faulkner's novel satirizes the militia as inept. It also did not help that even in times of war, colonies refused to pass appropriations to pay soldiers whose families were left to starve. See Elizabeth Cometti, "Women in the American Revolution," *The New England Quarterly* 20, no. 3 (1947): 329–46.

21. Abraham Lincoln, "Speech to the Springfield Scout Club," August 14, 1852, cited in Uviller and Merkel, *The Militia and the Right to Arms*, 123–24.

22. Cress, *Citizens in Arms*; Uviller and Merkel, *The Militia and the Right to Arms*, ch. 4.

23. Hadden, *Slave Patrols*, 43.

24. Uviller and Merkel, *The Militia and the Right to Arms*, 65–66.

25. Carl T. Bogus, "The Hidden History of the Second Amendment," *U.C. Davis Law Review* 31, no. 2 (1998): 339.

26. Linda Kerber, *Women of the Republic: Intellect and Ideology in Revolutionary America* (Chapel Hill: University of North Carolina Press, 1980), 102.

27. Cress, *Citizens in Arms*; Reinders, "Militia and Public Order in Nineteenth-Century America," 83; Uviller and Merkel, *The Militia and the Right to Arms*, 65–66.

28. Kaufman, "'Americans and Their Guns,'" 88–102.

29. William H. Riker, *Soldiers of the States: The Role of the National Guard in American Democracy* (Washington, DC: Public Affairs Press, 1957); Uviller and Merkel, *The Militia and the Right to Arms*, ch. 4.

30. Morgan, *Inventing the People*, ch. 7; Uviller and Merkel, *The Militia and the Right to Arms*, ch. 4.

31. Heather Cox Richardson, *West from Appomattox: The Reconstruction of America after the Civil War* (New Haven, CT: Yale University Press, 2007).

32. Ricardo A. Herrera, *For Liberty and the Republic: The American Citizen-Soldier, 1775–1861* (New York: New York University Press, 2015), 10–11.

33. Franklin, *The Militant South*, 181–82; Stephen Kantrowitz, *Ben Tillman and the Reconstruction of White Supremacy* (Chapel Hill: University of North Carolina Press, 2000), 34; David Zucchino, *Wilmington's Lie: The Murderous Coup of 1898 and the Rise of White Supremacy* (New York: Atlantic Monthly Press, 2020), 284–85, 380.

34. Franklin, *The Militant South*, 172–73.

35. Reinders, "Militia and Public Order in Nineteenth-Century America," 82.

36. Franklin, *The Militant South*, 175; Herrera, *For Liberty and the Republic*, 65–66, 83.

37. Martha Derthick, *The National Guard in Politics* (Cambridge, MA: Harvard University Press, 1965), 16; Tom Goyens, *Beer and Revolution: The German Anarchist Movement in New York City, 1880–1914* (Chicago: University of Illinois Press, 2007); Kaufman, "'Americans and Their Guns.'" In addition to business owners subsidizing the cost of arming and training militia units, there is also evidence of businesses dismissing employees who were called in for militia duty or who were required to attend summer training, which created great ambivalence among citizen-soldiers, many of whom were themselves workers. Such practices further negatively affected the performance, cohesion, and stability of units. See Jerry Cooper, *The Rise of the National Guard: The Evolution of the American Militia, 1865–1920* (Lincoln: University of Nebraska Press, 1997), 54–55. Adjutants General also mustered out volunteers who came from communities or were employed in fields prone to strikes (e.g., miners). See Riker, *Soldiers of the States*, 50–59.

38. Kaufman, "'Americans and Their Guns'"; Harry S. Laver, *Citizens More Than Soldiers: The Kentucky Militia and Society in the Early Republic* (Lincoln: University of Nebraska Press, 2007). The internal democracy of militia companies does not mean that class differences did not play a role. Officers, whether selected or elected, tended to be members of the upper social class, and there were cases where militiamen refused to serve under officers they considered to have insufficiently high social standing. Morgan, *Inventing the People*, 169–70. According to Franklin, the ratio of "officers" to rank and file in some Southern states was as low as 1 to 16, compared to 1 to 218 in Massachusetts. The proliferation of titles allowed even working-class and lesser gentry, such as small farmers, tavern keepers and shop owners, to claim social status. See Franklin, *The Militant South*, ch. 9. For additional anecdotes and commentary on militia uniforms and style, see Riker, *Soldiers of the States*.

39. Derthick, *The National Guard in Politics*, 18; Franklin, *The Militant South*, ch. 9.

40. NRA, *Americans and their Guns: The National Rifle Association Story through Nearly a Century of Service to the Nation* (Harrisburg, PA: Stackpole Company, 1967).

41. Mike McIntire, Glenn Thrush, and Eric Lipton, "Gun Sellers' Message to Americans: Man Up," *New York Times*, June 18, 2022, https://www.nytimes.com/2022/06/18/us/firearm-gun-sales.html.

42. Laver, *Citizens More Than Soldiers*, 120. According to Laver, pomp and circumstance served to recruit new members and ensure the financial prosperity of clubs in a highly dense and competitive organizational environment.

43. Franklin, *The Militant South*, 176–77.

44. Alexis de Tocqueville, *Democracy in America* (New York: Penguin Books, 2004 [1835]), 316.

45. Cooper, *The Rise of the National Guard*; Derthick, *The National Guard in Politics*; William T. Sherman, "Our Army and Militia," *The North American Review* 151, no. 405 (1890): 129–45; Roy Turnbaugh, "Ethnicity, Civic Pride, and Commitment: The Evolution of the Chicago Militia," *Journal of the Illinois State Historical Society (1908–1984)* 72, no. 2 (1979): 111–22.

46. Lt. Col. Ferdinand Lecomte, *The War in the United States: Report to the Swiss Military Department; Preceded by a Discourse to the Federal Military Society Assembled at Berne, August 18, 1862* (New York: D. Van Nostrand, 1863), 75; Franklin, *The Militant South*, 180; Herrera, *For Liberty and the Republic*, 97–99, 110.

47. Cooper, *The Rise of the National Guard*, 50.

48. Pratt, "Tin Soldiers," 17. Yet, the militia has significant institutionalized political power, especially in the South where Democrats vehemently opposed army centralization and professionalization of the armed forces at the expense of the party patronage system—see Stephen Skowronek, *Building a New American State: The Expansion of National Administrative Capacities, 1877–1920* (New York: Cambridge University Press, 1982), ch. 4.

49. Lane Crothers, "The Cultural Foundations of the Modern Militia Movement," *New Political Science* 24, no. 2 (2002): 221–34.

50. Kristin L. Hoganson, *Fighting for American Manhood: How Gender Politics Provoked the Spanish-American and Philippine American Wars* (New Haven, CT: Yale University Press, 1998), 1–15.

51. John K. Mahon, *The History of the Militia and the National Guard* (New York: Macmillan, 1983); Riker, *Soldiers of the States*; William C. Sanger, *Report on the Reserve and Auxiliary Forces of England and the Militia of Switzerland* (Washington, DC: Government Printing Office, 1903).

52. Uviller and Merkel, *The Militia and the Right to Arms*, 133–36.

53. Carol Anderson, *The Second: Race and Guns in a Fatally Unequal America* (New York: Bloomsbury, 2021), 60.

54. Herbert Aptheker, *American Negro Slave Revolts* (New York: International Publishers, 1983 [1949]); W. E. B. DuBois, *Black Reconstruction in America, 1860–1880* (New York: Simon & Schuster, 1999 [1935]); James Oliver Horton and Lois E. Horton, *In Hope of Liberty: Culture, Community, and Protest among Northern Free Blacks, 1700–1860* (New York: Oxford University Press, 1997).

55. Christian G. Samito, *Becoming American under Fire: Irish Americans, African Americans and the Politics of Citizenship during the Civil War Era* (Ithaca, NY: Cornell University Press, 2009), 20–24.

56. Jeffrey R. Kerr-Ritchie, "Rehearsal for War: Black Militias in the Atlantic World," *Slavery and Abolition* 26, no. 1 (2005): 1–34; William Cooper Nell, *The Colored Patriots of the American Revolution* (Boston: Robert F. Wallcut, 1855), https://docsouth.unc.edu/neh/nell/nell.html; Samito, *Becoming American under Fire*, 20–24.

57. Kerr-Ritchie, "Rehearsal for War," 19–20.

58. Otis A. Singletary, *Negro Militia and Reconstruction* (Austin: University of Texas Press, 2011 [1957]), loc. 155 of 3975, Kindle. Reconstruction militia were integrated forces, with many companies including both Black and White soldiers.

59. "General Orders No. 100: Instructions for the Government of the Armies of the United States in the Field," issued April 24, 1963. The Library of Congress offers a

detailed description at https://blogs.loc.gov/law/2018/04/the-lieber-code-the-first
-modern-codification-of-the-laws-of-war/.

60. Singletary, *Negro Militia and Reconstruction*, ch. 2.

61. Singletary, *Negro Militia and Reconstruction*, ch. 2.

62. Bruce A. Glasrud, ed., *Brothers to the Buffalo Soldiers: Perspectives on African-American Militia and Volunteers, 1865–1917* (Columbia: University of Missouri Press, 2011); Beth Taylor Muskat, "The Last March: The Demise of the Black Militia in Alabama," in *Brothers to the Buffalo Soldiers: Perspectives on the African-American Militia and Volunteers, 1865–1917*, ed. Bruce A. Glasrud (Columbia: University of Missouri Press, 2011); Jerry Cooper, *The Militia and the National Guard in America since Colonial Times: A Research Guide* (Westport, CT: Greenwood Press, 1993), 145.

63. Glasrud, *Brothers to the Buffalo Soldiers*; Samito, *Becoming American under Fire*.

64. Alwyn Barr, "The Black Militia in the New South: Texas as a Case Study," in *Brothers to the Buffalo Soldiers: Perspectives on the African-American Militia and Volunteers, 1865–1917*, ed. Bruce A. Glasrud (Columbia: University of Missouri Press, 2011); Roger D. Cunningham, "'They Are as Proud of Their Uniform as Any Who Serve Virginia': African American Participation in the Virginia Volunteers, 1872–99," in *Brothers to the Buffalo Soldiers: Perspectives on the African-American Militia and Volunteers, 1865–1917*, ed. Bruce A. Glasrud (Columbia: University of Missouri Press, 2011).

65. Glasrud, *Brothers to the Buffalo Soldiers*; Eleanor L. Hannah, "A Place in the Parade: Citizenship, Manhood, and African-American Men in the Illinois National Guard, 1870–1917," in *Brothers to the Buffalo Soldiers: Perspectives on the African-American Militia and Volunteers, 1865–1917*, ed. Bruce A. Glasrud (Columbia: University of Missouri Press, 2011); Muskat, "The Last March."

66. Brian E. Alnutt, "African-American Amusement and Recreation in Philadelphia, 1876–1926" (PhD diss., Lehigh University, 2003), 31–33.

67. Hannah, "A Place in the Parade," 86–88; Ulysses Lee, *The Employment of Negro Troops* (Washington, DC: Center for Military History, United States Army, 2001 [1963]), 4: "Lithographs of troops in action and of military heroes were common in Negro homes."

68. Jason Kaufman, *For the Common Good? American Civic Life and the Golden Age of Fraternity* (New York: Oxford University Press, 2003); Franklin, *The Militant South*, ch. 9; Laver, *Citizens More Than Soldiers*, 113. According to Laver, in the mid-nineteenth century, weapons became so central to the social status of militia companies and so essential to clubs' brand and image that fights erupted between groups and brawls within units in efforts to secure government-issued weapons (p. 118).

69. David Adams, "Internal Military Intervention in the United States," *Journal of Peace Research* 32, no. 2 (1995): 197–211.

70. Cooper, *The Rise of the National Guard*, 53; J. D. Dickey, *The Republic of Violence: The Tormented Rise of Abolition in Andrew Jackson's America* (New York: Pegasus Books, 2022); Reinders, "Militia and Public Order in Nineteenth-Century America"; Ida B. Wells-Barnett, *On Lynchings* (Mineola, NY: Dover Publications, Inc., 2014 [1892]).

71. Reinders, "Militia and Public Order in Nineteenth-Century America," 90–94.

72. Cooper, *The Rise of the National Guard*, 46–47.

73. Reinders, "Militia and Public Order in Nineteenth-Century America," 90–94.

74. Morgan, *Inventing the People*, 173; Laver, *Citizens More Than Soldiers*; Mahon, *The History of the Militia and the National Guard*; Michael E. McGerr, *The Decline of*

Popular Politics: The American North, 1865–1928 (New York: Oxford University Press, 1986). Also see Skowronek, *Building the American State*, 85–120.

75. Franklin, *The Militant South*; Glasrud, *Brothers to the Buffalo Soldiers*; Patrick A. Lewis, "The Democratic Partisan Militia and the Black Peril: The Kentucky Militia, Racial Violence, and the Fifteenth Amendment, 1870–1873," *Civil War History* 56, no. 2 (2010): 145–74.

76. Carole Emberton, "The Limits of Incorporation: Violence, Gun Rights, and Gun Regulation in the Reconstruction South," *Stanford Law and Policy Review* 17 (2006): 619.

77. Franklin, *The Militant South*, ch. 9.

78. Morgan, *Inventing the People*, 169–73.

79. Kaufman, *For the Common Good?*; Reinders, "Militia and Public Order in Nineteenth-Century America," 87.

80. These militia were organized on the model of the German rifle clubs that existed even before the Civil War. Kaufman, "'Americans and Their Guns,'" 90. According to the *New York Times* of the time, the Lehr und Wehr Verein even after it was disbanded by the state continued to exist as a private armed organization, and six such groups participated in episodes of labor unrest at the time of the Haymarket riots. The newspaper quoted witnesses from within the labor movement ("agitators") whose conclusion was that the organization was "training to fight the police. They have drilled in their halls and have steadily increased in numbers. . . . They are Socialists of the ultra-type. Every Socialist who is in favor of the dynamite is among them. The most of them have served in the army in the old country and hate government and law"—"The Lehr Und Wehr Verein," *New York Times*, July 20, 1886.

CHAPTER 4

1. Howard Schuman et al., *Racial Attitudes in America: Trends and Interpretations* (Cambridge, MA: Harvard University Press, 1997), ch. 3.

2. John Jost and Orsolya Hunyady, "The Psychology of System Justification and the Palliative Function of Ideology," *European Review of Social Psychology* 13, no. 1 (2003).

3. John T. Jost et al., "Social Inequality and the Reduction of Ideological Dissonance on Behalf of the System: Evidence of Enhanced System Justification among the Disadvantaged," *European Journal of Social Psychology* 33, no. 1 (2003): 13–36. For example, women are more likely than men to believe that they deserve lower pay, and African Americans more likely than White people to use meritocratic explanations for racial income differentials.

4. R. Gordon Kelly, *Mother Was a Lady: Self and Society in Selected American Children's Periodicals, 1865–1890* (Westport, CT: Greenwood Press, 1974), xvii.

5. Allison P. Anoll, Andrew M. Engelhardt, and Mackenzie Israel-Trummel, "Black Lives, White Kids: White Parenting Practices Following Black-Led Protests," *Perspectives on Politics* (2022): 1–18, https://doi.org/10.1017/S1537592722001050; A. Filindra and C. Burnett, "Who Should Control Education Policy? White Racial Attitudes and Support for Citizens' Involvement in Education Policymaking," paper presented at the 2023 conference of the Midwest Political Science Association, Chicago, April 13–16, 2023.

6. David Tyack, "Monuments between Covers: The Politics of Textbooks," *American Behavioral Scientist* 42, no. 6 (1999): 922–32.

7. Nikole Hannah-Jones, "The 1619 Project," *New York Times Magazine*, August 14, 2019, https://www.nytimes.com/interactive/2019/08/14/magazine/1619-america -slavery.html; Kimberle Williams Crenshaw, "Twenty Years of Critical Race Theory: Looking Back to Move Forward," *Connecticut Law Review* 43, no. 5 (2011): 1253–1354.

8. Hannah-Jones, "The 1619 Project"; Crenshaw, "Twenty Years of Critical Race Theory."

9. Leslie S. Kaplan and William A. Owings, "Countering the Furor around Critical Race Theory," *NASSP Bulletin* 105, no. 3 (2021): 200–218.

10. Crenshaw, "Twenty Years of Critical Race Theory."

11. Benjamin Wallace-Wells, "How a Conservative Activist Invented the Conflict over Critical Race Theory," *The New Yorker*, June 18, 2021, https://www.newyorker .com/news/annals-of-inquiry/how-a-conservative-activist-invented-the-conflict-over -critical-race-theory.

12. Matthew S. Schwartz, "Trump Tells Agencies to End Trainings on 'White Privilege' and 'Critical Race Theory,'" *NPR.org*, September 5, 2020, https://www.npr.org/ 2020/09/05/910053496/trump-tells-agencies-to-end-trainings-on-white-privilege -and-critical-race-theor; Kathryn Schumaker, "What Is Critical Race Theory and Why Did Oklahoma Just Ban It?" *Washington Post*, May 19, 2021, https://www.washington post.com/outlook/2021/05/19/what-is-critical-race-theory-why-did-oklahoma-just -ban-it/.

13. University of Massachusetts Amherst, "University of Massachusetts Amherst/ WCVB December 2021 National Poll," UMass Poll, December 2021, https://polsci .umass.edu/sites/default/files/CRTandRaceinAmericaCrosstabs.pdf.

14. Bernard Bailyn, "Education in the Forming of American Society: An Interpretation," in *History of Education: Major Themes, Debates in the History of Education*, ed. Roy Lowe (London: Routledge Falmer, 2000), 3–8.

15. Tyack, "Monuments between Covers."

16. Elizabeth Gillespie McRae, *Mothers of Massive Resistance: White Women and the Politics of White Supremacy* (New York: Oxford University Press, 2018).

17. Willis Mason West, *American History and Government* (Boston: Allyn & Bacon, 1913).

18. Maxine Seller and Andrew Trusz, "High School Textbooks and the American Revolution," *The History Teacher* 9, no. 4 (1976): 535–55; Joel Taxel, "The American Revolution in Children's Fiction: An Analysis of Historical Meaning and Narrative Structure," *Curriculum Inquiry* 14, no. 1 (1984): 7–55; Donald Yacovone, *Teaching White Supremacy: America's Democratic Ordeal and the Forging of a National Identity* (New York: Pantheon Books, 2022).

19. Taxel, "The American Revolution in Children's Fiction," 16; NRA, *Americans and their Guns: The National Rifle Association Story through Nearly a Century of Service to the Nation* (Harrisburg, PA: Stackpole Company, 1967), 1–15.

20. Edmund S. Morgan, "Slavery and Freedom: The American Paradox," *The Journal of American History* 59, no. 1 (1972).

21. Karen L. Cox, *Dixie's Daughters: The United Daughters of the Confederacy and the Preservation of Confederate Culture* (Gainesville: University Press of Florida, 2003); Ethan J. Kytle and Blain Roberts, *Denmark Vesey's Garden: Slavery and Memory in the Cradle of the Confederacy* (New York: The New Press, 2018).

22. Alexander H. Stephens, "Cornerstone Speech," Savannah, Georgia, March 21, 1861, https://www.battlefields.org/learn/primary-sources/cornerstone-speech.

23. James M. McPherson, *The Mighty Scourge: Perspectives on the Civil War* (New York: Oxford University Press, 2009), chs. 1–2.

24. Charles A. Beard and Mary R. Beard, *The Rise of American Civilization*, vol. 2 (New York: Macmillan Company, 1927).

25. McPherson, *The Mighty Scourge*, 5; Twelve Southerners, *I'll Take a Stand: The South and the Agrarian Tradition* (Baton Rouge: Louisiana State University Press, 2006 [1930]).

26. McPherson, *The Mighty Scourge*, 6–7.

27. Mike Konczal, "How Radical Change Occurs: An Interview with Historian Eric Foner," *The Nation*, February 3, 2015, https://www.thenation.com/article/archive/how-radical-change-occurs-interview-historian-eric-foner/.

28. George Fredrickson, *The Black Image in the White Mind: The Debate on Afro-American Character and Destiny, 1817–1914* (New York: Harper and Row, 1971), 51–56.

29. Donnarae MacCann, *White Supremacy in Children's Literature: Characterizations of African-Americans 1830–1900* (New York: Routledge, 1998), 235. McCann quotes Woodrow Wilson on the war in the Philippines as saying: "In the wrong hands,—in hands unpracticed, undisciplined,—[liberty] is incompatible with government. Discipline must precede it,—if necessary, the discipline of being under masters" (p. 237).

30. Jabez Lamar Monroe Curry, *A Civil History of the Government of the Confederate States* (Richmond, VA: B. F. Johnson Publishing Co., 1903); William A. Dunning, "Reconstruction, Political and Economic," in *The American Nation: A History*, ed. Albert Bushnell Hart (New York: Harper & Brothers, 1907); Edward A. Pollard, *The Lost Cause Regained* (New York: G. W. Carleton & Co., 1868). On the "Lost Cause," see Gary W. Gallagher, *Causes Won, Lost, and Forgotten: How Hollywood and Popular Art Shape What We Know about the Civil War* (Chapel Hill: University of North Carolina Press, 2008).

31. Eric Foner, *The Second Founding: How the Civil War Remade the Constitution* (New York: W. W. Norton & Co., 2019); Konczal, "How Radical Change Occurs."

32. W. E. B. DuBois, *Black Reconstruction in America, 1860–1880* (New York: Simon & Schuster, 1999 [1935]); Eric Foner, *Reconstruction: America's Unfinished Revolution, 1864–1877* (New York: Harper & Row Publishers, 1988), preface, xix.

33. Douglas Martin, "Shelby Foote, Historian and Novelist, Dies at 88," *New York Times*, June 29, 2005, https://www.nytimes.com/2005/06/29/books/shelby-foote-historian-and-novelist-dies-at-88.html.

34. David W. Blight, *Race and Reunion: The Civil War in American Memory* (Cambridge, MA: The Belknap Press of Harvard University Press, 2001).

35. Cox, *Dixie's Daughters*; Kytle and Roberts, *Denmark Vesey's Garden*; McRae, *Mothers of Massive Resistance*; McPherson, *The Mighty Scourge*.

36. William E. Hemphill, Marvin W. Schlegel, and Sadie W. Engelberg, *Cavalier Commonwealth: History and Government of Virginia* (New York: McGraw-Hill, 1957).

37. Rod Andrew, *Long Gray Lines: The Southern Military School Tradition, 1839–1915* (Chapel Hill: University of North Carolina Press, 2001); Alexander McCauley, *Marching in Step: Masculinity, Citizenship, and the Citadel in Post–World War II America* (Athens: University of Georgia Press, 2009); Ian Shapira, "At VMI, Black Cadets Endure Lynching Threats, Klan Memories and Confederacy Veneration," *Washington Post*, October 17, 2020, https://www.washingtonpost.com/local/at-vmi-black-cadets-endure-lynching-threats-klan-memories-and-confederacy-veneration/2020/10/17/3bf53cec-0671-11eb-859b-f9c27abe638d_story.html.

38. Kate Shuster, "Teaching Hard History," Southern Poverty Law Center, January 31, 2018, https://www.splcenter.org/20180131/teaching-hard-history.

39. Dana Goldstein, "Two States, Eight Textbooks, Two American Stories," *New York Times*, January 12, 2020, https://www.nytimes.com/interactive/2020/01/12/us/texas-vs-california-history-textbooks.html.

40. John Bodnar, *Remaking America: Public Memory, Commemoration and Patriotism in the Twentieth Century* (Princeton, NJ: Princeton University Press, 1992), 14–15.

41. Blight, *Race and Reunion*, 80.

42. Tony Horwitz, *Confederates in the Attic: Dispatches from the Unfinished Civil War* (New York: Vintage Books, 1999); Kytle and Roberts, *Denmark Vesey's Garden*.

43. "Carter to the rescue? U.S. Left pushes America toward in Haiti," Article, *Human Events* 50, no. 28 (1994).

44. Meagan Flynn, "The KKK Is Featured in a Florida Courthouse Mural. Lawyers Are Demanding Its Immediate Removal," *Washington Post*, July 14, 2020, https://www.washingtonpost.com/nation/2020/07/14/kkk-mural-florida/?utm_campaign=wp_main&utm_medium=social&utm_source=facebook.

45. In recent decades, and especially with the election of Barack Obama, African Americans have established their own reenactment events that focus on celebrating the history and accomplishments of the United States Colored Troops (USCT). These events are separate from White-dominated reenactments of major Civil War battles. Yet, in a way, they serve as sites of system justification. Patricia G. Davis, "The Other Southern Belles: Civil War Reenactment, African American Women, and the Performance of Idealized Femininity," *Text and Performance Quarterly* 32, no. 4 (2012): 308–31.

46. Charles H. Gillespie, "Pathetic Night Scene in Veterans' Great Reunion," *Pittsburg Press*, July 1, 1913, 3.

47. James O. Farmer, "Playing Rebels: Reenactment as Nostalgia and Defense of the Confederacy in the Battle of Aiken," *Southern Cultures* 11, no. 1 (2005): 46–73.

48. Gregory Hall, "Selective Authenticity: Civil War Reenactors and Credible Reenactments," *Journal of Historical Sociology* 29, no. 3 (2016): 413–36.

49. Farmer, "Playing Rebels," 46–73; Stephen Gapps, "Mobile Monuments: A View of Historical Reenactment and Authenticity from Inside the Costume Cupboard of History," *Rethinking History* 13, no. 3 (2009): 395–409.

50. Ludwig Olson, "The South Did Rise: Confederates Victorious in Blue-Gray Competition at Winchester, VA," *The American Rifleman* 115, no. 7 (July 1967): 28–29; "North-South Skirmish," *The American Rifleman* 101, no. 7 (July 1953): 13–15.

51. Sidney Porter, "Something about Early Telescope Sights," *Arms and the Man* 62, no. 21 (1917): 407; "Protective Coloration for the Sammies," *Arms and the Man* 62, no. 16 (1917): 308.

52. Col. H. P. Sheldon, "An Armed Citizenry," *The American Rifleman* 88, no. 9 (1940): 6–7.

53. C. B. Lister, "Re-Dedication," *The American Rifleman* 89, no. 5 (1941): 4.

54. "The General" Sculpted Canteen, "a richly detailed canteen honor[ing] Civil War General Robert E. Lee," in honor of the 150th anniversary of the Civil War. "Robert E. Lee's Canteen (advertisement)," *America's 1st Freedom* 14, no. 8 (2013); Stonewall Jackson, Cold-Cast Bronze Tribute: "Stonewall Jackson's strong faith, brilliant military maneuvers and unflinching courage in battle made him General Robert E. Lee's right-hand man. Now, in honor of the renowned Civil War leader we

present the Stonewall Jackson Cold-cast Bronze Tribute." For $99.95, satisfaction guaranteed. "Stonewall Jackson Cold-Cast Bronze Tribute (advertisement)," *America's 1st Freedom* 14, no. 4 (2013); "A Monument to Civil War Heroism, Leading the Way: Robert E. Lee, Cold-Cast Bronze Sculpture (advertisement)," *America's 1st Freedom* 13, no. 4 (2012); "The official Robert E. Lee collector knife. Robert E. Lee, leader of the Confederate army, won the respect of North and South alike," *America's 1st Freedom* 4, no. 2 (2003); "Robert E. Lee official Confederate ring, 'An inspiring symbol of Southern courage and honor.'" "Robert E. Lee was more than just the greatest General of the Civil War, he was a man of Southern dignity, spirit, and loyalty. Wear the ring that lets the world know that you share these qualities! (advertisement)," *America's 1st Freedom* 4, no. 3 (2003); "The official Robert E. Lee Civil War Collectors Watch: 'He first served the United States with such distinction that President Abraham Lincoln offered him full field command. But Robert E. Lee could not abandon his native soil, and sided with the Confederacy. As a supreme military leader, he triumphed again and again against overwhelming odds (advertisement)," *America's 1st Freedom* 3, no. 9 (2002).

55. Mike McIntire, Glenn Thrush, and Eric Lipton, "Gun Sellers' Message to Americans: Man Up," *New York Times*, June 18, 2022, https://www.nytimes.com/2022/06/18/us/firearm-gun-sales.html.

56. Kevin M. Levin, *Searching for Black Confederates: The Civil War's Most Persistent Myth* (Chapel Hill: University of North Carolina Press, 2019); *The United States Army & Navy Journal*, "The Colored Troops," March 18, 1866, 508.

57. At least one book about a former slave who fought for the Confederacy was featured in the *American Rifleman*. See Minor Ferris Buchanan, *Holt Collier: His Life, His Roosevelt Hunts, and the Origins of the Teddy Bear* (Jackson: Centennial Press of Mississippi, 2002); "Holt Collier: His Life, His Roosevelt Hunts and the Origin of the Teddy Bear," *The American Rifleman* 181, no. 2 (February 2003): 19; Olson, "The South Did Rise," 28–29.

58. Levin, *Searching for Black Confederates*, 124.

59. Edmund L. Drago, *Hurrah for Hampton! Black Red Shirts in South Carolina during Reconstruction* (Fayetteville: University of Arkansas Press, 1998).

60. Stephen Robinson, "'To Think, Act, Vote, and Speak for Ourselves': Black Democrats and Black 'Agency' in the American South after Reconstruction," *Journal of Social History* 48, no. 2 (2014): 363–82. For a contemporary analysis of Black partisan politics, see Ismail K. White and Chryl N. Laird, *Steadfast Democrats: How Social Forces Shape Black Political Behavior* (Princeton, NJ: Princeton University Press, 2020).

61. See especially the debate between Washington and DuBois: Booker T. Washington, "Atlanta Compromise Speech," in *The Booker T. Washington Papers*, ed. Louis R. Harlan (Urbana: University of Illinois Press, 1974 [1895]); W. E. B. DuBois, *The Souls of Black Folk* (New York: Oxford University Press, 2007 [1903]).

62. Glenda Elizabeth Gilmore, *Defying Dixie: The Radical Roots of Civil Rights, 1919–1950* (New York: W. W. Norton & Co., 2009).

63. "*Gods and Generals*," said the historian Steven Woodworth, "brings to the big screen the major themes of Lost Cause mythology that professional historians have been working for half a century to combat. In the world portrayed in the movie, slavery has nothing to do with the Confederate cause. Instead, the Confederates are nobly fighting for, rather than against, freedom." Steven E. Woodworth, "Film Review: Gods

and Generals," National History Education Clearinghouse (blog), August 16, 2011, https://teachinghistory.org/nhec-blog/25077.

64. McPherson, *The Mighty Scourge.*

65. McCann, *White Supremacy in Children's Literature*, 238–40.

66. Elizabeth Cobbs, "Fighting on Two Fronts: World War One, Women's Suffrage, and John Pershing's 'Hello Girls,'" *South Central Review* 34, no. 3 (2017): 31-47.

67. Tyack, "Monuments between Covers."

CHAPTER 5

1. Mike McIntire, Glenn Thrush, and Eric Lipton, "Gun Sellers' Message to Americans: Man Up," *New York Times*, June 18, 2022, https://www.nytimes.com/2022/06/18/us/firearm-gun-sales.html.

2. David W. Blight, *Race and Reunion: The Civil War in American Memory* (Cambridge, MA: The Belknap Press of Harvard University Press, 2001), chs. 3, 6.

3. NRA, *Americans and their Guns: The National Rifle Association Story through Nearly a Century of Service to the Nation* (Harrisburg, PA: Stackpole Company, 1967), ch. 3. William C. Church also served as the editor of the *Army & Navy Journal*, which was established by Republican elites concerned about the national press's criticism of the Civil War and its effect on morale, especially among soldiers and draft-age civilians. Church's mission was to produce a journal for the services that was of "unquestionable loyalty" to the Union. Donald N. Bigelow, "A Journal of 'Unquestionable Loyalty,'" *New York History* 27, no. 4 (1946): 444–57.

4. Scott R. McMichael, *A Historical Perspective on Light Infantry* (Fort Leavenworth, KS: US Army Command and General Staff College, 1987); Steven T. Ross, *From Flintock to Rifle: Infantry Tactics, 1740–1866* (London: Frank Cass, 1979). This changed in the late nineteenth century when Prussia beat France in the Franco-Prussian war of 1870. The German army used a new generation of breach-loading rifles and new tactics which were widely credited with winning them the war against a vastly superior opponent.

5. Robert Reinders, "Militia and Public Order in Nineteenth-Century America," *Journal of American Studies* 11, no. 1 (1977); William H. Riker, *Soldiers of the States: The Role of the National Guard in American Democracy* (Washington, DC: Public Affairs Press, 1957).

6. Jason Kaufman, *For the Common Good? American Civic Life and the Golden Age of Fraternity* (New York: Oxford University Press, 2003); John K. Mahon, *The History of the Militia and the National Guard* (New York: Macmillan, 1983).

7. NRA, *Address, Annual Reports, and Regulation for Rifle Practice, 1873–1878* (New York: Raynold & Whelpley, 1877), 7.

8. Jeffrey A. Marlin, "The National Guard, the National Board for the Promotion of Rifle Practice, and the National Rifle Association: Public Institutions and the Rise of a Lobby for Private Gun Ownership" (PhD diss., Georgia State University, 2013), 75–76; NRA, *Americans and Their Guns: The National Rifle Association Story through Nearly a Century of Service to the Nation* (Harrisburg, PA: Stackpole Company, 1967), ch. 8.

9. NRA, *Americans and Their Guns*, 88–89.

10. NRA, *Americans and Their Guns.*

11. In this era, "militarism" was often used in reference to building a large standing army. Therefore, being "anti-militaristic" did not mean pacifist or against war; rather,

it was a reference to supporting martial republicanism and a decentralized, citizen-soldier-based military force. See William C. Church, "What Constitutes 'Militarism'?" *The American Army & Navy Journal*, October 3, 1914.

12. Martha Derthick, *The National Guard in Politics* (Cambridge, MA: Harvard University Press, 1965); Marlin, "The National Guard."

13. Derthick, *The National Guard in Politics*, 16; Marlin, "The National Guard," 125–26.

14. Derthick describes such a pamphlet dated from 1884 and titled "Joining the Militia, or the Comic Adventures of a Recruit"—Derthick, *The National Guard in Politics*, 18.

15. Derthick, *The National Guard in Politics*.

16. Derthick, *The National Guard in Politics*.

17. Riker, *Soldiers of the States*; Congressional Research Service, *The Posse Comitatus Act and Related Matters: The Use of the Military to Execute Civilian Law* (Washington, DC: CRS Report, 2018), https://fas.org/sgp/crs/natsec/R42659.pdf. The concept of a Posse Comitatus has republican origins: it empowers a local political authority, typically the sheriff, to mobilize the town's (White male) citizens in order to preserve the peace. Although the principle is generally obsolete, in several states there are statutes that enable local law enforcement to seek the assistance of citizens in executing warrants. David Kopel, "The Posse Comitatus and the Office of Sheriff: Armed Citizens Summoned to the Aid of Law Enforcement," *Journal of Criminal Law and Criminology* 104, no. 4 (2015): 761–850.

18. Derthick, *The National Guard in Politics*. The rules governing the conduct of the US Army specified that soldiers and officers could not be publicly critical of the President, Congress, or the courts. After the Civil War, this limit on Army personnel's free speech rights was interpreted to include direct lobbying of elected officials. This relationship between the military and Congress was officially codified in the Uniform Code of Military Justice in 1950.

19. Recognizing that extant volunteer forces would not be sufficient to defeat Germany, the federal government introduced the draft in 1917 on the eve of America's entry into World War I. This was over the strenuous objections of the NRA. See especially: "Universal Service and the Emergency," *Arms and the Man* 62, no. 2 (1917): 28–29. However, after World War II, the NRA reversed its position and strongly supported universal service based on the expectation that the Association would provide marksmanship training to draftees. See C. B. Lister, "Universal Service," *The American Rifleman* 93, no. 1 (1945): 5; C. B. Lister, "Universal Military Service," *The American Rifleman* 93, no. 2 (1945): 5; C. B. Lister, "False Conception," *The American Rifleman* 93, no. 3 (1945): 5. Neither idea became reality.

20. Marlin, "The National Guard," 84–92. NRA, *Report of the National Rifle Association of America, A Patriotic Association* (New York: National Rifle Association, 1902), 19–21.

21. NRA, *Americans and Their Guns*. Theodore Roosevelt, Elihu Root, and William Howard Taft were all life members of the NRA.

22. NRA, *Report of the National Rifle Association*, 19–21.

23. "To Encourage American Marksmanship," *Washington Tribune*, August 4, 1904, 4. The same source says that the proposed legislation included an annual appropriation of $1,000,000 for the marksmanship program along with the option for the NRA "to purchase at cost rifles resembling those now in use in the Regular Army and sell

them at a slight advance to those who wish to practice, and ammunition as near cost as possible."

24. NRA, *Report of the National Rifle Association*, 19–20.

25. NRA, *Report of the National Rifle Association*, 21.

26. NRA, 21.

27. NRA, 21. William C. Church was such a major supporter of military preparedness that in the wake of World War I he extolled "German militarism," which he defined as the country's military preparedness. Church, "What Constitutes 'Militarism?'"

28. Marlin, "The National Guard," 84–92.

29. William C. Sanger, *Report on the Reserve and Auxiliary Forces of England and the Militia of Switzerland* (Washington, DC: Government Printing Office, 1903), 7, 9.

30. Sanger, *Report on the Reserve and Auxiliary Forces*, 94.

31. Sanger, *Report on the Reserve and Auxiliary Forces*. In the report, Sanger made the distinction between "militarism" and the citizen-soldier model, which implies that even in the early twentieth century, martial republicanism was to some degree perceived as antithetical to the "militarism" of a standing army.

32. James Parker, "The Militia Act of 1903," *The North American Review* 177, no. 561 (1903): 284.

33. NRA, *Americans and Their Guns*, 132; Jeffrey L. Rodengen, *NRA: An American Legend* (Ft. Lauderdale, FL: Write Stuff Enterprises, 2002), 82–83. As NRA editor in chief, C. B. Lister claimed in the pages of the *American Rifleman* in 1950, "it is evident that . . . the Congress has recognized the NRA as a quasi-governmental organization since 1902. The establishment of the National Board for the Promotion of Rifle Practice and the Office of the Director of Civilian Marksmanship are both the direct result of the NRA's continuing effort to promote small-arms training in the Armed Services and among civilians." C. B. Lister, "The Director of Civilian Marksmanship: The National Board for the Promotion of Rifle Practice," *The American Rifleman* 98, no. 3 (March 1950): 33.

34. NRA, *Americans and Their Guns*, 130.

35. 114 Cong. Rec. S13363, Debates on "Omnibus Crime Control and Safe Streets Act of 1968," https://www.govinfo.gov/content/pkg/GPO-CRECB-1968-pt10/pdf/GPO-CRECB-1968-pt10-6-1.pdf, quoting the *Congressional Quarterly* from April 10, 1968.

36. Rodengen, *NRA: An American Legend*, 128–30.

37. According to then NRA Director C. B. Lister, among other responsibilities, the DCM was to "maintain an alphabetical index of all NRA members who have purchased arms from the DCM, indicating the date of purchase and the type of gun." Ironically, this was a form of government registration which the NRA not only agreed to, but participated in. For a specific and sizable subsection of gun owners, all of them NRA members, the US government had a record of not only the fact that they owned firearms, but also the make and model of those weapons that came from the US military. Lister, "The Director of Civilian Marksmanship," 34.

38. On the UFA, see Charles V. Imlay, "The Uniform Firearms Act," *American Bar Association Journal* 12, no. 11 (1926): 767–69.

39. "Marksmen Are Made Not Born," *The Daily Picayune*, December 2, 1908, 8.

40. United States Senate, *To Regulate Commerce in Firearms: Hearings before the United States Senate Committee on Commerce, Subcommittee on S. 885, S. 2258 and S. 3680 (May 28–29, 1934)* (Washington, DC: US Government Printing Office, 1934). Excerpt from the hearing: "Senator Copeland: Have you made attacks on these bills?

General Reckord: Yes; we have. Senator Copeland: Have you made attacks on the committee? General Reckord: On the committee? Why, no, sir," United States Senate, *To Regulate Commerce in Firearms*, 10. In these hearings, the NRA went on record that they had no relationship with gun manufacturers, something that changed in the post–World War II era (p. 12). Excerpt from the hearing: "Senator Copeland: I noticed in your testimony before the House committee that you spoke of the fact that you were representing the adjutants general. . . . What have the adjutants general to do with the sale of firearms to citizens? General Reckord: I don't think they have an interest in it, except the general interest, Senator, that the adjutant generals are the heads of military departments in the several States, and they are all interested in marksmanship, and in the citizenry of the country knowing how to shoot."

41. 114 Cong. Rec. S13362, Debates on "Omnibus Crime Control and Safe Streets Act of 1968," https://www.govinfo.gov/content/pkg/GPO-CRECB-1968-pt10/pdf/GPO-CRECB-1968-pt10-6-1.pdf, quoting the *Congressional Quarterly* from April 10, 1968.

42. A scandal in 1925 involving the NRA leadership underscored the point. Up until then, the association shared offices with the NBPRP. A government agency and a private entity were practically indistinguishable. However, the scandal forced the Board to relieve the NRA executive of his duties on the Board, vacate the premises, and move to a different location. The loss of immediate access to the Board and the publicity surrounding the scandal dealt a blow to the NRA. In a rebranding campaign in response to the scandals, the NRA took pains to distance itself from the secret organizations, such as the Second Ku Klux Klan, Masonic lodges, and other societies, which were popular in the 1920s. Much like the NRA, members of such groups sported uniforms, assigned their members military titles, and engaged in a variety of social activities. The NRA asserted that it was a patriotic, enlightened, and defense-oriented organization of sportsmen, a group for "*the average rifleman—no more, no less. The Association is not a mystical organization . . . it is rather an organization of everyday citizens who believe in the rifle as a means of recreation and national defense.*" Rodengen, *NRA: An American Legend*, 83.

43. Rodengen, *NRA: An American Legend*, 132.

44. Rodengen, 132. Captain G. M. Kellogg and Major A. F. Spring, "Use of Chemical by Law Enforcement Officers in Civil Disorders (Part II)," *The American Rifleman* 80, no. 2 (1932): 46–49. The 1932-1933 volume includes such articles in almost every issue.

45. Rodengen, *NRA: An American Legend*, 62–70, 94–114.

46. United States Senate, *To Regulate Commerce in Firearms*.

47. "Incidentally," *The American Rifleman*, April 1950, 4.

48. Lister, "The Director of Civilian Marksmanship," 32–34.

49. "To Encourage American Marksmanship," 4.

50. Barton C. Hacker, "The Machines of War: Western Military Technology 1850–2000," *History and Technology* 21, no. 3 (2005): 257.

51. Hacker, "The Machines of War," 255–300.

52. Hacker, "The Machines of War." US General Accounting Office, "Military Preparedness: Army's Civilian Marksmanship Program Is of Limited Value" (Washington, DC: GAO/NSIAD-90-171, 1990).

53. "Directors Meet and Discuss Important Questions," *The American Rifleman*, March 1940, 12–13; Church, "What Constitutes 'Militarism'?"

54. James B. Whisker, *The Citizen Soldier and United States Military Policy* (Great Barrington, MA: North River Press, 1979), 38–39.

55. Robert H. Collins, "Many Members of Minutemen in Rifle Clubs, DePugh Admits," *St. Louis Post-Dispatch*, August 17, 1964, 3A.

56. According to the ADL report, membership in a "gun club" provided a ready excuse for KKK members caught with weapons in their cars. Arnold Forster and Benjamin R. Epstein, *Report of the Ku Klux Klan* (New York: Anti-Defamation League of B'nai B'rith, 1965); "Klan Blamed for Violence: Anti-Defamation League Cites 'Gun Club' Front," *The Baltimore Sun*, June 15, 1965, 10.

57. An editorial in the *American Rifleman* that discusses the report says it was authorized under Title IV of the Civil Rights Act. However, this is likely a typographical error, since Title IV relates to desegregation of public schools. Title VI concerns racial discrimination by entities that receive federal funding, which is more readily applicable here. Regardless, it is telling that among what must have been the earliest civil rights investigations authorized by Congress, this one involved the CMP and the NRA. Unfortunately, I was not able to ascertain the findings of that portion of the report. The Library of Congress does not have an electronic or physical copy of this report and neither do any major libraries. The only available copy is housed in the US Army Heritage and Education Center in Carlisle, PA. Travel restrictions due to COVID-19 made it impossible to access this report. "The Private Army Hoax," *The American Rifleman*, September 1965, 16.

58. Josh Sugarmann, *National Rifle Association: Money, Firepower, Fear* (Washington, DC: National Press Books, 1992).

59. Whisker, *The Citizen Soldier and United States Military Policy*; "New Curbs Urged on Rifle Program," *New York Times*, February 13, 1966.

60. Sugarmann, *National Rifle Association*, 110.

61. Robert Wohlforth, "Our $300,000,000 Skeleton," *The North American Review* 236, no. 2 (1933): 101–8; US General Accounting Office, "Military Preparedness"; US General Accounting Office, Testimony before the Subcommittee on Readiness, Committee on Armed Services, House of Representatives: Evaluation of the Army's Civilian Marksmanship Program (Washington, DC: GAO/T-NSIAD-90-20, 1990).

62. The program's "stickiness" despite changing conditions is not surprising. The political scientist Paul Pierson has shown how government programs create positive returns that empower key beneficiaries and incentivize them to continue lobbying elected officials to continue such programs. Andrea Campbell has shown that this process creates politically engaged communities within the public. Paul Pierson, *Politics in Time: History, Institutions and Social Analysis* (Princeton, NJ: Princeton University Press, 2004).

63. Wohlforth, "Our $300,000,000 Skeleton," 103; Matthew Lacombe, *Firepower: How the NRA Turned Gun Owners into a Political Force* (Princeton, NJ: Princeton University Press, 2021).

64. Rodengen, *NRA: An American Legend*, 154–55.

65. Rodengen, 163–64.

66. Rodengen, 173–76; Reva B. Siegel, "Dead or Alive: Originalism as Popular Constitutionalism in *Heller*," *Harvard Law Review* 122, no. 1 (2008): 191–245.

67. Osha Gray Davidson, *Under Fire: The NRA and the Battle for Gun Control* (Iowa City: University of Iowa Press, 1998); Frank Smyth, *The NRA: The Unauthorized History* (New York: Flatiron Books, 2020).

68. There is significant variation in the type of information offered about civilian candidates in the 1920s to 1940s.

69. "1954 Directors Nominations," *The American Rifleman* 102, no. 1 (1954): 37.

70. "1984 Directors Nominations," *The American Rifleman* 132, no. 4 (1984): 58–63.

71. "1994 Directors Nominations," *The American Rifleman* 142, no. 3 (1994): 56–63.

72. For many of the candidates, I relied on the information provided on the website "NRA: On the Record" (https://nraontherecord.org). This is a website collecting quotes attributed to various NRA Board members. The site also includes a short biography for each member. Since these biographies do not serve the same purpose as the ones used to promote a candidacy, I only used this information to fill in strictly biographical information, not to rate the candidates in terms of their commitment to gun rights. The biographies allowed me to determine whether the individual: 1) had military experience; 2) was in business or a professional occupation, or was a farmer/rancher; 3) was a lawyer; 4) was an elected official, government employee, or law enforcement agent; and/or 5) worked or consulted for the NRA.

73. "New Directors Elected at Annual Members' Meeting," *The American Rifleman* 82, no. 2 (1934).

74. See: "NRA Information Page," *The American Rifleman*, through the 1960s.

75. "NRA Official Journal," *The American Rifleman* 126, no. 1 (1978): 61–64.

76. "NRA Official Journal," *The American Rifleman* 132, no. 12 (1984): 46–49.

CHAPTER 6

1. Jeffrey L. Rodengen, *NRA: An American Legend* (Ft. Lauderdale, FL: Write Stuff Enterprises, 2002), ch. 13: A Diverse Organization, 126–43.

2. David Kopel, Paul Gallant, and Joanne Eisen, "Ambrose E. Burnside: General, Governor, Senator, Civil Rights Activist and First President of the NRA," *America's 1st Freedom* 5, no. 11 (2004): 24–27.

3. David Kopel, "Freedom Fighters," *America's 1st Freedom* 16, no. 2 (2016): 36–40.

4. Kopel, Gallant, and Eisen, "Ambrose E. Burnside," 24–27.

5. George Fredrickson, *The Black Image in the White Mind: The Debate on Afro-American Character and Destiny, 1817–1914* (New York: Harper and Row, 1971), 273–74; Corey Robin, *The Enigma of Clarence Thomas* (New York: Metropolitan Books, 2019), 169; Ida B. Wells-Barnett, *On Lynchings* (Mineola, NY: Dover Publications, Inc., 2014 [1892]).

6. Kopel, Gallant, and Eisen, "Ambrose E. Burnside," 24–27.

7. Mark A. Keefe, "The Buffalo Soldier Rides Forever," *The American Rifleman* 140, no. 10 (1992): 26–27.

8. William C. Church, "War & Peace," *The United States Army & Navy Journal*, July 22, 1865, 760–61.

9. C. B. Lister, "Re-Dedication," *The American Rifleman* 89, no. 5 (1941): 4.

10. Rev. Pharcellus Church, "The Fugitive Slave Bill," *Liberator* (1831–1865), October 18, 1850, 166.

11. James Hudnut-Beumler, *In Pursuit of the Almighty's Dollar: A History of Money and American Protestantism* (Chapel Hill: University of North Carolina Press, 2007), 15–20.

12. Rev. Pharcellus Church, "The Slavery Question in the Alliance," *Christian Reflector* (1838–1848), April 1, 1847, 49.

13. Donald Bigelow, *William Conant Church and the* Army & Navy Journal (New York: Columbia University Press, 1952), 18–19.

14. Robert J. Scholnick, "*The Galaxy* and American Democratic Culture, 1866–1878," *Journal of American Studies* 16, no. 1 (1982): 69–80; Brook Thomas, "*The Galaxy*, National Literature, and Reconstruction," *Nineteenth-Century Literature* 75, no. 1 (2020): 50–81.

15. Bigelow, *William Conant Church and the* Army & Navy Journal, 70.

16. *Army & Navy Journal*, March 12, 1864, quoted in Bigelow, 167.

17. Bigelow, *William Conant Church and the* Army & Navy Journal, 166–67. This argument is reminiscent of the "revisionist school" arguments of the 1940s which suggested that it was not fundamental social and economic differences between North and South that led to the conflict, and that instead it was an extremist minority on both sides—fanatical abolitionists and Southern fire-eaters—who stirred up hatred for their own partisan purposes. See James M. McPherson, *The Mighty Scourge: Perspectives on the Civil War* (New York: Oxford University Press, 2009), 6–7.

18. McPherson, *The Mighty Scourge*, 18–19, 71, 90. Church's conservative Republican leanings are also evident in his denunciation of the Confiscation Acts meant to punish those who aided in the Rebellion in the South. William C. Church, "The Policy of Confiscation," *The Galaxy. A Magazine of Entertaining Reading* (1866–1878), 1867.

19. David W. Blight, *Race and Reunion: The Civil War in American Memory* (Cambridge, MA: The Belknap Press of Harvard University Press, 2001), ch. 6.

20. Jeffrey A. Marlin, "The National Guard, the National Board for the Promotion of Rifle Practice, and the National Rifle Association: Public Institutions and the Rise of a Lobby for Private Gun Ownership" (PhD diss., Georgia State University, 2013), 87. Beauregard was the officer in command who ordered the attack on Fort Sumter, SC, that started the Civil War. He received a pardon in 1868 from Andrew Johnson. In 1876, Ulysses Grant reinstated his right to run for public office. From 1879 to 1888, he served as Adjutant General for the Louisiana state militia.

21. Blight, *Race and Reunion*, chs. 6 and 8.

22. Bigelow, *William Conant Church and the* Army & Navy Journal, 166–67; Church, "War & Peace," 761.

23. "'Sah-Junt' Is Supreme," *Army and Navy Journal*, January 5, 1918, 684.

24. "National Rifle Association Proclaims 'No Color Bar,'" *The Chicago Defender*, December 6, 1947, 7; "Black Panthers and Blind Kittens," *The American Rifleman* 118, no. 9 (1970): 20; Keefe, "The Buffalo Soldier Rides Forever," 26–27; Kopel, Gallant, and Eisen, "Ambrose E. Burnside," 24–27.

25. "National Rifle Association Proclaims 'No Color Bar,'" 7; "2,000 to Start Training Today at Camp Smith: 102d Medical Regiment, 10th Infantry to Open National Guard Season Cavalry at Pine Plains 102d Engineers Triumph in State Rifle Match," *New York Herald Tribune* (1926–1962), June 14, 1936, 12; "Jersey National Guard Closes Another Highly Successful Training Season at Sea Girt: Last Two Units To Break Camp Start for Home . . . Only Late Encampment of Negro Militia Remains," *New York Herald Tribune*, August 30, 1936, 30; "Negro Gun Clubs Cause of Concern in Congress," *Chicago Daily Defender (Daily Edition)* (1960-1973), April 8, 1964, 23.

26. "Mayor Reed Shot Well: Manchester Official and Middlesex Traps . . . of 12 Chosen to Shoot at Sea Girt Two Are Negros One Is Porto Rican," *Boston Daily Globe* (1872-1922), July 22, 1906, 9; Hanson W. Baldwin, "Rifle Championship Is Sought by 1,728 . . . Groups Are Composite of Chinese and Hawaiians, Brokers and Bricklayers Are on Camp Perry Firing Lane," *New York Times*, September 10, 1931, 16. For examples of press mentions of Black National Guardsmen in rifle training or competition at the

state level, see "Captain Kellner Wins Cascade Rifle Match," *The Sun* (Baltimore, Md.) (1837–1995), August 9, 1931, 12.

27. Bernard C. Nalty and Morris J. MacGregor, *Blacks in the Military: Essential Documents* (Wilmington, DE: Scholarly Resources, Inc., 1981).

28. Bruce A. Glasrud, ed., *Brothers to the Buffalo Soldiers: Perspectives on African-American Militia and Volunteers, 1865–1917* (Columbia: University of Missouri Press, 2011).

29. Laura Browder, *Her Best Shot: Women and Guns in America* (Chapel Hill: University of North Carolina Press, 2006).

30. Content analysis of the *American Rifleman* from the 1960s shows that mentions of the word "lady" or "ladies" were frequently associated with formal events for NRA leaders' spouses, such as the "Ladies Luncheon." "Ladies' Day at Creedmoor: The Director of the National Rifle Association Entertaining the Ladies," *New York Times*, June 27, 1878, 3; "Rifle Range and Gallery: Pertaining to Rifle Shooting," *Forest and Stream; A Journal of Outdoor Life, Travel, Nature Study, Shooting, Fishing, Yachting* (1873–1930), August 27, 1910, 352; Rodengen, *NRA: An American Legend*, 50, 117, 27–32.

31. NRA Convention Advertisement, Notes from Other Conventions, *The American Rifleman* 99, no. 9 (1951): 29.

32. National Rifle Association, *Address, Annual Reports, and Regulation for Rifle Practice, 1873–1878* (New York: Raynold & Whelpley, 1877), 19–21.

33. For example, see the Colt ad in the July 1951 issue of *The American Rifleman* 99, no. 11 (1951).

34. Rodengen, *NRA: An American Legend*, 117. This NRA-sponsored book makes it a point to highlight prominent women associated with NRA shooting events or the NRA leadership. "Girl Shooter in Third Place Tie," *Boston Daily Globe*, September 18, 1923, 15; "Three Possibles Dethrone Girl Pistol Champion: Al Hemming Beats Gloria Jacobs by Point; Walsh Wins Again," *The Hartford Courant*, July 6, 1940, 4; William McDonald, "Sharp Shooter," *The Sun* (Baltimore, MD), March 7, 1948, 145.

35. "Shooting Champs," *The American Rifleman* 101, no. 8 (1953): 22–23—"Maryland's attractive Maria Hulseman will run up against tough competition."

36. "Shooting Champs," 22–23.

37. "Hale Trophy for Jersey Marksmen," *The Trenton Times*, August 29, 1906, 2. Over the years, a very small number of women participated in civilian competitions, and their names were mentioned in the *American Rifleman*.

38. The collection only misses 1945, which was not available through interlibrary loan. Some individual issues across the years were also not available. For some years, the NRA published only eleven issues, with November/December or June/July issues combined in one.

39. "Urban Gun Enthusiast and NRA Commentator Colion Noir with America's Rifle: The AR-15," *America's 1st Freedom* 17, no. 8 (2016): cover. "Urban" is a common implicit reference to African American communities—a "dog whistle" or covert way to express derogation without using racial epithets.

40. Two-time National Women's Pistol Champion Lt. Gail N. Liberty of the US Air Force, in a picture supplied by the Air Force, *The American Rifleman* 112, no. 5 (1964): cover.

41. Ms. Judy Warden, nineteen, a June bride on her honeymoon, shot skeet at Tupelo, Mississippi—*The American Rifleman* 116, no. 10 (1968); an unnamed visitor to the

Smoky Mountain Gun Collectors booth at the NRA Annual Meetings and Exhibit, *The American Rifleman* 115, no. 6 (1967).

42. "All 19 ladies shown competed at Camp Perry this year. Top left, Mrs. Lillian Geer, an English grandmother, talks rifles with Sharon Hickey, 9, of Anchorage, Alaska, probably the youngest regular smallbore competitor.... The dazzling ladies in red, the Pistolettes of the Tonawandas Sportsmen's Club, Buffalo, NY, shot in regular team competition mostly with Hi-Standards," *The American Rifleman* 119, no. 10 (1971); "Mary Keys of Springfield, Va., was one of the star smallbore performers at the National Championships.... An All-American in her second year at East Tennessee State University," *The American Rifleman* 120, no. 10 (1972); Olympic medalists, *The American Rifleman* 132, nos. 9 and 10 (1984); "Karen Monez of Weatherford, Tex.... the first woman to win the smallbore rifle three-position national championship," *The American Rifleman* 134, no. 10 (1987).

43. "Kim Rhode, at age 17, became the youngest woman shooter ever to win an Olympic Gold Medal. She earned her gold in Atlanta in 1996. For more on Kim, who symbolizes the best and brightest of NRA's future, turn to Wayne LaPierre's column on p. 10," *The American Rifleman* 144, no. 3 (1997).

44. *The American Rifleman* 144, no. 7 (1997); *The American Rifleman* 140, no. 4 (1993); *The American Rifleman* 144, no. 9 (1997).

45. *The American Rifleman* 140, no. 10 (1993); *The American Rifleman* 141, no. 1 (1994).

46. *The American Rifleman* 151, no. 12 (2004); *The American Rifleman* 154, no. 3 (2007); *The American Rifleman*, 153, no. 11 (2006).

47. *The American Rifleman*, 112, no. 5 (1964).

48. "McCain-Palin vs. Obama-Biden: A Clear Choice for Gun Owners," *The American Rifleman* 155, no. 11 (2008), 62. According to Nielsen, 38.4 million people watched Obama's speech, compared to 37.2 million who watched Palin's. Leigh Holmwood, "Sarah Palin Republican Convention Speech Watched by 37 million in US," *The Guardian*, September 5, 2008, https://www.theguardian.com/media/2008/sep/05/ustelevision.tvratings. John McCain announced Sarah Palin's nomination as his Vice President on August 29, 2008. Yet, the *American Rifleman* mentions her only in the November and December issues, whereas McCain is mentioned in the August, September, and October issues as well.

49. "Shaneen Allen: Single Mother, Lawful Citizen, Gun Owner and ... Prisoner of New Jersey," *America's 1st Freedom* 15, no. 10 (2014): cover.

50. "Genocide Begins with Gun Bans," *America's 1st Freedom* 7, no. 8 (2006): cover.

CHAPTER 7

1. Mike McIntire, Glenn Thrush, and Eric Lipton, "Gun Sellers' Message to Americans: Man Up," *New York Times*, June 18, 2022, https://www.nytimes.com/2022/06/18/us/firearm-gun-sales.html.

2. Jack E. Owen, "The Influence of Warfare in Colonial America: On the Development of British Light Infantry," *Army History* 44 (1998): 20–30; Priya Satia, *Empire of Guns: The Violent Making of the Industrial Revolution* (Palo Alto, CA: Stanford University Press, 2018).

3. C. B. Lister, "Our Responsibility," *The American Rifleman* 89, no. 6 (1941): 4.

4. "The Value of Marksmanship," *Arms and the Man* 62, no. 3 (1917): 46.

5. C. B. Lister, "Independence Day 1776–1940," *The American Rifleman* 88, no. 7 (1940): 2.

6. Kathleen Belew, *Bring the War Home: The White Power Movement and Paramilitary America* (Cambridge, MA: Harvard University Press, 2018); James W. Gibson, *Warrior Dreams: Paramilitary Culture in Post-Vietnam America* (New York: Hill and Wang, 1994). The NRA was never a contemporaneous critic of that war. As an establishment organization, it was more concerned with the accuracy of the weapons used on the battlefield. See E. H. Harrison, "What's Ahead for the M16? An Expert Takes a Look," *The American Rifleman* 136, no. 1 (1968).

7. Francis Fukuyama, "The End of History?" *The National Interest* 16 (1989): 3–18.

8. Jennifer Carlson, *Citizen-Protectors: The Everyday Politics of Guns in an Age of Decline* (New York: Oxford University Press, 2015).

9. Jeffrey L. Rodengen, *NRA: An American Legend* (Ft. Lauderdale, FL: Write Stuff Enterprises, 2002), 149.

10. Wayne LaPierre, "Standing Guard: Looking at the Map You Understand the Power of Your Presence in America," *America's 1st Freedom* 2, no. 1 (2001): 10.

11. Charlton Heston, "President's Column," *America's 1st Freedom* 2, no. 1 (2001): 12.

12. David Cole, "Mandatory Firearms Training?—What If We Had Mandatory Free Speech Training," *Ammoland Shooting Sports News*, June 13, 2014, https://www.ammoland.com/2014/06/mandatory-firearms-training/#axzz6wMruQbjY.

13. Interestingly, the exception to mandatory firearms training and government involvement that comes in the form of subsidies is schools. In the wake of the Newtown shooting which led to the death of dozens of primary school children, the NRA suggested mandatory shooting and firearms safety training for school-age children—regardless of whether their parents approve. The NRA also proposed federal subsidies to support ranges and to purchase ammunition for shooting clubs. See Kayla Ruble, "NRA Commentator Suggests Mandatory Gun Training in Schools," *Vice. com*, July 24, 2014, https://www.vice.com/en/article/qvamj7/nra-commentator-suggests-mandatory-gun-training-in-schools. More recently, states have started to reduce the number of training hours required for teachers carrying firearms at schools.

14. John R. Lott Jr., "Reducing Access to Guns Makes People Sitting Prey," *America's 1st Freedom* 2, no. 1 (2001): 72. The US Supreme Court in *Heller* agreed with the view that requirements to keep arms unloaded and locked constituted undue interference with the exercise of one's right to self-defense. "We must also address the District's requirement (as applied to respondent's handgun) that firearms in the home be rendered and kept inoperable at all times. This makes it impossible for citizens to use them for the core lawful purpose of self-defense and is hence unconstitutional."

15. Wayne LaPierre, *Guns, Rights, and Terrorism* (Nashville, TN: Thomas Nelson, Inc., 2003), 124–25.

16. Mary E. Aitken et al., "Parents' Perspectives on Safe Storage of Firearms," *Journal of Community Health* 45, no. 3 (2020); Erin Renee Morgan, Anthony Gomez, and Ali Rowhani-Rahbar, "Firearm Ownership, Storage Practices, and Suicide Risk Factors in Washington State, 2013–2016," *American Journal of Public Health* 108, no. 7 (2018): 37–43; Erin R. Morgan et al., "Firearm Storage and Adult Alcohol Misuse among Washington State Households with Children," *JAMA Pediatrics* 173, no. 1 (2019): 882–88.

17. Lister, "Our Responsibility," 4.

18. Lister, 4.

19. Louis F. Lucas, "A Place to Shoot," *The American Rifleman* 108, no. 8 (1960): 16.

20. Lister, "Our Responsibility," 4; C. B. Lister, "Powder Smoke: Fire Power," *The American Rifleman* 88, no. 1 (1940): 4.

21. Bill Shadel, "Report to Riflemen," *The American Rifleman* 93, no. 7 (1945): 23.

22. Lister, "Powder Smoke: Fire Power," 4.

23. Corp. Jim Norington, "From the Ground Up," Letter to the Editor, *The American Rifleman* 91, no. 4 (1943): 39.

24. Bill Shadel, "Where Are the Riflemen?" *The American Rifleman* 93, no. 5 (1945): 6-7, 13.

25. Frank G. McGuire, "Snipers—Specialists in Warfare," *The American Rifleman* 115, no. 7 (1967): 28-29.

26. Lister, "Powder Smoke: Fire Power," 4.

27. Lister, "Our Responsibility," 4.

28. Lister, 4.

29. Lister, 4.

30. Norington, "From the Ground Up," 39.

31. Tom Clancy, "Foreword," in *NRA: An American Legend*, ed. Jeffrey L. Rodengen (Ft. Lauderdale, FL: Write Stuff Enterprises, 2002), ix.

32. Louis F. Lucas, "The Future of Firearms in America," *The American Rifleman* 108, no. 5 (1960): 18.

33. C. C. Finn, "Letter to the Editor," *Arms and the Man* 68 (1920): 13.

34. Charles Atwell and Marvin Rapp, "Buckskin Rifleman," *The American Rifleman* 91, no. 11 (1943): 6-8.

35. William D. Adler, *Engineering Expansion: The U.S. Army and Economic Development, 1787-1860* (Philadelphia: University of Pennsylvania Press, 2021); Heather Cox Richardson, *West from Appomattox: The Reconstruction of America after the Civil War* (New Haven, CT: Yale University Press, 2007).

36. Col. Charles Askins, "Close Encounters of the Right Kind," *The American Rifleman* 132, no. 9 (1984): 36-37; Ashley Halsey, "The Air Gun of Lewis and Clark," *The American Rifleman* 132, no. 8 (1984): 36-37, 80.

37. "90th NRA Annual Meetings & Exhibit: The Guest Speaker," *The American Rifleman* 109, no. 6 (1961): 27.

38. Satia, *Empire of Guns*.

39. Atwell and Rapp, "Buckskin Rifleman," 6-8.

40. Satia, *Empire of Guns*; Kevin M. Sweeney, "Firearms Ownership and Militias in Seventeenth- and Eighteenth-Century England and America," in *A Right to Bear Arms? The Contested Role of History in Contemporary Debates on the Second Amendment*, ed. Jennifer Tucker, Barton C. Hacker, and Margaret Vining (Washington, DC: Smithsonian Scholarly Press, 2019), 54-71.

41. Sweeney, "Firearms Ownership and Militias," 54-71.

42. Satia, *Empire of Guns*.

43. Clancy, "Foreword," ix.

44. Rejections of Indian claims to land predate the early nineteenth century. In fact, conflict between colonists who speculated on land west of the Appalachians and the British authorities who had agreed on a ban on speculation in Western lands in exchange for Native American cooperation contributed to the grievances that led to the American Revolution. See Woody Holton, *Forced Founders: Indians, Debtors, Slaves, and the Making of the American Revolution* (Chapel Hill: University of North Carolina

Press, 1999), ch. 1; Alan Taylor, *American Revolutions: A Continental History, 1750–1804* (New York: W. W. Norton & Co., 2016).

45. "Your Fellow Sportsmen (NRA Membership Application)," *The American Rifleman* 105, no. 7 (1957).

46. Gary Lantz, "Confessions of a Gun Nut," *America's 1st Freedom* 3, no. 8 (2002): 28–30.

47. Clancy, "Foreword," ix.

48. Clancy, "Foreword," vii. It is telling that even in 2002, this NRA-promoted book ignored Native Americans' claims to Western lands and insisted that this was land without titles.

49. John Hope Franklin, *The Militant South* (Cambridge, MA: The Belknap Press of Harvard University Press, 1956); Harry S. Laver, *Citizens More Than Soldiers: The Kentucky Militia and Society in the Early Republic* (Lincoln: University of Nebraska Press, 2007); Satia, *Empire of Guns*.

50. Richard Uviller and William G. Merkel, *The Militia and the Right to Arms, or How the Second Amendment Fell Silent* (Durham, NC: Duke University Press, 2003), 285–86; Sweeney, "Firearms Ownership and Militias," 54–71.

51. Lantz, "Confessions of a Gun Nut," 28–30.

52. Jon Hurwitz and Mark Peffley, "Playing the Race Card in the Post–Willie Horton Era: The Impact of Racialized Code Words on Support for Punitive Crime Policy," *Public Opinion Quarterly* 69, no. 1 (2005): 99–112.

53. C. B. Lister, "All to the Good," *The American Rifleman* 98, no. 6 (1950): 10; Thomas L. Washington, "The President's Column," *The American Rifleman* 142, no. 8 (1994): 60.

54. National Rifle Association, *Americans and Their Guns: The National Rifle Association Story through Nearly a Century of Service to the Nation* (Harrisburg, PA: Stackpole Company, 1967), 10–17.

55. LaPierre, "Standing Guard," 10.

56. C. B. Lister, "The Most Uncommon Thing," *The American Rifleman* 89, no. 3 (1941): 4.

57. Tali Mendelberg, *The Race Card: Campaign Strategy, Implicit Messages, and the Norm of Equality* (Princeton, NJ: Princeton University Press, 2001); Mark Peffley and Jon Hurwitz, *Justice in America: The Separate Realities of Blacks and Whites* (New York: Cambridge University Press, 2010).

58. Lucas, "The Future of Firearms in America," 11.

59. "90th NRA Annual Meetings & Exhibit," 27. The title of the article includes the phrase "The Guest Speaker"

60. "Letters to the Editor," *The American Rifleman* 127, no. 5 (1979): 6.

61. Askins, "Close Encounters of the Right Kind," 71.

62. Charlton Heston, *The Courage to Be Free* (Kansas City, KS: Saudade Press, 2000), 41.

63. Lantz, "Confessions of a Gun Nut," 28–30.

64. NRA, *Americans and Their Guns*, 10–17.

65. David R. Roediger, *The Wages of Whiteness: Race and the Making of the American Working Class* (New York: Verso Books, 2003).

66. Louis F. Lucas, "Build NRA," *The American Rifleman* 108, no. 1 (1960): 14.

67. "The NRA and Civil Defense," *The American Rifleman* 98, no. 11 (1950): 34.

68. Willis Mason West, *American History and Government* (Boston: Allyn & Bacon, 1913).

69. James Fenimore Cooper, *The Leatherstocking Tales* (New York: D. Appleton & Company, 1873); Atwell and Rapp, "Buckskin Rifleman." For one account of the atrocities committed against Natives by White settlers, see Taylor, *American Revolutions.* The frontiersman myth also ignores the role the US Army, the Regulars, played in Western expansion. See Adler, *Engineering Expansion.*

70. George C. Neumann, "Firearms of the American Revolution, Part I," *The American Rifleman* 115, no. 7 (1967): 17.

71. Otis Williams, "A Better Hunt," *The American Rifleman* 104, no. 11 (1956): 50–51.

72. West, *American History and Government*, 146. Also see NRA, *Americans and Their Guns*, 10–17; Robert J. Spitzer, *The Politics of Gun Control*, 4th edition (Washington, DC: CQ Press, 2008 [1995]).

73. McGuire, "Snipers—Specialists in Warfare," 28–29; James E. Serven, "Powder Horns with a Message," *The American Rifleman* 108, no. 12 (1960): 33–35; James E. Serven, "Theodore Roosevelt," *The American Rifleman* 112, no. 8 (1964): 51–53; Glenn R. Vernam, "Granddad Was a Realist," *The American Rifleman* 93, no. 8 (1945): 26–27.

74. Col. H. P. Sheldon, "The New Rifle," *The American Rifleman* 88, no. 1 (1940): 5.

75. Heston, *The Courage to Be Free*, ch. 7, "Dr. King Didn't Dream of Ice-T." "Rap often celebrates the violence of inner-city neighborhoods, and some black performers excel at it, while greedy entertainment magnates rake in millions from the messages of hate and promiscuity it often inspires."

76. In a discussion of Native Americans in Brazil, a 1954 *American Rifleman* article noted that "It seems the Indians were a lazy lot, content to knock off work for the rest of their lives as soon as they had acquired the most prized possession in the jungle, a rifle. Unfortunately for this rosy philosophy, the big rubber plantations demanded a steady labor supply. Still the Indians refused to work once they 'had earned money enough to buy' a rifle. The noble-minded plantation owners hit on a very simple solution. They introduced the 'trade gun' as the standard wage for their laborers. This was a calculatedly inferior weapon designed to be utterly worthless after 40 or 50 rounds were fired. Even though a poor peon might retire for a while after he'd earned his rifle, sooner or later he'd be back when his weapon had spent its short life." Richard M. Detwiler, "Shooting Money," *The American Rifleman* 102, no. 8 (1954): 36–37.

77. "Shooting Clubs and National Defense," *The American Rifleman* 112, no. 8 (1964): 16.

78. Lister, "The Most Uncommon Thing," 4.

79. "Year Marked by Increased Strength and Activity," *The American Rifleman* 101, no. 5 (1953): 13–15.

80. "Universal Service and the Emergency," *Arms and the Man* 62, no. 2 (1917): 28–29. The NRA strongly disapproved of the Selective Service Act, which established the draft in World War I.

81. "Hold Fast!" *The American Rifleman* 88, no. 11 (1940): 8.

82. NRA, *Americans and Their Guns*, 10–17.

83. "Year Marked by Increased Strength and Activity," 13–15.

84. See, for example, William C. Church, "What Constitutes 'Militarism'?" *The American Army & Navy Journal*, October 3, 1914; Garrett Underhill, "Under the Red Star: The Russian Rifle," *The American Rifleman* 89, no. 8 (1941): 7–12.

85. Lt. John Scofield, "The Implements of War: Children of the Sun," *The American Rifleman* 89, no. 2 (1941): 27–33; NRA, *Report of the National Rifle Association of America, A Patriotic Association* (New York: National Rifle Association, 1902); NRA, *Annual Report of the National Rifle Association of America* (no publisher, 1905).

86. Scofield, "The Implements of War," 27.

87. Scofield, 29.

88. C. B. Lister, "Unpleasant Facts," *The American Rifleman* 93, no. 9 (1945): 5. The *American Rifleman* accused the Army of operating based "cliques," such as Annapolis and West Point, that prioritized their own interests over the public good and thus opposed universal service. This sharp criticism of the Army is quite unusual given the tight relationship between the NRA and the US military establishment. This may have contributed to the loosening of ties between the two that is observed in the postwar era. C. B. Lister, "Officer Education," *The American Rifleman* 93, no. 10 (1945): 5.

89. Shadel, "Report to Riflemen," 23. This is the only mention of concentration camps that I found in the magazine.

90. C. B. Lister, "Universal Service," *The American Rifleman* 93, no. 1 (1945): 5; C. B. Lister, "Universal Military Service," *The American Rifleman* 93, no. 2 (1945): 5; C. B. Lister, "False Conception," *The American Rifleman* 93, no. 3 (1945): 5; C. B. Lister, "Fog of Words," *The American Rifleman* 93, no. 7 (1945): 5.

91. Lister, "False Conception," 5.

92. C. B. Lister, "Veterans' Return," *The American Rifleman* 93, no. 8 (1945): 5.

93. Heston, *The Courage to Be Free*; Wayne LaPierre, *Guns, Crime and Freedom* (Downers Grove, IL: Liberty Group, 2011 [1994]).

94. Donald R. Kinder and Lynn M. Sanders, *Divided by Color* (Chicago: University of Chicago Press, 1996).

95. "Law and Order," *The American Rifleman* 112, no. 7 (1964): 16; Heston, *The Courage to Be Free*.

96. Lt. Col. Walter Stokes, "The Business of Flinching," *The American Rifleman* 93, no. 7 (1945): 14–15.

97. "The Misuse of Firearms," *The American Rifleman* 112, no. 3 (1964): 16.

98. Lister, "Our Responsibility"; Raymond J. Stan, "The NRA and National Defense," *The American Rifleman* 89, no. 9 (1941): 7–9; "The Faces of the Opposition," *The American Rifleman* 115, no. 11 (1967): 18.

99. Louis F. Lucas, "Firearms and Public Opinion," *The American Rifleman* 108, no. 2 (1960); C. B. Lister, "Politics and Propaganda," *The American Rifleman* 88, no. 9 (1940); "The U.S. Justice Department, Izvestia, and the *New Yorker*," *The American Rifleman* 116, no. 6 (1968).

100. Lucas, "Firearms and Public Opinion," 14.

101. Heston, *The Courage to Be Free*, 33.

102. Lantz, "Confessions of a Gun Nut," 28–30.

103. "The Illegal Use of Guns," *The American Rifleman* 112, no. 12 (1964): 16.

104. Lucas, "Firearms and Public Opinion," 14.

105. "The Armed Citizen," *The American Rifleman* 113, no. 11 (1965): 17.

106. Lucas, "Firearms and Public Opinion," 14.

107. "Good-by Guns? [*sic*]," *The American Rifleman* 108, no. 12 (1960): 11.

108. Lucas, "The Future of Firearms in America," 11. Already in 1960, the NRA seemed to imply that there are categories of facts, and "true facts" is one such cat-

egory. This type of distinction became crucial in the Trump era politics of "alternative facts."

109. Joseph B. Stevens, "Pick Up Your Pen," *The American Rifleman* 118, no. 3 (1950): 31.

110. Maj. Gen. Bryce Poe, "Before You Write That Letter," *The American Rifleman* 108, no. 1 (1960): 46. These articles caution voters to be exceedingly deferential and polite to legislators—a major change to the contemporary, highly contentious, and even violent discourse.

111. "Good-by Guns? [*sic*]," 11.

112. "Inform Your Legislator," *The American Rifleman* 109, no. 1 (1961): 8.

CHAPTER 8

1. The role of the criminal trope, including its racialized connotations, in gun culture and gun narratives has been the subject of several studies. See for example: Alexandra Filindra and Noah J. Kaplan, "Racial Resentment and Whites' Gun Policy Preferences in Contemporary America," *Political Behavior* 38, no. 2 (2016): 255–75; Alexandra Filindra, Noah J. Kaplan, and Beyza Buyuker, "Racial Resentment or Modern Sexism? White Americans' Outgroup Attitudes as Predictors of Gun Ownership, Rationales for Ownership, & NRA Membership," *Sociological Inquiry* 91, no. 2 (2021): 253–86; Jennifer Carlson, "Police Warriors and Police Guardians: Race, Masculinity, and the Construction of Gun Violence," *Social Problems* 67, no. 3 (2019): 399–417. I pay less attention to the indirect role of criminals in fomenting corruption within the Republic.

2. Maj. Gen. Bryce Poe, "Before You Write That Letter," *The American Rifleman* 108, no. 1 (1960): 46.

3. David J. Garrow, *The FBI and Martin Luther King, Jr.: From Solo to Memphis* (New York: Open Road, 2015); Peniel E. Joseph, *Waiting 'Til the Midnight Hour* (New York: Henry Holt & Co., 2007); Kenneth O'Reilly, "The FBI and the Civil Rights Movement during the Kennedy Years—From the Freedom Rides to Albany," *The Journal of Southern History* 54, no. 2 (1988): 201–32; US Department of Justice, Short Report Submitted to Congress by Attorney General A. Mitchell Palmer, November 15, 1919, "A Report on the Investigation Activities of the Department of Justice: Letter from the Attorney General Transmitting in Response to a Senate Resolution of October 17, 1919, a Report on the Activities of the Bureau of Investigation of the Department of Justice against Persons Advising Anarchy, Sedition, and the Forcible Overthrow of the Government," 66th Congress, 1st session, Senate document (Washington, DC: G.P.O., 1919), https://libproxy.berkeley.edu/login?qurl=https%3A%2F%2Fwww.heinonline .org%2FHOL%2FPage%3Fhandle%3Dhein.beal%2Finaclett0001%26id%3D1 %26collection%3Dbeal%26index%3Dbeal.

4. Carlson, "Police Warriors and Police Guardians," 399–417.

5. "The Faces of the Opposition," *The American Rifleman* 115, no. 11 (1967): 18.

6. "Hoplophobia: A Modern Scourge," GunLaws.com, n.d., https://www.gunlaws .com/GunPhobia.htm. The term "hoplophobe" is attributed to gun rights activist Jeff Cooper and is defined in Jeff Cooper, *Fireworks* (Sommerville, MA: Wisdom Publishing, 2021 [1980]). Hoplophobia is "an unreasoning, obsessive neurotic fear of weapons as such, usually accompanied by an irrational feeling that weapons possess a will or consciousness for evil, apart from the will of their user. Not equivalent to normal

apprehension in the presence of an armed enemy." Sarah Thompson, *Hoplophobia Explored—Raging against Self Defense: A Psychiatrist Examines the Anti-Gun Mentality* (Hartford, WI: Jews for the Preservation of Firearms Ownership, 2000); https://www.gunlaws.com/Hoplophobia%20Analysis.htm.

7. "Alabama Legislature Opposes Dodd Bill," *The American Rifleman* 115, no. 8 (1967): 55.

8. Mark Chesnut, "Proud to Stand with NRA," *America's 1st Freedom* 17, no. 8 (2016): 6.

9. "Alabama Legislature Opposes Dodd Bill," 55.

10. "Realistic Firearm Controls," *The American Rifleman* 112, no. 1 (1964).

11. "Why Americans Own, Shoot, and Collect Guns," *The American Rifleman* 111, no. 4 (1963): 12.

12. "How the 1968 Gun Act Creates 'Criminals,'" *The American Rifleman* 119, no. 10 (1971): 20.

13. "Neuroticism in Chicago," *The American Rifleman* 116, no. 10 (1968): 13.

14. Harlon B. Carter, "Unity: Key to Defeat of Prop. 15," *The American Rifleman* 131, no. 1 (1983): 18–19.

15. "A Knowledge of Existing Laws," *The American Rifleman* 111, no. 3 (1963): 12; "Why Americans Own, Shoot, and Collect Guns," 12.

16. Irvine Reynolds, "Gun Controls and the News Media," *The American Rifleman* 122, no. 11 (1974): 42–43.

17. "Inform Your Legislator," *The American Rifleman* 109, no. 1 (1961): 8.

18. C. B. Lister, "Training—How Long?" *The American Rifleman* 93, no. 6 (1945): 5.

19. Joseph B. Stevens, "Pick Up Your Pen," *The American Rifleman* 118, no. 3 (1950): 31.

20. W. Roy Hunt, "These Policemen Teach Teen-Agers to Be Straight Shooters," *Guns* 6, no. 4 (1960): 16–18.

21. Frank C. Daniel, "The Gun Law Problem," *The American Rifleman* 101, no. 2 (1953): 16–18.

22. Daniel K. Stern, "Winning Public Support for Shooting," *The American Rifleman* 108, no. 5 (1960): 53–54.

23. Charlton Heston, *The Courage to Be Free* (Kansas City, KS: Saudade Press, 2000), 20.

24. "A National Sullivan Law," *Arms and the Man* 68, no. 14 (1920): 8.

25. "The Faces of the Opposition," 18.

26. Louis F. Lucas, "The Future of Firearms in America," *The American Rifleman* 108, no. 5 (1960): 11.

27. Gary Lantz, "Confessions of a Gun Nut," *America's 1st Freedom* 3, no. 8 (2002): 28–30.

28. "Cam's Corner: Stand Tall, NRA Members," *America's 1st Freedom* 19, no. 5 (2018): 20.

29. "The Faces of the Opposition," 18.

30. Carter, "Unity: Key to Defeat of Prop. 15," 18–19. Also see Tom Clancy, "Foreword," in *NRA: An American Legend*, ed. Jeffrey L. Rodengen (Ft. Lauderdale, FL: Write Stuff Enterprises, 2002), ix: "the ones who dislike the idea of [civilian-owned] firearms are those who, unlike Jefferson, do not think the average citizen can be trusted."

31. Dr. Michael S. Brown, "New Anti-Gun Strategy Doomed to Fail," *America's 1st Freedom* 2, no. 1 (2001): 14.

32. Bob Boatman, "The American Gun Show Heritage," *America's 1st Freedom* 2, no. 1 (2001): 54–56.

33. C. B. Lister, "Guns and Butter," *The American Rifleman* 98, no. 9 (1950): 10.

34. C. B. Lister, "Re-Dedication," *The American Rifleman* 89, no. 5 (1941): 4.

35. "Alabama Legislature Opposes Dodd Bill," 55.

36. "Logic and Reason," *The American Rifleman* 110, no. 2 (1962): 16.

37. Heston, *The Courage to Be Free*, 20–25.

38. Stacy Washington, "Stacy on the Outs," *America's 1st Freedom* 18, no. 7 (2017): 33–36.

39. Wayne LaPierre, "Standing Guard: Looking at the Map You Understand the Power of Your Presence in America," Standing Guard, *America's 1st Freedom* 2, no. 1 (2001): 10.

40. "Political Ad," *America's 1st Freedom* 4, no. 1 (2004): 37-38.

41. Heston, *The Courage to Be Free*, 20.

42. LaPierre, "Looking at the Map," 10.

43. Hamilton v. Accu-Tek, 62 F. Supp. 2d 802 (EDNY 1999); James O. E. Norell, "Judge Dred: Activist U.S. District Court Judge Jack Weinstein . . . Will Be on the Bench for the NAACP Lawsuit," *America's 1st Freedom* 4, no. 5 (2003): 48–50; Timothy D. Lytton, *Suing the Gun Industry: A Battle at the Crossroads of Gun Control and Mass Torts* (Ann Arbor: University of Michigan Press, 2009).

44. Alex Yablon, "George Soros Is Not the Gun Grabber the NRA Says He Is," *The Trace*, November 6, 2018, https://www.thetrace.org/newsletter/soros-not-the-gun -grabber-nra-says-he-is.

45. James O. E. Norell, "Hypocrisy: George Soros' Anti-Gun Vision for America," *The American Rifleman* 152, no. 4 (2004): 16, 82.

46. James Jay Baker, "Voting Freedom First," *America's 1st Freedom* 2, no. 1 (2001): 28–29. Soros has argued in favor of regulated capitalism. See George Soros, "The Capitalist Threat," *Atlantic*, February 1997, https://www.theatlantic.com/magazine/ archive/1997/02/the-capitalist-threat/376773.

47. "How Bad Can He Be?" *America's 1st Freedom* 5, no. 11 (2004): 40–41.

48. Norell, "Hypocrisy," 16, 82.

49. Wayne LaPierre, "Standing Guard: Michael Moore's Mob Is Being Harnessed into a One-Time Voting Block," *The American Rifleman* 152, no. 9 (2004): 10.

50. Stephen Eric Bronner, *A Rumor about the Jews: Antisemitism, Conspiracy, and the Protocols of Zion* (New York: Oxford University Press, 2000).

51. "How Bad Can He Be?" 40–41.

52. LaPierre, "Standing Guard: Michael Moore's Mob," 10.

53. Wayne LaPierre, "Standing Guard: The Radical Left Hates What George W. Bush Represents," *The American Rifleman* 152, no. 8 (2004): 10.

54. Norell, "Hypocrisy," 16, 82.

55. "The Private Army Hoax," *The American Rifleman* 112, no. 9 (1965): 16.

56. "United We Stand," *The American Rifleman* 113, no. 1 (1965): 16.

57. C. B. Lister, "Happy New Year," *The American Rifleman* 98, no. 1 (1950): 10.

58. Karen Mehall, "Letter from the Editors," *America's 1st Freedom* 2, no. 1 (2001): 6.

59. Lister, "Happy New Year," 10.

60. C. B. Lister, "Politics and Propaganda," *The American Rifleman* 88, no. 9 (1940): 4.

61. C. B. Lister, "Invasion," *The American Rifleman* 91, no. 2 (1943): 11.

62. Wayne LaPierre, "In Today's Democratic Party, Democrat Equals Socialist," *America's 1st Freedom* 19, no. 3 (2018): 8.

63. Ashley Halsey, "Those Irrepressible 'Rules for Revolution,'" *The American Rifleman* 118, no. 9 (1970): 10. In the article, the NRA acknowledges that the "Rules" were a hoax, but also suggests that C. B. Lister published an article in the August 1946 issue of the *American Rifleman* in which he suggested that the document was authentic. According to the *New York Times*, extreme right groups of the 1960s such as the John Birch Society, and several racist and anti-Semitic publications, popularized the document again in the post–Civil Rights era. The document became so popular that in 1970 it could be found on the bulletin boards of local police stations. Donald Janson, "Communist 'Rules' for Revolt Viewed as Durable Fraud," *New York Times*, July 10, 1970, 1. The "Rules" have persisted to this day and there is even a self-published book on the subject dated 2020, by an author of multiple conspiracy-oriented books.

64. Ashley Halsey, "Look Who Opposes Civilian Marksmanship," *The American Rifleman* 115, no. 8 (1967): 38–40.

65. Wayne LaPierre, "The Coming Socialist Wave That Will Drown Your Guns," *America's 1st Freedom* 19, no. 3 (2018): 32–35.

66. Reynolds, "Gun Controls and the News Media," 42–43.

67. "The Faces of the Opposition," 18.

68. Will N. Graves, "How the Soviet Controls Guns," *The American Rifleman* 115, no. 1 (1967): 42–45.

69. "Gun Control in the Third Reich: Disarming the Jews and 'Enemies of the State,'" *The American Rifleman* 163, no. 3 (2015). The article is a review of Stephen Halbrook's book, which makes the argument that "the Nazi regime made use of gun control to disarm and repress its people and consolidate power." The persecution and extermination of Jews and Hitler's political opponents was possible because these groups could not defend themselves with firearms. See Stephen Halbrook, *Gun Control in the Third Reich: Disarming the Jews and "Enemies of the State"* (Oakland, CA: The Independent Institute, 2013).

70. Graves, "How the Soviet Controls Guns," 42–45; Garrett Underhill, "Under the Red Star: The Russian Rifle," *The American Rifleman* 89, no. 8 (1941): 7–12.

71. Chris W. Cox, "A Freedom Fighter to Never Forget: Otis McDonald (1933–2014)," *The American Rifleman* 162, no. 7 (2014): 15–16.

72. Albert H. Jenkins, "Back of the Soviet 'National Matches,'" *The American Rifleman* 88, no. 6 (1934): 5–8.

73. James O. E. Norell, "The Cover Up," *America's 1st Freedom* 12, no. 10 (2011): 33–36.

74. The NRA repeated charges that the IRS targeted conservative organizations for audit. See Wayne LaPierre, "Stop Obama's Lawlessness," *The American Rifleman* 152, no. 10 (2014): 12.

75. The NRA claims that a UN Arms Trade Treaty to control the proliferation of small arms is an attempt to subvert the US Constitution through international agreements. For about a decade, the organization used the Obama administration's willingness to partake in the treaty as evidence of corruption and tyranny. See Chris W.

Cox, "Vote to Save Us All: Only Pro-Gun Candidates Can Confront Obama's Last Two Years," *The American Rifleman* 152, no. 11 (2014): 66–67; "LaPierre Fights for Gun Owners at United Nations," *America's 1st Freedom* 13, no. 9 (2012): 14.

76. Igor Derysh, "NRA's Silence on Police Violence Is Deafening—Its Members' Attacks on Black Victims Are Worse," *Salon*, July 9, 2020, https://www.salon.com/2020/07/09/nras-silence-on-police-violence-is-deafening--its-members-attacks-on-black-victims-are-worse; Adam Serwer, "The NRA's Catch-22 for Black Men Shot by Police," *Atlantic*, September 13, 2018, https://www.theatlantic.com/ideas/archive/2018/09/the-nras-catch-22-for-black-men-shot-by-police/570124.

77. NRA Staff, "An Attack on Our Cops Is an Attack on All of Us," *America's 1st Freedom* 17, no. 9 (2016): 34–35.

78. Rosalie Chan, "NRA Honors Heroism of Police in Dallas," *Time*, July 8, 2016, https://time.com/4398364/nra-honors-heroism-of-police-in-dallas-shooting.

79. NRA Staff, "An Attack on Our Cops Is an Attack on All of Us," 34–35.

80. Wayne LaPierre, "This Election Year Your NRA Membership Is Obama's Greatest Fear," *The American Rifleman* 162, no. 2 (2014): 49–52; NRA Staff, "An Attack on Our Cops Is an Attack on All of Us," 34–35.

81. Laurie Lee Dovey, "Bushmaster: Military DNA for Hunting, Home, and Competition Arms," *America's 1st Freedom* 11, no. 11 (2010): 52–53; J. Edgar Hoover, "The Shooting FBI," *The American Rifleman* 93, no. 7 (1945): 10–13; Capt. C. M. Kellogg and Maj. A. F. Spring, "Use of Chemicals by Law-Enforcement Officers in Civil Disorders (Part V)," *The American Rifleman* 80, no. 6 (1932): 45–47. This article is part of a series of articles on the topic.

82. See for example the April 1993 cover of *The American Rifleman*, which features ideal-type NRA members, including a police officer. Also see ads included in chapter 5.

83. "The Armed Citizen," *The American Rifleman* 115, no. 1 (1967): 45.

84. Lantz, "Confessions of a Gun Nut," 28–30.

85. Barbara Renner, "Helpless?" *America's 1st Freedom* 3, no. 8 (2002): 27.

86. Kayla Ruble, "NRA Commentator Suggests Mandatory Gun Training in Schools," *Vice. com*, July 24, 2014, https://www.vice.com/en/article/qvamj7/nra-commentator-suggests-mandatory-gun-training-in-schools.

87. These patterns shifted substantially in recent decades. See Carlson, "Police Warriors and Police Guardians."

88. F. A. Sternberg, "Letter to the Editor," *Arms and the Man* 68, no. 19 (1920): 18.

89. Lister, "Invasion," 11.

90. Lister, 11.

91. "A National Sullivan Law," 8.

92. "A Justly Merited Veto," *Arms and the Man* 62, no. 7 (1917): 128.

93. Jac Weller, "The Sullivan Law," *The American Rifleman* 110, no. 4 (1962): 33–34.

94. "A National Sullivan Law." The NRA reversed its position on stricter penalties in the 1930s and to this day remains a strong advocate of very strict criminal penalties for gun crimes.

95. Ashley Halsey, "Who Guards America's Homes?" *The American Rifleman* 115, no. 5 (1967): 16.

96. Lister, "Re-Dedication," 4.

97. Wayne LaPierre, *Guns, Crime and Freedom* (Downers Grove, IL: Liberty Group, 2011 [1994]), 110.

98. "NRA Official Defends Terms Used in Letter," *Washington Post*, May 1, 1995, https://www.washingtonpost.com/archive/politics/1995/05/01/nra-official-defends -terms-used-in-letter/eb75fcd2-faa9-49b9-8f31-04701763b5a1.

99. "The Clinton Gun Card: Go to Jail Without It," *The American Rifleman* 142, no. 2 (1994): 49.

100. LaPierre, *Guns, Crime and Freedom*, 189.

101. Kim Murphy and Kem Ellingwood, "Mexico Demands Answers on Guns," *Los Angeles Times*, March 11, 2011, https://www.latimes.com/archives/la-xpm-2011-mar-11 -la-naw-mexico-guns-20110311-story.html.

102. LaPierre, "Stop Obama's Lawlessness," 12.

103. Wayne LaPierre, "We Must Act to Stop Obama's Transformation of Our Constitution," *The American Rifleman* 162, no. 5 (2014): 12.

104. James W. Porter, "We Must Vote to Preserve the Rule of Law," *The American Rifleman* 162, no. 9 (2014): 14.

105. Jeffrey L. Rodengen, *NRA: An American Legend* (Ft. Lauderdale, FL: Write Stuff Enterprises, 2002), 170.

106. In February through April 1993, the FBI led a siege of the Branch Davidians' compound in Waco, Texas, after charges that the group was amassing weapons and the leader, David Koresh, was sexually abusing minors. The siege concluded with an FBI assault on the compound which led to the deaths of 76 people, including 25 children. On the Waco siege, see "Report of the Department of the Treasury Bureau of Alcohol, Tobacco, and Firearms Investigation of Vernon Wayne Howell Also Known as David Koresh," September (Washington, DC: US Government Printing Office, 1993), https:// ia800209.us.archive.org/17/items/reportofdepartme00unit/reportofdepartme00unit .pdf.

107. "NRA Official Defends Terms Used in Letter."

108. "U.S. Department of Justice, Report of the Ruby Ridge Task Force to the Office of Professional Responsibility of Investigation of Allegations of Improper Governmental Conduct in the Investigation, Apprehension, and Prosecution of Randall C. Weaver and Kevin L. Harris" (Washington, DC: US Government Printing Office, 1994), https://www.justice.gov/sites/default/files/opr/legacy/2006/11/09/rubyreportcover _39.pdf.

109. Jim Oliver, "The Randy Weaver Case: A Federal Fiasco," *The American Rifleman* 141, no. 11 (1993): 40–43.

110. "Ruby Ridge: Federal Law Enforcement on Trial," *The American Rifleman* 144, no. 1 (1996): 32–35, 59–61.

111. Oliver, "The Randy Weaver Case," 40–43.

112. "Ruby Ridge: Federal Law Enforcement on Trial," 32–35, 59–61.

113. Heston, *The Courage to Be Free*, 426–27.

114. LaPierre, *Guns, Crime and Freedom*, 194–95. *The American Rifleman* reprinted a letter from the BATF to the US Attorney's office in Idaho in which Weaver was characterized as "active in White supremacy activities," but without context or commentary. The magazine underlined these words, which clearly suggests that they wanted to focus readers' attention on this dimension of the case. "Ruby Ridge: Federal Law Enforcement on Trial."

115. Mark England and Darlene McCormick, "The Sinful Messiah," *Waco Tribune-Herald*, February 27, 1993, https://wacotrib.com/news/branch_davidians/ sinful-messiah/the-sinful-messiah-part-one/article_eb1b96e9-413c-5bab-ba9f

-425b373c5667.html; Sara Rimer and Sam Howe Verhovek, "Growing Up under Koresh: Cult Children Tell of Abuses," *New York Times*, May 4, 1993; "Report to the Deputy Attorney General on the Events at Waco, Texas: Child Abuse" (Washington, DC: US Department of Justice, 1993), https://www.justice.gov/archives/publications/waco/report-deputy-attorney-general-events-waco-texas-child-abuse.

116. Pierre Thomas, "Waco Probe Faults ATF in Cult Raid," *Washington Post*, September 30, 1993, https://www.washingtonpost.com/archive/politics/1993/09/30/waco-probe-faults-atf-in-cult-raid/3bac3282-43e7-4f39-91ef-3e14be1f24d0/?utm_term=.d62f525313cc; Edward S. G. Dennis, "Evaluation of the Handling of the Branch Davidian Stand-off in Waco, Texas, February 28 to April 19, 1993," US Department of Justice, October 8, 1993, https://www.justice.gov/archives/publications/waco/evaluation-handling-branch-davidian-stand-waco-texas-february-28-april-19-1993.

117. Elizabeth Swasey, "NRA Woman's Voice," *The American Rifleman* 141, no. 10 (1993): 22.

118. Jonathan Mummolo, "Militarization Fails to Enhance Police Safety or Reduce Crime but May Harm Police Reputation," *Proceedings of the National Academy of Sciences* 115, no. 37 (2018): 9181-86.

119. Swasey, "NRA Woman's Voice," 22. The allegation that Texas CPS had found no evidence of child sexual abuse is not true. The US Department of Justice report says: "From Interview by Texas Social Worker Joyce Sparks, Children's Protective Services Investigations supervisor, Waco, interviewed a young girl, a former compound resident, on February 22, 1993: '[She] entered the cult when she was about three or four years old. . . . We asked her if she could think of any reason that any of the children at the compound would not be safe and as we got into this discussion, she brought up the topic of sexual abuse. She described herself as special and treated differently than other children. She talked about spending time alone with David and although this was "scary" she felt "privileged." She explained to us that on one occasion, when she was ten years old, her mother left her in a motel room with David Koresh. He was in bed and he told [her] to come over to him. She got into the bed. David had no pants on. He took off her panties and touched her and then got on top of her.'" See: US Department of Justice, Short Report to the Deputy Attorney General on the Events at Waco, Texas; VII: Child Abuse. See also: Robert K. Corbin, "The President's Column," *The American Rifleman* 142, no. 4 (1994): 49.

120. Corbin, "The President's Column," 49.

121. Corbin, 49.

122. James Boward, "Spawn of Bubba: Just When You Thought It Was Safe to Go to the Polls—Clinton's Minions Rise Up From the Ooze!" *America's 1st Freedom* 3, no. 10 (2002): 53.

123. Ida B. Wells-Barnett, *On Lynchings* (Mineola, NY: Dover Publications, Inc., 2014 [1892]).

124. C. J. Bloom and Waldo E. Martin, *Black against Empire: The History and Politics of the Black Panther Party* (Berkeley: University of California Press, 2016); Cynthia Deitle Leonardatos, "California's Attempts to Disarm the Black Panthers," *San Diego Law Review* 36 (1999): 947-96; Bobby Seale, *Seize the Time: The Story of the Black Panther Party and Huey P. Newton* (Baltimore, MD: Black Classics Press, 1991).

125. Meghan G. McDowell and Luis A. Fernandez, "'Disband, Disempower, and Disarm': Amplifying the Theory and Practice of Police Abolition," *Critical Criminology* 26, no. 3 (2018): 373-91; Paige Fernandez, "Defunding the Police Will Actually Make

Us Safer," *ACLU*, June 11, 2020, https://www.aclu.org/news/criminal-law-reform/defunding-the-police-will-actually-make-us-safer; Rashawn Ray, "What Does 'Defund the Police' Mean and Does It Have Merit?" Brookings, June 19, 2020, https://www.brookings.edu/blog/fixgov/2020/06/19/what-does-defund-the-police-mean-and-does-it-have-merit.

126. NRA Staff, "An Attack on Our Cops is an Attack on All of Us," 34–35.

127. "Black Panthers and Blind Kittens," *The American Rifleman* 118, no. 9 (1970): 20.

128. My review of the *American Rifleman* issues from 1985 to 1995 showed no mention of the MOVE bombing. The racial politics of the MOVE case are complicated. Complaints about the group were issued by Black neighbors, and the order for the bombing was issued by Philadelphia Mayor Goode, who was Black.

129. Lindsay Neward, "The Day Philadelphia Bombed Its Own People," *Vox.com*, August 15, 2019, https://www.vox.com/the-highlight/2019/8/8/20747198/philadelphia-bombing-1985-move; Beverly C. Tomek, "Move," *The Encyclopedia of Greater Philadelphia*, 2017, https://philadelphiaencyclopedia.org/essays/move/.

130. Matt DeLong and Dave Braunger, "Breaking Down the Dashcam: The Philando Castile Shooting Timeline," *Star Tribune* (Minneapolis, MN), June 21, 2017, https://web.archive.org/web/20201204183122/https://www.startribune.com/castile-shooting-timeline/429678313.

131. NRA Institute for Legislative Action, "As the nation's largest and oldest civil rights organization . . . ," Facebook, July 8, 2016, https://www.facebook.com/NationalRifleAssociation/photos/a.10150117108031833.307969.22561081832/10154483218346833/.

132. Alanna Vagianos, "NRA Spokeswoman Was Forced to Discuss Philando Castile during Heated Debate," *Huffington Post*, July 10, 2017, https://www.huffpost.com/entry/nra-spokeswoman-was-forced-to-discuss-philando-castile-during-heated-debate_n_59637764e4b02e9bdb0e0e9e.

133. Kelly Cohen, "Dana Loesch Explains Why the NRA Didn't Defend Philando Castile," *Washington Examiner*, August 10, 2017, https://www.washingtonexaminer.com/dana-loesch-explains-why-the-nra-didnt-defend-philando-castile; Nick Wing, "NRA Spokeswoman Blames Philando Castile for Getting Killed," *Huffington Post*, August 11, 2017, https://www.huffpost.com/entry/dana-loesch-nra-philando-castile_n_598ce48fe4b090964295fa09.

134. NRA Staff, "An Attack on Our Cops Is an Attack on All of Us," 34–35.

135. Richard A. Oppel, Derrick Bryson Taylor, and Nicholas Begel-Burroughs, "What to Know about Breonna Taylor," *New York Times*, April 26, 2021, https://www.nytimes.com/article/breonna-taylor-police.html (2021).

136. Dana Loesch, "Charges in the Breonna Taylor Case," Dana Loesch's Chapter and Verse (blog), September 23, 2020, https://danaloesch.substack.com/p/charges-in-the-breonna-taylor-case.

CHAPTER 9

1. Robert Dowlut, "Right to Keep and Bear Arms: A Right to Self-Defense against Criminals and Despots," *Stanford Law and Policy Review* 8 (1997): 35. Dowlut is quoting Mao Zedong.

2. Robert J. Cottrol and Raymond T. Diamond, "The Second Amendment: Toward

an Afro-Americanist Reconsideration," *Georgetown Law Journal* 80 (1992): 309–45; Stephen Halbrook, *Gun Control in the Third Reich: Disarming the Jews and "Enemies of the State"* (Oakland, CA: The Independent Institute, 2013); Stephen P. Halbrook, *That Every Man Be Armed: The Evolution of a Constitutional Right* (Albuquerque: University of New Mexico Press, 2013).

3. District of Columbia v. Heller, 554 U.S. 570 (2008): 25: "That history showed that the way tyrants had eliminated a militia consisting of all the able-bodied men was not by banning the militia but simply by taking away the people's arms, enabling a select militia or standing army to suppress political opponents."

4. A version of this ideology, albeit one reflective of the social position of African Americans, is evident in Justice Clarence Thomas's beliefs about the role of firearms in American politics. See Corey Robin, *The Enigma of Clarence Thomas* (New York: Metropolitan Books, 2019), chs. 8–9.

5. C. B. Lister, "All to the Good," *The American Rifleman* 98, no. 6 (1950): 10.

6. Ashley Halsey, "Look Who Opposes Civilian Marksmanship," *The American Rifleman* 115, no. 8 (1967): 41.

7. C. B. Lister, "Oath of Allegiance," *The American Rifleman* 88, no. 9 (1940): 2.

8. "Skilled Marksmen in Viet Nam," *The American Rifleman* 113, no. 12 (1965): 16.

9. For example, see advertisements in the September 1961 issue.

10. Membership ad featured in *The American Rifleman* 89, no. 2 (1941): 64.

11. Raymond J. Stan, "The NRA and National Defense," *The American Rifleman* 89, no. 9 (1941): 8.

12. Louis F. Lucas, "Citizen-Soldiers and Civil Defense," *The American Rifleman* 109, no. 12 (1961): 16. Also see C. B. Lister, "Re-Dedication," *The American Rifleman* 89, no. 5 (1941): 4.

13. "The NRA and Civil Defense," *The American Rifleman* 98, no. 11 (1950): 34.

14. J. Edgar Hoover, "The Shooting FBI," *The American Rifleman* 93, no. 7 (1945): 10–13; Captain G. M. Kellogg and Major A. F. Spring, "Use of Chemical by Law Enforcement Officers in Civil Disorders (Part II)," *The American Rifleman* 80, no. 2 (1932): 46–49; Col. George O. Van Orden, "Retraining the Returning G.I.," *The American Rifleman* 93, no. 8 (1945): 10–13; Sgt. Walter Peters, "Sniper Killer," *The American Rifleman* 93, no. 2 (1945): 27; Lt. Paul Saunier, "The Shore Patrol," *The American Rifleman* 93, no. 2 (1945): 8–11; Lt. John Scofield, "Cost: One Village," *The American Rifleman* 93, no. 3 (1945): 14–16; James E. Serven, "Theodore Roosevelt," *The American Rifleman* 112, no. 8 (1964): 51–53; Col. H. P. Sheldon, "An Armed Citizenry," *The American Rifleman* 88, no. 9 (1940): 5–8.

15. The latest reference to the derogatory term "the Japs" that I identified was in 1994. It is an excerpt from a letter that the magazine received in 1944, reprinted in a column that publishes short selections from the magazine's archive. "Our crack shots are far more confident, nervy and dangerous. They go out of their way to get action. A Marine private, a crack pistol shot from Montana, asked me to go out with him on patrol. He said that if we had two M-l rifles and two pistols, we could jump any gang of Japs up to twenty, but that we shouldn't tackle over thirty. I declined the invitation! Maj. James R. Bright. APO, San Francisco. [June 1944]." "Second Shots," *The American Rifleman* 142, no. 6 (1994): 80.

16. Halsey, "Look Who Opposes Civilian Marksmanship," 38–40; Lister, "Re-Dedication," 4; C. B. Lister, "Happy New Year," *The American Rifleman* 98, no. 1 (1950):

10; "The U.S. Justice Department, Izvestia, and the New Yorker," *The American Rifleman* 116, no. 6 (1968).

17. Jason Morgan Ward, *Defending White Democracy: Making of a Segregationist Movement and the Remaking of Racial Politics, 1936–1965* (Chapel Hill: University of North Carolina Press, 2011); Jeff Woods, *Black Struggle, Red Scare: Segregation and Anti-Communism in the South, 1948–1968* (Baton Rouge: Louisiana State University Press, 2004).

18. Lucas, "Citizen-Soldiers and Civil Defense," 16.

19. Robyn Thomas, "The NRA Is Complicit in the Attack on the Capitol," Giffords (blog), January 14, 2021, https://giffords.org/blog/2021/01/the-nra-is-complicit-in-the -attack-on-the-capitol/. A search of the NRA's website for the word "Capitol" produced no articles that mentioned the January 6 insurrection.

20. Lucas, "Citizen-Soldiers and Civil Defense," 16.

21. NRA, *Americans and Their Guns: The National Rifle Association Story through Nearly a Century of Service to the Nation* (Harrisburg, PA: Stackpole Company, 1967); Jeffrey L. Rodengen, *NRA: An American Legend* (Ft. Lauderdale, FL: Write Stuff Enterprises, 2002).

22. Over the years, *The American Rifleman* has offered various analyses and criticisms of the Sullivan Act, for example Jac Weller, "The Sullivan Law," *The American Rifleman* 110, no. 4 (1962): 33–36. According to this article, the Sullivan Law was politically motivated, its true intention being to control and punish the political opponents of Tammany Hall and laborites not aligned with the bosses. The act passed without resistance because it was framed as an anti-crime bill and legislators did not realize the true scope and purpose of the law. The act proved useful to New York City police seeking to arrest and convict organized crime figures. The article concludes: "the absence of some form of gun law in a city such as New York is unthinkable today."

23. Mass. Gen. L., Chap. 395, Act of May 29, 1926; Ark. Acts 1923, Ch. 430 (the law was repealed within two years because it was deemed unenforceable: Ark. Acts 1925, p. 1047, Act No. 351); Mich. Public Acts 1925; No. 313; N. C. Laws 1923, Ch. 106; Charles V. Imlay, "The Uniform Firearms Act," *American Bar Association Journal* 12, no. 11 (1926): 767–69; Sam B. Warner, "Uniform Pistol Act," *Journal of Criminal Law and Criminology* 29, no. 4 (1938): 529–54; Franklin E. Zimring, "Firearms and Federal Law: The Gun Control Act of 1968," *The Journal of Legal Studies* 4, no. 1 (1975): 133–98.

24. C. B. Lister, "Problems as Well as Progress Expected in 1937," *The American Rifleman* 85, no. 1 (1937), 5–6.

25. Warner, "Uniform Pistol Act," 531–32. Zimring, "Firearms and Federal Law," 133–98.

26. On the NRA's perspective on the UFA, see NRA, *Americans and Their Guns*, 291–92. In fact, this provision was contested by the US Revolver Association (USRA) as discriminatory against its members. The NRA lobbied strongly for the UFA as an alternative to the Sullivan Law. The NRA's leader, C. B. Lister, chastised then New York Governor Franklin D. Roosevelt for his veto of the UFA. C. B. Lister, "Governor Roosevelt Upholds Sullivan Law," *The American Rifleman* 80, no. 5 (1932): 20–21.

27. The first gun regulation enacted by the federal government was in 1916, when a tax of 10 percent was levied on pistols and revolvers purchased for private use. In 1926, Congress held hearings on legislation that would ban the carry of pistols, revolvers, and other concealable firearms and also prohibit the transporting of such firearms through

the mail system. No organization testified in opposition to this bill. United States Senate, *To Regulate Commerce in Firearms: Hearings Before the United States Senate Committee on Commerce, Subcommittee on* § 885, § 2258 and § 3680, 73rd Cong. (1934): 40; Zimring, "Firearms and Federal Law." According to Zimring, more than 100,000 people were registered as firearms dealers by the 1960s, making it impossible for the Department of the Treasury to monitor their activities.

28. This exemption is discussed in the debates over the 1968 Omnibus Crime Control and Safe Streets Act. Supporters of gun control were explicitly concerned about the possibility of NRA members who had a criminal record could still get access to firearms through the NRA via a government program. See especially: 90 Cong. Rec. S13320–25 (May 15, 1968) (statement of Sen. Dodd), https://www.govinfo.gov/content/pkg/GPO-CRECB-1968-pt10/pdf/GPO-CRECB-1968-pt10-6-1.pdf.

29. United States Senate, *To Regulate Commerce in Firearms*, 40.

30. Josh Sugarmann, *National Rifle Association: Money, Firepower, Fear* (Washington, DC: National Press Books, 1992).

31. Stephen P. Halbrook, "To Keep and Bear Their Private Arms: The Adoption of the Second Amendment, 1787–1791," *Northern Kentucky Law Review* 10 (1982): 13–40; Don B. Kates, "The Second Amendment: A Dialogue," *Law and Contemporary Problems* 49, no. 1 (1986): 143–50.

32. *The Right to Keep and Bear Arms: Report of the Subcommittee on the Constitution of the Committee on the Judiciary*, 97th Cong. S. rep (1982), https://books.google.com/books?id=UE3h11ce2VgC.

33. Ronald Reagan was the first president to appear at the NRA national conference. The July 1983 cover of *The American Rifleman* depicts Reagan with Harlon Carter at the NRA event under the title "President Reagan Voices Support for NRA's Objectives."

34. Sugarmann, *National Rifle Association*, 60.

35. Sanford Levinson, "The Embarrassing Second Amendment," *The Yale Law Journal* 99, no. 3 (1989): 650–51.

36. Dowlut, "Right to Keep and Bear Arms"; Halbrook, *Gun Control in the Third Reich*.

37. Charlton Heston, *The Courage to Be Free* (Kansas City, KS: Saudade Press, 2000); Wayne LaPierre, *Guns, Crime and Freedom* (Downers Grove, IL: Liberty Group, 2011 [1994]).

38. Stephen A. Halbrook, "What Made the Nazi Holocaust Possible? Gun Control," *America's 1st Freedom* 15, no. 2 (2014): 72.

39. Dowlut, "Right to Keep and Bear Arms."

40. Daniel D. Polsby and Don B. Kates, "Of Holocausts and Gun Control," *Washington University Law Quarterly* 75, no. 3 (1997): 1237–76; Joshua Horwitz and Casey Anderson, *Guns, Democracy, and the Insurrectionist Idea* (Ann Arbor: University of Michigan Press, 2009).

41. Karl Hess, "Should You Own A Gun?" *Guns Magazine*, February 1959, 46.

42. Heston used the phrase in a 1997 speech, and LaPierre attributes the phrase as originating with Heston. See Wayne LaPierre, *Guns, Rights, and Terrorism* (Nashville, TN: Thomas Nelson, Inc., 2003).

43. See especially Joyce Lee Malcolm, "The Right to Be Armed: The Common Law Legacy in England and America," in *A Right to Bear Arms? The Contested Role of History in Contemporary Debates on the Second Amendment*, ed. Jennifer Tucker, Barton C.

Hacker, and Margaret Vining (Washington, DC: Smithsonian Scholarly Press, 2019), 154–66. For the debates on the right to bear arms, see generally: Jennifer Tucker, Barton C. Hacker, and Margaret Vining, eds., *A Right to Bear Arms? The Contested Role of History in Contemporary Debates on the Second Amendment* (Washington, DC: The Smithsonian Institution, 2019); Bernard E. Harcourt, "On Gun Registration, Adolph Hitler, and Nazi Gun Laws: Exploding the Gun Culture Wars (A Call to Historians)," *Fordham Law Review* 73 (2004): 653–80; Robert J. Spitzer, "Don't Know Much about History, Politics, or Theory: A Comment," *Fordham Law Review* 73, no. 2 (2004): 721–29.

44. LaPierre, *Guns, Rights, and Terrorism*, 34–35; David B. Kopel, "It Isn't about Duck Hunting: The British Origins of the Right to Bear Arms," *Michigan Law Review* 93, no. 6 (1995): 1333–62.

45. Saul Cornell and Nathan Kozuskanich, eds., *The Second Amendment on Trial: Critical Essays on* District of Columbia v. Heller (Amherst: University of Massachusetts Press, 2013); Nathan R. Kozuskanich, "Rethinking Originalism: Bearing Arms and Armed Resistance in Pennsylvania," *American Journal of Legal History* 56, no. 4 (2016): 398–411; Jack Rakove, "A Challenge to *Heller's* Historical Interpretations," SCOTUS-blog, June 28, 2010, https://www.scotusblog.com/2010/06/mcdonald-challenging-hellers-historical-interpretations/; Robert Spitzer, "Gun Law History in the United States and Second Amendment Rights," *Law and Contemporary Problems* 80, no. 2 (2017): 55–83.

46. The Second Amendment "is the very product of an interest balancing by the people, and it surely elevates above all other interests the right of law-abiding, responsible citizens to use arms for self-defense," Thomas wrote. Furthermore, "to justify its regulation, the government may not simply posit that the regulation promotes an important interest." New York State Rifle & Pistol Association, Inc. v. Bruen, 597 U.S. __ (2022), 14.

47. *Bruen*, 14.

48. *Bruen*, 5–6.

49. *Heller*, 24–25.

50. Carl T. Bogus, "The Hidden History of the Second Amendment," *U.C. Davis Law Review* 31, no. 2 (1998): 309–408.

51. Jennifer Carlson, "Revisiting the Weberian Presumption: Gun Militarism, Gun Populism, and the Racial Politics of Legitimate Violence in Policing," *American Journal of Sociology* 125, no. 3 (2019): 633–82.

52. Mark Tunick, "John Locke and the Right to Bear Arms," *History of Political Thought* 35, no. 1 (2014): 50–69.

53. "Training Requirements FAQ," Texas Department of Safety, n.d., https://www.dps.texas.gov/section/handgun-licensing/faq/training-requirements-faq.

54. Mike McIntire, Glenn Thrush, and Eric Lipton, "Gun Sellers' Message to Americans: Man Up," *New York Times*, June 18, 2022, https://www.nytimes.com/2022/06/18/us/firearm-gun-sales.html.

55. *Bruen*, 71 (J. Alito, concurring).

56. Frank Smyth, *The NRA: The Unauthorized History* (New York: Flatiron Books, 2020), 235.

57. Reva B. Siegel, "Dead or Alive: Originalism as Popular Constitutionalism in *Heller*," *Harvard Law Review* 122, no. 1 (2008); Joseph Blocher and Darrell A. H. Miller, *The Positive Second Amendment: Rights, Regulation, and the Future of* Heller (New York:

Cambridge University Press, 2018), 167. Based on the same logic, government buildings should not be designated as "sensitive places" in which gun carry is prohibited (Blocher and Miller, 168).

58. Eddie Stewart, "Voting Out Anti-Gunners," Letter to the Editor, *America's 1st Freedom* 13, no. 9 (2012): 7.

59. *Heller*, 27.

60. Colleen E. Terrell, "'Republican Machines': Franklin, Rush, and the Manufacture of Civic Virtue in the Early Republic," *Early American Studies* 1, no. 2 (2003): 100–132.

61. *Bruen*, 3.

62. Dowlut, "Right to Keep and Bear Arms"; Halbrook, *That Every Man Be Armed*; Malcolm, "The Right to Be Armed," 154–66.

63. Heston, *The Courage to Be Free.*

64. Dowlut, "Right to Keep and Bear Arms."

65. Timothy Zick, "Framing the Second Amendment: Gun Rights, Civil Rights, and Civil Liberties," *Iowa Law Review* 106 (2020): 229–97.

66. Zick, 229–97.

67. Tyler Stovall, *White Freedom: The Racial History of an Idea* (Princeton, NJ: Princeton University Press, 2021), ch. 3.

68. Matthew Lacombe, *Firepower: How the NRA Turned Gun Owners into a Political Force* (Princeton, NJ: Princeton University Press, 2021).

69. Robert Dahl, *Democracy and Its Critics* (New Haven, CT: Yale University Press, 1989).

70. C. B. Lister, "Behind the Headlines," *The American Rifleman* 89, no. 2 (1941): 2.

71. William C. Church, "What Constitutes 'Militarism'?" *The American Army & Navy Journal*, October 3, 1914.

72. "Directors Meet and Discuss Important Questions," *The American Rifleman* 88, no. 3 (1940): 12–13.

73. Lister, "Behind the Headlines," 2. Maj. C. B. Thorne, "British Home Guard," *The American Rifleman* 98, no. 11 (1943): 26–27.

74. Lister, "Behind the Headlines."

75. Col. Boris D'Adamovitch, "Hunting Wolves on Sleds in Russia," *The American Rifleman* 80, no. 4 (1932): 17–18, 35.

76. William Odom, *The Soviet Volunteers: Modernization and Bureaucracy in a Public Mass Organization* (Princeton, NJ: Princeton University Press, 1973).

77. Garrett Underhill, "Under the Red Star: The Russian Rifle," *The American Rifleman* 89, no. 8 (1941): 7–12.

78. "A Tribute to the Sniper," *The American Rifleman* 91, no. 4 (1943): 16.

79. Underhill, "Under the Red Star," 7–12.

80. "Deep in a Well," *The American Rifleman* 91, no. 2 (1943): 41–42.

81. D'Adamovitch, "Hunting Wolves on Sleds in Russia," 17–18, 35.

82. Lister, "All to the Good," 10.

83. Weller, "The Sullivan Law," 33–36.

84. Laura Browder, *Her Best Shot: Women and Guns in America* (Chapel Hill: University of North Carolina Press, 2006).

85. Linda Kerber, *Women of the Republic: Intellect and Ideology in Revolutionary America* (Chapel Hill: University of North Carolina Press, 1980).

86. Amanda Collins, "The Real War on Women," *America's 1st Freedom* 14, no. 5 (2013): 40–43.

87. Darren LaSorte, "Would Gun-Banners Rather Nicole Carney Had Been Murdered?" *America's 1st Freedom* 18, no. 10 (2017): 64.

88. Kelly Young, "The Aging Defender," *The American Rifleman* 168, no. 1 (2020): 60–64.

89. Heston, *The Courage to Be Free*; LaPierre, *Guns, Crime and Freedom.*

90. Heston, *The Courage to Be Free.*

91. John R. Lott, "More Guns, Less Violent Crime," *The American Rifleman* 145, no. 1 (1997): 26.

92. James W. Potter, "Bloomberg's All-Consuming Agenda," *America's 1st Freedom* 14, no. 12 (2013): 10.

93. LaSorte, "Would Gun-Banners Rather Nicole Carney Had Been Murdered?" 64.

94. Jac Weller, "Is there Any 'Best' Firearm for Home Defense?" *The American Rifleman* 115, no. 5 (1967): 30–31.

95. Kimberly Corban, "Hillary's Enemies List: Kimberly Corban," *America's 1st Freedom* 17, no. 9 (2016): 50–51.

96. LaSorte, "Would Gun-Banners Rather Nicole Carney Had Been Murdered?" 64.

97. Frank Minter, "Hillary Clinton Runs against Gun Rights Because She Has To," *America's 1st Freedom* 17, no. 6 (2016): 47.

98. Collins, "The Real War on Women," 40–43; Mark Chesnut, "The Socialist Wave Is Powerful Enough to Threaten More Than Just Our Politics," *America's 1st Freedom* 19, no. 4 (2018): 39–41.

99. Chesnut, "The Socialist Wave," 39–41.

100. Corban, "Hillary's Enemies List: Kimberly Corban," 50–51.

101. Collins, "The Real War on Women," 40–43.

102. Collins, 40–43.

103. Edward G. Carmines and James A. Stimson, *Issue Evolution: Race and the Transformation of American Politics* (Princeton, NJ: Princeton University Press, 1989).

104. Alan I. Abramowitz and Steven W. Webster, "Negative Partisanship: Why Americans Dislike Parties But Behave Like Rabid Partisans," *Political Psychology* 39 (2018): 119–35.

105. Alexandra Filindra and Noah J. Kaplan, "Testing Theories of Gun Policy Preferences among Blacks, Latinos, and Whites in America," *Social Science Quarterly* 88, no. 2 (2017): 413–28; Mark Peffley and Jon Hurwitz, *Justice in America: The Separate Realities of Blacks and Whites* (New York: Cambridge University Press, 2010).

106. Jacob Appleby and Christopher M. Federico, "The Racialization of Electoral Fairness in the 2008 and 2012 United States Presidential Elections," *Group Processes & Intergroup Relations* 21, no. 7 (2018): 979–96; Alexandra Filindra, Beyza Buyuker, and Noah J. Kaplan, "Do Perceptions of Ingroup Discrimination Fuel Whites' Mistrust in Government? Insights from the 2012–2020 ANES and a Framing Experiment," *Polity*, November 23, 2022, https://www.journals.uchicago.edu/doi/10.1086/722763; Alexandra Filindra, Noah J. Kaplan, and Beyza E. Buyuker, "Beyond Performance: Racial Prejudice and Whites' Mistrust of Government," *Political Behavior* 44, no. 2 (2022): 961–79.

107. The claim is first made in the July 1990 issue. See J. Warren Cassidy, "Here We Stand: Remarks from Anaheim," *The American Rifleman* 138, no. 7 (1990): 7. For a recent example, see Oliver North, "This Election Requires Participation from 'Freedom's Army' of NRA Members," *The American Rifleman* 168, no. 10 (2018): 14.

108. David Kopel, "The Deacons for Defense and Justice," *America's 1st Freedom* 14,

no. 10 (2013): 28–30; David Kopel, "Jim Crow and the Racist Roots of Gun Control," *America's 1st Freedom* 11, no. 3 (2011): 42–46; David Kopel, Paul Gallant, and Joanne Eisen, "Gun-Packing First Lady," *America's 1st Freedom* 16, no. 5 (2015): 39–41; David Kopel, "Freedom Fighters," *America's 1st Freedom* 16, no. 2 (2016): 36–40.

109. Allen West, "The Tale of Two Organizations from the Perspective of an American Black Man," CNS News, September 10, 2018, https://www.cnsnews.com/commentary/allen-west/allen-west-tale-two-organizations-perspective-american-black-man. Similar claims were made earlier by Black business leaders in 2013—see Tom Kertscher, "The National Rifle Association Was 'Founded by Religious Leaders Who Wanted to Protect Freed Slaves from the Ku Klux Klan," Politifact, February 22, 2013, https://www.politifact.com/factchecks/2013/jun/05/harry-alford/nra-founded-fight-kkk-black-leader-says/.This is a false claim. The NRA's history and its own annual reports of the Reconstruction era do not in any way support this assertion.

110. Sugarmann, *National Rifle Association: Money, Firepower, Fear*.

111. Zick, "Framing the Second Amendment," 229–97.

112. William C. Church, "War & Peace," *The United States Army & Navy Journal*, July 22, 1865, 760–61.

113. With the possible exception of a single article on the Buffalo Soldiers monument in 1992. Mark A. Keefe, "The Buffalo Soldier Rides Forever," *The American Rifleman* 140, no. 10 (1992): 26–27.

114. Ashley Halsey, "Who Guards America's Homes?" *The American Rifleman* 115, no. 5 (1967): 16.

115. "Law and Order," *The American Rifleman* 112, no. 7 (1964): 16.

116. Halsey, "Who Guards America's Homes?" 16.

117. Alexandra Filindra and Noah J. Kaplan, "Racial Resentment and Whites' Gun Policy Preferences in Contemporary America," *Political Behavior* 38, no. 2 (2016): 255–75.

118. Zick, "Framing the Second Amendment," 229–97.

119. Sugarmann, *National Rifle Association: Money, Firepower, Fear*, 175.

120. Paul Taylor, "Powder Burn: As Gun-Control Advocates Hit a Bull's Eye or Two, the NRA Tries to Sharpen Its Aim," *Washington Post*, July 6, 1982, A1.

121. Heston, *The Courage to Be Free*.

122. For the psychological processes that undergird moral credentialing, see Daniel A. Effron, Jessica S. Cameron, and Benoît Monin, "Endorsing Obama Licenses Favoring Whites," *Journal of Experimental Social Psychology* 45, no. 3 (2009): 590–93.

123. Frederick Douglass, "Men of Color, To Arms!" *Douglass' Monthly*, March 21, 1863.

124. W. E. B. DuBois, "Close Ranks," *The Crisis* 16, no. 3 (1918).

125. Stokely Carmichael and Charles V. Hamilton, *Black Power: The Politics of Liberation* (New York: Random House, 1967); Peniel E. Joseph, *Waiting 'Til the Midnight Hour* (New York: Henry Holt & Co., 2007); Peniel E. Joseph, *The Sword and the Shield: The Revolutionary Lives of Malcolm X and Martin Luther King, Jr.* (New York: Basic Books, 2020).

126. Robert Franklin Williams, *Negroes with Guns* (Detroit, MI: Wayne State University Press, 1998 [1962]).

127. "Black Panthers and Blind Kittens," *The American Rifleman* 118, no. 9 (1970): 20.

128. Ida B. Wells-Barnett, *On Lynchings* (Mineola, NY: Dover Publications, Inc., 2014 [1892]).

129. Robin, *The Enigma of Clarence Thomas*, chs. 8–9.

130. LaPierre, *Guns, Rights, and Terrorism*. Justice Scalia's decision in *Heller* also suggests that Americans do maintain a right to revolution against tyranny; therefore, for the Court too, gun ownership is a political right of citizenship outside of military service.

131. C. Irvine Walker, Carolina Rifle Club, Charleston S.C., 1905 [1869], HathiTrust .org, 5–6, http://hdl.handle.net/2027/wu.89072984933.

132. Chesnut, "The Socialist Wave Is Powerful Enough," 39–40. Some make the link explicit. For example, Anne Coulter argues that "gun control laws were originally promulgated by Democrats to keep guns out of the hands of blacks. This allowed the Democratic policy of slavery to proceed with fewer bumps and, after the Civil War, allowed the Democratic KKK to menace and murder black Americans with little resistance." This statement ignores the historical fact of the partisan realignment. Ann Coulter, "Negroes with Guns," AnnCoulter.com, April 18, 2012, http://www.anncoulter .com/columns/2012-04-18.html.

133. Chris Pandolfo, "Watch: Black GOP Candidate Wields AR-15 to Defend Home from Ku Klux Klan Democrats in Viral Ad: 'Make Rifles Great Again,'" Blaze Media, July 6, 2022, https://www.theblaze.com/news/watch-arizona-gop-candidate-wields-ar -15-to-defend-home-from-ku-klux-klan-democrats-in-viral-ad.

134. One rare case of direct attribution of institutional complicity is found in a 2015 article that states: "At a time when law enforcement officials were sometimes indifferent to acts of violence perpetrated against African Americans (or in some cases even complicit in them), those seeking any protection at all had few other options." However, there is no further discussion of structural racism. "Defending Rosa Parks," *America's 1st Freedom* 16, no. 5 (2015): 45.

135. Halbrook, "What Made the Nazi Holocaust Possible?" 72. Scholars have pointed out the historical inaccuracies associated with this argument. See Horwitz and Anderson, *Guns, Democracy, and the Insurrectionist Idea*.

136. The word "holocaust" appeared from time to time in the context of war destruction in general, and especially nuclear war. I did not find discussions of the Jewish Holocaust in the issues under examination here.

137. LaPierre, *Guns, Crime and Freedom*, 86.

138. Heston, *The Courage to Be Free*, 29.

139. "Chatterbox 2.0," *America's 1st Freedom* 15, no. 2 (2014): 16.

140. David Kopel and Richard Griffiths, "Hitler's Control: The Lessons of Nazi History," *National Review*, May 22, 2003, https://www.nationalreview.com/2003/05/ hitlers-control-kopel-griffiths/.

141. Halbrook, "What Made the Nazi Holocaust Possible?"

142. David Kopel, "Covering the Screen in Blood," *America's 1st Freedom* 15, no. 4 (2014): 33–34.

143. Stovall, *White Freedom*, ch. 3.

144. Harcourt, "On Gun Registration," 653–80.

145. Michael S. Bryant, "Holocaust Imagery and Gun Control," in *Guns in American Society: An Encyclopedia of History, Politics, Culture, and the Law*, ed. Greg Lee Carter (Santa Barbara, CA: ABC-CLIO, LLC, 2012), 411–15.

146. Theodor W. Adorno et al., *The Authoritarian Personality* (New York: Harper, 1950); Robert Gellately, *Hitler's True Believers: How Ordinary People Became Nazis* (New York: Oxford University Press, 2020).

147. Stephen Halbrook, "Second-Class Citizenship and the Second Amendment in

the District of Columbia," *George Mason University Civil Rights Law Journal* 5, nos. 1–2 (1995): 3.

148. Chris W. Cox, "A Freedom Fighter to Never Forget: Otis McDonald (1933–2014)," *The American Rifleman* 162, no. 7 (2014): 16.

149. LaPierre, *Guns, Rights, and Terrorism*, 35.

150. G. W. Allport, *The Nature of Prejudice* (Cambridge, MA: Perseus Books, 1954).

151. Stanley Milgram, "Behavioral Study of Obedience," *The Journal of Abnormal and Social Psychology* 67, no. 4 (1963): 371–78.

152. Robert B. Cialdini and Melanie R. Trost, "Social Influence: Social Norms, Conformity and Compliance," in *The Handbook of Social Psychology*, vols. 1–2, 4th ed. (New York: McGraw-Hill, 1998).

153. Alexandra Filindra and Laurel Harbridge Yong, "How Do Partisans Navigate Intra-Group Conflict? A Theory of Leadership-Driven Motivated Reasoning," *Political Behavior* 44 (2022): 1437–58, https://doi.org/10.1007/s11109-022-09779-1.

154. Philip J. Cook and Kristin A. Goss, *The Gun Debate: What Everyone Needs to Know* (New York: Oxford University Press, 2020).

CHAPTER 10

1. John T. Jost, *A Theory of System Justification* (Cambridge, MA: Harvard University Press, 2020).

2. Jake Hodder, "Casting a Black Gandhi: Martin Luther King Jr., American Pacifists and the Global Dynamics of Race," *Journal of American Studies* 55, no. 1 (2021): 48–74; Anthony C. Siracusa, *Nonviolence before King: The Politics of Being and the Black Freedom Struggle* (Chapel Hill: University of North Carolina Press, 2021).

3. Deborah J. Schildkraut, *Americanism in the 21st Century* (Cambridge, UK: Cambridge University Press, 2011), chs. 1, 3.

4. Elizabeth Theiss-Morse, *Who Counts as an American? The Boundaries of National Identity* (New York: Cambridge University Press, 2009), ch. 1.

5. The online appendix may be accessed at https://alexandra-filindra.com/.

6. Schildkraut, *Americanism in the 21st Century*. This work is not focused on white Americans; instead, it includes a broad cross section of the American population.

7. Items that correlate equally with more than one factor and those that did not load on any factor were removed and the analysis was re-run. I used 0.4 as the cutoff point for inclusion. Alternate specifications of the indices do not change inferences based on the multivariate results.

8. This finding has implications for the theory of racial resentment, which posits that a commitment to liberalism guides White rejection of African Americans on the grounds of government dependence. See for example Donald R. Kinder and Lynn M. Sanders, *Divided by Color* (Chicago: University of Chicago Press, 1996).

9. This is the case for the reduced item indices as well (alpha$_{AMR}$=0.88; alpha$_{ICR}$=0.77).

10. The results also show that "thinking of oneself as American" and "feeling American," along with "respect for laws and institutions," fit together as part of a third, distinct construct. In subsequent analyses, I combined the thinking and feeling American items into a single "American identity" variable (alpha=0.84). Although both indices are positively correlated with the American identity variable, the correlation with AMR is stronger (r=0.39) than that with ICR (r=0.20).

11. Appendix table 10.1 also shows the results of a model for ascriptive republicanism, an index that excludes the martial items. The results for AMR and AR are identical. It is important to note that a short version of AMR based on four items produces substantively similar results in all models presented in chapters 10 and 11. These items are: being Christian, being of European ancestry, living in rural America, and listening to one's father (women). Reliability is a=0.81. A factor analysis shows that the four items fall on a single factor (eigenvalue=1.96). A fifth item, owning and carrying firearms, adds substantially to the index's reliability (a=0.85), but I excluded it from analyses because of its close relationship with many of the dependent variables.

12. Both items are established measures in the literature. See Ashley Jardina, *White Identity Politics* (New York: Cambridge University Press, 2019); and Kinder and Sanders, *Divided by Color.*

13. Lilliana Mason, *Uncivil Agreement: How Politics Became Our Identity* (Chicago: University of Chicago Press, 2018).

14. Alexandra Filindra, Noah J. Kaplan, and Beyza Buyuker, "Racial Resentment or Modern Sexism? White Americans' Outgroup Attitudes as Predictors of Gun Ownership, Rationales for Ownership, & NRA Membership," *Sociological Inquiry* 91, no. 2 (2021); Benjamin Dowd-Arrow, Terrence D. Hill, and Amy M. Burdette, "Gun Ownership and Fear," *SSM—Population Health* 8 (2019), https://doi.org/https://doi.org/10 .1016/j.ssmph.2019.100463.

15. Models using the AR index (excluding martial items) produce similar albeit somewhat weaker results. See Appendix table 10.2d.

16. Charlton Heston, *The Courage to Be Free* (Kansas City, KS: Saudade Press, 2000).

17. The effect of AMR on the ranking of rights is similar for men and women.

18. See Appendix table 10.3b. The interactions are null.

19. Pew Research Center, *Perspectives on Gun Owners, Non-Owners: Why Own a Gun? Protection is a Top Reason,* Pew Research Center (Washington, DC, 2013), https://www.pewresearch.org/politics/2013/03/12/why-own-a-gun-protection-is -now-top-reason/; Kim Parker, Juliana Menasce Horowitz, Ruth Igielnik, J. Baxter Oliphant, and Anna Brown, "America's Complex Relationship with Guns," Pew Research Center, June 22, 2017, https://www.pewresearch.org/social-trends/2017/06/22/ americas-complex-relationship-with-guns/.

20. Filindra, Kaplan, and Buyuker, "Racial Resentment or Modern Sexism?"

21. Alexandra Filindra and Noah J. Kaplan, "Racial Resentment and Whites' Gun Policy Preferences in Contemporary America," *Political Behavior* 38, no. 2 (2016).

22. See Appendix table 10.4b. The interactions do not contribute to the model and they are null.

23. Corey Robin, *The Enigma of Clarence Thomas* (New York: Metropolitan Books, 2019); Reva B. Siegel, "Dead or Alive: Originalism as Popular Constitutionalism in *Heller,*" *Harvard Law Review* 122, no. 1 (2008).

24. Heston, *The Courage to Be Free*; Wayne LaPierre, *Guns, Crime and Freedom* (Downers Grove, IL: Liberty Group, 2011 [1994]).

25. Mark Peffley and Jon Hurwitz, *Justice in America: The Separate Realities of Blacks and Whites* (New York: Cambridge University Press, 2010).

26. B. Keith Payne, Alan J. Lambert, and Larry L. Jacoby, "Best Laid Plans: Effects of Goals on Accessibility Bias and Cognitive Control in Race-Based Misperceptions of Weapons," *Journal of Experimental Social Psychology* 38, no. 4 (2002): 384–96.

27. For a similar approach, see: Filindra and Kaplan, "Racial Resentment and Whites' Gun Policy Preferences." For the IAT, see Anthony G. Greenwald et al., "A Unified Theory of Implicit Attitudes, Stereotypes, Self-Esteem, and Self-Concept," *Psychological Review* 109, no. 1 (2002): 3–25.

28. Michael Tesler, *Post-Racial or Most Racial? Race and Politics in the Obama Era* (Chicago: University of Chicago Press, 2016).

29. Results showed that including or excluding respondents who failed attention checks did not affect inferences. I opted to include all respondents.

30. When controls are included, the difference strengthens to p=0.02.

CHAPTER 11

1. Mark Tunick, "John Locke and the Right to Bear Arms," *History of Political Thought* 35, no. 1 (2014);Max Weber, *The Vocation Lectures* (Indianapolis, IN: Hackett Publishing Company, 2004 [1919]).

2. Charlton Heston, *The Courage to Be Free* (Kansas City, KS: Saudade Press, 2000); Wayne LaPierre, *Guns, Crime and Freedom* (Downers Grove, IL: Liberty Group, 2011 [1994]).

3. Corey Robin, *The Enigma of Clarence Thomas* (New York: Metropolitan Books, 2019); Robert J. Spitzer, *The Gun Dilemma: How History Is Against Expanded Gun Rights* (New York: Oxford University Press, 2022).

4. Steve Benen, "Second Amendment Remedies, 2014 Style," MSNBC, October 23, 2014, http://www.msnbc.com/rachel-maddow-show/second-amendment-remedies -2014-style.

5. Alex Seitz-Wald, "As Newsom Leads California Recall Polls, Larry Elder Pushes Baseless Fraud Claims," NBC News, September 13, 2021, https://www.nbcnews.com/ politics/elections/newsom-leads-california-recall-polls-larry-elder-pushes-baseless -fraud-n1279080.

6. Nick Corasaniti and Maggie Haberman, "Donald Trump Suggests Second Amendment People Could Act against Hillary Clinton," *New York Times*, August 9, 2016, https://www.nytimes.com/2016/08/10/us/politics/donald-trump-hillary -clinton.html; William Cummings, "Democratic Congressman Suggests Second Amendment Solution for Trump," *USA Today*, March 22, 2018, https://www.usatoday .com/story/news/politics/onpolitics/2018/03/22/democratic-congressman-suozzi -second-amendment-solution-trump/450923002/.

7. Michael Gershon, "Eric Greitens's 'RINO Hunting' Ad Shows the Radicalization Pipeline in the GOP," *Washington Post*, June 23, 2022, https://www.washingtonpost .com/opinions/2022/06/23/eric-greitens-rino-hunting-ad-must-be-rejected.

8. Shelly S. Hinck et al., "A Tale of Two Parties: Comparing the Intensity of Face Threats in the Democratic and Republican Primary Debates of 2012 and 2016," *Argumentation and Advocacy* 54, nos. 1–2 (2018): 104–21; Yunya Song et al., "Contagion of Offensive Speech Online: An Interactional Analysis of Political Swearing," *Computers in Human Behavior* 127 (2022).

9. Nathan P. Kalmoe and Lilliana Mason, *Radical American Partisanship: Mapping Violent Hostility, Its Causes and the Consequences for Democracy* (Chicago: University of Chicago Press, 2022).

10. Rebekah Herrick, Sue Thomas, and Kate Bartholomy, "Gender, Power, and Colleague Aggression in U.S. State Senates," *Political Research Quarterly* 75, no. 1 (2021);

Rebekah Herrick et al., "Physical Violence and Psychological Abuse against Female and Male Mayors in the United States," *Politics, Groups, and Identities* 9, no. 4 (2021): 681–98.

11. Alexandra Filindra and Laurel Harbridge Yong, "How Do Partisans Navigate Intra-Group Conflict? A Theory of Leadership-Driven Motivated Reasoning," *Political Behavior* 44 (2022): 1437–58, https://doi.org/10.1007/s11109-022-09779-1; Matthew H. Graham and Milan W. Svolik, "Democracy in America? Partisanship, Polarization, and the Robustness of Support for Democracy in the United States," *American Political Science Review* 114, no. 2 (2020): 392–409.

12. Kalmoe and Mason, *Radical American Partisanship*.

13. Larry M. Bartels, "Ethnic Antagonism Erodes Republicans' Commitment to Democracy," *Proceedings of the National Academy of Sciences* 117, no. 37 (2020), https://www.pnas.org/content/pnas/early/2020/08/26/2007747117.full.pdf; Beyza Buyuker, "Democracy and the 'Other': Outgroup Attitudes and Support for Anti-Democratic Norms," *Political Research Quarterly* (forthcoming).

14. Jacob Appleby and Christopher M. Federico, "The Racialization of Electoral Fairness in the 2008 and 2012 United States Presidential Elections," *Group Processes & Intergroup Relations* 21, no. 7 (2018): 979–96; Alexandra Filindra, Beyza Buyuker, and Noah J. Kaplan, "Do Perceptions of Ingroup Discrimination Fuel Whites' Mistrust in Government? Insights from the 2012–2020 ANES and a Framing Experiment," *Polity*, November 23, 2022, https://www.journals.uchicago.edu/doi/abs/10.1086/722763 ?journalCode=pol ; Alexandra Filindra, Noah J. Kaplan, and Beyza E. Buyuker, "Beyond Performance: Racial Prejudice and Whites' Mistrust of Government," *Political Behavior* 44, no. 2 (2022): 961–79.

15. Rand Corporation, "The Effect of Stand-Your-Ground Laws," Gun Policy in America, April 22, 2020, https://www.rand.org/research/gun-policy/analysis/stand -your-ground.html.

16. Neil MacFarquhar, "Suspect in Kenosha Killings Lionized the Police," *New York Times*, August 27, 2020, updated October 16, 2020, https://www.nytimes.com/2020/ 08/27/us/kyle-rittenhouse-kenosha.html.

17. Elyse Wanshel, "Florida's Gov. DeSantis Wants to Allow Armed Citizens to Shoot Looters and Rioters," HuffPost, November 11, 2020, https://www.huffpost .com/entry/floridas-gov-desantis-wants-to-allow-armed-citizens-to-shoot-looters-and -rioters_n_5fac0ccac5b6d647a39af5c0.

18. Jonathan Mummolo, "Militarization Fails to Enhance Police Safety or Reduce Crime but May Harm Police Reputation," *Proceedings of the National Academy of Sciences* 115, no. 37 (2018): 9181–86.

19. Tyler Stovall, *White Freedom: The Racial History of an Idea* (Princeton, NJ: Princeton University Press, 2021), ch. 3.

20. University of Massachusetts Amherst, University of Massachusetts Amherst/ WCVB December 2021 National Poll, https://polsci.umass.edu/sites/default/files/ CRTandRaceinAmericaCrosstabs.pdf.

21. BBC News, "Virginia Gun Rally: Thousands Converge on Richmond," January 20, 2020, https://www.bbc.com/news/world-us-canada-51180452; Ed Hornick, "Gun Rights Advocates Rally in Washington, Virginia," CNN, April 19, 2010, http://www.cnn .com/2010/POLITICS/04/19/second.amendment.rally/index.html.

22. "Man Carries Assault Rifle to Obama Protest—and It's Legal," CNN, August 17, 2009, https://www.cnn.com/2009/POLITICS/08/17/obama.protest.rifle/.

23. Mark Thompson, "When Protesters Bear Arms against Healthcare Reform," *Time*, August 19, 2009, http://content.time.com/time/nation/article/0,8599,1917356 ,00.html.

24. Joseph Blocher and Reva B. Siegel, "When Guns Threaten the Public Sphere: A New Account of Public Safety Regulation under *Heller*," *Northwestern University Law Review* 116, no. 1 (2021).

25. Tracy Garnar, Sione Lynn Pili Lister, and Jennifer Carlson, "Whiteness and Impunity," *Sociological Inquiry* 92 (2022): 597–622.

26. Timothy Zick, "Arming Public Protests," *Iowa Law Review* 104, no. 1 (2018).

27. Hahrie Han, Elizabeth McKenna, and Michelle Oyakawa, *Prisms of the People: Power and Organizing in 21st-Century America* (Chicago: University of Chicago Press, 2021).

28. Herrick et al., "Physical violence and psychological abuse," 681–98.

29. Kalmoe and Mason, *Radical American Partisanship*.

30. Sophia Moskalenko and Clark McCauley, "Measuring Political Mobilization: The Distinction between Activism and Radicalism," *Terrorism and Political Violence* 21, no. 2 (2009): 239–60.

31. Song et al., "Contagion of Offensive Speech Online"; Karen J. Greenberg, "Counter-Radicalization via the Internet," *The ANNALS of the American Academy of Political and Social Science* 668, no. 1 (2016): 165–79.

32. Bartels, "Ethnic Antagonism Erodes Republicans' Commitment to Democracy"; Matthew H. Graham and Milan W. Svolik, "Democracy in America? Partisanship, Polarization, and the Robustness of Support for Democracy in the United States," *American Political Science Review* 114, no. 2 (2020); Steven V. Miller and Nicholas T. Davis, "The Effect of White Social Prejudice on Support for American Democracy," *The Journal of Race, Ethnicity, and Politics* 6, no. 2 (2021).

33. George E. Marcus et al., *With Malice toward Some: How People Make Civil Liberties Judgements* (New York: Cambridge University Press, 1995); Thomas E. Nelson, Rosalee A. Clawson, and Zoe M. Oxley, "Media Framing of a Civil Liberties Conflict and Its Effect on Tolerance," *The American Political Science Review* 91, no. 3 (1997).

34. Alexander Hamilton, James Madison, and John Jay, *The Federalist Papers* (New York: Bantam Dell, 2003 [1787]). See especially *Federalist* 10.

35. Mia Bloom and Sophia Moskalenko, *Pastels and Pedophiles: Inside the Mind of QAnon* (Palo Alto, CA: Stanford University Press, 2021); Sophia Moskalenko and Clark McCauley, "QAnon: Radical Opinion versus Radical Action," *Perspectives on Terrorism* 15, no. 2 (2021): 142–46.

36. Varieties of Democracy (V-Dem), "Autocratization Turns Viral: Democracy Report 2021," V-Dem Institute, University of Gothenburg, 2021, https://www.v-dem .net/static/website/files/dr/dr_2021.pdf.

37. Filindra and Harbridge Yong, "How Do Partisans Navigate Intra-Group Conflict?"

38. B. Buyuker, A. J. D'Urso, A. Filindra, and N. J. Kaplan, "Race Politics Research and the American Presidency: Thinking about White Attitudes, Identities and Vote Choice in the Trump Era and Beyond," *Journal of Race, Ethnicity, and Politics* 6, no. 3 (2021): 600–641; Ashley Jardina, *White Identity Politics* (New York: Cambridge University Press, 2019); John Sides, Michael Tesler, and Lynn Vavreck, *Identity Crisis: The 2016 Presidential Campaign and the Battle for the Meaning of America* (Princeton, NJ: Princeton University Press, 2019).

39. Including or excluding the few voters who selected a third candidate does not change the interpretation of the results.

40. It is also important to note that for these dependent variables the interaction between AMR and partisanship is null. The same is true of the interaction between AMR and identification with the NRA, with the notable exception of the QAnon model. The interaction model suggests that even though NRA identifiers are generally more supportive of QAnon than people who do not identify with the group, the effect of AMR on support for QAnon is stronger among non–NRA identifiers than among NRA identifiers.

41. Eamon Whalen, "Across the Country, Republican Groups Are Holding 'Vigils' for January 6 'Patriot Martyrs,'" *Mother Jones*, January 6, 2022, https://www .motherjones.com/politics/2022/01/across-the-country-republican-groups-are -holding-vigils-for-january-6-patriot-martyrs/.

42. Carlton Larson, "Seditious Conspiracy Was the Right Charge for the January 6 Organizers," *Atlantic*, January 15, 2022, https://www.theatlantic.com/ideas/archive/ 2022/01/seditious-conspiracy-charge-january-6-organizers-treason/621251/.

CONCLUSION

1. US Senate Committee on Finance Minority Staff Report, *The NRA and Russia: How a Tax-Exempt Organization Became a Foreign Asset*, U.S. Senate (Washington, DC: US Government Printing Office, 2019), https://s3.documentcloud.org/ documents/6432520/The-NRA-Russia-How-a-Tax-Exempt-Organization.pdf; "The NRA Has Lost Influence, But the Culture It Created Remains," *PBS News Hour*, May 25, 2022, https://www.pbs.org/newshour/show/nra-remains-key-player-in-battle-over -gun-laws-but-is-its-unbreakable-grip-diminishing.

2. David Zucchino, *Wilmington's Lie: The Murderous Coup of 1898 and the Rise of White Supremacy* (New York: Atlantic Monthly Press, 2020).

3. District of Columbia v. Heller, 554 U.S. 570 (2008); McDonald v. City of Chicago, 561 U.S. 742 (2010); and New York State Rifle & Pistol Association, Inc. v. Bruen, 597 U.S. __ (2022).

4. To date, I have conducted in-depth interviews with twenty-seven elected officials at all levels of government and in various states. Robert Putnam, *Bowling Alone: The Collapse and Revival of American Community* (New York: Simon and Schuster, 2000).

5. Corey Robin, *The Enigma of Clarence Thomas* (New York: Metropolitan Books, 2019); Joshua D. Hawley, *Theodore Roosevelt: Preacher of Righteousness* (New Haven, CT: Yale University Press, 2015).

6. Josh D. Hawley, "Speech at the National Conservatism Conference," July 18, 2019, https://www.hawley.senate.gov/senator-josh-hawleys-speech-national-conservatism -conference.

7. Josh D. Hawley, "Keynote Address at the National Conservatism Conference on the Left's Attack on Men in America," November 1, 2021, https://www.hawley .senate.gov/senator-hawley-delivers-national-conservatism-keynote-lefts-attack-men -america.

8. Michael Gershon, "Eric Greitens's 'RINO Hunting' Ad Shows the Radicalization Pipeline in the GOP," *Washington Post*, June 23, 2022, https://www.washingtonpost .com/opinions/2022/06/23/eric-greitens-rino-hunting-ad-must-be-rejected/; Mike McIntire, Glenn Thrush, and Eric Lipton, "Gun Sellers' Message to Americans: Man

Up," *New York Times*, June 18, 2022, https://www.nytimes.com/2022/06/18/us/firearm-gun-sales.html.

9. Lilliana Mason, *Uncivil Agreement: How Politics Became Our Identity* (Chicago: University of Chicago Press, 2018).

10. Robert Draper, "The Arizona Republican Party's Anti-Democracy Experiment," *New York Times*, August 15, 2022, https://www.nytimes.com/2022/08/15/magazine/arizona-republicans-democracy.html.

11. Erin C. Cassese, "Partisan Dehumanization in American Politics," *Political Behavior* 43 (2021): 29–50; Stefano DellaVigna and Ethan Kaplan, "The Fox News Effect: Media Bias and Voting," *Quarterly Journal of Economics* 122, no. 3 (2007): 1187–1234; Joshua D. Clinton and Ted Enamorado, "The National News Media's Effect on Congress: How Fox News Affected Elites in Congress," *The Journal of Politics* 76, no. 4 (2014).

12. Jacob Appleby and Christopher M. Federico, "The Racialization of Electoral Fairness in the 2008 and 2012 United States Presidential Elections," *Group Processes & Intergroup Relations* 21, no. 7 (2018); Larry M. Bartels, "Ethnic Antagonism Erodes Republicans' Commitment to Democracy," *Proceedings of the National Academy of Sciences* 117, no. 37 (2020): 22752–59, https://www.pnas.org/content/pnas/early/2020/08/26/2007747117.full.pdf; Alexandra Filindra, Beyza Buyuker, and Noah J. Kaplan, "Do Perceptions of Ingroup Discrimination Fuel White Mistrust in Government? Insights from the 2012–2020 ANES and a Framing Experiment," *Polity*, November 23, 2022, https://www.journals.uchicago.edu/doi/abs/10.1086/722763?journalCode=pol.

13. Filindra, Buyuker, and Kaplan, "Do Perceptions of Ingroup Discrimination Fuel Whites' Mistrust"; Alexandra Filindra, Noah J. Kaplan, and Beyza E. Buyuker, "Beyond Performance: Racial Prejudice and Whites' Mistrust of Government," *Political Behavior* 44, no. 2 (2022): 961–79.

14. Draper, "The Arizona Republican Party's Anti-Democracy Experiment."

15. Nathan P. Kalmoe, "Fueling the Fire: Violent Metaphors, Trait Aggression, and Support for Political Violence," *Political Communication* 31, no. 4 (2014): 545–63.

16. Philip J. Cook and Kristin A. Goss, *The Gun Debate: What Everyone Needs to Know* (New York: Oxford University Press, 2020), 2–4.

17. Clifford Young and Sarah Feldman, "Guns in America," IPSOS Report, July 8, 2022, https://www.ipsos.com/en-us/news-polls/guns-america (2022).

18. Cook and Goss, *The Gun Debate*, 2–4.

19. Meredith Deliso, "Suspected Gunman Who Killed Judge Esther Salas's Son Disparaged Her as a Latina," ABC News, July 22, 2020, https://abcnews.go.com/US/suspect-deadly-shooting-called-federal-judge-esther-salas/story?id=71901734.

20. Josh Campbell, Jessica Schneider, Donie O'Sullivan, Paul P. Murphy, and Priscilla Alvarez, "FBI Investigating 'Unprecedented' Number of Threats against Bureau in Wake of Mar-a-Lago Search," CNN Politics, August 13, 2022, https://www.cnn.com/2022/08/12/politics/fbi-threats-maralago-trump-search/index.html.

Index

Tables are indicated with the letter *t* following a page number. Figures are indicated with the letter *f* following a page number.

Made in United States
North Haven, CT
24 September 2023

41911322R00215